On Love
and Loving

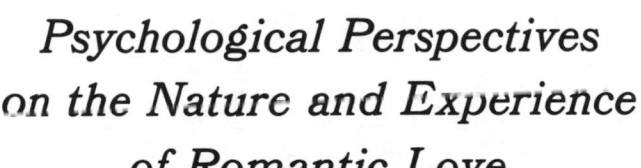

*Psychological Perspectives
on the Nature and Experience
of Romantic Love*

Kenneth S. Pope
and Associates

On Love
and Loving

 Jossey-Bass Publishers

San Francisco • Washington • London • 1980

ON LOVE AND LOVING
Psychological Perspectives on the Nature
and Experience of Romantic Love
        by Kenneth S. Pope and Associates

Copyright © 1980 by: Jossey-Bass Inc., Publishers
                       433 California Street
                       San Francisco, California 94104

                       &

                       Jossey-Bass Limited
                       28 Banner Street
                       London EC1Y 8QE

Library of Congress Cataloging in Publication Data

    Main entry under title:

    On love and loving.
        Bibliography: p. 336
        Includes index.
        1. Love—Psychological aspects.   I. Pope, Kenneth S.
BF575.L8048   152.4   80-8012
ISBN 0-87589-479-8

Manufactured in the United States of America

JACKET DESIGN BY WILLI BAUM

FIRST EDITION

Code 8037

The Jossey-Bass
Social and Behavioral
Science Series

Preface

If a little knowledge is a dangerous thing, we have been safe where love is concerned. In everyday clinical practice, as well as in theory and research, our work has generally lacked even an initial scientific knowledge of romance.

For reasons discussed in Chapter One, such fundamental human activities as falling in love have often been glossed over, ridiculed, or ignored entirely in scientific research and clinical practice. This history of ignorance has put practitioners at a genuine disadvantage. The psychodynamically oriented therapist needs a firm grasp of the relationship among love, transference, and countertransference (discussed in Chapters Seven and Thirteen). The group counselor needs information about love as a concept defining the relationship between two people of the opposite or same sex, about evolving patterns of loving, and about the influence of the women's movement on love and marriage as social institutions (see Chapters Four, Five, Six, Twelve, and Sixteen). The Victorian resistance to recognizing sex in childhood has largely been replaced by our refusal to take seriously romantic love in childhood. Yet, the child psychologist and psychiatrist, the social worker, and the teacher should be able to recognize and understand the earliest forms and patterns of love to work effectively and sensitively with youth (Chapters One, Two, and Ten). The marriage and family therapist requires practical knowledge about predictable stages of relationships, common problems faced by lovers, factors that influence the growth or disintegration of long-term relationships, and specific steps that other therapists have found useful in handling issues of love (Chapters Seven and Fourteen through Seventeen). Research findings about sex differences in romantic experience and behavior, crises—that can result in psychotic breakdowns, homicide, or suicide—precipitated by romance, the changing ways in which people love as they develop through adulthood, and the "loss of self" that is experienced in romantic loving are all topics of primary importance to clinicians and other human services workers. With expanded knowledge, they can develop practice that is informed by scientific research and investigation and remains true to one of the most vital and mysterious aspects of human life.

The intent of this book is to explore, from a variety of theoretical orientations (cognitive, behavioral, psychodynamic) and specializations (community psychology, psychotherapy, human development), a fascinating aspect of human life: romantic loving. The various chapters examine romantic love as it appears in the development of individuals, groups, families, and communities; as it is understood within some major theoretical frameworks; and as it touches vital human experiences or endeavors.

On Love and Loving is addressed primarily to social and behavioral scientists, although a diverse audience may find it interesting and useful. Romantic Love—a subject of seemingly infinite appeal and importance—has seldom been dealt with seriously by psychology and related fields, and not uncommonly they have generally been hostile or indifferent to the concept. When acknowledged at all, it all too often appears within the contexts of artificial laboratory experiments, idle speculation, or "pop" psychology.

In this book, the contributors attempt a careful, comprehensive exploration of major facets of romantic love. Along with a review of pioneering work (the false starts as well as the lasting discoveries), data from naturalistic observation, first person accounts, experimental studies, survey research, and clinical case material are brought together to test current hypotheses and to suggest new directions.

With its reviews of the literature and its current, comprehensive reference section, this volume can serve the professional as a source book and as a useful guide to continuing work in this area, demonstrating the possibility of creative, systematic, informed research and theory that remain true to human experience. It may also be of particular interest to those in other professions—literary criticism, the arts, the ministry, teaching, and counseling—who often look to psychology (with frequent disappointment) for some help in understanding and dealing with human behavior and experience. The book should enhance the reader's personal and professional growth.

The introductory chapter looks at how the concept of romantic loving evolved through the ages. Three major themes emerge, each emphasized as a defining aspect of romantic love by the succession of historical periods, and they are examined throughout the book from a variety of perspectives. The idea that knowing and being known are definitive aspects of romantic love (drawn from the earliest historical period) is addressed by Friedlander and Morrison, who use the psychoanalytic notion of idealization: "Although not exclusively, it is to a significant extent by virtue of the occurrence of idealization that romantic love can be distinguished from similar forms of interpersonal attraction phenomena." They posit that *not* knowing (completely) and *not* being known (completely) is a vital element of romantic loving. Livingston, however, uses a cognitive framework to discuss the "uncertainty" presented by the incompletely known loved one, the arousal generated by this uncertainty, and the positive experience of reducing this uncertainty. From the middle historical period came the notion of romantic love involving union, with its attendant ecstasy and terror. Among those who consider that concept in this volume are Weiner, who explores the "temporary losses of boundaries between lovers"; Farber, who describes the lovers' fear that fusing will lead to the self being "engulfed or overwhelmed"; Levenson and Harris, who devote much of their chapter to the experience of losing identity that frequently seems to occur when lovers join; and Geller and Howenstine, who note the number of initial schizophrenic breaks brought about by a dissolving sense of self triggered by the experience of "fusing" with a lover. The modern period's stress on the aspects of participation, continuing interaction, and acting together likewise is examined carefully in light of a variety of research data, contexts, and theoretical perspectives. Huesmann, for instance, develops the idea that "continuing love requires an ever-changing array of exchanges"; Csikszentmihalyi focuses on the lovers' working together to provide new, but manageable, challenges to each other; and Goethals stresses the "shared sense of collaboration."

The volume as a whole, however, is not limited to these themes. In addition to the introductory and concluding chapters, there are five parts: In Part One, which focuses on the development of the individual, the authors examine the role of romantic loving in the life of the child, the adolescent, the adult male, and the adult female. Part Two, which presents understandings of romantic loving from diverse theoretical perspectives, contains chapters on psychobiology, psychodynamic theory, information processing, and computer-simulated (algorithmically) romantic relationships. Part Three explores romantic loving within various contexts: the inner life of the individual, groups and their influence, and the broad community context in which temporal patterns emerge. Part Four focuses on the pathologies of love and the therapeutic process. Finally, in Part Five, the authors show how romantic loving provokes, encourages, threatens, frustrates, and enhances the development of personal identity.

I owe an immense debt to the following people for their work, support, suggestions, and love—each made contributions that were crucial and perfectly timed: Dale Booth, Phillip Howard Brakefield, Barbara Classon, Asenath LaRue, Hanna Levenson, Barbara McGraw, Lawrence Perrine, Kate and Kenneth Pope (my parents), Katherine Pope (my sister), Herta and Fritz Redlich, Joe Reese, Marie Reese, Dorothy and Jerome Singer, and Helen Woolf. That this volume came out at all, and that it turned out as well as it did, is, I am almost certain, quite a tribute to me; whereas all errors, weaknesses, and glaring omissions are undoubtedly due to those people I have just listed (and I advise the reader to address criticisms directly to them). I also want to thank everyone involved, particularly each of the authors, for having a kind and generous sense of humor about the major and minor tragedies of life, especially deadlines.

Los Angeles, California   Kenneth S. Pope
September 1980

Contents

Part Five: Love and the Sense of Self

Conclusion

The Authors

Kenneth S. Pope is director of psychological services at Gateways Hospital and Mental Health Center and assistant clinical professor of psychology at the University of California in Los Angeles. He received his B.A. degree (1968) in English literature from Southern Methodist University, his M.A. degree (1972) in English literature from Harvard University, where he was a Woodrow Wilson Fellow, and his Ph.D. degree (1977) in clinical psychology from Yale University; he completed his clinical internship at the Langley Porter Institute of the University of California Medical School, San Francisco.

Pope has been assistant professor of psychiatry and lecturer in psychology at the University of California, Los Angeles, staff psychologist at the Central County (Calif.) Mental Health Center, and clinical psychologist at the Brentwood Veterans Administration Medical Center. His journal articles include such topics as malpractice, the effects of fee assessment on psychotherapy, and sexual intimacy in psychology training. He is the coeditor of *The Stream of Consciousness: Scientific Investigations into the Flow of Human Experience* and *The Power of Human Imagination: New Methods of Psychotherapy* (both with J. L. Singer, 1978). Pope is a recipient of the Frances Mosseker award for fiction and the Belle Mayer Bromberg award for literature.

Mihaly Csikszentmihalyi is professor and chair, Committee on Human Development at the University of Chicago.

Linnda Durré is in private practice, La Jolla, California.

Barry A. Farber is assistant professor of psychology and education at Teachers College, Columbia University.

Steven Friedlander is a staff psychologist at the Langley Porter Institute, and an assistant professor of psychology at the University of California Medical School, San Francisco.

Jesse D. Geller is director of the Psychotherapy Section of the Connecticut Mental Health Center, and an associate professor of clinical psychology at Yale University.

George W. Goethals is senior lecturer on the psychology of personality at Harvard University and consultant in psychology to the Harvard University Health Services.

Charles N. Harris is in private practice, San Francisco.

Richard A. Howenstine is assistant professor of clinical psychology in psychiatry and lecturer in the Department of Psychology at Yale University.

L. Rowell Huesmann is professor of psychology and computer science at the University of Illinois at Chicago Circle.

Anne E. Kazak is a doctoral student in the Community and Clinical Training Program in the Department of Psychology at the University of Virginia.

Hanna Levenson is in private practice, San Francisco.

Diane D. Livingston, currently licensed in Texas, is pursuing further training in clinical psychology at the California School of Professional Psychology, Los Angeles.

Kenneth R. Livingston is assistant professor of psychology at Vassar College.

James C. Miller is director of the Clinical Training Program, and professor of psychology at George Washington University.

Delmont C. Morrison is chief psychologist of the Children's Service of the Langley Porter Institute, and professor of psychology at the University of California Medical School, San Francisco.

Donald C. Ransom is behavioral sciences coordinator of the Family Practice Residency Program at Santa Rosa, California, and associate professor at the University of California Medical School, San Francisco.

N. Dickon Reppucci is director of Community and Clinical Psychology Training, and professor of psychology at the University of Virginia.

Ross Rizley is assistant professor of psychology at Harvard University.

Jerome L. Singer is director of the Clinical Training Program and professor of psychology at Yale University.

Deborah C. Uchalik is a staff psychologist at Gateways Hospital and Mental Health Center, Los Angeles.

Myron F. Weiner is professor and assistant to the chairman, Department of Psychiatry of the University of Texas Health Science Center at Dallas.

On Love
and Loving

*Psychological Perspectives
on the Nature and Experience
of Romantic Love*

1

Defining and Studying Romantic Love

Kenneth S. Pope

Falling in love is madness, say some of the earliest writers. Dido in the *Aeneid*, Catullus in his poetry, Phaedra and Medea in the plays of Euripides—a savage insanity seizes them, tosses them around vigorously, and leaves them destroyed.

How far have we come from that classical conception of romantic love? By the seventeenth century, in a work called by Sir William Osler "the greatest medical treatise ever written by a layman," Robert Burton ([1651] 1963) declared that love was not only madness but also a "disease, frenzy, . . . hell." Among its more notable accomplishments, he asserts, are that "it subverts kingdoms, overthrows cities, towns, families, mars, corrupts, and makes a massacre of men; thunder and lightning, wars, fires, plagues, have not done that mischief to mankind, as this burning lust, this brutish passion. . . . Besides those daily monomachies, murders, effusion of blood, rapes, riot, and immoderate expense, to satisfy their lusts, beggary, shame, loss, torture, punishment, disgrace, loathsome diseases that proceed from thence, worse than calentures and pestilent fevers, those often gouts, pox arthritis, palsies, cramps, sciatica, convulsions, aches, compustions, etc., which torment the body, that feral melancholy which crucifies the soul in this life and everlastingly torments in the world to come" (pp. 192–193).

In his ability to delineate the effects of love in such detail, Burton surely owes a debt of gratitude to Sir Francis Bacon, who had observed more simply that "it is impossible to love and be wise." Writing at the end of the sixteenth century, Bacon ([1597] 1955, p. 28) suggests: "You may observe, that amongst all the great and worthy persons (whereof the memory remaineth, either ancient or recent), there is not one that hath been transported to the mad degree of love: which shews that great spirits and great business do keep out this weak passion." Bacon, suspected by some of having written Shakespeare's plays (for which, let us hope, Shakespeare offered him payment, if only in turn to write some of Bacon's essays), would certainly have found nothing surprising in Hamlet's reaction to love. Hamlet, according to Polonius' account:

> Fell into a sadness, then into a fast,
> Thence to a watch, thence into a weakness,
> Thence to a lightness, and, by this declension,
> Into the madness wherein now he raves . . .
> (Shakespeare [1602] 1957, II, 2, 157–160)

Not everyone, of course, wrote so gloomily of the etiology and course of this "disease." Some offered treatments. Sir John Suckling ([1658] 1963, p. 432), for instance, wrote to his cousin Charles: "Though your disease be in the number of those that are better cured with time than precept . . . I will adventure to pre-scribe to you and of the innocence of the physic you shall not need to doubt, since I can assure you that I take it daily myself." Goethe's Werther, however, thought only a procedure so radical as suicide would rid the body of this "malignant fever."

Truly modern conceptions of love came only in the late nineteenth and twentieth centuries, with the pioneers of the rigor-ous psychological, philosophical, and cultural theory. William James, in his classic *Principles of Psychology*, devoted a full two pages of these volumes to "Love." He traces love to "sexual im-pulses," but admits "these details are a little unpleasant to discuss"

(James [1890] 1950, vol. 2, p. 439). Elsewhere in the work, however, he discusses "disorderly and impulsive conduct" (Mania) and notes that "works on insanity are full of examples of these morbid insistent ideas, in obstinately struggling against which the unfortunate victim's soul often sweats with agony, ere at last it gets swept away" (p. 542). In his list of such afflictions, between "the craving for drink in real dipsomaniacs, or for opium or chloral in those subjugated" and the compulsion to wash one's hands repeatedly, appears love: "the passion of love may be called a monomania to which all of us are subject, however otherwise sane" (p. 543).

Like James, Freud traced the idea of love to sexual impulses (Reik [1941] 1976) and seemed rather puzzled by the whole matter. When asked by a French magazine to explore that aspect of love that went beyond sex, Freud replied: "Up to the present I have not found the courage to make any broad statements on the essence of love and I think that our knowledge is not sufficient to do so" (Reik, p. 25). And at the conclusion of his career he confessed, "We really know very little about love" (Reik, p. 25). Rarely did Freud or such psychoanalytic theorists as Fenichel (1945) deal seriously with falling in love without stressing the regressive qualities. Such regression was not necessarily without redeeming social value. Kris (1951) proposes that regression may be in the "service of the ego," and Balint (1959) suggests that progression itself may have the aim of regression. Such faint praise, however, continues to consider love "regressive."

Subsequent theorists have addressed love more directly. Askew (1965) believes it to be a neurosis; Koenigsberg (1967) says it represents a projection of competitiveness with the father; Becker (1973, p. 166) affirms Rank's assertion of the "bankruptcy of romantic love"; and Kilpatrick (1974) calls it "antisocial." De Rougement (1963, 1969), perhaps the most widely quoted modern authority on the subject, claims that romantic love enshrines suffering and death and is in fact contrary to life itself.

Romantic love, as it emerges from this admittedly biased sample of writings, is at best a primitive, regressive experience, at worst a plague. It is something long ignored by scientific research. Only in the last decade or so have such pioneers as Rubin (1970), Hatfield (Berscheid, Stephan, and Walster, 1971), and the Walsters (1978) undertaken creative, rigorous, systematic research into this topic. However, major compendia in the social and behavioral sciences are silent on the subject.

The purpose of this volume is to explore romantic love as it appears in the development of individuals, groups, and communities, as it is understood within some major theoretical frameworks, and as it touches a variety of human experiences or endeavors. This introductory chapter will note some patterns that may help to place the subject in perspective.

Defining Romantic Love

An initial working definition of romantic love might contain the following elements:

> A preoccupation with another person. A deeply felt desire to be with the loved one. A feeling of incompleteness without him or her. Thinking of the loved one often, whether together or apart. Separation frequently provokes feelings of genuine despair or else tantalizing anticipation of reuniting. Reunion is seen as bringing feelings of euphoric ecstasy or peace and fulfillment.

The adjective *romantic* is probably effective in telling us not so much what the concept includes as what it excludes. It does not refer to love of country, of God, of activities, or of things.

Romantic love can begin as a "crush" or "puppy love" in young children, and there seems to be no point at which one becomes too old to fall in love. Though romantic love seems to be most often directed toward someone of the opposite sex, it can also define the relationship between two people of the same sex. Frequently the presence (or sometimes merely thought) of the loved one can evoke specific physiological reactions: erections for the male and wetness for the female, a lump in the throat, sweaty palms, weak knees, cold feet, a pounding heart, butterflies in the stomach, and dizziness. But ultimately romantic love is a subjective state. As with the phenomenon of pain, an "outsider" may or may not be able to find physiological correlates or describe its etiology. "I'm in love" or "I'm in pain" seem to be statements not capable of solely external verification.

Unable to detect romantic love with certainty by counting behaviors or x-raying the human heart, we can nevertheless emphasize aspects that help set it apart from other human experiences. First, romantic love involves a *preoccupation* with another person. The lover is involved, enthusiastic; a major portion of her or his attention is directed to the beloved. Csikszentmihalyi, in Chapter Seventeen, develops a definition of romantic love based solely on this process of attending. Romantic love is not a casual undertaking, not an activity generally kept on the back burner. Those who are in love do not march to an indifferent drummer.

Second, romantic love involves, or at least allows the involvement of, the whole person. The relationship between lovers can be free, open, and unrestricted. This sets romantic love apart from other relationships which may also involve considerable enthusiasm, attention, and involvement, but in which the roles are *necessarily* unequal or restricting. In the relationship between a parent and an infant, for example, the parent is expected to provide food, shelter, and security to the infant whereas the infant is prevented, by nature, from reciprocating. In a supervisory relationship, one member exercises, by virtue of the relationship itself, an authority toward (or over) the other which cannot be reciprocal. The professional (for example, a doctor or lawyer) is expected, by the very nature of the relationship, to act in accordance with the client's interests, whereas the client is under no such obligation. The romantic relationship imposes no such constraints or necessary inequality. Like friendship, it is a "holistic" relationship.

Why, then, are not all romantic relationships—or all friendships, for that matter—equal? Why are there some romances in which one partner is clearly the "parent," the "supervisor," the "professional," or some role denied to the other? Why are there some romances in which one partner is clearly dominant? One cause, obviously, is the cultural stereotypes and expectations by which we have all been influenced to some degree. The "whole person" is often seen and reacted to predominantly in terms of certain group characteristics (for example, age, gender, race, wealth, I.Q., regional origins). These characteristics may influence any relationship the individual enters into: parental (parents may treat a male offspring differently than they would a female), supervisory (the white supervisor may treat black supervisees differently than white ones), professional, or romantic. But just as differential treatment based on such group characteristics as age, gender, or race is not *inherently* or *necessarily* or *definitionally* an aspect of the parental, supervisory, or professional relationship, differential status or treatment of any sort is not an integral part of romantic loving or of friendship.

Perhaps the major difference between intimate friendship and romantic love is that in romantic love a significantly greater proportion of attention is turned solely toward the other person: we immerse ourselves in another person. Epicurus maintained that *satis magnum alter alteri theatrum sumus* ("each is to the other a theater large enough"). Graham ([1711] 1963, p. 907) wished only to be "in the empire of thy heart, where I should solely be." Freud recognized that the more intense the romantic love between two people, the more they sufficed for each other. And perhaps most vividly, Lewis (1960, p. 98) wrote: "We picture lovers face to face but friends side by side; their eyes look ahead."

The feeling of romantic love, then, calls forth energetic involvement from the lovers. "All functions of the human mind are alive in every act of love," writes Tillich (1963, p. 137), and the lovers are involved primarily with (and in) each other, in a manner that can allow complete reciprocity.

Tracy, in Woody Allen's 1979 movie *Manhattan*, eloquently defines romantic love: "We have laughs together. I care about you. Your concerns are my concerns. We have great sex." All of which would hardly seem to justify the hero's shutting off this experience, let alone the harsh, rejecting assessments of romantic love mentioned in the opening of this chapter. How are we to account for the horror, fear, repulsion, or condescension (for example, love as regression) evoked by this experience?

To some extent, our views may have been shaped by the ways in which we evaluate the myths, dramas, and stories that portray the experience of love. Critics of romantic love, such as de Rougement (1963), lean heavily on works of art (for example, Tristan and Isolde) in which the lovers meet a particularly unhappy ending: death. De Rougement, in fact, identifies the experience of death, which many lovers meet in such stories, with the concept of love itself. Indeed, love stories with unhappy endings, in which one or both lovers die, are numerous; *Antony and Cleopatra*, *Romeo and Juliet*, and *Wuthering Heights* are but three examples. Yet to confuse the unhappy endings of these love stories with what is being revealed about the process of love is similar to confusing the unhappy ending of a tragedy with the theme of the tragedy. Whitehead (1925, p. 17) pursues the meaning of tragedy with considerable clarity: "The essence of dramatic tragedy is not unhappiness. It resides in the solemnity of the remorseless working of things. This inevitableness of destiny can only be illustrated in terms of human life by incidents which involve unhappiness. For it is only by them that the futility of escape can be made evident in the drama. This remorseless inevitableness is what pervades scientific thought. The laws of physics are the decrees of fate."

Love stories seek to convey the solemn, demanding, transforming, surprising process of the unrestrained involvement of two people in each other. To confuse this process with death and sad endings, as many critics do, is to believe that the famous O. Henry story is ultimately about the loss of a watch and some beautiful hair. Setting aside such misconceptions, we can perceive more clearly the source of genuine fear and distancing condescension evoked by love. If tragedy arouses us to feel pity and fear as we watch a human being intimately come to know his or her fate (with such intimacy that some critics have proclaimed that "character" *is* "fate"), love stories can arouse similar feelings as we watch a human being intimately come to know another human being (with such intimacy that metaphorically the two may become one).

One need not believe that each human being has a "heart of darkness" to recognize disturbances and rude shocks that can accompany the experience of getting to know another human being. Apprehending simply the physical attributes of another person—recognizing their burps, farts, snorts, wrinkles, sweat, age spots, moles, urination, and defecation, to name but a few personal characteristics of most people that are curiously absent from many a love song—is enough to turn many of us off, or at least to give us pause ("Would you mind closing the bathroom door, please?"). Swift expressed the devastatingly disconcerting effects of realizing that his beloved actually defecated:

> *"No wonder how I lost my wits;*
> *Oh! Celia, Celia, Celia shits!"*

Of course, it is not only the physical but also the other aspects of a human being that we encounter. And as we become increasingly involved with another person, we are like the four men in Dickey's novel *Deliverance*; off on a journey into the heart of

nature: we are likely to meet what we do not anticipate or comprehend, cannot control or easily assimilate. Unlike the jungle
cruise at Disneyland, the experience is not created for our amuse-
ment, comfort, and safety. As Becker (1973, p. 166) wrote: "Humans have wills and counter wills of their own, in a thousand ways
they can move against us, their very appetites offend us."

The awful (in the sense of inspiring awe) nature of love is
that it brings us up against another person in all her or his offen-
sive, threatening particularities and also that it makes us known in
the same way. We are without the guiding, reassuring constraints
or buffers provided by the limited reciprocity of professional,
parental, supervisory, and other such relationships.

The minds and bodies, the time and energy of lovers are
largely directed to knowing and being known by each other, to
creating a union, to participating in a shared life. I shall suggest in
the next section that these activities of romantic love have emerged
in turn and, one after another becoming manifest in Western history, have been considered defining or predominant. But the process of knowing and becoming known, of union, and of participation are not contradictory, mutually exclusive, or different in
importance. Each is of equal importance in the fulfillment of
romantic love.

Before looking at historical patterns, however, it is worth
pausing a moment to reflect on the claims that romantic love is,
if not destructive, then at least among the more primitive and
regressive activities people undertake. Does devoting ourselves to
another person in such a way genuinely seem less mature than
devotion to music, health, study, poetry, wealth, power, or sports?

An Early Period: To Know and Be Known

Ideal of Love in the Early Period. The central theme of the
earliest love stories—particularly those popular in the classical
period—was the difficult, dangerous, and remorseless process in
which lovers attempted to know each other. They sought a knowledge of not only what made the beloved human but also of what
made him or her different from all other humans. They acquired
a knowledge not only of the head but also of the heart and body.
Something of this expanded meaning of "to know" is caught up in
our phrase "to know in a Biblical sense." Likewise, the German

erkennen and the Greek *gnosis* embrace both the conventional meanings of knowing and also the union achieved through sexual intercourse and other intimate contact.

The conception of romantic love centered on this form of intimate knowing is clearly set forth in that work which, along with the *Iliad*, marks the foundation of Greek and European literature: the *Odyssey*. Odysseus and Penelope are deeply in love, wanting only to be with each other. Even when asked to fight for his country, Odysseus tries all means to avoid separation from her. When recruited by the army, he pretends to be crazy—a ruse that fails. At the end of the *Odyssey*, however, when the process of knowing is fulfilled, there occurs one of the most moving romantic passages in literature. "She flew weeping to his side, flung her arms about his neck and kissed him. . . . Then Odysseus in his turn melted, and wept as he clasped his dear and faithful wife to his bosom. As the sight of land is welcome to men who are swimming towards the shore, when Poseidon has wrecked their ship with fury of his winds and waves; a few alone reach the land, and these, covered with brine, are thankful when they find themselves on firm ground and out of danger—even so was her husband welcome to her as she looked upon him, and she could not tear her two fair arms from about his neck" (Homer, 1969, pp. 248-249).

Why does not this scene take place earlier? After all, Odysseus returns to Ithaca, his home, about halfway through the story (in book thirteen—there are twenty-four books in all). As Athena chides Odysseus in book thirteen, "Anyone but yourself on returning from so long a voyage would at once have gone home to see his wife" (p. 142). And even when the two lovers finally come into the physical presence of each other in book twenty-three, their son, Telemachus, is astounded that his mother does not there and then embrace her husband. "Mother—but you are so hard that I cannot call you by such a name—why do you keep away from my father in this way? Why do you not sit by his side and begin talking to him and asking him questions? No other woman could bear to keep away from her husband when he had come back to her after twenty years of absence, and after having gone through so much" (p. 246).

What seems senseless resistance to Athena and Telemachus is the private process of knowing and being known by each other. Odysseus, in the latter half of the epic, is going about what Athena comes to call "testing" his wife. And Penelope reciprocates. As she tries to explain to a baffled Telemachus: "We [Odysseus and Penelope] shall get to understand one another better by and by, for there are tokens with which we two alone are acquainted, and which are hidden from all others" (p. 246).

Penelope and Odysseus are able to achieve this mutual knowing, unlike Agamemnon and the house of Atreus whose romantic relationships are ever violent and unfulfilled. Agamemnon's one piece of advice to Odysseus—which is happily *not* heeded—is: "Be sure, therefore . . . and not be too friendly even with your wife. Do not tell her all that you know perfectly well yourself. Tell her a part only, and keep your own counsel about the rest" (p. 121).

The extent to which Odysseus and Penelope have identified themselves with this process of knowing and being known by the other is dramatized when Odysseus is deprived of the relationship. During that time, "My name," he tells Polyphemus, "is no one."

The importance of the beloved in all his or her particularities—aspects known only by the lovers and knowable only through love—is underscored heavily in this epic. Neither lover lacks other available and, in some senses, more attractive partners. Penelope's house is literally besieged by insistent suitors. Odysseus finds himself courted by women who, in beauty and some other respects, surpass Penelope, whom he describes as "this woman [who] has a heart as hard as iron" (p. 248). Making it clear to them that his heart belongs to another and that, when possible, he will continue his journey to Penelope, Odysseus nevertheless resides and sleeps with some who court him. The beautiful enchantress Circe is one of these. Another is Calypso, a goddess who wishes to marry him and make him immortal. Yet he spends his time on her island "sitting upon the beach with his eyes filled with tears" (p. 51). And his other partners are ever conscious of what Calypso calls "this wife of yours of whom you are thinking all the time day after day" (p. 52).

When someone is seeking solely a sexual relationship, or perhaps only companionship, any one of a number of available partners will suffice. In a romantic relationship, only the individual beloved, in his or her unique nature, will do.

It is not only what lovers put themselves through in order to "understand one another [in ways] which are hidden from all others," it is also the obvious enjoyment in, acceptance of, and reverence for the deeply human characteristics of the beloved that baffle outsiders such as Telemachus and Athena. Often when the lover carries on about the beloved, it seems as if he or she cannot really see or understand the beloved. If the lover saw with clear eyes—so goes the reasoning of the outsider, and perhaps of the beloved—he or she could not possibly embrace this person. And yet it is precisely this clarity of perception that is the foundation upon which the relationship rests. The lover's enthusiasm and excitement are evoked only by this one other human being, warts and all. And to the lover, this "truth is beauty." Shakespeare expresses quite directly this love that affirms the individual, as he or she exists beyond the customary ways by which things are classified and described.

> My mistress' eyes are nothing like the sun;
> Coral is far more red than her lips' red;
> If snow be white, why then her breasts dun;
> If hairs be wires, black wires grow on her head.
> I have seen roses damask'd, red and white,
> But no such roses see I in her cheeks;
> And in some perfumes is there more delight
> Than in the breath that from my mistress reeks.
> I love to hear her speak—yet well I know
> That music hath a far more pleasing sound;
> I grant I never saw a goddess go—
> My mistress, when she walks, treads on the ground;
> And yet, by heaven, I think my love as rare
> As any she belied with false compare.
>   (Sonnett CXXX)

And Joyce, when he reworked the story of Penelope and Odysseus, concluded by celebrating the theme of openness and deep understanding of the other, in all the beloved's troubling particulars.

The Frustration of Love in the Early Period. To attempt this sort of knowing is to risk failing at it, to risk deception. Penelope confesses to "shuddering all the time through fear that someone might come here and deceive me" (p. 249). The Trojan War itself is based on just this sort of deception, and the disruption of the love between Menelaus and Helen. After the war, Menelaus and Helen, who never stopped loving each other, are reunited and reestablish their relationship in a manner similar to that of Odys-

seus and Penelope. The Trojan War was launched when Menelaus
and his fellow Greeks undertook to recover Helen, who had been
taken away by the gods. Paris, asked to judge the fairest among
Juno, Venus, and Minerva, attended not to the three goddesses
but rather to the bribes they offered him. And in return, according
to Euripides and Stesichorus, he was given, not Helen, but a de-
ceptive semblance of her. Helen herself was swept safely away
to Egypt.

The deception that prevents "knowing," that frustrates
a deep mutual understanding between lovers is rampant in the life
of Agamemnon and the house of Atreus, is bemoaned by the lyr-
ical poets like Catullus, and is presented most charmingly by the
creators of the "new" comedy—Terence, Plautus, and Menander.
The standard plot, in both Roman and Greek comedy of this sort,
involves two lovers prevented from marrying because one of them
is simply the "wrong" person: he or she is not born into a sufficiently high social class, is not wealthy, and so on. Often the father
of one of the lovers prevents the marriage. The lovers seek help
from a clever, funny slave, who is skilled in the art of deception
(all of these stock characters endure; the clever slave appears as
Figaro in *Barber of Seville*). The slave undertakes an elaborate deception which, of course, results in catastrophe. But out of this
chaos comes a surprise: the *real* identity of the "flawed" lover is
discovered—a revelation to both lovers, the other characters, and,
supposedly, the audience as well. When this genuine identity of
the lover is known, all is transformed and the love is fulfilled.

Terror of Love in the Early Period. A third theme emerges
in this earliest period. Romantic love as intimate knowing and being known offers the ideal of fulfillment (Odysseus and Penelope,
the lovers of the new comedies) and the risk of frustration, of
failed knowledge (Agamemnon and the house of Atreus, Paris and
Helen); but it also offers the terror of fulfillment. And the terror
of love for this broad historical period concerned what would be
discovered in this intimate knowing: it is the fear of being discovered, caught, "found out." Nowhere is this prospect more ter-
rifyingly presented than in *Oedipus Rex*. The questions, puzzles,
and seeking for answers in *Oedipus Rex*, like the attempts by lovers
to know and understand each other, always transcend simple
factual information, always concern human identity. When the

Sphinx puts the riddle to the only person who can solve it (the romantic nature of his exchange is horrifyingly portrayed by Franz Stuck's famous portrait "Kiss of the Sphinx"), or when Oedipus initiates the great search for whoever caused the plague, the answers to these questions will strike at the heart of Oedipus's relationship to his beloved, of his identity as it emerges from and is known within that relationship. In this sense, the terror that we will be found out and known for what we are may seem worse than deception and the frustration of understanding between lovers.

A Middle Period: Union

As time passed, the understanding of romantic love gradually changed. Knowing and being known faded into the background, and the union of two people became the defining characteristic of love.

In this new period, as there had in the old, there appeared a popular treatise "on the art of love." These two texts are frequently quoted as a serious lover's presentation of the current "rules," a sort of combination tribute to love and a "how to do it" manual for the novice. But they are of little help to us for both are essentially antilove works—of the same type as many quoted at the opening of this chapter—written to ridicule or disparage, rather than to present and understand, the concept.

Early in the thirteenth century, Andreas Capellanus wrote his classic *De Arte Honeste Amandi*, often taken as the authoritative text of "courtly love." His opening statement that "love is suffering" and his detailed instructions to Walter on how to go about achieving his love give a morbid, constricted picture of romantic lóving. We may catch hints that his praise of the concept is less than sincere when he includes such advice as how to seduce a nun, but it is in the beginning of the last book that he gives the game away entirely: "You must read all this, my dear Walter, not as though you sought thence to embrace the life of lovers, but that being refreshed by its doctrine and having well learned how to provoke the minds of women to love, you may yet abstain from such provocation, and thus merit a greater reward" (Capellanus, 1969, p. 314). For Andrew the Chaplain believes romantic love to go against religion and holy law. "No man through any good deeds can please God so long as he serves in the service of love" (p. 315). To cite this, and similar, popular works as authoritative sources for the age's notions of romantic love is like citing Marx as a source of capitalist ideology.

Andreas adapted his title from Ovid's *Ars Amatoria*. And again, those who refer to this work as an expression and celebration of serious notions of love miss the point. As Lewis (1977, p. 6) wrote in a detailed analysis: "The very design of his *Art of Love* presupposes an audience to whom love is one of the minor peccadilloes of life, and the joke consists of treating it seriously— in writing a treatise, with rules and examples *en règle* for the nice conduct of illicit loves. It is funny, as the ritual solemnity of old gentlemen over their wine is funny. Food, drink, and sex are the oldest jokes in the world; and one familiar form of the joke is to be very serious about them. From this attitude the whole tone of *Ars Amatoria* flows." Among Ovid's advice for the aspiring lover: Don't visit her on her birthday—it'll cost too much.

Any dividing point between historical periods is, of course, somewhat arbitrary. But if we consider the second historical period to begin sometime around the tenth or eleventh century and to stretch into the sixteenth or seventeenth century, one difference in the expression of romantic love becomes immediately apparent: the latter age involves much more emphasis on adultery. If, as I am suggesting here, the union of the lovers—two becoming one—is the primary concern of this second historical period, then the adulterous nature of many of their love stories can be seen in its proper context. Particularly in the Middle Ages, when marriages were formed almost exclusively along economic or utilitarian lines, those who valued "true love" had to give serious thought to adultery. The claims of duty, ownership, and obligation between husband and wife were seen as antithetical to the expression of romantic love. The marriage bonds were one among many of the potential barriers that could frustrate lovers in their search for union. Even the rules of courtly love of the type laid down by Andreas Capellanus were quickly seen as impediments to the true joining of two people in love. *Sir Gawain and the Green Knight* humorously dramatizes the common rejection of these "rules."

Ideal of Love in the Middle Period. The ideal of complete union with the beloved is the central concern of this second broad historical period and finds its most fervent expression in metaphysical poetry. Again and again, this poetry picks up the theme, turning it over for another look. Lord Herbert of Cherbury puts it simply:

> *As one another's mystery*
> *Each shall be both*
> *Yet both but one.*

Cowley points to the explosive transformation:

> *Woe to her stubborn heart, if once mine come*
> *Into the self-same room,*
> *'Twill tear and blow up all within,*
> *Like a grenade shot into a magazine.*
> *Then shall Love keep the ashes, the torn parts,*
> *Of both our broken hearts:*
> *Shall out of both one new one make.*

And from Donne:

> *Love's riddles are, that though thy heart depart,*
> *It stays at home, and thou with losing savest it:*
> *But we will have a way more liberal*
> *Than changing hearts, to join them; so we shall*
> *Be one, and one another's all.*

And, in some of the most beautiful lines ever written, the conclusion of Donne's "A Valediction Forbidding Mourning," this idea finds expression. The speaker, about to leave on a journey that will separate him from his mistress, assures her:

> *Our two souls, therefore, which are one,*
> *Though I must go, endure not yet*
> *A breach, but an expansion,*
> *Like gold to air thinness beat.*
>
> *If they be two, they are two so*
> *As stiff twin compasses are two;*
> *Thy soul, the fixed foot, makes no show*
> *To move, but doth if the other do.*
> *And though it in the center sit,*
> *Yet, when the other far doth roam,*
> *It leans, and hearkens after it,*
> *And grows erect as that comes home.*

Such wilt thou be to me, who must
Like the other foot obliquely run:
Thy firmness draws my circle just,
And makes me end where I begun.

Frustration of Love in the Middle Period. The ideal of union was not always achieved. Many of the works of this period explore the difficulties lovers encounter when laws, customs, morals, previous commitments (including marriage), politics, heritage, and the various vicissitudes of life maintain a separation, prevent a union. The warring families of *Romeo and Juliet*, the sword that lies between Tristan and Isolde as they sleep "together," the fact that Guinevere would betray Arthur and Lancelot would lose his powers in battle should they consummate their union—these represent but a few of the barriers to union. In Shakespeare's *Antony and Cleopatra*, however, these barriers remain in the background and the process of a complete joining together—with all its attendant terrors of losing one's self, one's separate identity, one's "shape"—is seriously explored.

The play opens in Alexandria, in a room in Cleopatra's palace. Philo and Demetrius, friends of Mark Antony, are talking.

> Philo: *Nay, but this dotage of our general's*
> *O'erflows the measure. Those his goodly eyes*
> *That o'er the files and musters of war*
> *have glowed like plated Mars, now bend, now turn*
> *The office and devotion of their view*
> *Upon a tawny front. His captain's heart,*
> *Which in the scuffles of great fights hath burst*
> *The buckles on his breast, reneges all temper*
> *And is become the bellows and the fan*
> *To cool a gypsie's lust.*
> (Shakespeare [1607] 1970, I, 1, 1-10)

This passage, like those quoted in the opening of this chapter, depicts romance as a pathological process. It presents a good man fallen into some kind of dotage, a man once a fine soldier now merely a lover. And Antony himself agrees:

> Antony: *These strong Egyptian fetters I must break*
> *Or lose myself in dotage.*
> (I, 2, 130-131)

As Reik ([1941] 1976, p. 132) puts it: "The person whom love approaches does not welcome it as a guest but tries to chase it

away as an intruder." But Antony opens himself more and more
to Cleopatra, realizing that her wishes, feelings, and desires increasingly become his (a process that, as we shall see, is reciprocal).

> Cleopatra: *Antony will be himself.*
> Antony: *But stirred by Cleopatra.*
> (I, 1, 49-50)

He is not gently, subtly stirred, as one might be stirred by background music: he gives himself to her totally.

> Antony: *I go from hence*
> *Thy soldier, servant, making peace or war*
> *As thou affects.*
> (I, 3, 85-86)

This process is quite dramatic, obvious to those dealing with the
two lovers.

> Canidius: *So our leader's led . . .*
> (III, 7, 86)

Antony's opening himself up to Cleopatra seems to have no bounds:

> Antony: *Egypt, thou knewest too well*
> *My heart was to thy rudder tied by the strings*
> *And thou shouldst tow me after. O'er my spirit*
> *Thy full supremacy thou knewest, and that*
> *Thy beck might from the bidding of the gods*
> *Command me.*
> (III, 11, 61-66)

His calling her "Egypt" represents more than a recognition
of her formal identification with the country of which she is queen.
It is giving to the individual person an importance once accorded
only to such abstractions as the state. The lovers are willing to
give themselves to each other and no longer give military victories,
political advancement, and the concerns of nationalism their chief
allegiance.

> Antony: *Let Rome in Tiber melt and the wide arch*
> *Of the ranged empire fall! Here is my space.*
> *Kindgoms are clay . . .*
> (I, 1, 40-42)

> Cleopatra: *Melt Egypt into Nile . . .*
> (II, 5, 99)

Cleopatra: *Sink Rome ...*
(III, 4, 20)

Antony and Cleopatra are united to such an extent that the other characters of the play repeatedly mistake them for one another and comment on their blending.

Enobarbus: *Hush! Here comes Antony.*
Charmion: *Not he! The Queen!*
(I, 2, 80–81)

Caesar: *Antony is not more manlike*
Than Cleopatra, nor the queen of Ptolemy
More womanly than he ...
(I, 4, 5–7)

Terror of Love in the Middle Period. The terror of this experience is the sense of losing one's own identity. Philo speaks of "sometimes when he is not Antony" (I, 1, 67); and Antony himself fears: "I lose myself" (III, 4, 25). As he opens himself up for the two to become one, his self leaks out, empties out, melts away —and finally it seems as if he cannot even hold his physical shape.

Enobarbus: *... The full Caesar will*
Answer his [Antony's] emptiness.
(III, 13, 39–40)

Enobarbus: *Sir, sir, thou art so leaky*
That we must leave thee to thy sinking ...
(III, 13, 72–73)

Antony: *Authority melts from me.*
(III, 13, 110)

Antony: *Eros, thou yet beholdst me?*
Eros: *Ay, noble lord.*
Antony: *Sometimes we see a cloud that's dragonish;*
A vapor sometime like a bear or lion,
A towered citadel, a pendant rock,
A forked mountain, or blue promontory
With trees upon't that nod unto the world
And mock our eyes with air. Thou has seen these signs;
They are black vesper's pageants.
Eros: *Ay, my lord.*
Antony: *That which is now a horse, even with a thought*
The rack dislimns, and makes it indistinct
As water is in water.
Eros: *It does, my lord.*

Antony: *My good knave Eros, now thy captain is*
Even such a body. Here I am Antony;
Yet cannot hold this visible shape, my knave.

(IV, 14, 1-19)

In uniting, both lovers experience this terrifying process of seeming disintegration, of giving up a separate identity. And yet, as de Chardin puts it: "At what moment do lovers come into the most complete possession of *themselves*, if not when they are lost in each other?" (May, 1969, p. 311).

It is this sense of a new, deeper identity that each affirms at the conclusion of the play.

Cleopatra: *Now from head to foot*
I am marble constant.

(V, 2, 296-297)

Antony: *Behold this man.*

(IV, 8, 27)

A Modern Period: Participation

Modern Agonies of Love: Terror, Frustration and Control. Gradually, over the last three centuries, the focus of romantic love seems again to have shifted. Issues of control and dependence threaten an ideal love in which both lovers participate, in which both act even as they are acted upon, in which the feelings, needs, wills, and wants of both are affirmed by both.

Napoleon, having met Countess Walenska in the Tuileries, rendered an ultimatum—either she would love him or he would grind her people in the dust. More and more in the current age, the ideal of love has given way to technology, strategy, manipulation, and coercion. Napoleon demanded control: he shaped the relationship into threat and surrender. For the terror of romantic love in the modern period is of being out of control, of losing our autonomy, independence, and seeming freedom to accomplish whatever goals we set for ourselves. We have become a nation of "can-do" people—a nation that rejoices in putting a man on the moon, in being number one, in nailing the coonskin to the wall. From our earliest school days, we pledge never "to give or receive help" on examinations and in other related activities. The reciprocity and interdependence involved in romantic loving hardly coincide with the ideals of freedom, autonomy, and "being in charge" of our lives. Toffler (1970) has noted in *Future Shock* the research suggesting that those who are most successful in Modern America are those who are least heavily involved in relationships and are most able to disengage quickly, frequently, and without lingering pain. As long as we do not sublet our "personal space" on a long-term basis, we are in an ideal position to act independently, to adapt to the rapidly changing environment, and to maintain as orderly a life as possible. The ideal of romantic love in which two people freely participate, then, is frustrated by the creation of relationships that are controllable through: (1) the coercion of one partner by the other; (2) the use of technologies or strategies by which one or both partners maintain the semblance of a loving relationship while keeping themselves at a distance and "in control"; and (3) the giving of themselves over to what may be a delightful, terrifying, stressful, exhilarating experience only to the extent that they know they retain the ability to disengage without undue pain, energy, or interruption to the daily business of life (much as, when learning how to swim, we keep a watchful eye on the bank, always making sure we can thrash our way back and pull ourselves out of the water should we panic).

These frustrated (only in the sense of romantic love—they may be quite adaptive, useful, and pleasurable in other respects) relationships are common in the literature of the last three centuries. In the eighteenth century, rape became a phenomenally popular literary theme. Perhaps the most influential work was Richardson's *Clarissa*, in which Lovelace accomplishes his goal by drugging his beloved.

Interestingly, the use of drugs to maintain control in a relationship continues to the present, and even into our anticipations of the brave new worlds of the future. But whereas in the eighteenth and nineteenth centuries drugs were used by one person to control another, in the twentieth century they are chiefly used by the individual to control him or herself in the relationship. In Woody Allen's 1977 movie *Annie Hall*, the heroine demands Valium and marijuana before having sex. The drug is part of distancing herself and her feelings from the experience, and in one scene we actually see two images of her: one remaining in bed, the other getting up and walking away. Men have drugs available to them to prevent premature ejaculation. These ointments are actually local anesthetics, and the resultant "mature" ejaculation shoots forth from someone who has numbed himself to retain control. Actual drugs need not be used. Techniques have been developed that produce the same dulled awareness of the immediate experience, as this scene from Woody Allen's 1972 movie *Play It Again, Sam* presents:

> Linda: *What were you thinking about while we were doing it? Hmm?*
> Allan: *Willie Mays.*
> Linda: *Do you always think of baseball players when you're making love?*
> Allan: *It keeps me going.*
> Linda: *Yeah, I couldn't figure out why you kept yelling "slide."*

It is not only in sexual aspects of relationships that achieving or maintaining control is seen as crucial and for which numerous strategies and technologies, customs and habits have been developed. More generally, "lack of control"—or at least the sense of control—is seen as the cause of much that is wrong with our lives, and its amelioration as the way to set things right once again. A standard tome of psychoanalysis states quite unequivocally: "All neurotic phenomena are based on insufficiencies of the normal control apparatus" (Fenichel, 1945, p. 85). "Learned helplessness" as an explanatory mechanism for depression and other psychopathology is still another statement of the theme. Bandura's (1977) social learning theory emphasizes the crucial expectations of "self-efficacy"; Meichenbaum (1978) believes that "a sense of helplessness with regard to one's internal life is an important component of many presenting problems. Common to each of the imagery-based therapies is the teaching of imagery control" (p. 389); and Strupp (1970), reviewing the literature of psychotherapy, argues that the major implication of the various forms of psychotherapy has to do with the degree to which individuals learn to control their emotions or their impulsive activity.

If the adaptive, effective, efficient, and appropriate locus of control is internal, the modern ideal of romantic love as participation in something beyond the self (that is, participation in that to which one is vulnerable, over which one does not have maximal control, and in which one at best may be said to share responsibility with an equally important other person whose desires, feelings, plans, and understandings may be contrary to one's own) stands as an inconvenience or threat. Literature has tended to celebrate self-affirmation and freedom from such frustrated relationships. In 1894, Chopin wrote:

> But she saw beyond that bitter moment a long procession of years to come that would belong to her absolutely. . . . There would be no powerful will bending hers in that blind persistence with which men and women believe they have a right to impose a private will upon a fellow-creature. . . . And yet she had loved him—sometimes . . . what did it matter! What could love, the unsolved mystery, count for in the face of this possession and self assertion which she suddenly recognized as the strongest impulse of her being!
>
> "Free! Body and soul free!" she kept whispering.
>
> (Pearson and Pope, 1976, p. 132)

In 1862, Meredith wrote:

> Like sculptured effigies they might be seen
> Upon their marriage-tomb, the sword between,
> Each wishing for the sword that severs all.
>
> (Pearson and Pope, p. 129)

The sword that served as a temporary barrier to the complete union of Tristan and Isolde is now used by potential lovers to destroy the relationship entirely. The ability to retain control, if only the previously mentioned fail-safe ability to disengage entirely—quickly, effectively, efficiently—is cultivated, refined, and treasured. A popular book, *How to Fall Out of Love*, offers a "step-by-step guide" which includes such techniques as "silent ridicule" and "repulsion." The latter involves finding "a quiet place where you won't be disturbed. Then think of a scene in which you are about to have physical contact with the person you've loved. You are about to touch, embrace or kiss that person and just as you get close to him or her you see and smell that he or she is covered with ooze or excrement or whatever you find most repulsive. You pull back, not wanting to touch or kiss excrement, and as you turn away, suddenly everything is gone, including the person. The air is clear and sweet and you feel fresh and new" (Phillips and Judd, 1978, p. 74). Another book along these lines is *Letting Go*, which offers a "12-week personal action program to overcome a broken heart" (Wanderer and Cabot, 1978).

Many guidebooks on handling love suggest a sort of "object relations theory": The very real person who was, or is, or might have been a lover is conceived as an object over whose ability to affect us we maintain control. We withhold affirmation of them as people. We are ready to cover them with excrement mentally to make more real their lack of worth to us. As Dick Christie advises Allan Felix, when Nancy has left him, in Woody Allen's movie *Play It Again, Sam*:

> Dick: *Allan, you've invested your emotions in a losing stock.*
> *It was wiped out. It dropped off the board. Now what*
> *do you do, Allan? You reinvest. Maybe in a more stable*
> *stock. Something with long-term growth possibilities.*
> Allan: *Who are you gonna fix me up with, General Motors?*

The rape scene in Richardson's *Clarissa* makes vivid yet another facet of romantic love in relation to issues of control and dependence. Clarissa submits only when she is drugged. Insofar as romantic love invites us to modify our ideal of a securely internal locus of control, to recognize and affirm as vitally important someone else who can overwhelm us with his or her influence and effect upon us, the experience seems to resemble an addiction. As a recent book, *Love and Addiction*, puts it: "Interpersonal addiction—love addiction—is just about the most common, yet least recognized, form of addiction" (Peele and Brodsky, 1975, p. 17). *Letting Go* outlines reassuring steps for handling such an addiction when the supply dries up: "The first week of separation is the hardest. Suddenly you find yourself without the gratifying supply of love; you've been cut off 'cold turkey.' . . . The same principles of behavior therapy used successfully to treat people who are addicted to foods, drugs, alcohol and even sexual compulsions can be applied to your addiction to your former lover" (Wanderer and Cabot, 1978, p. 34).

Of course, an ounce of prevention can save us pounding mental images of our beloved with ooze and excrement, and preventive strategies (primary intervention) have been explored. Better, perhaps, than even the most painless and effective methods of kicking addictions is simply not to become addicted in the first place. Eighteenth-century literature's preoccupation with rape (with direct and indirect uses of force) gave way to the widespread pornography—not so publicly obvious or openly discussed as it is today—in the art and literature of the nineteenth century. Unlike seduction managed through drugs, direct force, threats, deception, obligation, or bartering, pornography need not involve any recognition or affirmation of another human being. Control is always ours: whenever we desire, whenever we are "through," we simply close the book, put away the pictures, or leave the theater. The appeal is obvious and overwhelming. A character in Albee's *Zoo Story* (1961) remarks that when we are young, pornographic pictures are a substitute for doing it with someone else; and when we get older, being with someone else becomes a substitute for the pictures. Even a person at high risk for "interpersonal addiction" can relax with pornography. It takes the worry out of being close.

A Modern Ideal of Loving. The main themes of romantic love—knowing and being known, union, and participation—are not mutually exclusive. All three have been present to some extent throughout history, though each historical age, as suggested here, seems to have cherished one as a first among equals. They represent the heart of romantic love: the careful, honest giving over of ourselves to knowing another human being even as we are known; the entering into a union with that person; the participating, with unlimited reciprocity, in a shared venture in which we are active and influencing the other even as the other acts and influences us. We neither hoard control of our own life nor thrust responsibility for ourselves into someone else's hands. Romantic love is the recognition and affirmation of both the self and someone else, no matter how flawed both may be. Though it may mean "you have to have a little faith in people," as Tracy urges in Woody Allen's *Manhattan*, it is the very opposite of distortion and idealization.

Coming full circle to the modern retelling of the story of Odysseus, James Joyce's *Ulysses*, we find Molly and Leopold Bloom—neither of them idealized in much of any sense. Molly, lying in bed, drifting off to sleep at the end of the book, reflects on herself and her husband (a clumsy, balding, fat, comic man of such particulars that it would seem that to recognize him as he is would prevent her from affirming him as important, desirable, and even in some ways wonderful to her). And yet,

> *The sun shines for you he said the*
> *day we were lying among the rhododendrons*
> *on Howth head in the grey tweed suit*
> *and his straw hat . . .*

> *yes first I gave him the bit*
> *of seedcake out of my mouth and it*
> *was leapyear like now yes 16 years*
> *ago my God after that long kiss I*
> *near lost my breath yes he said*
> *I was a flower of the mountains yes . . .*
> *that was one true thing he said in his*
> *life and the sun shines for you today*
> *yes that was why I liked him because*
> *I saw he understood or felt what a*
> *woman is . . . and 0 that awful deepdown*
> *torrent 0 and the sea the sea crimson*
> *sometimes like fire and the glorious*
> *sunsets . . . and then I asked him with*
> *my eyes to ask again yes and then*
> *he asked me would I yes to say*
> *yes my mountain flower and first*
> *I put my arms around him yes and*
> *drew him down to me so he could*
> *feel my breasts all perfume yes and*
> *his heart was going like mad and*
> *yes I said yes I will yes.*
>   (Joyce [1914] 1961, pp. 782–783)

Toward a Better Understanding of Romantic Loving

This chapter, an attempt to introduce the topic of romantic loving and to trace its history, has attended almost exclusively to poets and other artists. The patterns discerned here emerge from literature. There is always the issue of what artistic themes represent. Do these "fictions" present common experiences of the time and culture, new patterns that people may come to embrace (life tending to imitate art), fantasies enjoyed by the audience but never reflected in their lives, or simply the idiosyncratic vision of the individual artist? There is clearly a need to expand our understanding of these themes—and of romantic love more generally—beyond an almost exclusive reliance upon literary sources, however rich they may be.

This volume attempts a more inclusive, systematic exploration of romantic loving. The chapters to come will struggle to specify the defining characteristics of romantic loving; to explore the ways in which individuals experience love at different times in their development and in various contexts; to present, evaluate, and synthesize the evidence supporting the diverse notions we have come to believe about loving; and to help create a basis for understanding this phenomenon, a basis not only personal and artistic but also scientific.

2

Childhood

Steven Friedlander
Delmont C. Morrison

A precise and satisfactory definition of romantic love has eluded even those social scientists who have recently risen to the challenge of its scientific study. However, the phenomenon may be identified in one of its manifestations as an affectively charged subjective experience characterized by an intense longing for and preoccupation with another person. In the presence of this person the individual experiences powerful affect and physiological arousal; the individual aspires to be the exclusive recipient of the loved one's attention, interest, and approval, is painfully sensitive to indications of rejection, and is thus susceptible to feelings of jealousy when this aspiration goes unrealized. Pope has elaborated on this experience in Chapter One: "A feeling of incompleteness without him or her. . . . Separation frequently provokes feelings of genuine despair or else tantalizing anticipation of reuniting. Reunion is seen as bringing feelings of euphoric ecstasy or peace and fulfillment."

Consideration of this description, as well as a review of varying theoretical discussions of romantic love (for example, Berscheid and Walster, 1974; Capellanus [13th c.] 1969; Koenigsberg, 1967; Reik [1941] 1957; Rubin, 1974; Walster and Walster, 1978), reveal that at the core of this experience is an internal need state that is frustrated in its efforts to gain satisfaction. The implicated need states tend to be variations on the theme of narcissistic injury or threat to self-esteem and include the wish to rediscover the total love of infancy, to master the trauma of losing the original love object, to achieve perfection, to relieve anxiety, or to make sense of otherwise confusing and incomprehensible affective arousal. Hence, both a *need state* and its *frustration* are central to the romantic love experience, and both, in concert, set the stage for the third and perhaps most definitive component of the romantic love experience—*idealization* of the object. It is the idealization of the object that invests it with the qualities and characteristics that establish its desirability to the individual. And finally, it is this investiture and idcalization, in league with frustrated need state, that establishes the fourth and final component of the romantic love experience—the *fantasy* that possession of the object will satisfy the myriad of frustrated needs and thereby result in a blissful, conflict-free existence.

This conceptualization of romantic love accords the process of idealization an essential and definitive role in the romantic love experience. While recognizing that this is not the only factor that is operative in the occurrence of this phenomenon, we have chosen to focus our discussion on the role of idealization and fantasy. Our decision emerges from the belief that idealization and fantasy are the sine qua non of the romantic love experience, and that they have particular relevance to childhood in general. Hence, while acknowledging the prerequisite of a motivating, frustrated need, this chapter will focus on the idealized fantasy and the nature and development of romantic ideation in the child as they interrelate with the affective and interpersonal aspects of the romantic love experience. This focus represents a beginning attempt to integrate, or at least reconcile, the parallel phenomena of cognitive and affective development.

Although not exclusively, it is to a significant extent by virtue of the occurrence of idealization that romantic love can be distinguished from similar forms of interpersonal attraction phenomena, including, for example, liking (Berscheid and Walster, 1974; Rubin, 1974), companionate love (Walster and Walster,

1978), or attachment (Bowlby, 1969; Harlow, 1958). Thus, not surprisingly, the necessary conditions for the occurrence of idealization overlap with and add to those of the more general romantic love experience.

As already described, a frustrated need state, most often a threat to or actual loss of self-esteem, is an integral part of the romantic love experience and provides the impetus for idealization of the romantic object. The recognition of one's own imperfection and incompleteness is at the root of the idealized perception of the romantic object as self-sufficient, all-powerful, and omniscient—in a word, perfect. The object of romantic love is viewed as possessing all those characteristics that the individual lacks and which, if possessed, would restore the valued experience of self as complete and perfect. Thus the motive to possess the romantic object is related to the wish to achieve perfection and completeness (see Reik [1941] 1957).

In order to permit the attribution of such idealized characteristics to the romantic love object, the individual selected to serve this function is often one who is not readily available or knowable. In this way, a relative lack of familiarity and partial knowledge of the romantic object serve to facilitate the process of idealization. Similarly, obstacles to the attainment of the wished-for object also facilitate idealization, as well as generating frustration and painful anticipation. This frustration adds affective fuel to the process and thus kindles idealization of the object. Additionally, such obstacles tend generally to enhance the object's desirability, in part by supporting the inability to know the object fully. Myths and classical literature—Tristan and Isolde, Romeo and Juliet—contain this theme of unattainability, and empirical study tends to support this notion (Driscoll, Davis, and Lipetz, 1972). Of course, depending on the intensity of the individual's affective needs, the removal of such obstacles and exposure to increasing knowledge of the object may not completely mitigate continued idealization.

Manifestations of Romantic Love in Childhood

Consideration of our everyday vocabulary confirms the existence of romantic love in childhood. Puppy love, infatuation, and the ever-present crush immediately call forth images of childhood, and, not surprisingly, each is thus often preceded by the modifier "childish." In fact, it can be argued that romantic love, by definition, is childish and the special province of childhood. Moreover, the child's experience of romantic love can be regarded as the prototype and paradigmatic of the romantic love experience in adulthood. When an adult is smitten, the more intense the experience the more inclined we are to regard it as a "childish crush" and, not unusually, dismiss it as an index of immaturity. In fact, it would perhaps be more accurate to substitute "immature" for "childish" in describing such romantic love, for the reference is to the very special cognitive and affective qualities of the child that uniquely suit him or her to the experience.

From the adult perspective, these qualities—which include the abdication, loss, or distortion of reality in the service of idealization, and the surrender of self or loss of boundaries between self and object—may be childish. From a developmental perspective, however, these qualities are childlike and are descriptive of the child's very natural incompleteness: the ongoing and active involvement in the development and discovery of self, and hence, the fragile self-esteem; the still-fluid and permeable boundaries between self and other, resulting in an ever-ready capacity to share the qualities of the other and thereby own them; the relative lack of resources to satisfy, in reality, the many needs that are so characteristic of the developmental process; the struggle to make sense of and integrate the various confusing, powerful, and often overwhelming feelings experienced; and finally, the inherent requirement that these developmental challenges be negotiated in a manner consistent with the limited capacities specific to the child's level of cognitive development and general maturity. Although for the adult these characteristics might be regarded as immature or childish, they are the very essence of childhood and thus, for the child, they are both axiomatic and definitive.

The Family Romance. The essence of the romantic love experience in childhood is succinctly illustrated in the family romance, a complex set of interacting forces and circumstances that is often regarded as the paradigmatic romantic love experience. A major developmental task for the child is to move from a dependent state in the family, in which all basic needs are satisfied, to one in which satisfaction of needs can be obtained independently, outside the family constellation. The child has the unique experience of a prolonged and intense emotional attachment to a parent that is associated with need satisfaction and pleasure. The importance of this attachment is further enhanced by the fact that the child's limited cognitive capacities and narcissism contribute to the perception that this relationship is the most important, and perhaps the only one in which the parent is involved. With growing cognitive maturity, paralleled by increasing erotic feelings, the child must move from this state to one in which it is recognized that all needs can no longer be satisfied in this relationship and that he or she must compete with others, most typically the same-sex parent, for the valued opposite-sex parent's affection. Gorney (1979) has suggested that the functional value of the incest taboo, the factor ultimately responsible for this self-esteem damaging and frustrating realization, is to necessitate the child's movement away from dependence on the family and toward more autonomous functioning in society. Sexual and aggressive fantasies reach a pitch at this time, and in interaction with caretakers, most often the parents, the child discovers feelings, wishes, and other aspects of self that are undesirable and which produce anxiety. The highly valued opposite-sex parent is now forbidden to the child and thus less knowable. In short, the necessary conditions for idealization, and thus romantic love, are satisfied. The child longs to possess the forbidden opposite-sex parent, with whom an idealized relationship is fantasied.

Resolution of this complex conflict optimally occurs via identification with the same-sex parent. A persisting romantic fantasy with the opposite-sex parent as object would provide no resolution, and identification with the romantic object would be antithetical to optimal development. It is likely, however, that in the course of struggling with these conflicts the child may experiment with identification with the romantic object, choosing to take on characteristics of the object in an effort to accomplish the goal of possession. Identification with the object may in fact be an integral part of the romantic love experience in that it may represent a strategy intended to increase the likelihood of possessing the object. Indeed, if, as does Rubin (1974), we conceptualize romantic love as one variant of those phenomena described in the interpersonal attraction literature, then there is some empirical evidence for the wisdom of such a tactic. Thus Thelan, Dollinger, and Roberts (1975) have demonstrated that being imitated increased the imitated child's attraction to the imitator (see also McCall, 1974). Although identification with the romantic object may occur in the course of the family romance, various factors discourage this as a satisfactory ultimate resolution, and the child achieves partial gratification via identification with that person most highly valued by and who actually possesses the object—the same-sex parent (see Kagan, 1958).

The specific form and content of the various forces and protagonists in this family romance are thought by many to be the prototype of romantic love and to form the emotional template into which all subsequent romantic love experiences are fitted. In general, under the trauma of having to move out of the family, the previously experienced idealized state, in which the child's conception of self was more valued, is evoked. In the face of this, and subsequent experiences of narcissistic injury, the child seeks outside figures that will bolster self-esteem and satisfy frustrated needs. To the extent that the chosen figure is only partially known and unattainable, the frustration and narcissistic injury will fuel the idealization of the object whereby it is invested with extraordinary powers and virtues more or less specific and complementary to the child's frustrated needs. The romantic love process is thus set in motion, with the child striving to possess the object.

Romantic Love, Identification, and Hero Worship. To the extent that the chosen object becomes an ego-ideal rather than, or in addition to, a romantic love object, the child may identify with the object. The distinction between the choice of an identificatory model and that of a romantic love object, and the associated processes and motives of identification and romantic love (see Bronfenbrenner, 1960), is critical. Identification may be a more mature process in that it more clearly requires recognition of boundaries between self and object. In fact, the process associated with romantic love may be a developmental precursor of identification, as is clearly the case in the family romance. Further, the identification process and model do not necessarily involve idealization or a fantasied relationship, whereas these are necessary aspects of the romantic love experience. Finally, the motivating factors in the two phenomena are quite different. Freud ([1921] 1965, p. 47) summarized this distinction succinctly: "It is easy to state in a formula the distinction between an identification with the father and the choice of the father as an object. In the first case one's father is what one would like to *be*, and in the second he is what one would like to *have*."

This distinction between identification and romantic love, in terms of process, motive, and outcome, can become obscured, however, in those instances in which idealization of the identificatory model occurs. The blurring of the boundaries between the two phenomena is in part a consequence of the fact that the choice of an object for romantic love, and the nature of the associated process, will depend on factors related to the child's cognitive and psychosexual stage of development. For example, an equivalent or variant of the romantic love phenomenon, often occurring in latency-age children, is hero worship, in which the romantic object and identificatory model approach identity. Hence, fortified by the decreased internal press of drives, the latency-age child gradually moves into the external world in which issues of mastery and self-esteem loom most saliently. Responding to these specific issues and needs, the child may idealize a popular sports figure, a characteristic of *romantic* object choice, but then, consistent with the motive for identification, subsequently seek to become *like* that idealized person. Characteristics are attributed to the hero which, if duplicated in the child's self, would tend to enhance his or her ability to manage the associated developmental challenges. Additionally, the child's specific level of cognitive development will determine the extent to which the possession of concrete objects related to the hero is equated with the possession of the power and wished-for characteristics that have been attributed to the hero. Such acquisition of symbols that advertise similarity to the idealized hero is relatively commonplace. Hence, the child will insist on eating the breakfast cereal endorsed by a particular hero. Later in development, the same phenomenon is evidenced by the child who wishes to dress like or affect a hairdo similar to that of a particular person. Although the advertising industry capitalizes on this phenomenon, in certain instances such hero worship can play an important role in the socialization process. For example, Superman, who is all-powerful and knowing, is also an advocate of "truth, justice, and the American way." Thus, in the process of idealizing and subsequently striving to be like the hero, the child learns those qualities that are valued by the culture.

The manifestation of romantic ideation in the form of hero worship most typically casts the hero in a socially acceptable role.

However, the reverse side of romantic ideation, which has been ignored in the literature, constitutes an increasingly important phenomenon, the understanding of which will further our appreciation of the manner in which aggressive and sexual impulses find satisfaction in romantic fantasies. Cultural evidence for the idealization of the socially unacceptable or "negative" romantic object is apparent in the medieval worship of the devil, the glorification of criminal folk heroes—such as Jesse James and Bonnie and Clyde —and the recent idolization of rock music figures who intentionally project images of exaggerated evil, sexuality, and aggressiveness.

Although the same impulses and affect fuel the child's idealization of both forms of hero, in the more negative sexual and aggressive impulses are given overt expression. The content of the idealization process places special emphasis on power, both sexual and aggressive, and in this way assists the child in managing the rejected self and associated affect. Negative components of self are legitimized by virtue of their idealization, and the object is perceived as manifesting the unacceptable qualities without anxiety, guilt, or condemnation. Such romanticized figures characteristically possess these anxiety-producing, socially unacceptable qualities in a manner that, somewhat paradoxically, provides them with power, prestige, and pleasure. As a consequence of the child's capacity for romantic ideation and identification, the unacceptable aspects of the child's previously rejected self obtain acceptance and gratification.

In its somewhat nebulous place between identification and romantic love, the object of hero worship is often characterized by a vaguely unreal or storybook quality. The hero often seems a caricature whose attributes are undisguised reflections of the specific needs and conflicts with which the child is struggling. Similarly, heroes created by our culture seem specifically designed to facilitate idealization. They often possess a mysterious quality that precludes familiarity. Note, for example, Superman's alter ego and the Lone Ranger's mask of anonymity. Interestingly, consistent with the more general process associated with the "negative" romantic object, in these instances the same mystery and anonymity are present, but in an exaggerated and overt manner as seen in the members of one popular rock group who paint their faces for concerts and maintain their anonymity offstage by refusing to be photographed out of costume.

Impact on Development. It can be seen that inherent in this formulation of the relationship among identification, hero worship, and romantic love is the implication that romantic love, with the interactions between the child's affective needs and cognitive capacities that it entails, has the potential of exerting a significant effect on the child's developing self. Thus, in the process of striving to possess the object, the child may perceive that object as setting forth requirements or conditions that must be met in order to increase the chances of a successful outcome. To the extent that the object also functions as an ego-ideal, the likelihood of the child accommodating the perceived expectations or identifying with the object are proportionately increased. Moreover, the perceived requirements, which are likely a combination of real expectations and the child's projections of the ideal self, represent obstacles that the child attempts to overcome. In this process, the child acquires or takes on these idealized characteristics, thus moving closer in fantasy to attainment of the idealized relationship with the object. The ideal self is thus also more closely approximated, and self-esteem and a sense of mastery are thereby enhanced. As already suggested, the child's inclination to be like the romantic object or adopt the related idealized characteristics may be less a function of identification and more a result of the child's efforts to win the object's affection. Thus, Reik ([1941] 1957, p. 113) suggests that upon recognizing the possibility of losing the mother's love, a child will "demonstrate in his own behavior what he wants his mother to do to him. . . . He announces this wish by displaying his tenderness and affection toward his mother." Reik (p. 114) goes on to explain more generally that "our display of loving is the anticipation of love we desire from the other person. . . . We are both the other person whose love we yearn for and the beloved which we want to be. Our love is the unconscious advertisement of how we wish to be loved." However indirectly, such a process can result in substantial modifications of the self.

The Development of Romantic Ideation

We have described in a general way the manner in which the converging internal and external forces and the specific challenges of the developmental process combine to create the requisite conditions for the development of romantic love in childhood. Implicit in that description has been the central and moderating role played by the child's level of cognitive development in the process. With this background, we can now examine the manner in which the specific qualities of the child's cognitive functioning, in concert with the affective arousal characteristic of childhood, permit the occurrence of idealization and thus set the stage for the romantic love experience, as well as the more general development of romantic ideation.

Cognition. Romantic ideation is evidenced in the child who is preoccupied with images and wish-fulfilling fantasies characterized by an anticipated relationship with the chosen object in which frustrated needs are satisfied and anxiety reduced. The affective component, depending on the stage of development of the child, will manifest varying degrees of anxiety, eroticism, anger, frustration, and hope, and the ideational content associated with these affects will vary as a function of the child's chronological age, the level of cognitive development, and the nature of his or her interpersonal relationships. The content of the fantasy often serves a major adaptive function, enabling the child to cope with the many stresses of childhood, including and especially separation from his or her parents at a time when discovery of self is associated with low self-esteem. The romantic fantasy provides a compensatory image of the self when the child has a contrasting image of self that is unintegrated and associated with anxiety.

Egocentrism, as defined by Piaget (1952), is a lack of discrimination between self and object. The ideation and thinking patterns indicative of the child's cognitive state during the period of development associated with egocentrism have been described as primary process by Freud ([1915] 1957f), and sensori-motor intelligence and preoperational thought by Piaget (1952). Egocentrism is the dominant cognitive state of childhood, denoting a lack of discrimination between the child's own wishes, affects, perceptions, needs, and external reality. These factors greatly influence the child's perception and fantasies of objects, permitting the attribution of qualities to an object that support continued idealization without external validation. Because of the lack of self-observation, the child is relatively unaware of the influence of these factors on his or her perception of reality. Piaget outlined the types of experiences and interactions with the environment that modify cognitive organization, moving the child from a state of egocentric to reflective thought. Although the nature of egocentric thought changes considerably between birth and age twelve, the period of time covered in this discussion, the child demonstrates many characteristics of egocentric thought between the ages of five and twelve, the interval of time in which he or she seems most susceptible to romantic ideation. Even in those instances in which the child has developed a capacity for reflective thought, under stress, such as would occur during the Oedipus complex, the child might easily regress to egocentric thought. In such a cognitive state, the child has a reduced capacity to share another's view, and the object concept becomes less stable. This produces a less veridical perception and evaluation of the romantic object, with the child's own needs greatly influencing his or her evaluation of an object and thus promoting idealization. Reflective thought develops as the child is more capable of accommodation to the characteristics of objects and events and develops more self-observation and, eventually, reversible logic. These cognitive capacities are found in later developmental stages such as the periods of concrete and formal operations.

The child's proclivity for romantic ideation is enhanced by the predominance of the adaptive cognitive process of assimilation, or the tendency to understand novel stimuli and events in terms of previously formed schemata and current needs. Intimately related to assimilation are subordinate processes that further contribute to romantic ideation. For example, artificialism describes the child's tendency to understand natural processes in terms of human activity. Similarly, the quality of animism refers to the tendency to understand and attribute physical movements and events to intentional activity, and efficacy describes the child's sense that his or her wish, effort, or longing is somehow responsible for external cause-and-effect relationships. These cognitive tendencies combine to permit the misattribution of cause-and-effect, and thus enable the child to perceive the self and the romantic object as powerful. These preoperational cognitive styles are the building blocks of idealization and romantic ideation and enable the child to construct an environment and subjective universe consistent with current affective needs, thus permitting, if not indirectly facilitating, the development of romantic ideation. Knowledge of objects eventually moves from being influenced in this way by internally based needs that color the child's evaluation of the object to an accommodative balance between the child's internal evaluation of the object and the external, objective characteristics of that object.

Imaginary Playmate. The child's capacity to develop an object concept that is based more on the particular needs of the self than on an adequate comprehension of the limits of objects in space and time is central to the development of romantic ideation and is clearly demonstrated in the phenomenon of imaginary playmates. Play is a child's way of solving problems, contemplating difficult experiences, experimenting with new solutions, reliving old experiences, and restoring a sense of mastery and competence. Between the approximate ages of two and seven, the preoperational child is capable of representing or evoking images of reality through five interrelated semiotic functions—deferred imitation, mental imagery, graphic representation, verbal evocation, and symbolic play (Piaget, 1962).

It is as a result of the operation of these functions that the imaginary playmate acquires a quality of subjective reality for the child. As in the romantic love experience, the particular needs and conflicts of the child that are salient at any one time will lend form and substance to the imaginary playmate, providing him or her with the characteristics necessary to aid the child in managing the current challenge or conflict. The nature of the play in which the child will subsequently engage with the imaginary playmate will thus not only symbolize this conflict but will also provide a context in which the child can experiment with alternate forms of resolution.

The imaginary playmate most often emerges during the preoedipal and oedipal periods, between the ages of three and six. According to some, it may still be apparent in varying forms through the age of eleven or twelve (see, for example, Masih, 1978). Typically, the child will have only one or two imaginary playmates at a given time, and they are usually the same age as the child. They have special names, may resemble human beings or animals, and are frequently accorded magical powers. The imaginary playmate serves various functions for the child, but those most related to the development of the romantic object are compensatory. Thus, the imaginary playmate may make a sudden appearance when the child is in a stressful situation. This appearance represents the child's effort to provide the self with the sympathy, support, and nurture that are not forthcoming from others. The new playmate may serve a primarily nurturant function, or it may take on the role of a moral conscience, ideal self, or some other form of alter ego. By means of the creation of this fantasy figure, the child attempts to achieve an ideal state in which anxiety reduction is obtained through a system of thought that subordinates accommodation to assimilation. In the normal course of events, the child will later develop concrete and formal operational capacities that counterbalance the occurrence of those preoperational phenomena that permit the existence of an imaginary playmate. In cases of pathological development, the child may fixate or regress to a cognitive state in which the imaginary playmate continues to meet the child's narcissistic needs at the expense of accommodation to a stressful reality (Bettelheim, 1967). Kohut (1977) views the imaginary playmate as one of a succession of self objects in the normal development of narcissism, which include transitional objects, latent peer groups, adolescent gangs, adult fantasy, and adult work.

The imaginary playmate represents one manifestation of the romantic ideation typical of childhood and, as such, it bears a fundamental similarity to the romantic love experience. Both are motivated by a frustrated need state and represent the child's effort, in the absence of the skills and capabilities necessary to obtain gratification in the real world, to satisfy that need and restore a sense of well-being, mastery, and self-esteem. Similarly, fantasy and idealization play a primary role in both phenomena. Finally, in each of these instances of romantic ideation, it can be seen that the requirements for idealization, the essence of *romantic* love, are permitted and facilitated by the cognitive phenomena characteristic of childhood.

Developmental and Research Considerations

Transitions in Romantic Ideation. Our discussion of romantic love in the child has focused on idealization and fantasy as the necessary and definitive components of the romantic love experience, and has attempted to show how the specific cognitive and affective qualities of childhood permit and promote the occurrence of this process. Given the intimate relationship between romantic love and these developmental considerations, the nature of the experience will undergo transformations with advancing maturity. In the child, idealization serves as a cognitive simplification for the challenge of expressing one's impulses, avoiding harm, and obtaining satisfaction and security. This process serves an adaptive function at a particular time when the child's cognitive capacities permit him or her to operate comfortably with dichotomous and conflicting conclusions, in which complex associations, generalizations, and categories cannot be conceptualized, and real satisfaction is not possible. As the child matures cognitively and becomes less egocentric, such inconsistencies become more difficult to entertain. Emerging cognitive and affective maturity brings with it greater possibility for real satisfaction. When this is not the case, regression to the fantasies of childhood may occur.

As the child becomes increasingly able to conceive of the self as a stable object, the capacity to perceive others more realistically is developed, and the predisposition to idealization concomitantly reduced. This gradual establishment of a stable sense of self, occurring during the preoperational period, which enables the child to make discriminations between self and others, also enhances the corresponding capacity for reciprocity in relationships. In this process, the child learns that others possess characteristics superior to those of the self, and that these can be shared and acquired through the processes of learning, conformity, and winning affection. That is, in contrast to the compensatory fantasies involved in romantic ideation, reality-based cognitive operations must be employed in order for reciprocity in relationships to exist (see Kohlberg, 1969). The cognitive capacities to group objects on the basis of similar attributes and to form categories help to establish the concept of similarity and difference. The capacity to see similarities between oneself and others and to enter into relationships based on mutual satisfaction play a major role in developing attachments to others that are more stable and less susceptible to the influence of romantic ideation.

Our conceptualization of the idealization process in childhood is equally applicable to the occurrence of similar phenomena in later life. An important difference, however, is that with the capacity for reflective thought the adult can observe the process, recognize its distorting effect, and temper behavior and judgment so as to take these factors into account. Lacking reflective thought, the child does not do this and maintains the conviction that the fantasy is, or can be, realized.

Romantic Love vs. Mature Love? Our formulation of romantic love in childhood has excluded consideration of the needs, wishes, and well-being of the romantic object. We have taken a very different stance on romantic love than those who define love as requiring that the satisfaction, needs, and well-being of the beloved be of at least equal importance to the individual as his or her own (for example, Csikszentmihalyi, in this volume; Fenichel, 1945; Sullivan, 1953a; Weiner, 1978). We regard such a relationship, variously described as mature love, caring (Rubin, 1974), or companionate love (Walster and Walster, 1978), as quite distinct from the *romantic* love experience (see Walster and Walster, 1978). In fact, to a considerable extent, the conditions necessary for romantic love, as outlined in this chapter preclude such companionate or mature love, in which intimacy, reciprocity, and a full knowledge and appreciation of the beloved enhance rather than interfere with the process.

This distinction, with the inherent implication that romantic love is therefore immature or childish, has received considerable theoretical attention (for example, Gediman, 1975; Kernberg, 1974b; Walster and Walster, 1978). Is the adult in the throes of the romantic love experience thereby revealing developmental immaturity and psychic defect? Although we have addressed romantic love as manifest in childhood, we have done so in a way that emphasizes its status as a developmental phenomenon intimately tied to the individual's efforts to manage and negotiate the stresses and challenges characteristic of a particular developmental stage. We have called attention to the potentially adaptive, as opposed to compensatory, function that romantic ideation in general, and love in particular, can serve. Given the perspective that developmental challenges characterize the entire life span and are thus not exclusive to childhood (for example, Erikson, 1963; Levinson, 1978), it is not surprising that these phenomena are repeatedly evident at points in the life cycle other than childhood.

It has been suggested that romantic love is the precursor of that love which is characterized by caring and concern for the beloved (see Walster and Walster, 1978). We have suggested that romantic ideation and love precede the development of the child's capacities to secure gratification in the real world. It may thus be the case that romantic love and ideation represent the beginning efforts of the individual to manage unfamiliar and anxiety-producing developmental challenges, the successful negotiation of which requires skills and abilities that are as yet undeveloped or absent. To the extent that such fantasy activity substitutes for the development of those capacities necessary for substantial gratification in the real world, the process may have adverse consequences and signal immaturity. However, to the degree that it serves as a transition to and aid in the development of the requisite abilities, as it optimally does in the child, romantic ideation and love may contribute to and facilitate the developmental process. From this perspective, romantic love is childish only in the sense that it, like most everything else, makes its first appearance in childhood.

Implications for Research. We have presented a particular perspective on the development of romantic love and ideation in children which generates hypotheses that can be scientifically evaluated. Such study would serve generally to enhance our understanding of romantic ideation in general, and love in particular, as well as the manner in which such phenomena contribute to ongoing developmental adaptation.

Many of these possibilities are self-evident but may nevertheless be worth noting. Initially, case studies of romantic love and ideation, with individuals at critical points in the developmental process, would provide preliminary data regarding the viability of the perspective presented in this chapter. Also, in a structured interview, do children report the occurrence of romantic ideation and the romantic love experience? General hypotheses might then be evaluated in a more controlled context. For example, assessment of the particular developmental challenges confronting individuals of selected ages might be compared to the nature of concurrent romantic ideation, independently measured, perhaps by the use of content analysis of projective storytelling techniques or content of play. Projective stimuli in these procedures might include a "hero" for a child, or an "ideal mate" for an adult, and analysis of the characteristics attributed to these romantic objects compared to the nature of the salient developmental task. The hypothesized relationship between the *content* of romantic ideation and the specific psychological components of the developmental challenge can, in this way, be assessed. Additionally, the *nature* of romantic ideation can similarly be evaluated, with special attention to whether it is of the adaptive, problem-solving variety, or in the service of a primarily compensatory function.

More specific propositions of the current formulation of romantic love are also available for empirical test. Thus, in the romantic love experience, are children, in fact, oblivious of the needs and well-being of the romantic object? The inclination to test such a proposition immediately crystallizes the very troublesome and general issue of methodology in the study of romantic phenomena. Their implicit subjective and elusive nature is perhaps a primary reason that researchers have ignored this very significant aspect of human experience. However, creative and pioneering study, and the development of new methodologies, will permit exploratory research of such questions and result in more specific hypotheses that are amenable to traditional methodology. For example, a controlled laboratory study, employing familiar procedures, could be designed to assess the effects of obstacles to the attainment of an object on subsequent evaluation of that object, thus providing a test of a primary postulate of the formulation of the idealization process herein presented.

The problem of the scientific study of such subjective, personal phenomena, with the implicit risk of artificializing the process being studied, might be partially avoided by addressing our attention to the phenomena *in vivo*. A naturally occurring phenomenon that appears, on the surface, to be related to romantic ideation and love is that of the "teacher's pet." Systematic evaluation, from a developmental perspective, of the content and possible function of this phenomenon, including its behavioral and implicit cognitive manifestations, of both the child *and* teacher, each as subject and object, might be most illuminating. On the assumption that both individuals are facing developmental challenges, albeit of a different nature, the intensive study of this phenomenon seems to hold great potential for clarifying, elaborating, and testing many of the assumptions on which our formulation has been based.

3

Adolescence

Barry A. Farber

Picture a couple walking hand-in-hand on a mild spring day. Or try to remember the exquisite excitement you felt upon awakening on a day when you knew you would be seeing that special person. The imagery of love is familiar to us all regardless of age. And, as the chapters within this section clearly indicate, romantic love can occur at all stages of human development even if, as Broderick (1966) suggests, it needs to be progressively redefined with age. Yet, despite its ageless quality, romantic love has traditionally been conceptualized by social scientists, as well as by novelists and poets, as if it were essentially an adolescent phenomenon. Rubin (1970) defined romantic love as "love between unmarried opposite-sex peers, of the sort which could possibly lead to marriage" (p. 266); Freud (1921) spoke of love as the "young man's sentimental passion"; and poet Robert Graves (1973) has written lyrically of the "love of love" in young eyes. Moreover, the relevant research in the last decade has focused almost exclusively on the nature of romantic love in high school or college students.

That romantic love should be identified with adolescence is not surprising. Romantic love is bound up in intense, emergent feelings of sexuality and in an expanding sense of self-feelings we experience initially and most powerfully during adolescence. Although affectional drives are present during childhood, as seen in Chapter Two, it is only during adolescence, usually one or two years following pubescence, that affection and sexual drives can be synthesized and consciously focused upon the same individual (Freud, 1921; Lidz, 1976). Adolescence is also that period when we generally fall in love with a willing partner for the first time. Kephart (1967), for example, found that "infatuation" generally occurred for the first time at age thirteen and "love" at age seventeen. Although love affairs and boyfriend-girlfriend relationships among preadolescents have been reported (Broderick, 1966; Broderick and Fowler, 1961; Broderick and Rowe, 1968; Hamilton, 1929), these attachments are not likely to be reciprocal (Broderick, 1966), nor are they likely to have the intensity of eroticism that characterizes love during adolescence and adulthood (Jersild, 1963). Finally, romantic love and adolescence share a common descriptive vocabulary within our language. Both concepts are frequently described as intense, overwhelming, passionate, consuming, exciting, and confusing.

Taken together, these data suggest that our adult conceptions of romantic love emerge primarily from the experiences we have had during adolescence—experiences that range from early adolescent "crushes" to mid-adolescent dating, sexual experimentation and first heterosexual love, to late-adolescent premarital relationships. This chapter will: describe the major physiological, cognitive, and emotional changes that affect adolescents' experience of friendships, sexuality, and love; examine the nature of romantic love within each of the three phases of adolescence; review the research on adolescent love; and discuss how changes in our cultural patterns may be affecting the experience of adolescent love.

Romantic Love in Adolescence: General Considerations

Adolescence is a time of physical, cognitive, and emotional changes. It begins with the physiological changes accompanying pubescence. It involves changes in the adolescent's ways of thinking about the world. And it is, as Erikson (1956) has noted, a time to define one's identity—a task usually requiring the formation of significant relationships with the opposite sex. For the purposes of this chapter, adolescence will be divided into three major over-lapping periods: early adolescence, including the one- to two-year prepubertal phases when physiological changes begin*; mid-adolescence, beginning twelve to eighteen months after pubescence; and late adolescence, beginning at about age sixteen or seventeen.

Most of us are familiar with the physiological changes of adolescence: the rapid increase in general body growth, including the size of the genital organs, the gradual appearance of secondary sex characteristics, and the occurrence of menarche in girls. These overt physical manifestations of puberty are accompanied too by the emergence of intense sexual feelings which may cause excitement, frustration, and/or confusion. Frequently there is a consuming interest in everything sexual. "Many a child's first acquaintance with the encyclopedia results from the persistent rumor that there is detailed sexual information in it" (Group for the Advancement of Psychiatry, 1968, p. 77). Sexual talk and jokes, and heterosexual daydreams and masturbatory fantasies, are also part of this preoccupation with sexual matters. Emergent feelings of sexuality may also, at least initially, engender much anxiety and cause some adolescents to retreat into the safety of a same-sexed group. Teasing, bantering, and competition between groups of boys and girls may also serve to partially attenuate this sexual anxiety. However, usually within a year or two following pubescence, sexual impulses have catalyzed the formation of tentative boy-girl relationships.

The cognitive changes accompanying adolescence are less obvious and less well understood but they too are critical determinants of the phenomenology of adolescent love. Foremost among these changes is the adolescent's new ability to engage in *formal operational thinking* (Piaget, 1950)—to begin to be able to plan ahead, to test hypotheses, to reason abstractly, and to think about oneself in objective terms. Elkind (1967, 1968, 1978) has written extensively of the implications of these cognitive changes for the

---

*The prepubertal growth spurt starts between the ages of ten and eleven in most girls and between the ages of twelve and thirteen in most boys. Girls mature about two years earlier than boys with the median age of menarche in the United States now about 12.7 (Reiter and Kulin, 1972).

adolescent's interpersonal development. He notes, for example, that with the onset of formal operations, adolescents not only become more concerned with their own self-image but also with the image they feel others have of them. Adolescents, however, often wrongly assume that everyone must be thinking the same way they are (*adolescent egocentricism*). Thus they assume that others are as obsessed with their behavior and appearance as they are themselves. This may account for the high degree of self-consciousness during adolescence. "The boy who stands in front of the mirror for two hours combing his hair is probably imagining the reactions he will produce in the girls, and the girl applying her makeup is probably imagining the admiring glances that will come her way" (Elkind, 1970, p. 68).

A related phenomenon is the adolescent's assumption that his or her feelings and convictions are unique, and that others, particularly parents, cannot possibly understand them. This assumption, which Elkind calls "a personal fable," manifests itself most dramatically in the tragedy of teenage suicides ("no one understands my pain and despair") and the glory of teenage love ("no one has ever felt this way before"). The story of Romeo and Juliet beautifully illustrates the universal power of these themes. This form of egocentricism does, however, ultimately dissipate as adolescents fall in love, learn to integrate the feelings of others, and gradually establish relationships of mutual intimacy.

Finally, the development of formal operations affects the nature of intimate relations during adolescence. As the adolescent's capacity for introspection increases, he or she seeks to share these personal and profound thoughts with a carefully chosen other—someone who will respect and confirm one's innermost feelings. As Mitchell (1976, p. 276) has observed: "Adolescents who experience the heightened passion of sexual stimulation reinforced by the soul stimulation of genuine intimacy almost invariably conclude that they are 'in love.'"

Romantic Love in Early Adolescence: Chum Relationships and Crushes

During early adolescence (one to two years before and after the onset of puberty), both males and females remain primarily in same-sex groups. Here they may compete, show off, gossip, and exchange sexual information in relative safety. Here too they begin to gain the interpersonal skills that will later be used in both mixed-sex groups and opposite-sex relationships. At this time, however, movement of the two sexes toward each other is impeded initially by the differences in size and then by the differences in the sexual maturity of boys and girls of the same age and educational level (Lidz, 1976).

Romantic love during this developmental period most often appears in the form of either "chum relationships" or "crushes." Crushes are feelings of infatuation, with strong elements of idealization, directed toward either peers or older, emulated adult figures. Chum relationships are intimate and often tender same-sex friendships. Both types of relationships involve loving someone like oneself and as such they represent a natural midway point in the progression from self-love to the love of another (Lidz, 1976).

Both Friedenberg (1959) and Sullivan (1953a) have emphasized the importance of same-sex chums for the later development of adult forms of intimacy. Chum relationships are marked by hours spent "hanging out" together—playing or shopping or mostly just exchanging views on parents, friends, teachers, and life in general. These relationships teach adolescents to trust their feelings, to be tender, to accept another's well-meaning intrusiveness, to provide and receive honest personal criticism. Chums also teach each other how good it feels to care for another person.

In contrast to the depth of feeling displayed in chum relationships, crushes on opposite-sex peers appear to be both superficial and transitory. At their peaks, however, these relationships may involve frequent meetings, some physical affection, teasing, letter writing or phone calling, and even intense jealousy, particularly among girls (Landis, 1940). Crushes focused on adult figures usually involve more overt forms of romantic idealization and hero worship but they are obviously nonreciprocal relationships. In reviewing autobiographical accounts of crushes and puppy love, Kiell (1964, p. 127) has noted the following common elements: purity and intensity of affect, an overpowering sweetness, a gentle melancholy, ambivalent sensations of confidence and awkwardness, and a sense of helplessness when the object of desire does not respond or is unaware of the "relationship."

Crushes may appear in children as young as ten or eleven. Research, as well as clinical evidence, suggests that girls have more frequent and intense crushes and that they are less inhibited in sharing or displaying their feelings. A group of girls on the school playground may discuss their love for a handsome classmate or the teacher down the hall; or, alone in her room, a girl may fantasize meeting the rock star whose posters adorn every wall in her room. In the mid 1960s, the Beatles' visits to the United States were punctuated by the hysteria of groups of enraptured female fans (although certainly not all were early adolescent!). Television images of the pleading, crying, shrieking audience were vivid testimony to the emotional intensity of their feelings. Today the profits of those who seek to capitalize on the intensity of such crushes through the manufacture of such items as T-shirts, posters, and fan magazines can hardly be overestimated.

During a phase when adolescents are still self-conscious and tentative in approaching each other, crushes may be suitable substitutes for burgeoning heterosexual interest (Ausubel, 1954). Broderick (1966) has suggested that crushes are "practice emotions" and that their significance lies in the fact that young people may feel, express, and fantasize their love without risk of rejection. Lidz (1976) has noted that crushes are part of the process of movement away from dependency on parents, and that new objects of attachment provide ideals that may ultimately be incorporated in a young person's emerging identity. Blos (1962) and Friedenberg (1959) have both observed that crushes impel, as well as prepare, adolescents to seek heterosexual companionship.

During this stage of development, adolescents do in fact seek heterosexual companionship through dating. At ages ten to eleven, about 25 percent of boys and girls have had a date; by age thirteen, 75 percent of boys and girls have had dates (Broderick, 1966). Dating at this time primarily consists of spending time together at school, going to parties together, or occasionally "going out" (to the movies, for example) with other couples. By age twelve or thirteen, there may be more reciprocity between sweethearts—a fact that may reflect an important step away from the largely imaginary characters of earlier relationships and toward real romantic interaction (Broderick, 1966). Still, in this early stage of adolescence, heterosexual relationships continue to reflect the narcissistic character of late childhood: self-preoccupation is common and genuine emotional involvement is rare (Conger, 1973).

Romantic Love in Mid-Adolescence:
Dating, Sexual Exploration, and "First Love"

Love—romantic, heterosexual, and reciprocated—comes to some during the latter stages of mid-adolescence. But some preparation is necessary. During the early stages of this period, same-sex groups gradually change to mixed groups, providing the individual with greater opportunities for becoming more comfortable and confident with opposite-sex peers (Dunphy, 1963). Fantasy has also served to prepare the adolescent for heterosexual involvement. Fantasy enables the individual to try on new behaviors and emotions, and shared fantasies may reassure the individual that his or her interest, even preoccupation, with the opposite sex is normal. Whereas the daydreams of ten- to twelve-year-olds are dominated by adventure and activity, by thirteen or fourteen, adolescents of both sexes are primarily fantasizing about romance, sex, and achievement (Gottlieb, 1973). For example, before an individual falls in love, he or she may strongly identify with one of the classic themes of rock-and-roll songs—that of finding one's true love. And in the earliest stages of love, before the intensity of the relationship has been mutually acknowledged, love is primarily experienced in fantasy: any number of environmental events—a romantic picture, a beautiful song, the sight of other lovers—can stimulate feelings of overwhelming tenderness and joy.

Heterosexual friendships, including dating, increasingly become the norm during mid-adolescence, so that by age fourteen or fifteen, 80 percent of adolescents are dating, some (25 percent) as frequently as once weekly (Broderick, 1966). Heterosexual relationships act as a positive feedback loop: contact between the sexes leads to desires for further contact, and behavior, speech, and thoughts become increasingly concerned with satisfying the need for heterosexual involvement.

Sex, of course, plays a critical, albeit not fully understood, role during this developmental period. It is not clear, for example, to what extent adolescents consider sex and romance as orthagonal concepts. At least for some individuals, sexual activity is motivated primarily, if not exclusively, by sexual impulses, fantasies, and curiosity and may be basically unrelated to romantic involvement; others, however, even at this stage, consider sex as one aspect of a total loving relationship. It is also not entirely clear what effect gender has on the relationship between sex and romance. The traditional view holds that males at this stage are erotic and females romantic; and that for males sex takes priority over love, whereas for females sexual activity is subordinate to the need for a loving relationship (Douvan and Adelson, 1966; Ehrmann, 1959; Stone and Church, 1957). These gender roles, however, may be in the process of breaking down as females in American society become more comfortable in asserting their own sexual needs.

Interest in the opposite sex may not stem entirely from either erotic or romantic sources. The need to maintain self-esteem during this developmental period is more likely to derive from opposite-sex friends than from those of the same sex. Interest in the opposite sex may also be a function of the expectations and subtle pressures of parents, of peer group rewards for demonstrated prowess with members of the opposite sex, and of wishes to emulate older friends and relatives, particularly siblings.

Adolescents must be prepared not only biologically and socially to fall in love but also psychologically and emotionally. For example, many observers feel that a sense of tenderness is a prerequisite to falling in love (Friedenberg, 1959; Kernberg, 1976b). Tenderness has its original basis in infancy and childhood but its capacity for mature expression first develops during early adolescent chum relationships. Then, with the advent of formal operational thinking, tenderness becomes related to a growing capacity for concern for others, awareness of self, and empathic thought. Another prerequisite to falling in love is the adolescent's need to feel independent, to psychologically relinquish the security of his or her nuclear family. This separation may be difficult and anxiety-provoking but it also involves a psychological confirmation of prior successful relationships with family members and friends.

The experience of falling in love for the first time is surely one of our most poignant memories. Saying "I love you," hearing "I love you"; thinking constantly and joyfully of the other; secretly dreaming of an idyllic future together; expressing thanks to your personal God for your fortune; wanting to spend all your time together; smiling, gazing, and holding hands, all with the same wonderfully obvious meaning; sharing quiet, peaceful moments; hearing "your song"; whispering your private endearments and nicknames; writing letters that could never express enough; speaking on the phone for never enough time; needing so much to please; feeling that you have found your purpose and meaning in life; feeling important, complete, and full of self-respect; wanting nothing to change, ever; anticipating the pain of separation and the joy of reunion; feeling that you could never be happier or so much in love; indeed, feeling that no one could ever experience such happiness or be so much in love.

The experience of falling in love involves a number of psychological changes for the adolescent. Certain residual elements of preadolescence and early adolescence—most notably self-absorption and grandiosity—are gradually shifted from the self to one's love partner. This accounts for the idealization that is frequently involved in love affairs. In fact, as Blos (1962) points out, if love takes the form of extreme infatuation, then this shift of "narcissistic energy" may leave the self emotionally and physically depleted, even to the point where the individual may recklessly endanger his or her health by failing to eat, sleep, or even drive properly. Even in less extreme cases, however, a first love often includes recognizably narcissistic components. That is, individuals are likely to fall in love with those persons of the opposite sex whom they could have been or would like to have been. For example, a young man may identify with the cheerfulness or athletic ability of his girlfriend; or, a young woman may identify with the assuredness, or even rebelliousness, of her boyfriend. Falling in love may also precipitate a related process—that of securing one's sense of gender identity (Blos, 1962; Douvan and Adelson, 1966; Lidz, 1976). As the relationship grows, adolescents "transfer" those sex-alien tendencies left over from preadolescence to their partners. This affirmation in turn facilitates movement toward the establishment of a more general, secure sense of self.

The adolescent in his or her mid-teens is now more comfortable with the physical and cognitive changes of puberty. He or she is ready to try on new roles, emotions, and behaviors; willing to explore the inner feelings of self and others; and eager to learn about the adult world and all its prerogatives, particularly those of a sexual nature. Falling in love is the grandest part of the mid-adolescent experience of self-exploration.

Romantic Love in Late Adolescence:
The Development of Intimate Relationships

From birth on, the individual has been engaged in a myriad of interpersonal relationships in which new roles and behaviors have been explored. Some behaviors will not "feel" right, or will not meet with social approval, and will drop out of a person's repertoire; other behaviors, however, will feel comfortable and will become integrated into the personality. This process is constant and gradual and also occasionally difficult, particularly during the earlier stages of adolescence when, with the onset of formal operational thinking, the choice of behaviors, values, friends, and interests becomes more conscious. However, in the last stage of adolescence, the individual integrates earlier experiences and develops a more consistent view of self and others. If during early adolescence and mid-adolescence the individual is "trying on" new roles, in late adolescence he or she is "selecting" a more or less permanent personal identity.

An integral part of identity formation is the development of the capacity for *intimacy*—learning to share and trust and fuse with another without fear that the self will be engulfed or overwhelmed. These two processes—the attainment of a personal identity and the attainment of a capacity for intimacy—are interactive. A well-integrated sense of identity includes perceptions of oneself as a loving human being and is therefore dependent upon prior romantic experiences. Conversely, the ability to love intimately— to engage in a relationship marked by mutuality and a genuine concern for another—is to a great extent contingent upon achieving a stable sense of identity. "Only as a person begins to feel more secure in his identity is he able to establish intimacy with himself and with others, both in friendships and eventually in a love based, mutually satisfying sex relationship with the opposite sex" (Erikson, 1965, p. 328).

It is therefore not until the period of late adolescence that individuals become capable of what psychoanalysts call "genital love"—a fusion of genital satisfaction, tenderness, and concern for another. Each of these components may have existed in love relationships of an earlier period; they may even have fused temporar-

ily at some point. But it is not until this developmental era—when a more stable sense of identity allows for sexual fulfillment to exist concomitantly with feelings of tenderness and concern—that these elements can securely coexist in a relationship. The achievement of genital love transforms the act of falling in love into the state of being in love (Kernberg, 1976b).

An alternative, although related way of viewing the phenomenon of late adolescent love is through the conceptual framework of Harry Stack Sullivan. According to Sullivan (1953a), older adolescents learn to integrate their previously conflicting needs for sexual satisfaction, security, and intimacy. Sexual needs, previously a source of anxiety, can now be expressed unabashedly within the context of a secure relationship; the needs for sex and intimacy, previously kept separate, can now be focused upon the same partner, and one's lover can now also be one's best friend; and finally, the need for intimacy, previously fulfilled by hours spent talking with same-sex friends, can now be satisfied within a heterosexual relationship.

Given these changes, what then is the phenomenology of romantic love during late adolescence? The tenderness of love, originally expressed toward parents and later toward chums and opposite-sex partners, is still present; and the excitement of sex and the joy of mutual idealization that is experienced during mid-adolescence is present during relationships of late adolescence as well. But now, as has been indicated, these feelings are merged to a greater extent than previously. Moreover, as individuals become less self-centered and less narcissistic, there is a strong element of concern for the other. Now those in love begin to experience their partners as equally important to themselves; indeed, the satisfactions and happiness of the partner begin to feel good to the self. There is also a greater sense of differentiation and complementarity in the relationship—there is no longer a strong desire for one's partner to be an opposite-sex mirror image of oneself. Instead, partners tend to fulfill each other's needs and "complete" each other. Now different values can be tolerated and appreciated; there is a more genuine sense of respect and admiration that includes aspects of, but goes beyond, the reflexive idealization of previous relationships. There is a feeling of strength and comfort derived from the partner, and there is a feeling of expansiveness as well, a sense that one is transcending one's limitations with the help of one's partner. Falling in love during this period may also involve a greater appreciation of culture, art, history, and nature (Kernberg, 1976b). In short, the full expression of intimacy within a romantic love relationship appears to satisfy and fulfill the self, the love partner, and even nature. It is not difficult to understand how the sum of these feelings could lead two people to pledge their love eternally and enter into marriage.

Love is an exhilarating feeling. But what of those who do not or cannot share in this experience? Some, whose sense of personal identity has not yet been firmly established, intuitively feel that a love relationship would be too much to bear—that the intimacy and responsibilities demanded would be beyond their emotional capacity. These individuals may be envious of others' relationships and saddened by the lack of love in their lives but often they sublimate their needs for sexual and emotional intimacy through intense involvement in work, sports, art, or hobbies. Others may feel that they are ready for love but in fact avoid meeting potential partners or refrain from becoming seriously involved in a relationship. These individuals withold their intimacy, fearing the profound sadness and feelings of worthlessness that may ensue from rejection. Some of these individuals may have previously experienced these dysphoric feelings in relationships with families, peers, or earlier romantic partners and may refuse to risk being hurt again.

Lack of love produces loneliness—a feeling we have all experienced at times but one which, in its more permanent condition, may lead to a state of self-abasement and even desperation. According to Erikson (1968a), if by late adolescence or early adulthood an individual has not been involved in a romantic love relationship, he or she may settle instead for a series of impersonal relationships. And although this pattern may not appear to hamper an individual's ability to succeed in the world, it may result in a permanent sense of depersonalization, a feeling of never having found oneself.

Finally, what of those who having allowed themselves to be vulnerable and having successfully entered into a love relationship now awake one day to find the relationship disintegrated? As we would expect, they become depressed. They feel sad and cry.

They feel a loss of self and self-esteem and may even regress to a point of infantile helplessness and dependency (Goethals, 1973). They may socially withdraw. They feel anxious and incomplete. They often feel inconsolable and believe that they will never again experience happiness, much less the ecstasy of love. They sometimes develop neurovegetative signs of depression, including loss of appetite, sleep disturbances, psychomotor retardation, and loss of sexual desire. They may even wish to do away with themselves —and sometimes actually do so. Tennov (1973), for example, suggests that suicide and even suspicious car accidents frequently represent the tragic consequences of terminated young love affairs. Yet, although it may be impossible to exaggerate the intensity of despair experienced immediately following the breakup of a relationship, nearly all of those who do get hurt eventually recover. Most adolescents, in fact, prefer to deal with the pain of this situation by talking with a friend rather than a trained psychotherapist (Farber and Geller, 1977). And so, with the passing of a few interminable months, even those who earlier discounted the possibility of reentering society now find themselves once again willing to risk being hurt in order possibly to reexperience the inimitable pleasures of love.

Research on Romantic Love

Research on romantic love has increased substantially since Rubin's (1970) germinal paper on the "measurement of romantic love." To a great extent this research, like most psychological research, has been carried out on populations of high school and college students. The findings therefore have particular relevance for the study of romantic love in adolescence.

According to Walster and Walster (1978), 97 percent of Americans fall in love at least once during their lifetimes. Research has begun to shed light on how and with whom this occurs. First of all, it is easier for people to fall in love if they love themselves (Burns, 1976); however, those who are low in self-esteem but do not happen to fall in love are likely to love and trust their partners more than those blessed with feelings of high self-esteem (Dion and Dion, 1975). Individuals are more likely to fall in love with those who are equally attractive (Silverman, 1971; Walster, Aronson, Abrahams, and Rottman, 1966), as well as with those who live nearby (Clarke, 1952). In high school, black males, only children, and those from working-class homes are more likely to have romantic partners (Larson, Spreitzer, and Snyder, 1976). Individuals tend to fall in love for the first time at age thirteen (and later look back upon it as an infatuation) (and then fall in love again more romantically at age seventeen or eighteen) (Kephart, 1967). And a slightly higher proportion of men (20 percent) than women (15 percent) are likely to know that they are in love by the time of their fourth date. In general, romantic love is related to feelings of affiliation and dependency, absorption (feeling free to confide in one's partner), and caring (Rubin, 1970); it may also include elements of physical attraction and idealization (Driscoll, Davis, and Lipetz, 1972). Those in love are likely to stand closer to each other (Byrne, 1971) and spend more time looking at each other than nonromantic couples (Goldstein, Kilroy, and Van de Voort, 1976; Rubin, 1970). If, after falling in love, individuals find the relationship going badly, it may be because they have either been comparing their partners to others or they have been too frequently hostile or contemptuous (Driscoll, Davis, and Lipetz, 1972). Apart from such usual remedies as flowers and apologies, lovers may find that parental interference in the relationship may intensify their feelings of love (Driscoll, Davis, and Lipetz, 1972). Such efforts notwithstanding, there is still about a 45 percent chance that young couples involved in a steady, several-month-long relationship will one day break up; furthermore, there is only a 15 percent chance that ending the relationship will be a mutual decision (Hill, Rubin, and Peplau, 1976).

Another major focus of the research has been on examining how males and females differ in their conceptualizations of romantic love. Rubin (1970) found that men and women love equally intensely, and Good (1976) reported no sex differences in the proportions of men and women believing in romantic love. Other research, however, has found significant differences in the ways that men and women experience romantic love. Women report having been in love more frequently (Dion and Dion, 1973). And women also experience their love affairs more intensely—that is, they admit to more "symptoms" of love (Kanin, Davidson, and Scheck, 1970), report a greater sense of euphoria during their relationships (Dion and Dion, 1973; Kephart, 1967), feel more romantic (Tennov, 1973) and place a greater emphasis on love (Knox and Sporakowski, 1968), find their love affairs more rewarding (Dion and Dion, 1975), and rate their partners more positively (Black and Angelis, 1974). However, Hobart (1958) as well as Fengler (1974) found that men were more romantically inclined than women. Men also seem to become involved more quickly in a love affair (Kanin, Davidson, and Scheck, 1970) and seem less inclined to terminate a relationship (Hill, Rubin, and Peplau, 1976). In fact, when a relationship is finally ended, men appear to become more depressed and self-deprecating (Hill, Rubin, and Peplau, 1976).

For the most part, the literature on romantic love has focused on: (a) definitions of the concept, and (b) specifications of the psychosocial correlates of falling in and out of love. The literature, still in its infancy, has not yet begun to look at the phenomenological aspects of romantic love in adolescence. In fact, the current research methodology—questionnaires, rating scales, and personality inventories—although adequate and necessary for the demographic study of the incidence and types of romantic love, is inadequate to the task of investigating the phenomenological experience of love. For example, we still need to know what being in love means to those who experience it. How do people "know" when they are in love? What does each partner do to show love to the other? How does being in love affect the rest of one's life, including relationships with others? When and how do partners tell each other that they are in love? How is this responded to? Where do we get our ideas of how to act when in love? How do past relationships influence falling in love the second or third time? In short, researchers have not yet attended to the details of this process, assuming perhaps that romantic love is ineffable, or adequately described only by poets.

Adolescent Love in the Age of Narcissism

As we enter the 1980s, we bear with us the cultural legacy of the 1970s—a decade that has been characterized as an age of entitlement, individualism, and narcissism (Lasch, 1978; Malcolm, 1971; Slater, 1976). During this period we acted, it is said, as if we had inalienable rights to virtually every desire and as if our actions had no consequences for those around us. Furthermore, the youth of America—the so-called "me generation"—were considered the foremost proponents of this attitude. Not only did youth want its way but wanted it immediately.

It is difficult to validate scientifically these assumptions regarding changing values in American society. We can neither accurately assess the ubiquity of these values during the past decade nor predict the enduring influence of these values for a generation of adolescents in the coming decade. However, if these assessments of contemporary American values are correct, then we would expect to note changes in the nature of interpersonal contacts, including the experience of romantic love. And, in fact, there is much evidence to suggest that substantial changes in these relationships have occurred in the last decade, although there is little agreement on the direction and value of these changes. One view is that adolescents are forming relationships that are increasingly transient and sexual and decreasingly intimate and romantic; that they are forming these relationships with little effort or psychic investment and disbanding them at the first signs of difficulty or inconvenience; that they are primarily concerned with satisfying individual needs within the relationship; and that above all else, they are afraid of intimacy and commitment (Hendin, 1975; Kilpatrick, 1974; Shippers, 1978). Indeed, according to Margaret Mead (1970), the central psychological problem for youth in the seventies has been a "crisis of commitment."

In a related vein, Kilpatrick (1974) has suggested that adolescents have "de-mythologized" love and stripped it of its romantic foundations. His argument is that romantic love is based on the premise of pursuing the unattainable and that for this generation of adolescents everything (including sexual relations) and everyone (including individuals of all ages, religions, classes, and ethnic groups) are easily attainable. Furthermore, he states, several other cultural trends—including the disinclination for adolescents to postpone gratification, the trend toward convergence of sexual roles, and the increasing emphasis on communal rather than dyadic relationships—have all served to diminish the intensity, mystery, and excitement of romantic love.

Those who have pointed to a decline in the quality of romantic love have frequently used studies of popular music to corroborate their views. In the forties and fifties, songs were basically romantic in nature—they dealt with steady relationships, marriage, and "the glory of love." In the sixties and seventies, however, the lyrics of songs became more explicitly sexual and less emphatically romantic—relationships were no longer assumed to be permanent, and one's motivation for finding a partner could just as well be hedonistic as romantic (Carey, 1969; Kilpatrick, 1974; Shippers, 1978). In this regard too, a study of a currently popular woman's magazine revealed a thematic trend toward greater freedom in premarital relationships and an increased use of more explicit language in describing sexual intimacies and problems (Hurowitz and Gaier, 1976).

There is, however, a very different way of looking at today's adolescents, even assuming that they are affected by the culture of narcissism that surrounds them. It is a view that asserts that adolescents are now more interested and capable of intimacy than they were a generation ago; that they are more open, honest, and caring in their relationships; and that shifts in the direction of individual self-discovery and self-expression have resulted in an increased emphasis on meaningful relationships (Coleman and others, 1972; Conger, 1975; Malcolm 1971). Consistent with this viewpoint, changing patterns of sexual behavior have resulted not in promiscuity but in a greater acceptance of sex within the context of steady relationships (Conger, 1975; Dreyer, 1975; Lewis and Burr, 1975; Luckey and Nass, 1969; Sorenson, 1973).

Those who have attempted to predict cultural norms for the 1980s have envisioned a generation of morally responsible, self-sacrificing adolescents who are less restricted by traditional assumptions regarding appropriate sex-role behavior (Kennedy, 1979; Toffler, 1980). Perhaps the narcissistic elements in our culture have made falling in love more problematic for adolescents. And perhaps too, as Rubin (1973) predicts, there will be more casual friendships and fewer enduring relationships in the future. Still, it is difficult to conceive of a time when romantic love will ever lose its passion and appeal, particularly among adolescents. Two decades ago, Friedenberg (1959) commented that the passion of adolescent love frightens us and makes us envious. We should expect no less a reaction in the decades to come.

4

Adulthood: Men

Jesse D. Geller

Richard A. Howenstine

This chapter concerns the unfolding of romantic love in the lives of adult men. Many sources of inspiration have guided our approach to this majestic theme. We bring to this work our experiences as men, friends, lovers, husbands, and fathers. In our efforts to struggle with romantic love, as psychotherapists and scholars, we are particularly indebted to Barzun (1961), Levinson and others (1978), Loewald (1978), and Schafer (1976). They have convinced us that a comprehensive investigation of romantic love would include and specify the interrelations among the bodily changes that men label romantic love, the subjective experience and meanings, both conscious and unconscious, of these bodily changes, the expressive and instrumental ways in which men love romantically, the interpersonal modes (heterosexual, homosexual) within which men love romantically, and the situational, historical, and developmental contexts in which these events take place. To realize such a goal would require the study of romantic love, conjointly, from the multiple vantage points of biology, history, psychology, and sociology. Existing theories and research on romantic love have rarely integrated these now disparate perspectives. There is in fact a lack of information and research about the genesis, development, and vicissitudes of romantic love in the adult male. To seek clarity about these complex issues is worthy of a lifetime's commitment. We regard the discussion that follows as a "work in progress." Our hope is to encourage clear and systematic thinking about the evolving experiences, meanings, and functions of romantic love during adulthood.

Men As Romantic Lovers

Romantic love is an elusive concept that defies singular definition. Traditionally, romantic love has been viewed as an abstract noun, that is, as an entity with a name of its own and adjectivally designated properties of its own. Because the concept synthesizes into one commanding image complex and paradoxical themes, a wide variety of different and sometimes antithetical properties have been attributed to romantic love. A partial listing of these characteristics includes passion, tenderness, joy, anger, envy, hate, security, excitement, novelty, anxiety, intrigue, power, frustration, danger, elation, disorganization, and ecstasy (Walster and Walster, 1978). In other words, men are used to thinking of the characteristics of romantic love, and not of themselves as romantic lovers. Schafer (1976) has concluded that this mode of thinking predisposes men to concretize and personify the concept of love. Thus men "speak of what *it* is, what *it* does, of *its* properties, and *its* tendencies, of *its* source and *its* influence" (p. 271). Such a view encourages a belief in the existence of a fundamental category of consciousness that can unequivocally be called romantic love, despite evidence to the contrary. There is research to suggest that the same visceral and autonomic changes (for example, a flushed face, a pounding heart) occur in various emotional and nonemotional states (Woodworth and Schlosberg, 1954), and that the same state of physiological arousal can be labeled in terms of a great variety of emotions (Schachter, 1964). Such findings indicate that the subjective experience of romantic love is always mediated by a personal interpretation. Or to paraphrase Ortega y Gasset (1957), love, in its very essence, is choice. Anthropomorphizing romantic love, however, permits men to disavow responsibility for their choices. It is commonplace to hear men claim that romantic love "caused" their behavior. For these reasons, we advocate implementation of Schafer's (1976) recommendation that only verbs and adverbs be used when discussing romantic love. When presenting our own views, we shall try to speak of loving romantically as a *how* or as a *thus* rather than as a reified metaphor.

The Facts and Fictions of Romantic Love. Social scientists, however, have relied heavily on the use of reified metaphors when speaking of romantic love. For example, in his writings, Freud used the term *libido* to denote the sexual energy that is directed toward the mental representation of a loved person. Schafer (1976, p. 280) has recently acknowledged that at its root libido is a "pseudo-scientific poetic metaphor which enables psychoanalysts to endow discussions of sex, pleasure, and love with the (presumed) dignity of mechanics, hydraulics or electrostatics."

Social scientists have also been vulnerable to collapsing the distinction bewteen the social facts and fictions of romantic love. In 1962, Albert Ellis offered the following composite portrait of the romantic lover. We believe his rendering illustrates this trend.

> The romantic lover is unrealistic, he over evaluates and fictionalizes his beloved. He is verbal and aesthetic about his love. He is aggressively individualistic. He insists utterly on his own romantic love choice, and on all but absolute lack of restraint in that choice. He is . . . demanding . . . perfectionistic . . . antisexual. He acknowledges the value of sexuality only when it is linked to love. He is . . . changeable, frequently going from one violent passion to another. He is jealous, often intensely so, of his beloved. He tends to emphasize physical attractiveness above all else. He is . . . sentimental, . . . passionate and intense. He is supposed to love madly and to be violently in love, rather than affectionately loving. Finally, in today's world, the romantic lover invariably stresses marrying only for love, and is likely to believe that one should never remain married when love dies. For him, too, the death of love from his marriage tends to become sufficient license for every sort of adultery [Ellis, 1962, p. 32].

Ellis calls these "the *facts* of love." Psychoanalysts might recognize in this portrait the purportedly universal tendency among men to design situations that reawaken the oedipal theme and its corresponding affects. Yet Ellis's rendering does not grow out of an exact empirical representation of the ways in which today's men love romantically. In its essential features, this summary description owes more to the love literature, particularly that of the Middle Ages, than to empirically replicable observations about contemporary men. The justification for such an approach follows presumably from the generally accepted assumption that romantic love represents the historical persistence of Courtly Love. Yet the historical significance of Courtly Love itself is enmeshed in controversy.

   The Art of Courtly Love, written by Andreas Capellanus early in the thirteenth century, represents the first effort to record a "system of courtly love." The basic idea of Courtly Love, as described by Capellanus, is that "the lady is to be worshipped, that she is to be intensely desired and ardently pursued, not only because of her intrinsic beauty and nobility, but because of her capacity to endow the man with virtue through her acceptance of him. The lady, in turn, is to judge her pursuer, not on the basis of incidental qualities, but on the basis of his character, the latter being defined and demonstrated through the performance of acts of gentleness and courtesy" (Capellanus, 1969, p. 40). Social scientists have tended to read Capellanus's book as an accurate description of a way of life found in the so-called "Courts of Love." From the text they have inferred that medieval romanticism was an exceptionally class-limited form of love, invariably adulterous, and conducted in a ritual-like fashion. Scholars tend to agree that Courtly Love, as an idea, originated as a revolt against the sexual repressiveness of early Christianity and its doctrine of marriage. There are eminent medievalists, however, who doubt whether Courtly Love as a social institution every existed. For some, Capellanus's book exemplifies a rather vague complex of literary conventions (Halverson, 1970). Still others argue that Capellanus's treatise should be read as a "spoof" and/or that the "rules" of Courtly Love were instructions for a court "game" (Donaldson, 1965). Thus, in its very origins, romantic love challenges our notions of "reality" by threatening the distinction between fact and fiction. Consequently, at the center of many perennial debates about romantic love can be found a delicate and reciprocal relation between the social reality of romantic love and the unique imaginative metaphors that influential men have used to convey the idea of romantic love. Throughout history, there have been "fictional" representations of romantic love that have been experienced by their audiences as accurate sociological descriptions. Such works of art are "exemplary" (Sontag, 1966); they invite us to imitate them. Their creators are likely to become our romantic heroes. For many of our peers, this privileged status is currently occupied by such men as Woody Allen, Jackson Browne, Bob Dylan, Dustin Hoffman, Mick Jagger, Paul McCartney, Paul Mazursky, Eric Rohmer, Philip Roth, Paul Simon, François Truffaut, John Updike, John Voight, Neil Young, and so on. Perhaps it is during adolescence that we are most vulnerable to imitating such artists' eloquent images of romantic love.

As Ortega y Gasset (1957, p. 24) realized, romantic love has been so extensively eulogized that "before experiencing it we all know about it, place high value on it, and are resolved to practice it, like an art or profession."

Empirical Study of Adult Development. The longitudinal and/or biographical study of adult development, like the study of romantic love, is just beginning. Whatever data are available suggest that we have been guided by fundamental misconceptions in our thinking about adult men. The pioneering studies of R. L. Gould (1972), Levinson and others (1978), and Vaillant (1977) indicate that the process of entry into adulthood is far more lengthy and complex than has usually been imagined. Their work further suggests that the capacity to love romantically evolves during adulthood in accordance with developmental principles and timetables. By contrast, it has been traditionally assumed that romantic love is "a young man's sentimental passion" (Freud, 1921) and that adolescence is the last developmentally given period in the evolution of the personality. With few exceptions (Jung, 1971; Erikson, 1968b), theorists have represented adulthood as a plateau, with personality changes taking place only under the impact of massive stress due to environmental trauma or the reactivation of childhood conflicts.

The psychoanalytic concept of transference is indispensable to understanding the historical dimension of a man's love life. Yet it too has carried with it the erroneous implication that each new romance is a "mere repetition" of early familial attachments, including their inherent frustrations and disruptions. Freud ([1915] 1953e, p. 387) maintained that "there is no love that does not reproduce infantile prototypes." In the essay "The Dynamics of Transference" ([1912] 1953d, p. 313), he wrote that the childhood capacity to love "forms a cliché" or stereotype in the person which perpetually repeats and reproduces itself as life goes on. Although emotions originally felt toward one or the other parent are undoubtedly revived when we "fall in love," we are not condemned to mindless reenactment of our early love relations throughout the life cycle. Even if a man's loving relationships are burdened with conflicts enduring since childhood, the quality and substance of these conflicts will undergo decisive changes in response to the unique challenges of each developmental era. This conclusion is supported by the theory and findings of Levinson and others (1978) as well as Loewald's (1978) reformulation of the psychoanalytic concepts of transference and narcissism.

The integration of these complementary frameworks would permit research that locates a man and his efforts to love romantically within his ongoing biographic context. We have relied heavily on these works to develop the hypothesis that men manage the complexities of loving romantically in ways that are influenced profoundly by the ever-changing sociocultural conditions and developmental tasks that confront us as we age. Our primary aim in the next section will be to present the framework of Levinson and others (1978) for the analysis of adult development. Once this is presented, we shall turn our attention to the following questions: Does our culture support or undermine men's efforts to love romantically? How do men reconcile the dualities of love: the tensions between longing and consummation, sexuality and tenderness, being loved and loving, passion and harmony, and so on? How does loving romantically contribute to psychological growth and development? What psychological functions does loving romantically serve at different stages of the life cycle?

A Model of Adult Development

The concept of "life structure" is fundamental to the biographical approach of Levinson and others (1978) to understanding adult development. Levinson (p. 41) defines life structure as "the basic pattern or design of a person's live at a given time" and suggests that it is composed of three integrated components: one's sociocultural world, one's self, and one's mode of participation in society. He visualizes the life structure as a "tapestry" which inherently interconnects the sociocultural world in which a person is embedded, the person's relationship with the external world, and his personality as it is reflected in these relationships. In other words, for Levinson the self or personality is an intrinsic element of the life structure, and not a separate entity. The self in Levinson's theory is comparable to the psychoanalytic concept of character. Such concepts account for the stability, consistency, and predictability of our reactions to internal and external events. The sociocultural world, however, "provides a landscape, a cast of characters, a variety of resources and constraints out of which a man fashions his own life" (p. 42). The theory thus deals with the evolving process of mutual interpenetration between these components, rather than with personality development per se. When Levinson speaks of adult development, he is referring to the evolution of the life structure.

According to this theory, a life structure is viable "if it works in the world" and suitable to the extent that it allows a man to "live out crucially important aspects of his self" (p. 54). A life structure may be both viable and suitable (a dream come true), viable but not suitable (externally viewed as successful but experienced as corrupt or empty), suitable but not viable (experienced as meaningful but economically and socially unrewarded or scorned), or none of these (disastrous from societal and self perspectives). Since the "self" contains more wishes, talents, fantasies, values, modes of action, ideals, and potentialities than can be expressed within any single life structure, flaws and contraindications can be found in all men's lives.

To understand a particular man's evolving life structure, it is necessary to clarify the key choices he has made and how he has dealt with their resulting consequences. The most important choices in adult life have to do with work, family, friendships, and love relationships. From Levinson's perspective, to choose something means to form a relationship with it: "The relationship becomes a vehicle for living out certain aspects of the self and for participating in the world" (p. 18). The major components of a life structure thus include the person's relationships with self, with other individuals, with groups, symbols, organizations—with any aspect of the social or physical world that has significance for the person.

Although lives differ widely in the nature and patterning of these components, the biographical analyses of Levinson and others (1978) revealed two consistent themes: Most men make their occupation and their marriage-family relationships the central components of their life structure, and the live structure evolves through a relatively orderly sequence during the adult years. The essential nature of the sequence consists of an alternating series of stable and transitional periods. The stable periods ordinarily last some six to eight years, the transitional periods four to five years. The primary developmental task of a stable period is to build a life structure. To do so, a man must make crucial life choices, form a structure about them, and pursue his goals and values within that framework. The primary developmental task of a transitional period "is to terminate the existing structure and to work toward the initiation of a new structure. This requires a man to reappraise the existing life structure, to explore various possibilities for change in the world and in the self, and to move toward the crucial choices that will form the basis for a new life structure in the ensuing stable period" (p. 100).

The findings of Levinson and others (1978) further indicates that each new transitional and stable period is rendered unique because of the changing constellation of developmental tasks that confront us as we age.* As an example, the transition into early adulthood (roughly ages seventeen to twenty-two) carries with it the special task of separating from one's family of origin. The distinctive character of the period extending from twenty-two to twenty-eight follows from the overriding task of balancing exploration of the possibilities for adult living with the antithetical task of making a commitment to a stable life structure. By contrast, the shift from early adulthood to middle adulthood (roughly ages

*Levinson and others (1978) acknowledge that the age linkages of the adult stages represent a preliminary picture of the timetable of the periods, and that they are suggestive rather than conclusive. Nevertheless, Gould (1972) has independently arrived at a similar sequence of periods in adult personality development.

forty to forty-five) revolves around men's efforts to integrate life's key polarities: young/old, male/female, destruction/creation, separation/attachment, and so on.

At mid-life, moreover, the reality and inevitability of one's personal death and the finitude of time force themselves, painfully, on the attention of men. Neugarten (1978, p. 97), in a study concerning the changing time perspective in middle age, reported that "life is restructured in terms of time-left-to-live rather than time-since-birth." Jaques (1965) maintains that these changes are primarily responsible for the essential features of the "mid-life-crisis."

Loving romantically can serve enduring and changing, diverse and contradictory functions during these successive transformations of the life structure. In our culture, "romantic solutions" (Becker, 1973) to problems in living appear to be a particularly conspicuous feature of transitional periods, irrespective of the era in which they occur. For many young men, romantic love is synonymous with sexual love. For these men, romantic love can serve as a rhetorical device to obtain the pleasures of sexual gratification with a variety of women. During the transition into adulthood, men are also seeking an affirmation of their autonomy and competence. Loving romantically is frequently the pathway for realizing these goals and the catalyst that precipitates the creation of a first, provisional life structure. In our culture, for example, men tend to marry during the early adult transition. Divorce and marital problems, however, have tended to peak during the developmental period which Levinson refers to as the "age thirty transition." During the mid-life transition, a man may seek in romantic love a reaffirmation of his youthfulness and potency or the opportunity to "break out" of an existing life structure. Extramarital affairs which serve this latter function can either help a man correct the imbalances of early adulthood or can further contribute to the disharmonies inherent in a life structure. If they are experienced as taking place "outside" of the life structure, such romantic relationships, in our experience as psychotherapists, are not likely to be enduring. They appear to be in their very essence transitional or preparatory relationships. In our clinical work, we have also found that whereas the emphasis in young adulthood is upon being loved romantically, men at mid-life seem to be more preoccupied with their capacity to love the other romantically. Men at mid-life and beyond also appear to be more comfortable with the "effeminizing" influence of loving romantically. R. L. Gould's (1972, p. 526) findings similarly indicate that in the fifties there is a "mellowing and warming up." He reports that men come to value their own spouses more as a source of companionship and are less likely to regard them as a parent or as a source of supplies during this era. Loewald's (1978) theorizing lends further support to the view that loving romantically holds the promise of healing the structural flaws in our personalities. He has demonstrated how transference, in its nonpathological meaning, can be understood as "the dynamic of psychological growth and development" (p. 47). Loewald's reasoning, based upon Kierkegaard's notion of the "dialectic of repetition," is that repetitions of transference paradigms during adulthood contain aspects of novelty as well as an active and imaginative reorganization and elaboration of early love relations, and that consequently our love relations do not remain determined by the unmodified power of infantile prototypes.

It is generally assumed that it is in their romantic choices that men reveal their essential natures. In the following sections of this chapter, we shall examine how romantic choices, as a component of the life structure, are saturated with self and by the conditions of, and opportunities provided by, our sociocultural world. This presentation will focus on three trends that may change decisively the ways in which men love romantically: our culture's reevaluation of romanticism, the impact of the "new feminism" on work and sexual relationships, and our culture's growing preoccupation with narcissism.

The Romantic Vision of Reality

In 1880, Thomas Hardy wrote: "Romanticism will exist in human nature as long as human nature lasts. The point is (in imaginative literature) to adopt that form of romanticism which is the mood of the age" (Orel, 1969, p. 189). Hardy's statement recognizes two distinct but related meanings of the word *romantic*. Following Barzun (1961), we shall refer to these meanings as "intrinsic romanticism" and "historic romanticism."

Intrinsic Romanticism. As a result of the works of Barzun (1961) and Schafer (1970), we have come to view "intrinsic romanticism" not merely as a product of literary ingenuity but rather as an archetypal perspective on "reality testing." At the core of intrinsic romanticism, Barzun has identified "the effort to create order out of experience individually required" (p. 94). The romantic emphasizes action and involvement in the world, admires energy, and idealizes individuality, self expression, and authenticity. Extending the work of Frye (1957), Schafer has revealed that the terms *comic*, *tragic*, and *ironic* similarly refer to the "visions of reality" that emerge whenever the imaginative mind confronts the world. According to Schafer, these four organizing or structural principles shape each man's mode of comprehending the form and content of human situations and the changes they may undergo. Each represents a broad outlook, a theory of life, and a style of understanding and representing everyday ideas and judgments. In complex combinations, they define each man's overall "vision of reality." Clashes between such visions cannot be settled by simple appeals to the "evidence." As these visions influence the determination of facts and their interrelations and implications, men who are generally considered to be realistic and objective can therefore be expected to disagree in all sorts of ways about romantic love. Similarly, the loving relationships of those men whose life structures are saturated with the romantic vision can be expected to be quite different from those for whom it occupies a peripheral position.

In the romantic vision as formulated by Schafer (1970, p. 31), "life is a quest or a series of quests. The quest is a perilous, heroic, individualistic journey. Its destination or goal combines some or all of the qualities of mystery, grandeur, sacredness, love, and possession by or fusion with some higher power or principle (Nature, Virtue, Beauty, etc.). The seeker is an innocent, adventurous hero, and the quest ends, after crucial struggles, with exaltation." The reward of the quest usually is or includes a wife. In mythic literature, "this bride-figure is ambiguous, her psychological connection with the mother in the Oedipus fantasy is insistent, and she is often found in a perilous, forbidden, or tabooed place" (Frye, 1957, p. 193).

The study by Levinson and others (1978) of male adult development indicates that the archetype of the quest embraces essential aspects of men's lives. This study suggests that romantic dreams are not confined to adolescence, nor is the failure to relinquish adolescent dreams a sign of immaturity. Apparently, most men have a dream about how their lives should be as adults. This dream, according to Levinson, has its roots in childhood but fundamentally changes over time and involves an image, or sense, of one's self in the world. Levinson's findings suggest that throughout early adulthood a man's preoccupation tends to be with himself and the creation of his dream. Other people tend to be valued for what they contribute to his quest. In their attempts to translate this dream into a social reality, many men depend on "a special woman." Levinson suggests that the special woman "helps to animate that part of the self that contains the Dream . . . she shares it, believes in him as its hero, gives it her blessing, joins him on the journey and creates a 'boundary space' within which his aspirations can be imagined and his hopes nourished . . . the special woman can foster his adult aspirations while accepting his dependency, his incompleteness and his need to make her into something more than (and less than) she actually is" (p. 109). It is with such women that men often fall in love.

A prevailing assumption in the literature is that romantic lovers are unmindful of reality because they idealize their special women (Walster and Walster, 1978). In their structure, romantic quests are analogous to dreams and wish fulfillment daydreams (Frye, 1957). It does not necessarily follow, however, that romantic lovers are unrealistic or oblivious to complicating details, especially when considering romantic love as a basis for marriage. In his pioneering empirical studies, Rubin (1973) has demonstrated that men undisputedly recognize love as a prerequisite to marriage —not unreasoning love of the "head-over-heels" variety and not love that transcends all obstacles and barriers, but love nonetheless. In the terms of this discussion, Rubin's findings indicate that unqualified romanticism, as reflected in the belief that love can transcend barriers of race, religion, and social class, rarely describes the totality of a man's relationship to romantic love.

Historically, the romantic vision has been most often paired with comic and tragic perspectives on love (Frye, 1957). The unqualified hopefulness of many young lovers represents the commingling of comic and romantic perspectives on romantic love. The comic vision, with its emphasis on optimism, ultimate reconciliations, and sexual gratification unburdened by pain, promises endings that are simply happy. But, as Kafka asserted, "the decisive moment in human development is a continuous one" (1946, p. 279). Adult development, like marriage, is about the "morning after" and brings with it a growing appreciation of the difficulties of loving romantically. Thus a sense of the tragic begins to temper naive romanticism as we age. The tragic vision confronts us with the realization that the essential conditions of love include the loss of opportunities entailed by every choice, the inevitable clashes between passion and duty, inescapable ambivalence, and the insidious influence of unresolved unconscious processes on loving romantically.

When asked why he had waited till his eighties to divorce his wife, an octogenarian replied, "We were waiting for the children to die." Whatever humor one finds in this joke derives, perhaps, from the tension between its romantic and ironic undercurrents. The ironic vision shares with the tragic vision a readiness to seek out paradoxes, contradictions, and the absurdities of human existence. However, whereas the emotionally overcharged and grandiose inclinations of romantic lovers are supported by the tragic vision, the detachment and self-deprecatory thrust of the ironic vision undermines the very terms of romantic thinking. The heroics, enchantment, idealizations, and blissful joy of loving romantically contrast starkly with the ironic effort not to take any aspect of oneself or others too seriously. We believe that today the struggle to integrate the seemingly incompatible modes of romance and irony is endemic in our culture.

Of the lovers of his day, Tolstoy remarked, "Many people's love would be instantly annihilated if they could not speak of it in French" (Morton, 1889, p. 23). Romantic loving requires a comfort with expressiveness and a capacity to yield to the concrete immediate presence of the other. However, as society has become "psychologized" and infused with a sense of irony, many men have increasingly become "spectators" of themselves. Consequently, many modern men are usually too self-conscious to engage in the rhetoric and esthetic refinements of romantic love. Such predicaments are exemplified in the films of Woody Allen. In *Annie Hall* and *Manhattan*, Allen's romantic lovers are trying self-consciously to offset genuineness and mockery, commitment and withdrawal, earnestness and absurdity, satire and sentiment. Tension between romance and irony can also give rise to disjunctions between subjective experience and expressivity. Apparently, this trend is widespread among men. In *Family Circle* magazine, Balswick (1979, p. 110) advises troubled readers that many men who love their wives are "unable" to tell them. Rubin's (1973) findings similarly indicate that men are more reluctant than women to express the euphoric feelings that accompany "falling in love." Although they will admit to fewer of the "symptoms" of love, men appear to fall in love more quickly and to cling more tenaciously to a dying affair than women. Durkheim (1951) found that three times as many men as women commit suicide after a disastrous love affair. Hill, Rubin, and Peplau (1976), in their study of unmarried couples, found that usually the women decided whether and when an affair should end; the men seemed to stick it out to the bitter end. It was also the man who suffered most (felt more depressed, more lonely, less happy and less free) after the breakup. Women were far more resigned and thus were better able to pick up the pieces of their lives and move on. Rubin's studies, in part, have addressed the question, Are men or women more romantic? His results led him to conclude that the answer depends on which criteria are used to define the essential features of romantic love.

Historic Romanticism. Whereas romanticism as a characteristic of human beings, or certain human beings, is perennial, romanticism as a historical movement may become cultivated, dominant, or devalued in any given period. Extraordinary events appear to stimulate and justify historic romanticism. Barzun (1961) has discerned that romantic periods in history are those that support the creation of a new society different from, and on the ruins of, its immediate forerunner. In the past, cultures were regarded as romantic to the extent that they were characterized by "a return to the Middle Ages, a love of the exotic, an exaggeration of individualism, a liberation of the unconscious, a reaction against the scientific method, a revival of pantheism, idealism, and Catholicism, a rejection of artistic conventions, a preference for emotions, a movement back to nature or a glorification of force" (p. 13). Such cultural conditions not only lent weight and color to our ancestors' experience of romantic love but also perhaps, in the last analysis, determined their particular form.

    In recent history, these values have been held, either explicitly or implicitly, as "the enemy of reason, science, and democracy"

(Barzun, 1961, p. 15). In politics, romanticism has been seen as resulting in the excessive authority that leads to totalitarianism and/or the excessive individualism that leads to anarchy. Literary critics have equated romanticism with easy sentimentality, self-indulgence, utopian aspirations, irrationalism, escapism, indolence, and insanity. In the psychoanalytic community, the romantic vision has been viewed as regressive and childlike, naive and simplistic. "Spurious" is often used as a synonym for romantic in academic journals. It is therefore not surprising to find that scholars, as well, have recently emphasized the perils and illusions of romantic love. Pessimism regarding the possibilities of integrating romantic love into an enduring relationship is commonplace. The most eloquent and frequently quoted spokesman for this point of view has been de Rougement:

> Romance is by its very nature incompatible with marriage even if the one has led to the other, for it is the very essence of romance to thrive on obstacles, delays, separations, and dreams, whereas it is the basic function of marriage daily to reduce and obliterate these obstacles. Marriage succeeds only in constant physical proximity to the monotonous present. . . . Romance is . . . incapable of establishing a durable marriage, and it is not an act of courage but one of absurdity to marry someone forever because of a fever that endures for two months [1963, p. 80].

Although the conditions we now live in are different from those of any prior civilization we are once again living in extraordinary times. During the writing of this chapter, a test-tube baby celebrated her first birthday. The elderly are experimenting with eroticized relationships and living arrangments for which we have no previous models. In a highly publicized trial, a wife sued her husband for rape and then sought a reconciliation. As we enter the 1980s, fundamental changes are occurring in our culture's conceptions of masculinity. It is becoming increasingly difficult to define, in the abstract, sex-role characteristics as either male or female. American films are increasingly portraying men as vulnerable, sensitive, and trusting and not as "macho." Freud's ([1905] 1957j) assumption that the sexual inclinations of all men evolve from "polymorphous perversity" and "bisexuality" embodies today a program of reform for gay activists. In their inquiries regarding fantasy patterning during sexual stimulation for both homosexual and heterosexual couples, Masters and Johnson (1979) reported a high incidence of cross-preference fantasy. Homosexual men and women imagined heterosexual interactions, and, conversely heterosexual men and women had homosexual fantasies. Sexologists rarely talk about romantic love but instead focus on the behavior of the human sexual apparatus. Nevertheless, their work has sensitized men to the problems that have followed their insistence on *dividing* lovemaking into foreplay and sexual intercourse. A recent survey of the readership of *Psychology Today* indicates that an androgynous ideal is gaining popularity in our culture (Tavris, 1977).

Concomitantly, there are suggestions that men are questioning the suitability of achievement-dominated life structures. American men today, in unprecedented numbers, are investing their personal relations, especially those with women, with greater emotional importance. A *Playboy*-financed Louis Harris survey of American male values found that men rank love second only to health as their most important need (Brozan, 1979). Many men are active participants in the culturally diffuse yet pervasive "consciousness movement." The emphasis here is upon such values as expressiveness, direct immediate experience, and spontaneity. In parallel, antiromantic opposition to these trends is also growing. Lasch (1978, p. 30), for example, argues that "the current preoccupation with self-discovery, psychic growth, and intimate personal encounters represents unseemly self-absorption, romanticism run rampant." Taken together, these trends suggest that our culture is going through a painful reevaluation of the values associated with historic romanticism.

Work, Sex, and the New Feminism

Of all the reform movements that began in the 1960s, none appears as enduring as women's efforts to achieve equality with men. There is *less* support today to men's claim of superiority than during any other historical era. We fundamentally agree with Farber's (1976, p. 163) conclusion: "In its efforts to redress sexual, social, political, economic, artistic, historical, and religious inequalities, the new feminism has thrown into question all those institutions under whose auspices men and women have sought to combine their lots and join their fates."

The division of labor between the sexes is being irreversibly changed. Half of the women in this country are in the paid labor force, including 46 percent of those with children (Kahne, 1975). Whereas the working wife was a "deviant" role a half century ago, it may soon be the unpaid housewife who feels social pressure to justify her role. A recent survey of upper-middle-class professional husbands suggests that coping with the stresses of dual-career marriages, role differentiation, and the relentless chores of daily life enhances personal growth and leads to a more rewarding marital relationship (Nadelson and Eisenberg, 1977). The privileges of the upper middle class include the possibility of doing work that inspires and gratifies romantic strivings. Finding work that is both suitable to the self and viable in the world is far more problematic for the poor and uneducated. Nevertheless, working-class men pride themselves on the hard work and personal sacrifice they are making as "breadwinners." Many in the past made a "gift" of these sacrifices to their wives and children. Today, according to Goode, "they are told that it was not a gift at all. . . . In fact their wives earned what they received. If work was a sacrifice, they are told, so were all the services, comforts, and self deprivations that women provided" (Friedan, 1979, p. 5). The change that Goode believes most disturbs man "is a loss of centrality, a decline in the extent to which they are the center of attention. Boys and grown men have always taken for granted that what they were doing was more important than what the other sex was doing. Women's attention was focused on them. Nowadays, the center of attention has shifted more to women" (p. 6). Male reactions to these shifts often include a sense of being unlovable, demeaned, and betrayed. Some men claim that the women's movement is destroying the very cornerstone of men's sexual identity, is responsible for unleashing anxiety, envy of women, dread, hostility, and exhaustion, and is the main cause of the increase in divorce, separation, and wife battering everywhere in the United States. Whether such claims exaggerate the negative impact of the women's movement has yet to be comprehensively investigated.

When such studies are conducted, we anticipate that they will reveal that men express changing attitudes toward the democratization of male-female relationships at different stages of their lives. For example, the values that Freud expressed in his scientific critiques of romantic love (published in 1910, 1912, and 1918)

were "more advanced" than the attitudes that can be discerned in
his love letters to his fiancée, Martha Bernays (E. L. Freud, 1961).
Freud wrote approximately 900 letters to his fiancée during their
four-year engagement. In these letters, he expressed the belief that
equality between the sexes would mean "the disappearance of the
most lovely thing the world has to offer us: our ideal of womanhood" (p. 76). Freud's ideal young woman was possessed of
"charm, beauty, goodness" and aroused erotic passions in men
while remaining passive herself. In his own engagement, Freud conveyed the idea that courtship consisted of masculine initiative
overcoming girlish passivity and reticence. Yet, in his later scientific studies, Freud concluded that sexuality must be freed from
inclinations toward domination and submission if we are truly to
love persons as persons rather than as surrogates for our lost
parental love. Rieff (1961, p. 184) puts it this way: "Freud advanced an ideal of love purged of parental influences, an exchange
of equals."

The sexual aspects of romantic relationships, as well as the
division of labor between the sexes, are being altered profoundly
by women's efforts to achieve equality with men. Males in our
culture have traditionally been socialized to offer some degree of
commitment to get sex, whereas women have been socialized to
bargain with sex to get commitment (Maddock, 1973). This dilemma found expression during the 1950s in the dialectical caricatures
of the "sexpot" and the "nice girl." Up until recently, this splitting tendency was paralleled by and also encoded in the paralyzing
edict that no man would marry a woman who was not a virgin.
This age-old virgin/whore dichotomy is being fundamentally as-
saulted today by the collapse of chivalry, the modern woman's increasingly insistent demand for sexual fulfillment, the scientific
demystification of female sexuality, and strenuous propaganda on
behalf of "open marriage" and "creative divorce," as well as the
ever-present possibility that any given marriage will end in divorce.

Divorced people used to be considered failures, misfits,
neurotics, selfish immoralists. Today divorces, although still invariably traumatic, can be obtained without stigma and without
jeopardizing careers—even in such sensitive fields as politics or
the ministry. A century ago there was only one divorce per thirty-
two marriages in a given year, nowadays there is one divorce for
every two marriages. Moreover, divorce no longer means the end

to married life. Today four out of five divorced people remarry. And, although many more young people are delaying marriage, 90 percent of young men and approximately 95 percent of young women will marry (U.S. Bureau of the Census, 1975).

Census Bureau figures show that, since 1970, the number of unmarried people of the opposite sex sharing a household has doubled from 654,000 to 1.3 million. With such shifts in mind, Farber (1976, p. 165) concluded: "Courtship at best represented a rather stylized manner in which two people could come to know each other before sex and/or marriage. A young man and young woman today are more apt to begin with sex, and for the kinds of knowing which follows, we have no ready word." Owing to a growing climate of permissiveness, the availability of efficient contraceptives, legalized abortions, and the promotion of sex as a "healthy" bodily function, young adults today have more sexual freedom than any previous generation. Their music and modes of dancing emphasize consummation rather than longing. Few of the colleges they attend retain parietal rules, many have coed dormitories. Such trends both reflect and legitimize the pursuit of sexual pleasure as an end in itself. Taboos against adultery also appear to be weakening. The latest Kinsey report indicates that growing numbers of married women are participating in extramarital sexual relationships (Weinberg, 1976). It seems reasonable to conclude that men no longer treat women as "ladies" and that modern sexual imagination supports a preoccupation with variety and multiplicity. These and other "facts" represent symbolic shifts that have great significance for the ways in which men love romantically.

The Failures of Love

The conflict-laden dialectic between the thinking man and his penis has not been reconciled by the growing range of sexual possibilities in the modern world. Sontag (1966) has discerned that a prevailing theme of serious literature is the failure of love. She maintains that the modern cult of love "is the main way in which we test ourselves for strength of feeling, and find ourselves deficient" (p. 47). Lasch (1978) claims that as women have become more accessible as sexual partners, they have also become more threatening. He has observed that "formerly men complained about women's lack of sexual response; now they find this response intimidating and agonize about their capacity to satisfy it," and that "the famous Masters and Johnson report on female sexuality added to these anxieties by depicting women as sexually insatiable, inexhaustible in their capacity to experience orgasm after orgasm" (p. 193).

Taken together, these observations suggest that men today simultaneously overvalue yet are pessimistic about the healing possibilities of sexual love. The changing role of religion and/or spirituality in our culture is deeply implicated in this predicament. For two thousand years, among Christians and Jews, suffering has been a hallmark of a man's "seriousness" (Sontag, 1966). Resisting the temptations of premarital sex or an extramarital affair provided evidence of one's character or seriousness. The allure of unrequited romantic love was particularly appealing to those who were seeking confirmation of their ability "unselfishly" to renounce private desires. Americans no longer believe, with certainty, that "God is on our side." The growing popularity of Eastern philosophy and meditational practices suggests that many young men in our culture are measuring their seriousness today by their ability to evade or transcend suffering and achieve tranquillity (Farber and Geller, 1977). Traditionally, the emphasis has been on subordinating and controlling the body as a prerequisite for spiritual advancement. As our culture increasingly aspires to a life of the body, the relinquishment of "earthly love" for "divine love" has become more problematic, even for Catholic priests. In the wake of our culture's repudiation of the ascetic traditions of Judaism and Christianity, there has appeared a growing readiness to acknowledge that "every man can be subject, if he so chooses, to undifferentiated sexual arousal" (Farber, 1976, p. 170). (The popularity of Erica Jong's [1973] "zipless fuck" suggests that many women too are given to "undifferentiated lust.") Yet, because they are still confined by the generalized prohibitions that their religious traditions bequeathed them, many young men today share with Alexander Portnoy the complaint that they are "sex maniacs" (Roth, 1969). At thirty-three, Portnoy tells his analyst:

> "And, Doctor, your Honor, whatever your name is—it seems to make no difference how much the poor bastard actually gets, for he is dreaming about tomorrow's pussy even while pumping away at today's. . . . Please, let us not bullshit one an-

other around about 'love' and its duration. Which is why I ask;
how can I marry someone I 'love' knowing full well that five,
six, seven years hence I am going to be out on the streets hunting down fresh new pussy—all the while my devoted wife, who
has made me such a lovely home, et cetera, bravely suffers her
loneliness and rejection? How could I face her terrible fears?
I couldn't. How could I face my adoring children? And then
the divorce, right. The *child* support, the *alimony*, the *visita-
tion* rights. Wonderful prospect, just wonderful" [p. 123].

As a result of hormonal changes, men experience their lust
with less urgency as they grow older. Over age fifty, psychic erections become rarer, direct friction is often required to stimulate an
erection, and orgasm may not be reached with every act of intercourse. This physiologically mediated change may be variously
interpreted. As Masters and Johnson (1975, p. 69) discovered:
"The susceptibility of the human male to the power of suggestion
with regard to his sexual prowess is almost unbelievable." Many
men become more passionate and sensual lovers as they age. Intimacy does not flourish if one fears "premature ejaculation."
Prolonged lovemaking deepens the possibilities of intimacy. Many
men, however, interpret the same bodily changes as evidence of
their waning masculinity. Such men are particularly vulnerable to
a variety of sexual dysfunctions. For example, although impotence
is never due to "age" alone, one fourth of the men surveyed by
Weinberg (1976) were impotent by the age of sixty-five and one
half by seventy-five.

A profound loss of self-esteem invariably accompanies the
fear that one is incapable of "successful lovemaking" or of making
a permanent commitment to a woman. Men in general are reluctant to explore candidly the intimate details of their romances,
be they successful or unsuccessful. Even in our sexually permissive
culture, romantic lovemaking, on the whole, is still conducted in
private. Psychotherapists have privileged access to this private
realm. A "therapeutic" outlook and sensibility pervades our contemporary views on romantic love. It is not surprising therefore
that psychotherapists, including Erich Fromm (1956), Rollo May
(1969), and Otto Kernberg (1976b), have become the dominant
theoreticians of love in our time. They report that psychotherapists are being consulted, in increasing numbers, by individuals
who are suffering from characterological problems highlighted by

schizoid or narcissistic detachment. The presenting complaints of such individuals prominently include feelings of emptiness and in-authenticity, the inability to mourn, an unappeasable hunger for exciting experiences to fill a sense of inner void, promiscuous pan-sexuality, avoidance of dependence, and a simultaneous yearning for yet dread of intimacy (Guntrip, 1969; Kernberg, 1976b). Such individuals, on the one hand, appear to be able to gratify, impul-sively, their sexual impulses; on the other hand, on closer inspec-tion they are found to be profoundly alienated from their bodies. Their emotional inaccessibility precludes receptivity to the intern-al and external cues of romantic love. For these reasons, "many patients with a narcissistic personality structure have never fallen or been in love" (Kernberg, 1976b, p. 186). The inability to "fall in love," in other words, is coming to be regarded as a sign of sig-nificant psychopathology.

If two people truly are to join together, and not just place their bodies at each other's disposal, both must render themselves vulnerable, and each must be able to receive the gift of the other. In order to realize this goal, a man must be able to manage the continuous interplay and mutual shaping of the "active-rational" and "sensuous-receptive" modes of experiencing (Deikman, 1974). Models of consciousness invariably include such a bimodal concep-tion of two opposite but complementary modes of experiencing (Ornstein, 1971). Each mode is typically associated with a distinc-tive constellation of physiological and psychological characteristics, and each is deeply implicated in men's capacity to experience and sustain romantic love. In the "rational-active" mode, a person func-tions to manipulate or act upon the environment. Sympathetic nervous activity and striate muscle activity predominate. Atten-tion is maintained on external events, and the goal-oriented be-havior of normal waking consciousness prevails. By contrast, in the "sensuous-receptive" mode, a person functions to let in sen-sory aspects of the environment. Parasympathetic nervous activity and sensory-perceptual activity predominate. Attention is focused inward on internal events, muscle tension is decreased, and para-logical thought characterized by intuition and sensation assume prominence (Dosamentes-Alperson, 1979).

In his efforts to blend these divergent modes of experiencing, a man may become one-sided and have only one mode available to him, he may vacillate in an unintegrated fashion between them, or ideally he may balance harmoniously the continuous interplay between these modes. Historically, the active-rational and sensuous-receptive modes have been erroneously equated with activity and passivity. Activity and passivity in turn have been designated as masculine and feminine inclinations. Such sex-role stereotyping has unfortunately fostered a skewed distribution of these modes of functioning in men and women. Sociological authorities such as Parsons and Bales (1955) maintain that the self-esteem of females has traditionally been more dependent upon interpersonal-social factors and expressiveness than is the self-esteem of males, who are believed to be more dependent on individualistic and instrumental criteria (for example, achievement) of relative worth. In fact, dominant social stereotypes view competence, independence, competition, and intellectual achievement as qualities inconsistent with femininity but as positively related to masculinity and psychological health (Broverman and others, 1970).

Don Juans are apt to be viewed as "antisocial" because they are in rebellion against these cultural stereotypes. Don Juans violate the "truism" that women live for love and men live for work. Don Juans are lovers of love; they devote their greatest energy to being uninterruptedly in love with women. Ortega y Gasset (1957, p. 27) further suggests that they "are not the men who make love to women but the men whom women make love." According to psychiatric theorists, this trend suggests that their heterosexual seductions are in the service of camouflaging passive, feminine, homosexual trends (Reich, 1949). Don Juans may be capable of inspiring romantic love in women but they may also be incapable of truly loving romantically. Along with the narcissistically disabled, they may perform "it" rather than live "it." Such interpretations may in part express the ambivalence with which Don Juanism has been regarded by men. As Fowles (1964, p. 281) asserted: "For every Don Juan, a hundred would like to be Don Juan." Ortega y Gasset (1957) agrees with this estimate. He maintains that, with few exceptions, men can be divided into three classes: "those who think they are Don Juan, those who think they have been Don Juan, and those who think they could have been but did not want to be. The last are the ones who propose, with worthy intention, to attack Don Juan and perhaps decree his dismissal" (p. 170).

The Healing Potential of Romantic Love

Paradoxically, fulfillment of many romantic strivings, including "infantile" wishes, is possible only when an individual has "grown up." The findings of Levinson and others (1978) indicate that young men are novice lovers, husbands, and fathers. They are in general not capable of highly loving, sexually free, and emotionally intimate relationships because the guiding energy during early adulthood tends to be narcissistic. As previously noted, the love a man experiences for his special woman, during early adulthood, largely derives from her dedicated support of his dream, and not from an appreciation of her in her own right. The endogenous efforts of the self to right itself after such imbalances and one-sided emphases of early adulthood crucially define the experience of mid-life. The gradual emergence of the flaws and inevitable contradictions inherent in a narcissistic life structure consequently provoke, with heightened urgency, efforts at reconciliation as middle adulthood approaches. For example, the man at mid-life who has been "married to his career" may seek in romantic love opportunities to heal the disharmonies in his life structure. For such men, the capacity to love romantically may begin to express itself, perhaps for the first time. Many men rediscover or discover romantic love with their wives and/or seek romantic love in extramarital relationships during the transition into middle adulthood. As this occurs, neglected aspects of self are reexperienced and reappropriated. Risks are taken. New sources of energy are unleashed. As Farber (1976, p. 165) has recognized, real man/woman talk and sexuality promises "the exciting possibility of receiving and offering a range of perceptions and sensibility whose otherness can be uniquely and surprisingly illuminating." In other words, we are affirmed and come to know ourselves in the process of disclosing ourselves to our lovers.

A major appeal of new love during transitional periods may be the opportunity to rewrite one's narrative history. Unencumered by a shared past and the wounds inflicted by the sheer dailiness of existence, new lovers listen effortlessly and speak candidly. During this process, the past may be reenacted, mourned, reappraised, and integrated. To further explore the ways in which romantic love can contribute to growth and individuation, we must first clarify the distinction between object love and narcissistic love.

Psychoanalysts maintain that throughout life the opposing claims of narcissism and object love, striving for reconciliation, characterize all erotic relationships. Narcissism is our first erotic disposition in the sense that before we know that other bodies exist and/or what it is to like other bodies, we direct our libido towards our bodies. Narcissism so conceptualized does not refer primarily to love of self in contrast to love of others but rather to a "primordial love-mentation" which, according to Loewald (1978, p. 39), "does not structure or divide reality into the poles of inner and outer, subject and object, self and others." Following Loewald, we shall refer to this process as "identificatory love." Object love, by contrast, refers to a mode of relatedness in which oneself as subject and the other as object are established at least to the extent that there is some awareness that there are differences between the other's needs, desires, feelings and one's own.

Most developmental theorists now agree that in the early stages of life such boundaries are not yet established (Mahler, Pine, and Bergman, 1975). The prototype* for identificatory love is the infant-mother unity or bond. Identificatory love enables children to enrich themselves, to take into themselves aspects or traits of their parents. Thus, in early childhood, this process plays a prominent role in the formation and consolidation of the self. However, this process continues in far more complex ways in later developmental stages as well. In adulthood, the suspension or blurring of the boundaries between self and other can be seen in psychosis, in some drug-related and ecstatic stages, and in situations of deep intimacy between people. In her work, "Parenthood As a Developmental Phase," Benedek (1959) reported that there is also a "normative symbiosis" on the part of the adult parent to the developing child which similarly makes possible a blurring of self-definition.

Approach-avoidance motifs dominate the literature on romantic love. At their root can be found the joys and perils of identificatory love. From the perspective of self-other differentiation, romantic loving can be experienced as deeply enriching and/or as terrifying. A man may "fall in love" but he "makes love." Roman-

---

*A prototype may be defined as an event, actual or symbolic, that is prefigurative, prior in time, and causally related to later behavior (Rieff, 1961). Transference, as Rieff has recognized, is but one instance of the power of prototypes.

tically inspired lovemaking requires the capacity to tolerate "the manifold, simultaneous and/or shifting heterosexual and homosexual, pregenital and genital identifications activate in the context" (Kernberg, 1976b, p. 222). Identificatory love promises the romantic lover, as George Bernard Shaw recognized, "a celestial flood of emotion and exaltation of experience" (Barzun, 1961, p. 127), not merely orgasms.

Many schizophrenic "first breaks," during early adulthood, are precipitated by the dissolving sense of self brought about by the experience of merging or fusing with a lover. Such individuals are still uncertain about their identity as separate beings and consequently experience "reengulfment" (Mahler, Pine, and Bergman, 1975) with a caring other as a threat to their individuality, cohesion, and stability.

Consciousness and choice imply a commitment to, rather than an identification with, the external other. To the extent that a man acknowledges that he can be sexually aroused by and love more than one women at a time, he will be burdened by the arbitrariness of his romantic and marital choices. Identificatory love lends authority, reassurance, even a sense of inevitability to one's choices. The push toward commitment is strengthened if a man can experience at crucial and delicate moments a merged identity with his lover. He can, moreover, overcome temporarily his loneliness to the extent that he can achieve a sense of oneness with his lover. According to Bertrand Russell (1930), it is the fear of loneliness that prompts most men to marry.

It is through the medium of identificatory love that a man can also achieve transcendence of his narcissistic self-absorption or a cancellation of the self. For men who are confronting the reality and inevitability of their own personal death, this "spiritual" aspect of romantic loving can assume problematic importance. Near the end of his life, Rilke (1978, p. 28) wrote: "Is it easier for lovers? Ah, they only manage, by being together, to conceal each other's fate!" In their efforts to come to terms with growing old and dying, men, especially those who are alienated from the collective visions that guide their culture, seek to reinvent for themselves "the project of spiritually" (Sontag, 1969). They may come to rediscover with Pavese (Sontag, 1966, p. 46) that "love is the cheapest of religions," and that loving romantically can provide

them with relief from worldly concerns or with a way of getting
out of themselves and onto a higher plane of existence. In *The
Denial of Death*, Becker (1973, p. 28) concludes that the failure of
romantic love, in its guise as a "personal religion," to reconcile the
existential contradiction "between a symbolic self, that seems to
give man infinite worth in a timeless scheme of things, and a body
that is worth about 98¢" is a defining feature of our time.

Although romantic loving can only anesthetize pain temporarily, identificatory love can also promote growth and change.
Loving romantically promises men the possibility of developing
attributes or modes of functioning that are not adequately represented in their own personalities. For example, obsessional men
often fall in love with hysterical women and vice versa, because
they see each other as complementary to their own style, and indeed they are. (See Chapter Thirteen.) The hysteric style is viva-
cious, emotional, empathic, and spontaneous. The obsessional
style, by contrast, is more contained, intellectualized, logical, and
controlled. As Barnett (1971, p. 75) has documented: "These
factors of outward style aid in the initial idealization each makes
of the other. The hysteric sees the obsessional as the strong silent
man, profound, organized and successful, while the obsessional
views the hysteric as being warm, vital, loving and fun. Both see in
the other's outward style evidence of precisely those characteristics they would like to see in themselves. They see in the other
an opportunity for change and growth, a complementary relationship which may be therapeutic for their own inadequacies and lia-
bilities or, at the very least, might enhance their own experience."
The fate of these initial idealizations is often problematic, as Barnett has detailed. The literature on marriage has in fact emphasized the pathological aspects of forsaking an individual identity
for merged identity (Wexler and Steidl, 1978). We shall, however,
conclude this essay by citing one further example of how the iden-
tifactory components of loving can serve as a "force or power that
not only brings people together, but equally brings oneself together
into that one individuality which we become through our identifications" (Loewald, 1978, p. 40).

The desire to fuse with a lover, according to Ortega-y-Gasset
(1957, p. 37), usually "culminates in a more or less clear desire to
leave, as testimony of the union, a child in whom the perfections

of the beloved are perpetuated and affirmed." A child is neither the father's nor the mother's but a "personified union" of the two. Today's young adults, especially those who are pursuing dual-career marriages, are often in severe conflict about their urge to have children. Having children has become burdened by the weight-iness of decisions that are premised disproportionately on the "rational-active" mode. Erikson (Adams, 1979) has recently urged psychoanalysts to be alert to the possibility that just as sexual re-pression characterized the Victorian era, repression of the urge to have children may characterize the future.

The implications of choosing not to have children are pro-found. Childless couples can devote their full energies to each other. They have the freedom to cultivate desire and experiment with a relationship that approximates perpetual courtship. In their work, they can also express their "procreative" urges and concern for future generations. However, the decision not to have children can weaken the idea of a permanent commitment to each other. Children may also help to reconcile the opposing claims of narcis-sism and object love. It is in their relationship to their children that men most closely approximate the ideal of loving unselfishly and unconditionally. Vicarious participation in a child's crushes and romances provides men with opportunities to reexperience, perhaps with greater clarity, the unfinished business of their own youth. Erikson's (1968b) work suggests that mature concern for one's children encourages a decisive turn toward intimacy, genera-tivity, and integrity rather than toward isolation, stagnation, self-absorption and despair in later adulthood. The identificatory com-ponents of a man's love for his children can therefore facilitate the heroic quest for personal integration, which may not be achievable, according to Jung (Campbell, 1971), until the fifth decade of life.

In our time, the creative and constructive role that romantic love can play in fostering personal integration needs to be reaf-firmed. A renewal of this belief will require continued and arduous revision of the dualities of love which this "work in progress" has briefly discussed.

5

Adulthood: Women

Deborah C. Uchalik
Diane D. Livingston

The absence of a solid theoretical framework of romantic love makes it difficult to discuss the experience of romantic love in adult women. Yet this experience is a universal phenomenon. Women of all shapes, sizes, and colors experience the joys of new love. Romantic love knows no social class, economic, educational, or age limitations. Grandmothers, women in prison, lonely women, women in business, country women, all experience, in their own individual ways, the happiness, inspirational moments, and fantasies of romantic love. In spite of such diversity of experience, however, there is no reliable description of how women really experience romantic love.

Our conclusions about the female romantic love experience are complicated by the fact that nearly all of the writing that has been done in this area represents men's views of women's loving.

Note: The authors wish to thank William Aitken for his editorial comments and suggestions.

What we do know of women's actual experience is largely derived from research performed with college students, women discussing love among themselves, and the love lives of women characters in popular novels and magazines. Although these are certainly limited sources of information, they provide a starting point for looking at romantic love in women.

This chapter will attempt to take a holistic approach to describing the role of romantic love in the lives of women. Because a woman's experience of romantic love is influenced by the social, cultural, and psychological views of her time, information from these areas will be considered within the context of female development and the formation of love relationships. It is hoped that many new thoughts, research ideas, and positive personal experiences will evolve from these considerations.

The Concept of Romantic Love

A number of definitions of romantic love have already been put forth in this volume. Pope's conception of romantic love in Chapter One includes elements of preoccupation with the beloved, total involvement in the love relationship, a sense of incompleteness without the other, despair when the loved one is absent and ecstasy upon being reunited. Romantic love is exciting, inspiring, and transforming. Rubin (1970) defined romantic love by drawing upon a wide range of literary and psychological conceptualizations. Factor analysis of his resulting love scale revealed three principal components: an affiliative and dependent need, a predisposition to help, and an orientation of exclusiveness and absorption.

Romantic love also might be conceptualized physiologically. During the process of falling in love, one experiences a state of physiological arousal, evidenced, for example, in increased cardiovascular and respiratory activity. Depending on one's socialization experiences, alterations in attention, affect, thought, and behavior occur in response to a specific set of stimuli, namely those associated with the individual focused upon as a lover.

The state of physiological arousal that accompanies falling in love resembles the body's response to stress and is also reminiscent of the behavior changes produced by stimulant drugs. Euphoria, decreased need for sleep, increases in arousal and alertness, increased motor activity, and augmentation of learning and performance all characterize amphetamine-induced arousal and the early stages of romantic love. This state of arousal serves a number of important functions at the beginning of a love relationship. It permits the development of attachment bonds and facilitates conditioning of physical, emotional, and behavioral stimuli associated with the new lovers. If during this process, communication, intimacy, and affection develop, then the initial romantic period may merge into a continued love relationship. As McCary (1975) notes, mature love represents a process of personal growth and awareness of the partner's individual needs. However, if the relationship remains dependent on the initial level of novelty, idealistic expectation, and sexual excitement and ecstasy, it is unlikely that mature love will develop, and the relationship will probably be short-lived. (Of course, there may be those for whom short-lived relationships are not unwelcome, for they then permit new romantic opportunities. Surely, part of the mystique of romantic love is the fantasy of love lost and the delicious hurt and pain that then ensues before a new love is found.)

Growing Up Female—Developmental Factors and Romantic Love

The process of learning to love romantically is indeed a complex one. The adult woman's conceptions of romantic love and her response in love relationships have at their foundation the romantic experiences of her childhood and adolescence.

A modern American woman coming of age absorbs a host of messages from family, educators, and the media as to the appropriate role behavior of females in love relationships. For the preschool girl, in the process of developing a female identity, these influences can have potent implications for her adjustment as an adult in romantic partnerships.

To begin with, children generally do not receive any direct information about love from their parents (Walster and Walster, 1978). Thus the young girl's first ideas about romance and love are a function of her sharing in love experiences with her family and her observation of love models in her immediate environment and the media. The young female observes interactions between her parents and begins to develop a sense of the behaviors her mother engages in to elicit a romantic response from her father. Likewise, she learns the differential contingencies that govern her receiving attention from adult males and females in her environment. When is she rewarded for looking pretty? Are similar values placed on physical contact with men and women? The degree to which she observes and receives physical and verbal exchanges of caring will influence her early ideas about giving and sharing love. As the preschool female internalizes feminine role behaviors through observation of her mother model, she may also learn that romantic love is linked with her most acceptable future status, that of wife and mother.

Outside of the interpersonal sphere, the female growing up in America receives considerable support for the romantic ideal of love. Nursery school fairy tales are replete with examples of romantic love. Most of these (for example, Cinderella, Sleeping Beauty) promote love of the happily-ever-after variety and depict the fruition of romance with woman's status defined by her relationship with men (for example, wife of a king, admirer of an explorer) (Weitzman and others, 1972). Female cartoon characters swoon over their heroes. And Barbie and Ken allow the young girl to practice the rituals of courtship and romance with the perfect (though certainly not normative) couple.

It is unfortunate that there is little empirical evidence specifying how different types of models or reinforcement contingencies affect attitudes and values toward romantic love in young girls. The application of methodologies used to investigate female role behaviors and personality characteristics (Williams, 1977) to the study of romantic love could provide a useful source of identifying early influences on female adult romantic behavior.

However, it is important to be aware that even before adolescence, a girl has established values regarding the importance of romantic love. She has learned that romantic love plays a role in her identity and choice of life goals and that there are specific ways to elicit romantic and other love responses from others. She may not engage in these behaviors often, but they are available to her as she develops into adolescence and comes into more direct contact with romantic love experiences.

The period of adolescence represents a time of self-discovery and experimentation with values and social behaviors in preparation for adult roles. Physiologically, the emergence of secondary sex characteristics accentuates the development of adolescent sexuality and progression toward manhood or womanhood. Interpersonally, the adolescent passes from a period of crushes and romantic fantasies to idealized real romantic experiences and then to an integration of romantic love with the intimate sharing of sexual interchange and mature love. Autonomy, security, and confidence in oneself also develop during these years and serve as important prerequisites to forming enduring love relationships.

For the adolescent girl, romantic love occupies much of her fantasy life. Boys are a priority topic in conversations among girls. Romantic love is linked closely with the adolescent values of popularity, sociability, and attractiveness. Being able to attract a desirable partner becomes a highly emphasized goal. A girl's status (even in high school) is at least partially determined by how often she dates and the status of the boys that she sees. If she can attract an upper-class or college man, her popularity and desirability to other boys is certainly enhanced.

The teenage girl is well instructed in the "how to's" of romance by a plethora of magazines published just for her. She learns strategies for attaining the standards of physical attractiveness and social grace that will get *him* to call. She must play hard to get but be neither too aloof nor too aggressive. She should act interested but not be too easy. She should have (or fake) good nails, shiny hair, and round breasts. Indeed, during adolescence the American female learns to make an art of attracting a man. For many women, this aspect of early indoctrination comes to be regarded as an integral part of the process of falling in love and staying there.

Overidentification with media standards does not allow the adolescent female to develop a sense of her own worth. She may never experience the realities of romantic love but rather become enmeshed in her falsified image of romance. She may associate superficial traits and acceptance by males with romantic love so convincingly that she never really falls in love but rather "falls in love with love." Thus she will be unable to experience the genuine joys, insecurities, and exciting moments of adolescent romance.

She may also be unable to learn to share romantic love, an aspect of the process that both heightens its intensity and paves the way for sharing more intimate love experiences.

Although the influence of the media on attitudes and behavior cannot be denied, media standards need not exert a major influence on the adolescent female's romantic love behavior. The development and reinforcement of alternative value systems that emphasize individual goals and achievements over adherence to media standards are likely to minimize media effects on behavior. For the female who has developed a sense of herself that includes her own strengths and weaknesses, a romantic love relationship can become more personal and fulfilling. She can learn to experience intimacy, caring, and conflict resolution. Romantic love can be her unique experience, rather than a goal in and of itself. It is especially important, after all, that the adolescent female learn how to discriminate her own feelings, attitudes, and behavior in romantic love. She will soon be an adult, probably choosing a permanent love partner. She must understand herself as she is, not as the media defines her, if she is to select a partner who will allow her to develop as an individual and as a lover.

As for the young adult woman, she is at a critical choice point in her life, deciding whether and when she wants a career and/or marriage. She brings into the decision-making process many of the fantasies and experiences of romantic love of childhood and adolescence. She faces a number of societal imperatives that are likely to affect her choices. These include: (1) romantic love will or should lead to marital bliss; (2) much of a woman's worth as a person and lover depends on her physical attractiveness; and (3) a woman should strive for a permanent relationship with a male partner.

Research on Romantic Love in Women

College has provided a convenient testing ground for researchers interested in women's attitudes and values concerning romantic love. Although there are many problems inherent in objectifying a concept such as romantic love, the experience of social psychologists in assessing research variables related to interpersonal attraction and social bond formation has led to the development of valid measuring scales for studying romantic love, for example, Rubin's (1970) scales for loving and liking.

A number of studies have assessed general correlates of romantic love in young women. For the most part, research supports the idea that women and men do not differ in the degree of love expressed for their romantic partners (Black and Angelis, 1974; Rubin, 1970). Some researchers, however, have noted that women do in fact admit to more "symptoms" of romantic love than men (Kanin, Davidson, and Scheck, 1970), and report a greater degree of euphoria during their love relationships (Dion and Dion, 1973). Although these latter findings may suggest that women are more romantically inclined than men, they may also indicate that women are simply more comfortable than men in admitting such feelings. Further research, utilizing consistent measurement techniques to assess comparable romantic-love-related variables, is needed before firm conclusions regarding male and female attitudes and values toward romantic love can be drawn.

Within the contex of specific relationships, researchers have noted that college women tend to be more pragmatic and less romantically idealistic about love than their male counterparts. Coombs and Kenkel (1966) assessed women's partner preference at a computer dance. Prior to the dance, women rated characteristics such as intelligence, campus status, dressing style, and dancing ability as important in a partner, while men expressed a single strong preference for physical attractiveness. After the dance, men indicated greater satisfaction with their partners than did women; they felt more "romantic attraction" and were more optimistic about the possibility of a happy marriage with their partner.

Dion and Dion (1973) examined responses made by male and female undergraduates on an Attitudes Toward Love scale. Whereas more women than men reported experiencing romantic love, women disagreed more than men with idealistic and cynical attitudes about love.

Finally, Hill, Rubin, and Peplau (1976) assessed, among other variables, attitudes toward romantic love in a college dating sample through repeated administration of Rubin's liking and loving scales over a two-year period. The authors noted that women were significantly less likely than men to cite "desire to fall in love" as an important reason for entering a relationship. Whereas

men were quicker to fall in love, women were more likely to fall
out of love. They appeared to be more aware of problems in unsuccessful relationships than did men. The research to date thus
supports the notion that women tend to be more pragmatic, rather
than romantic, about their love relationships.

Dion and Dion (1973) propose a functional role for romantic love as an explanation for the unexpected absence of romantic
ideals in their female sample. They suggest that romantic love may
serve different purposes for women than for men. Because women
usually contribute less economically to heterosexual relationships,
they have more to gain in a social system where marriage is based
on romantic love. "Since women in contemporary American society generally contribute less to economic subsistence in marriage,
they should be more prone than men to value romantic love in
pragmatic terms as a basis for marriage rather than for purely idealistic reasons. Thus, for females, romantic love may primarily serve
to induce males into marriage" (p. 56).

Hill, Rubin, and Peplau (1976) provide an additional interpretation for this apparent phenomenon of female romantic prag-
matism. Because women in our society are reinforced more than
men for social-emotional behaviors, Hill suggests they may be
more aware of qualitative aspects of their interpersonal relationships. Consequently, women may ascribe considerable significance
to interpersonal factors within romantic love relationships. They
may be more sensitive to interactional and internal cues that suggest that a relationship is not up to par. This reliance on a wide
range of social and emotional cues may explain why women appear to be more pragmatic than men in their selection and maintenance of long-term romantic love relationships.

Although the research to date provides a valuable starting
point for understanding the role of romantic love in women's lives,
studies thus far have focused on attitudes and values and their
associations with romantic love and relationship variables. The
unique, individual, subjective quality of romantic love, however,
renders the study of the process of its development a herculean
scientific venture. Yet understanding the dynamic changes that
ensue as romantic love unfolds would aid in discerning its purpose
in adult women's lives.

Statements concerning the purpose of romantic love in women's lives are certainly speculative. Whereas Geller and Howenstine, in Chapter Four, note men's tendencies to seek "romantic solutions" at transition periods in their lives, similar observations have not been made for women. Pursuit of romantic love for its ecstatic potential constitutes a rationale for romantic involvement in both sexes. As men and women embark on the transition to early adulthood, the process of romantic love must reconcile the discrepancies that exist between their goals and style of living and the idealized love of adolescence. Romantic love cannot occur in a vacuum.

Social-Cultural Considerations. For women, the need to experience and establish a love relationship is complicated by the previously mentioned societal proscriptions regarding love, sex, and marriage. Psychological writings on women and love have labeled them as insecure and weak, as modeling themselves after men's images of them. As a consequence, women are seen as fearful of having their true selves discovered in a love relationship (Reik [1941] 1976). Women's dependence on men for their sense of individuality limit the extent to which they can develop a mature love relationship. This position has been supported by a number of authors (Reik [1941] 1976; Winthrop, 1973).

Not all writings dealing with women and love have taken this stance. Horney (cited in Williams, 1977) notes how women are influenced by a social system that encourages women to love, admire, and serve men and to adapt themselves to the lives of the men they love. In such a system, women experience a lowering of confidence in their own abilities and self-esteem. Women become dependent on men. Horney's clinical work with women in conflict over their expected roles as lovers and their personal goals led her to conclude that the overvaluation of love relationships with men produced conflict in many women's lives. Women need to love, but to be able truly to express themselves in love relationships, they also must develop a sense of their own autonomy. Although autonomy can be achieved, the pressures for women to follow the prescribed role patterns can impede the process.

The overvaluation of heterosexual love, coupled with the pressure on a woman to "hook a man" who is an asset to her economic and social status, can set the stage for false romantic experiences in adulthood, just as preoccupation with physical image did in adolescence. If a woman views romantic love as a goal rather than a process, if attention to external attributes supersedes the interpersonal excitement, ecstasy, and sharing of a romantic love, if she does not develop a sense of confidence and autonomy, then even as an adult she may not experience true romantic love or develop the basis for a mature love relationship.

For many women of the 1970s and 1980s, the romantic ideal has been expanded to include finding a man who is sensitive, emotionally expressive, and intelligent, along with a host of other traits. The following interchange from *Combat in the Erogenous Zone* by Ingrid Bergis (1972, p. 210) illustrates this conflict well:

> "My aunt recently said to me, "You want too much. You aren't willing to compromise. Men will never be as sensitive or aware as women are. It's just not in their natures. So you have to get used to that, and be satisfied with something else."
> "What else?"
> "Either sexual satisfaction or theoretical intelligence or being loved and *not* understood or else being left alone to do the things you want to do."
> "But those aren't enough."
> "They have to be."
> "Then I'd rather do without love altogether."
> "You'll have to."

The search for this complex, perfect partner can be an additional source of falsification of the romantic love experience for women. Focusing on specific partner qualities, trying to find a partner who meets all of one's criteria for a mate, negates the process of discovery innate to romantic love. In our attempts to eradicate all pain and suffering from our lives, we may also be losing much of the joy and potential for closeness. True love implies the acceptance of even the undesirable aspects of the other. The process by which two individuals adapt their independent selves to their mutual needs is the process by which romantic love merges with mature love. Women's search for perfection in love needs include an acceptance of its imperfections if romantic love is to be experienced fully and mature love is to ensue.

Romantic Love in Committed Relationships. In the context of a committed relationship such as marriage, the true test of romantic love is delivered. The transition to the married state carries with it emotional, economic, and social interdependence. The realities of married life appear to influence romantic idealism and attitudes toward love.

Newly married couples tend to hold a strong belief in the interpersonal power of love rather than in romantic love (Knox and Sporakowski, 1968). Early in marriage, couples tend to value love and affection, sexual satisfaction, emotional interdependence, and temperamental interaction (Burgess and Wallin, 1953). As role structure in the relationship increases, particularly with the addition of children, married couples tend to believe more strongly in conjugal-rational love, that is, love that is calm, rational, and based on realism and mutual trust. When the children leave home, many years after the initial romance, both romantic and conjugal love feelings are experienced strongly (Munro and Adams, 1978).

Although women report greater happiness in a new marriage than their husbands, they begin to lose their romantic illusions between the early and middle years of marriage (Bell, 1971). It is not surprising that women should be less romantically inclined as they adjust to marriage. First, the married woman is likely to experience considerable stress as she is called upon to meet the needs of her husband, the demands of parenthood, and her own personal goals (Donelson, 1977). The very routine of living together is less consistent with the ideals of romantic love than the days of dating, planning a future together, and discovering each other. Second, as marital partners notice the shortcomings of their idealized mate, they are likely to experience disappointment, rage, and even hatred. The "real" person they married exists in sharp contrast to the romantic courtship fantasies of marriage.

Resolution of this conflict depends on the couple's respect for each other as individuals and ability to share even the intimate emotion of hatred. The occurrence of conflict along with the continued perception of novelty, interest, and excitement within the other person will permit mature love to deepen.

For the woman who has sacrificed her independence and made much of her sense of worth dependent on her spouse, romantic reality testing can call into question her choice of life goals and she may adjust by means of acquiring self-esteem outside of her relationship with her husband. If she is highly dependent on romance per se, for a feeling that she and life are worthwhile, she may choose extramarital relationships rather than interpersonal confrontation as a means of restoring romance into her life. Such relationships, however, merely recapture the superficial essence of romantic love. The heightened excitement of an extramarital affair certainly seems preferable to the routine and uncomfortable moments of conflict with one's partner. Yet the adult woman, like the adolescent, is "in love with love" and is destined repeatedly to experience frustration and unhappiness. Although a romance may provide a temporary renewal of spirits, the realities of the absence of love in her life and her own need for personal growth and achievement remain.

As women's roles become more flexible, greater opportunitys for growth of romantic and mature love exist in marriage. Couples engaged in activities outside of the home that enhance their own sense of autonomy can bring greater security and opportunity for sharing into the relationship. Sharing of common daily life routines can provide an additional opportunity for greater merging of couples' lives and the growth of love.

Romance Between Women. The potential for expressing romantic love within an enduring relationship is not limited to the married state. Although most attention has been directed at romantic love within heterosexual dating and marriage, some women choose romantic relationships with other women. Because the lesbian life-style is not sanctioned in this heterosexual society, little information is available on the development of romantic love between homosexuals. In both literature and psychoanalytic writings, the sexual component of lesbianism is emphasized to the exclusion of the love relationship.

Courtship, romantic idealization, and the sharing of mature love are not restricted to heterosexuals. Peplau and others (1978) note that women involved in long-term relationships with other women report high levels of emotional and sexual satisfaction as well as equality of power. All lesbian women (contrary to stereotype) are not the same. Some women are more romantic than others. Women who value exclusivity and permanence in love relationships are more likely to believe in traditional romantic conceptions of love.

Romantic love can be experienced in many ways. Some women choose to abandon the traditional model of romantic interaction with a male partner in favor of a relationship where power and independence are less likely to be defined by sex-role standards. Considerably more research is needed on the development and expression of romantic love between women, with particular awareness by researchers of their own heterosexual standards in interpreting findings.

Sexuality and Romantic Love. The mystique of romantic love is nowhere better expressed than in the allure of a potential sexual encounter with one's beloved. The excitement of sexual attraction, coupled with fantasies of future erotic moments to be shared, are an integral component of romantic love. Sexual interest serves as one highly motivating force that brings two individuals together during the initial phases of a romantic love relationship. Continued sexual expression with a loving partner offers the opportunity for developing closeness within the most intimate of personal exchanges. As a love relationship develops and two individuals come to respect and appreciate each other, sexual intimacy becomes a shared experience in which both romantic and mature aspects of love can be expressed.

Women's sexuality, as perceived by males and females, has been influenced to a great extent by proscriptive societal standards of sexual behavior coexisting with a media image that flagrantly overemphasizes a woman's potential as a sex partner. During adolescence, females learn that love is desirable but sex is forbidden. The teenage girl may even begin to develop aspects of her personal identity relative to her sexual behavior: "Does she or doesn't she?" The adult female has been viewed traditionally as linking sex with emotional intimacy. How many women have asked in the early phases of falling in love: "If I give in tonight, will he respect me in the morning?"

Sexual standards in America have eased considerably since the days of "save yourself for the man you love." For the female of the 1950s, sexual experience was associated primarily with being in love (Ehrmann, 1959). Women's sexual partners are no longer the men they plan to marry (Bell and Chaskes, 1970). Studies of college females of the 1970s reveal considerable variability in standards of sexuality and its relationship to love. Questionnaire responses of dating college couples indicated that while females were less permissive about casual sex, both men and women agreed that sex is acceptable in love relationships. The mutual decision to abstain from sex or the time of first intercourse was not correlated with measures of romantic love. Furthermore, sexual satisfaction was *not* more closely associated with love for women than for men (Hill, Ruben, and Peplau, 1976).

Young couples do appear to differ in their attitudes about the relationship between romantic love and sex. In the Hill, Rubin, and Peplau (1976) study, couples classified as sexual moderates (first intercourse one month or later after dating onset) were more likely than abstainers or sexual liberals to see "time for love to grow" as a necessary prerequisite for sexual interaction to occur. However, when they were assessed over a two-year period, no differences were noted between the three groups with respect to reports of love and relationship progress or deterioration. This latter finding tends to argue against the notion that sexual permissiveness impairs the development of mature love relationships. Although sexual mores have become more relaxed in the last decade, the decision to engage in sexual activity is a mutual one, most influenced by the values of the individuals involved in the romantic relationship.

Many single women are not involved with a steady romantic partner. Although more females today do enjoy casual sex, for the many women now in their twenties and thirties, raised with the value of virginity, the sexual standards of today produce conflict. The modern woman should be sexually liberated. However, if she believes that sexual intimacy should go hand in hand with potential romantic involvement, then pressure to engage quickly in sexual activity with a new partner may lead to disappointment and hurt when further intimacy does not develop.

Research on the nonattached woman's attitude about romantic love and sexuality in our culture today is lacking. Yet the fact that more women are choosing to remain single longer suggests that women's attitudes and behavior concerning romantic love and sexuality deserve investigative attention. Likewise, studies addressing these issues in lesbian women and older married women would facilitate our understanding of the development of romantic love and sexual intimacy within the context of long-term involvements.

Conclusions

Romantic love is an important part of the adult lives of all women. Although socialization and societal expectations regarding women's roles affect her expression of love, each woman is an individual who learns her own unique ways of expressing and obtaining romantic love. Central to the experience of romantic love and its convergence with mature love is a woman's sense of autonomy and personal security. Definition of herself via another person's status or achievement precludes her partaking in an individual unique experience of love and reduces it to the superficialities of day-to-day media living.

Women's changing status and greater role flexibility provides them with new freedom for personal growth and greater opportunity to share in the positive aspects of romantic love with less pressure to see it as a means to the goal of marriage and security. Changing sexual values, acceptance of singlehood, and acceptance of women as achievers allow them more freedom to learn about loving. Considerable research is needed before we can fully understand the process of the romantic experience in all women in all types of relationships. Romantic love and the romantic ideal are not lost—they merely change as women's lives and their roles in society are altered. The coming generation of females in America will have much to offer in showing us their ways of adapting romantic love to their lives.

6

Psychobiological Bases of Romantic Love

Ross Rizley

Recent advances in evolutionary theory, particularly those concerned with the emergence of social and altruistic behavior (for examples Wilson, 1975, 1978), shed new light on the phylogenetic development of what we, in this culture, call "romantic love." The primary purpose of this chapter is to draw attention to the evolutionary and biological significance of romantic love, and to suggest that our appreciation and understanding of this remarkable human phenomenon will be greatly increased if we consider love as a form of altruistic social behavior which, at least in the past, has contributed to the survival of the species. The evolutionary perspective suggests that romantic love once played an important role in pair bonding and thus contributed greatly to reproductive success. In our current, evolutionarily novel environment, it may no longer have the same function or significance. The question we pose then is what, if any, reproductive advantages were conferred on those strongly affected by romantic love throughout our evolutionary history, and do these advantages still hold true?

Definition of Romantic Love

The basic phenomenology and "symptomatology" of romantic love has remained relatively constant since the beginnings of recorded history. Early descriptions of "love sickness," for example, that were presented by Sappho in the sixth century B.C. (see Rubin, 1974) are remarkably similar to modern-day accounts. Regardless of the cultural diversity in its expression, the romantic love "syndrome" is remarkably consistent across centuries and across cultures.

There are several important properties of romantic love, properties that any definition of the phenomenon should acknowledge. First, one of the most significant aspects of romantic love is its speed of occurrence. As the expression "love at first sight" suggests, romantic bonds can develop remarkably quickly between individuals who hardly know each other. In fact, romantic love often develops despite very real flaws or disadvantages associated with the love object. It is significant that romantic lovers move quickly from the position of being complete strangers to one of total intimacy and commitment. The rapidity of this transition from strangers to partners attests to the strong biological and evolutionary bases for romantic love.

A second significant property of romantic love is its robustness. Love, at least in its early phases, can be nearly irreversible despite very strong social, economic, or political pressures operating to undo the romantic bond. In the "Romeo and Juliet" prototypic case, lovers value each other above all else despite numerous very real difficulties and obstacles. Clearly, once formed, the romantic bond is not easily broken.

A third significant "fact" about romantic love is that it does not depend on similarities in background, custom, attributes, or beliefs. The emotional reactions involved in romantic love do not demand that the beloved be a known quantity, similar to the lover. Romantic love often functions to bond very dissimilar people despite the fact that one might expect greater wariness and suspiciousness of those who are different or unfamiliar to us.

A fourth significant property of romantic love is that it occurs between genetically unrelated individuals. Despite the propinquity and opportunity presented by close relatives, it is rare to find romantic attraction expressed to genetically closely related individuals, unless the genetic relationship is unknown to the involved parties. The evolutionary significance of the object choice will be remarked upon later, but suffice it to say that romantic love seems to function to bond together very quickly two genetically unrelated strangers, and the bond is robust enough to endure, in fact even to flourish, under exceedingly difficult conditions.

Given these significant properties of the romantic bond, how might one define romantic love? Most attempts are based on the phenomenology of the experience, that is, how it feels to the person in love. From a scientific, evolutionary point of view, however, it may be advantageous to define romantic love without appealing to conscious experience or subjective reports of emotions. With this in mind, *we define the dyadic social relationship of romantic love as a rapidly formed, temporally robust attachment between two genetically unrelated individuals*. Sexual attraction can be expressed directly and overtly or indirectly through attempts to approach, touch, caress, and mate with the loved one. Biologically, romantic love produces an orienting response toward the love object, in whom the lover invests a great deal of "biologically scarce" attention (see Chapter Seventeen).

The phenomenology and expression of romantic love are highly dependent upon cultural factors and individual learning experiences. Similarly, the relationship between romantic love and more formalized social bonds, such as marriage, is again very much a function of cultural rules and patterns. But the core "love" reaction is biologically preset and predetermined. Romantic love is a psychobiological reaction that functions, even under difficult conditions, to increase the proximity, and hence the probability of mating, of two genetically unrelated individuals.

It should be emphasized that we have not excluded from the class of romantic love relationships those between two members of the same sex. The evolutionary significance of homosexual romantic love is not necessarily different from that of heterosexual love. It too may confer a reproductive advantage on the genotype that possesses a tendency toward romantic love, despite the fact that the homosexual relationship does not directly produce offspring. The reproductive advantage is conferred altruistically on close relatives who share the genotype of the homosexual individual (see Wilson, 1978).

Parallel Between Romantic Love and Grief

We believe that romantic love is a psychobiological reaction analogous to, and in some sense the converse of, grief (see Averill, 1968). The comparison of love and grief is instructive. Cultures vary enormously in their approaches to loving and grieving. Both often occur suddenly and unpredictably. Both have significant and undeniable physiological impact and urgency. Both influence our social, cognitive, motoric, emotional, and biological functioning. Both loving and grieving are core, psychobiological reactions, the very impact and severity of which attest to their very basic biological role. Their evolutionary significance may lie in the fact that both love and grief help assure group cohesiveness in species where the maintenance of social bonds is helpful to survival.

To pursue the analogy somewhat, consider the relationship between grieving and mourning. Averill (1968) defines grieving as a basic psychobiological reaction that has remarkable consistency across cultures. Mourning, however, is the culturally prescribed way of dealing with grief and is determined by the mores and customs of the society. Grief and mourning may occur quite independently of each other, although in general the two are closely related.

We believe that romantic love is analogous to grief in that both are complex psychobiologically predetermined behavior patterns consisting of stereotyped psychological and physiological reactions. However, just as grief is distinct from mourning, love is distinct from marriage, courtship, and all of the socially prescribed customs and rules governing the expression of attraction, pair bonding, and mating. The fact that there exist extreme variations in cultural expressions of both grief and romantic love should not obscure the basic fact that both are biologically patterned reactions based on neurochemical and hormonal processes. Given a biological organism and physiochemical and neurochemical substratum for behavior, it is clear that the individual's physiological and biological inheritance is an important determinant of the romantic love reaction. We believe that although individuals who experience romantic love or grief act in culturally determined ways, they do exhibit stereotyped patterns of psychological and physiological reactions that are relatively constant across cultures and centuries. The point is simply that certain features of romantic love relationships are sufficiently uniform and strong so as to represent a core, psychobiological reaction. In general, love is occasioned by the development or expectation of development of a new significant object, typically another person. Love arises, then, through the formation or expectation of formation of a new social relationship. While the culture may determine to a large extent the specific expression of love, its key evolutionary feature has been that it is a reaction that rapidly and robustly bonds two genetically unrelated strangers in such a way that mating is highly likely.

It is possible that social and cultural developments could lead to a society that completely masks or eradicates both loving and grieving. The thousands of societies that have existed during recorded history are enormously variable in their expressions of love and grief. This is to be expected, given that societies mold their mores and customs to the specific demands of their environment. Nonetheless, the flexibility is not limitless. If we ignore the culturally induced aspects of love and focus instead on the biologically significant commonalities, we can begin to piece together an image of love removed from any specific cultural or temporal features. If we look beneath the cultural variations, there are general features of romantic love that match our expectations based on evolutionary theory. Romantic love, even today, is an expression of a very basic, ubiquitous, biologically and genetically based reaction, the significance of which can only be understood in a reproductive context. Moreover, many of the apparent paradoxes about love are predictable and understandable if we only consider the circumstances under which strong romantic love developed and hence the circumstances under which it was adaptive.

Evolutionary View of Romantic Love

The evolutionary biologist views the human as a reproductive system. Traits developed in the species so as to maximize its reproductive success in its usual environment. The fundamental insight of the principle of natural selection is that in any one generation, the carriers of different genotypes make unequal contributions to the hereditary endowment of succeeding generations. Those genotypes (and associated phenotypes) that efficiently transmit their genes to future generations are reproductively successful. Natural selection perpetuates those genotypes that promote survival and reproduction in the environments that the species regularly encounters. If we assume that romantic love is an expression of a psychobiological reaction based on complex gene actions, we must ask ourselves in what ways the phenotypic expression of these gene effects may have enhanced the reproductive success of the species *in those environments typically encountered.* How might romantic love—that is, rapid and robust attachment to a genetically unrelated stranger for the purpose of pair bonding—have proven adaptive to individuals possessing it in great degree? The answer to this question must first involve consideration of the average environment inhabited by our ancestors.

Until perhaps 10,000 years ago, when agriculture developed, populations were organized as small hunter-gatherer bands. Members of each group were genetically related, and social structure was based on kinship or genetic relatedness of group members. Nonrelatives probably interacted only rarely throughout most of human evolutionary history (Wilson, 1978; Alexander, in press). Once humans developed rudimentary group-living skills and escaped the overriding influence of large predators, small groups of kin became one another's chief competitors and sources of mortality (see Alexander and Noonan, in press). Interaction with nonrelatives was relatively uncommon and dangerous.

One additional factor must be mentioned at this point. Environments present problems to organisms which they must solve in order to survive and reproduce. However, environments change in unpredictable ways. One of the most effective reproductive "strategies" is to maximize diversity in offspring so that one maximizes the chances that offspring will survive and reproduce regardless of subsequent, unpredictable changes in the environment. As Wilson (1978, pp. 122–123) notes: "Diversity is the way a parent hedges its bets against an unpredictably changing environment. . . . Diversity, and thus adaptability, explains why so many kinds of organisms bother with sexual reproduction. They vastly outnumber the species that rely on the direct and simpler, but in the long run, less prudent modes of sexless multiplication." Wilson points out that sex is not designed primarily for reproduction, nor is the primary function the giving and receiving of pleasure. The reason sexual reproduction is favored over asexual reproduction is that diversity is favored in natural selection, and sex creates diversity.

It is only when we mate with a genetically unrelated individual that maximal diversity in offspring genotype can develop, hence maximal assurance of reproductive success. The need to reproduce sexually with genetically unrelated individuals has important implications for the development of romantic love.

Consider the problem facing a hypothetical male ancestor who lived in a small kinship band that survived through hunting and gathering. To be reproductively successful, he had two possible strategies. The first was what has been called "pure" nepotism, where one gives benefits to a genetic relative expecting nothing in return except an increased reproduction of the genes shared with the recipient of the altruism. Here the individual does not mate but behaves altruistically toward close relatives, increasing their reproductive success and indirectly insuring that at least some of the shared genes will be passed on to offspring (Alexander, in press). This sort of altruistic behavior which only indirectly results in genes being passed on to offspring may underlie homosexual love and bonding (see Wilson, 1978).

The second more common strategy for reproductive success was for our ancestor to locate an appropriate mate of the opposite sex to whom he was genetically unrelated (or very distantly related) and reproduce sexually. Unfortunately, genetically unrelated individuals were one's chief source of mortality, and hence were realistically to be feared. Hence, once our ancestor located a genetically unrelated individual who might be an appropriate mate, his extreme suspiciousness, wariness, and fear had to be overcome. The forces of attraction had to be greater than those of fear. Overwhelming, powerful attraction had to be generated rapidly under the less than ideal conditions of extreme arousal, anxiety, fear, and realistic danger. Moreover, the attraction had to be strong enough to override protective tendencies and fight or flight reactions. An equally strong emotional attraction had to be generated in the potential mate to overcome her fear and wariness of strangers and draw her away from her own group of kin into a new and unfamiliar social group. The love bond had to be robust enough to endure despite less than optimal circumstances. All of this had to occur to ensure mating with an unrelated individual.

Alexander (in press), discussing "falling in love," states: "Humans, apparently everywhere, tend to select as mates individuals with whom they have had relatively few social interactions, or, in some cases, who are even poorly known; and at least in our own society we draw them rapidly from strangeness to ultimate intimacy and make them long-term or lifetime partners, usually in what must be referred to as the dearest of all biological enterprises. There is much evidence in music, art, and literature that few events are more dramatic in human sociality than falling in love—*falling*, it seems to me, across the chasm from social strangeness to social intimacy" (p. 32 of preprint). It is clear that romantic love can provide the cement for social and sexual relationships between genetically unrelated individuals and that its parameters meet the requirements we would demand based on an evolutionary analysis of ancestral lifestyles and environments. Love is rapid, robust, irreversible (within limits), and it generally bonds one to appropriate (generally heterosexual) sex objects to whom one is genetically unrelated. It undeniably functions to increase dramatically the probability of mating. In the process of evolution, individuals whose genes endowed them with exceptional capacity to "fall in love" may have had greater reproductive success because of their increased probability of mating with genetically unrelated individuals. The genetic diversity so created is highly favored by natural selection.

There are other reproductive benefits conferred by romantic love. The most obvious is that love ensures stable attachments. Greater stability in male-female bonds must have conferred a reproductive advantage on the participants, especially given the long period of helplessness and dependency of the human infant and the needs for specialization of labor in order to survive. As Wilson (1978, pp. 139–140) notes: "Human beings, as typical large primates, breed slowly. Mothers carry fetuses for nine months and afterwards are encumbered by infants and small children who require milk at frequent intervals through the day. It is to the advantage of each woman of the hunter-gatherer band to secure the allegiance of men who will contribute meat and hides while sharing the labor of child-rearing. It is to the reciprocal advantage of each man to obtain exclusive sexual rights to women and to monopolize their economic productivity. If the evidence from hunter-gatherer life has been correctly interpreted, the exchange has resulted in near universality of the pair bond and the prevalence of extended families with men and their wives forming the nucleus. Sexual love and the emotional satisfaction of family life can be reasonably postulated to be based on enabling mechanisms in the physiology of the brain that have been programmed to some extent through the genetic hardening of this compromise."

It is interesting to consider that the wide variety of human sexual and romantic behaviors may have evolved precisely to increase the stability of the pair bond. Among species other than man, it appears that those that have evolved long-term bonds are also the ones that have developed elaborate courtship rituals. Human beings are unusually active sexually and have developed elaborate sexual activities that have little, if anything, to do with reproduction. As Wilson (1978, p. 141) notes: "If insemination were the sole biological function of sex, it could be achieved far more economically in a few seconds of mounting and insertion." Elaborate sexual behavior and foreplay facilitates bonding, and more secure bonding increases the couple's reproductive success. The fact that the sexual responsiveness of the human female has become nearly continuous is most likely attributable to the fact that sexuality facilitates bonding, and bonding confers a Darwinian advantage by more tightly joining the members of primitive human bands. Unusually frequent (by the standards of other species) sexual intercourse among humans cements the pair bond (see Wilson, 1978).

To summarize, romantic love can be understood only when we consider its operation and consequences in the environments in which it originally emerged and developed, and hence, in the environment in which it was originally adaptive. For hundreds of generations, our ancestors lived in social groups composed primarily of small numbers of kin. Genetically unrelated individuals lived in bands that were hostile, dangerous, or competitive. There were few genetically unrelated members of the opposite sex with whom one had regular contact. Robust romantic love occurring quickly under conditions of high arousal and danger was necessary to overcome fear and wariness and to bond a couple in a relatively permanent fashion, greatly increasing the chances that they would mate. By creating genetic diversity and allowing for stable pair bonding and specialization of labor, romantic love most likely contributed to reproductive success.

It is not surprising that the experience of falling in love seems puzzling and irrational in our very different, modern world. What we experience has its roots far back in our evolutionary past. It may no longer seem necessary, since we have developed structured, safer, and more predictable ways of identifying and meeting potential mates. Strong, overriding emotions of romantic involvement may even seem dysfunctional today, where more rational unions may have many social, economic, or political advantages. However, rapid, irreversible attachments to strangers are still so very likely that many societies suppress the expression of romantic love and eliminate the conditions favorable to its development (for example, by segregating the sexes, arranging early marriages, and so on). This attests to the strength of the basic psychobiological pair-bonding process.

Although this account is speculative and certainly oversimplified, it is important to view romantic love from a biological and evolutionary perspective. We cannot understand the operation and significance of complex emotional responses without considering how they have emerged over time and how they might have functioned to increase reproductive success. Romantic love is clearly an important adhesive process underlying human social attachments. It alters the individual's chances of reproductive success by increasing the genetic diversity of offspring and by ensuring continuity and quality in the care of offspring. The neurochemical and hormonal processes underlying the psychobiological romantic love reaction are activated by appropriate (that is, evolutionarily meaningful) experiences and increase the individual's chances of finding an appropriate mate. As capricious as romantic love may seem at times in our modern world, falling in love may be a biologically patterned, highly organized way of choosing a mate which has proven successful over thousands of years of evolution. For this reason, attempts to tamper with its natural operation should not be taken lightly.

7

Healthy and Pathological Love— Psychodynamic Views

Myron F. Weiner

Romantic love involves the bonding or attachment of persons, but it is more than an epiphenomenon of the biological drive for perpetuation of the species. Romantic love encompasses a range of behavior that transcends pairing for reproduction, safety, or security. It is a uniquely human experience.

A Psychodynamic Definition of Romantic Love

Let us examine, from the psychodynamic point of view, Pope's working definition of romantic love as set forth in Chapter One:

> A preoccupation with another person. A deeply felt desire to be with the loved one. A feeling of incompleteness

114

without him or her. Thinking of the loved one often, whether together or apart. Separation frequently provokes feelings of genuine despair or else tantalizing anticipation of reuniting. Reunion is seen as bringing feelings of euphoric ecstasy or peace and fulfillment.

Psychodynamicists as divergent as Otto Fenichel and Harry Stack Sullivan assert that adult romantic love goes beyond Pope's definition. Adult romantic love involves concern for one's beloved as well as preoccupation with him or her and a desire for proximity. Fenichel (1945) and Sullivan (1953a) agree that when the satisfaction or security of another person (for that person's sake) is as significant as one's own satisfaction or security, love exists. In this respect, there is concurrence with Csikszentmihalyi's definition of love as the investment of attention in another with the intention of realizing that person's goals. When concern for one's beloved is solely to ensure one's own source of narcissistic supplies, an immature love exists and is a potential basis for significant difficulties in the love relationship.

A prerequisite to adult romantic love is the development of a certain level of intrapsychic and interpersonal maturation. In the psychoanalytic view, adult love requires successful completion of the oral, anal, and oedipal phases of psycho-sexual development. That is, one distinguishes one's self and one's own needs from others', develops a sense of autonomy and self-direction, and sufficiently disentangles from the sexualized attachment to parents to love a person for himself or herself and not because of his or her similarity to, or dissimilarity from, a parent. This view is also in accord with Sullivan (1953a) for whom the capacity for adult love marks the transition from childhood to preadolescence.

A psychodynamic view of romantic love considers the intrapsychic processes that underlie the preoccupation with one's beloved and also notes the nature of this preoccupation. "Thinking of the loved one often" as well as having "feelings of genuine despair or else tantalizing anticipation of reuniting" when separated are part of an intrapsychic process that includes the repetition compulsion—the tendency to relive unconsciously aspects of one's past in order to master traumas or to return to highly rewarding earlier modes of living or thinking. It also involves partial ego regression and a partial attempt at primitive incorporation of the be-

loved. Projection of one's repressed infantile feelings of helplessness and omnipotence as well as one's need for an external source
of narcissistic supplies are partly responsible for two necessary
ingredients of romantic love: the nurturing attitude toward one's
beloved and the overvaluation of one's beloved.

Mutual nurturing at the most regressed levels is readily observable. When two adults spoon-feed each other while simultaneously consuming each other with their eyes, they are in love.
Each accepts the other's most basic needs and is willing to provide
them—feeding and physical closeness.

Freud (1921) saw the sexual instinct as the biological drive
underlying love and suggested that the first historical motive for
love beyond mere sexual release was based on the awareness that
the need for sexual release recurs and necessitates the continued
presence of a partner. He noted that the loved person is relatively
free from criticism, that his or her characteristics are valued more
highly than similar characteristics in unloved persons, and are
more highly valued than they were in the same person before he or
she became the object of love. He called this falsified judgment
idealization and suggested that one's beloved substitutes for one's
own unattained ego-ideal.

The repetition compulsion occurs in many love relationships.
Men and women choose marital partners who remarkably resemble
emotionally important aspects of their parents. The children of
abusive parents frequently marry abusive spouses. Children of alcoholic parents often marry alcoholics, sometimes more than once.

Selection of a love partner resembling one's other-sexed parent does not always denote a pathological oedipal fixation. One
learns from parents how to mesh comfortably with others. People
seek what is familiar. A mature adult will seek, just as will an immature person, a style of interaction that he or she has found rewarding, and this usually has its roots in the parent-child relationship. The mature person does not regress and seek loving responses
in the manner of a child. Instead, the ease in relating to a person
who has attributes of the other-sexed parent facilitates the mature
tie between lovers. The mature person's ties to his or her parents
form a partial framework for adult love relationships. For the immature person, they form rigid confines.

Another regressive aspect of love manifests when lovers who
were formerly autonomous find they can barely endure a day's

separation and, in spite of an adequate supply of external narcissistic gratification, now find that the adoration of the beloved is not only the preferred source but also the only source that matters. Regression also manifests in the sense of incompleteness when apart, wholeness when together, and the loss of physical boundaries experienced during orgasm and even less intense forms of intimacy.

Jealousy is part of falling in love and can be explained in simple economic terms as a type of vigilance. If another person is one's most important source of emotional supplies, one can hardly afford to lose that person. Therefore, one guards the beloved to be certain that his or her emotional supplies are not given away, borrowed, or stolen. There are other factors in jealousy, such as the projection of one's own impulse to search for other potential lovers.

Monogamy is a recent and relatively uncommon practice, according to Ford and Beach (1951). Of the 185 societies they studied, 84 percent allowed men to have more than one wife. Monogamy is not the most reproductively efficient system of mating. Monogamous pairing heightens jealousy because it fosters dependence on one person as a primary source of gratification. Additionally, separation of the nuclear family from the extended family increases the demands made on each marital partner. A pathological source of jealousy is the feeling that one is not deserving of love, that one has hoodwinked one's lover and must keep him or her from discovering a more deserving and desirable love object.

Overvaluation of one's beloved goes hand in hand with another phenomenon of love relationships: narcissistic vulnerability to one's beloved. One's beloved is above criticism by others, and one will defend him or her against others. However, one is highly vulnerable to the beloved's neglect, broken promises, or inconsiderate acts. The injuries may be suffered quietly or may give rise to a lover's quarrel, the otherwise inexplicable hostile behavior of two people whose love would enable them to forgive, were they not regressed in the relationship and in a state of heightened vulnerability.

In summary, adult romantic love is psychodynamically characterized by:

1. a wish to be united with one's beloved, emotionally and sexually
2. temporary losses of boundaries between lovers

3. overvaluation of one's beloved
4. some relationship to one's infantile love objects
5. the ability to recognize the needs of another and to differentiate them from one's own
6. the satisfaction of one's beloved's needs being of equal importance to the satisfaction of one's own (a form of altruism)
7. vigilance over one's beloved to prevent his or her loss
8. narcissistic vulnerability to the beloved

Developmental Aspects of Romantic Love

Harlow's (1959) work indicates that one must have had the earlier experience of consistent love and nurturance to be able to seek it appropriately and to express it in turn.

Temporary losses of boundaries between lovers indicates a temporary regression to the earliest levels of psychosexual development, when one was not able to differentiate one's self from one's environment. The overvaluation of the beloved is partly the fulfillment of the wish to return to the sense of omnipotence presumably experienced in infancy.

Basically, love is a uniting—a denial of one's aloneness in the world and an attempted restitution of the original mother-child symbiosis, a partial recapitulation of the oral stage of psychosexual development. For men and women alike, the most primitive threat to the self that stems from loving is the fear of being engulfed and of losing one's individuality. This is the threat experienced by orally fixated men and women for whom the primary psychological danger in a relationship is annihilation through dissolution of their ego boundaries. It is as if one could be absorbed or engulfed. Individuals with strong oral fixations can see others only as sources of gratification or frustration. They remain attached only as long as the beloved is gratifying or as long as there is no greater available source of gratification. These individuals immediately strike out against their lovers when frustrated. They feel entitled to gratification but have little awareness of the give-and-take that makes a mutually rewarding relationship. Their situation is like that of the infant who can only respond to frustration with a tantrum: there is only diffuse reaction to frustration without the conscious ability to solicit or reward giving.

A person strongly fixated at the anal level (everyone, incidentally has multiple fixations at immature levels of psychosexual development) engages in a perpetual struggle for control—projecting on his loved one the wish to control, fearing loss of the beloved if he or she cannot control the beloved or if he or she does not submit to the beloved's control. It is control or be controlled.

One can see unresolved oedipal difficulties in men who marry women similar to their mothers or women who seek to marry men as powerful as their idealized fathers. In speaking of marital relationships, one must consider both sides of the situation. A man who wishes to be treated like a child can powerfully shape the behavior of his mate, so that a woman who is merely aggressive can be molded into a castrator. Resolution of oedipal difficulties by falling in love with a powerful parent-surrogate also helps resolve problems of aggression. One's own aggression can be discounted as a reaction to an outside force. One sees oedipal victories: men who actually displace the father and become their mother's primary love object. Needless to say, it is difficult for these men to marry or to maintain a marital relationship.

The man who marries a woman for her ability to control others is disappointed to find that he is controlled and not loved. The woman who seeks a powerful father-substitute finds that she is loved but that she cannot be controlled. The man's submission to his mother-substitute engenders her contempt; the woman's demands to be treated as an unconditionally loved child stimulate anger.

Oedipal love fails to fulfill two important requirements of adult love: recognizing the separate needs of another and placing one's beloved's needs on a par with one's own. The oedipally fixated person's self-involvement or narcissism clouds his or her view of others and places his or her needs above all others'.

In adolescence, children begin to loosen their emotional ties to their parents, to emerge from fantasy and from their childish self-involvement. They also struggle with a reawakened attraction to the parent of the opposite sex, which partly determines their choice of first love. While mourning the loss of their parents and attempting to separate from the oedipal parent, teenagers experience the emergent life-style of "being in love."

Boys' idealization of the beloved derives some of its intensity and quality from a normal degree of mother fixation, according to Blos (1962). The first choice of a heterosexual love object is commonly determined by the physical or mental similarity or dissimilarity to the other-sexed parent.

Girls flee an oedipal attachment by falling in love with and marrying boys similar to, or opposite from, their fathers but, in the process, do not relinquish their fathers. They fail to take the developmental step, substitute another father, and establish a child-parent relationship with their spouses. The oedipal theme can be acted out in still another way. The adolescent girl feels her mother does not understand her father and that her mother is unduly critical of him. She falls in love with a boy whose most important attribute is that he is misunderstood or mistreated, symbolically competing with and revenging herself upon her mother.

An individual's ability to establish an adult romantic love relationship is determined not only by his or her level of psychosexual maturation but also by the realistic pressures that may heighten object need and/or engender a degree of regression. A man whose wife is chronically ill may fall in love with his secretary. A woman who has recently left home to embark on a career may fall in love with her mentor. A severely ill man may fall in love with his nurse.

Relationship Aspects of Romantic Love

Romantic love is not sufficient to maintain an intimate relationship. Maintaining intimacy requires that the relationship be high on the couple's list of priorities, and that it not be eclipsed by career concerns or by the needs of the children. Because people change, spouses' attitudes or opinions do not remain static. There must be communication of these changed feelings and attitudes. An intimate relationship requires commitment and communication in addition to mature romantic love.

A love relationship changes over time. With maturation, and because of events within and outside the relationship, the partners change internally and in relation to each other. Unequal rates of personal development are major problems in love relationships. Individuals who had much in common at the beginning of a love relationship may have little of mutual interest within five, ten, or twenty years because of differing growth opportunities or differing responses to life events. One person may react to an event as a growth-inhibiting trauma, whereas another seizes it as an opportunity for greater mastery.

It is possible to delineate a series of five repetitive stages in a love relationship. These stages, taken together, compose what may be called a love cycle. An intimate relationship that lasts over a significant period of time will go through many partial or full love cycles as the people change individually and as partners in the relationship.

The first stage of a love cycle is early courtship—the pre-falling-in-love stage. In this stage, the lovers-to-be are on their best behavior. They size up each other as sources of direct gratification, asking themselves if the other can meet their needs for affection, nurturnace, attention, or even limit-setting. They also assess each other as sources of indirect gratification, looking to see what can be admired in the other. Each measures his or her emotional and physiologic responses to the other but also finds himself or herself inexplicably drawn toward the other.

Walster and Walster (1978) point out that certain "sets", including sexual frustration and danger, predispose toward the formation of romantic relationships. Viewed from another standpoint, these situations heighten object need (Weiner, 1978). At early stages of psychosexual development, clinging or attachment behavior results from object need (Bowlby, 1969). Being in love, like attachment behavior, is merely a special case of object relationship.

The second stage of romantic love is "falling." Falling pertains to the partially involuntary, partially voluntary reduction of the lovers' ordinary interpersonal barriers, which are lowered to allow the other "in" and which lead to the feeling of emotional and physical fusion. It is at this stage that idealization of one's partner is at its height. Because one's ordinary defenses and interpersonal expectations are only suspended and not abandoned, there still exists the potential for friction between the lovers. When one fails to meet the other's needs or expectation, a narcissistic injury occurs. One of the lovers may fail to meet a direct need, such as affection, or an indirect need, such a failing to behave ideally in public. The result is the accusation that "you don't love me any more," based on the presumption that adequate love would guarantee an adequate supply of narcissistic needs. This second stage of romantic love may well be designated the honeymoon stage. It lasts variable periods of time, usually extends beyond the marital honeymoon, and is followed by a stage designated by Walster and Walster (1978) as companionate love.

The transition from romantic to companionate love comprises the last three stages of the love cycle. Stage three is unmasking. Ordinarily, people cannot maintain courtship behavior for long. In time, less ideal attributes show, whether failure to use underarm deodorant or disrespectful behavior to one's mother-in-law. Discovery of these aspects of one's beloved is painful not only because of the real difficulties they cause but also because one is enhanced by one's beloved's idealness. After all, one is known by the company one keeps.

One might expect that a mature adult's discovery of imperfections in his or her beloved would be met with a shrug of the shoulders and understanding acceptance. One must remember, however, that falling in love involves a partial regression of ego functions. As previously mentioned, it involves partial suspension of interpersonal defenses and of one's critical judgment, and allows formerly repressed urges for fusion to reemerge. It is therefore no surprise that lovers are readily wounded by trivial acts committed or omitted by each other. Suspending one's defenses against input also lowers the censorship on output. And what comes out are the most elemental responses to the threat of injury or abandonment.

Unmasking involves expectations as well as behavior. Each partner in a love relationship has expectations unstated early in the relationship. One may withold revealing an expectation that might offend until the relationship is firmly cemented or until marriage is consummated. For example, a man who enjoys fellatio may conceal his expectation of fellatio as a regular sexual practice because of concern that his beloved will see him as less than ideally masculine (a projection of his own concern). Some expectations are not made explicit because they are assumed. Culturally accepted stereotypes of "masculine" or "feminine" behavior are frequently assumed and not agreed upon. Certain expectations are undisclosed because they were not consciously formulated until triggered within the context of the love relationship. Others do not emerge because they have been repressed, or have been repressed and projected, or rationalized.

In stage four, the disappointed lovers attempt to force their beloveds to become what they were thought to be or were expected to become. The lovers make suggestions to each other if the disappointment is minimal and berate each other if the disappointment is great. The lovers may not be able to comply with each others' push to change. After all, their former idealness was not a true perception but an illusion or a wish. If the partners' perceived changes are real, the outlook for resolution by action is better. If the problem is that one can no longer completely idealize his or her partner, the resolution can only come through a change in attitude. Ordinarily, real changes in behavior are most likely to eventuate if encouraged in a caring manner, and are less likely if demanded in a selfish, demeaning way. One must use the reward (or punishment) that best motivates one's beloved. To do so requires knowledge of one's partner and/or great persistence in attempting various methods of persuasion.

Stage five is the stage of resolution. Illusion is recognized as illusion. The undesired behavior or attitude is completely changed, partially changed, or does not change at all. Or, the behavior or attitude, when better understood, is found acceptable. There may be compromise, with a partial change in behavior of one partner and a partial change in the attitude of the other partner toward the behavior that persists. The ability to reach mutually satisfying resolutions sets the tone of the love relationship—whether it will be a series of stalemates, whether it will be a power struggle, or whether the legitimate needs of each will be recognized and dealt with so that each has maximum opportunity for individual fulfillment while remaining a rewarding, effective partner in the love relationship. The ability to resolve conflicts of interest is the main criterion by which one can predict if the love relationship will become stagnant or if it will foster growth and development of the partners. The capacity to come to satisfactory conflict resolution is the hallmark of a truly adult love relationship, for it is not based on idealization but on increasing acceptance of the other as he or she really is.

Because lovers change over time, aspects of the love cycle are repeated in all but the most stagnant relationships. New expectations arise. New disappointments occur. Both must be dealt with if the relationship is to nourish and enhance the lovers.

Pathological Loving

Romantic love, like any other human attribute, is subject to perversion. Some of the perversions of love relationships are extreme submissiveness, bondage, masochistic attachment, and love addiction.

Extreme submissiveness exaggerates certain normal features of falling in love. In this instance, one lives only through one's beloved. One is nothing and the beloved is everything. Falling in love becomes a perversion if one's primary sexual excitement stems from feeling insignificant in relation to one's partner (Fenichel, 1945). This overestimation of the beloved is a participation in one's partner's greatness, a partial regaining of one's lost and projected omnipotence.

A damaging bondage can result from extreme overvaluation of one's beloved, as in a Romeo and Juliet syndrome. The lovers' capacity for self-love is completely drained and they sacrifice their self-interest for the supposed interest of the beloved, or in the interest of being at the beloved's side. In this type of devotion, which resembles a sublimated devotion to an abstract ideal, the critical aspect of the ego-ideal disappears. The beloved is right in all that he or she does or wants, and conscience does not judge any act done for the sake of the beloved. The beloved is in the place of the ego-ideal. Dying for one's lover is like dying for one's country; the relationship transcends life.

There is a continuum between bondage and identification as a form of love. In identification, the ego is enriched with the properties of the person with whom it identifies. In a bondage relationship, the ego surrenders itself to the beloved which it has substituted for its most important constituent. In identification, the person with whom one has identified has been lost or relinquished. He or she is set up again in the ego, which modifies itself after the lost person. In love-bondage, the loved person is retained. There is overinvestment of the ego's energy in the beloved. Where ordinary love substitutes the beloved for the ego-ideal, love-bondage substitutes the beloved for the entire ego (Fenichel, 1945).

Masochistic love is commonly seen in clinical practice. Many factors predispose a person to victimize himself or herself for the sake of another. Some people operate on a limited-goods concept of interpersonal relations. If one gains, another must be depleted. One can receive only at another's expense. A mother may teach her child that he prospers only by virtue of her suffering, and that what the child obtains results from the mother giving up something for herself (Greenburg, 1964). In psychodynamic terms, this attitude can be a resolution of anal conflicts in which autonomy is surrendered for the sake of security. The person remains fixated at a stage of oral dependence.

Certain people who are incapable of recognizing the needs of others and of putting the needs of others on a par with their own, nevertheless repeatedly fall in love or seek to be in love. The affection or affirmation these individuals receive from others plays the same role as food in food addiction. Although unable to return love, the love addict needs to feel loved as a means to provide oral gratification. The love addict, when in love, has no interest in the real personality of his or her partner and can be in love with one person today and another tomorrow. The love addict has not become a complete individual and requires participation in a greater union to feel his or her own existence.

Mrs. Z, a twice-divorced woman, came to treatment for several years with the sole hope of finding an appropriate suitor. She was vaguely aware that some aspect of her personality was working against her but was never able to understand that her sexual favors in no way compensated for her inability to see her partners' other needs. In spite of above-average intelligence, it was difficult for her to perform simple clerical jobs because they detracted from her greater goal of finding a marital partner. She is now in the early stages of her third marriage to a man whom she regards as well off and is beginning to alienate him by her overspending and her inability to share him with his adolescent children.

Delusional Love. Seeman (1978) investigated a group of women who had delusions of being loved; she described two subtypes. The first type had a phantom lover. These women were usually schizophrenic. They clung to their delusional lovers for a lifetime. He was seen as an ordinary person with an active interest in obtaining the woman's affection, but who did not dare to approach her. These women were timid, dependent, and had little real heterosexual experience. Seeman postulated that the delusion served as a defense against low self-esteem, sexuality, and the aggression of others.

The second group, which Seeman called erotomania proper, was a healthier group of women who were impulsive, aggressive, and sexually active. They imagined they were loved by powerful, prominent men. They renounced their imaginary lovers every few months, experienced depression, and moved along to another delusional love. Seeman suggested that these women may have been defending against homosexual urges and their own competitiveness, and that they may have exaggeratedly enhanced themselves because they doubted their worth or because they had little sense of identity as individuals.

Pathological Relationships. A pathological relationship compromises the human needs of one or both of the partners to the extent that there is subjective discomfort (which may not be perceived as stemming from the relationship) or malfunction of the couple as parents or members of a larger society. For example, a spouse may feel depressed but be unaware that his subjective discomfort is the result of unreasonable expectations of himself that are compounded by his spouse's similar expectations. Malfunction as parents is illustrated by parents who cannot acknowledge grown children as adults. Malfunction as members of a larger society is seen in its most pathological form as a shared psychosis, *folie à deux* (Lasègue and Falret [1877] 1964).

Love is not enough to sustain an intimate relationship. There must be mutual involvement in areas of living that each partner regards as worthwhile. In many instances, these other interests eclipse romantic or companionate love as the principal sustaining factor in the relationship. In heterosexual relationships, children are the most frequent bond. Homosexual lovers commonly share careers or hobbies. The disappearance of love as the primary bond frequently becomes evident in heterosexual partners when the children become self-sufficient. In pathological relationships in which there is little love but great need felt for the marital partner, steps may be taken to ensure that the children remain thoroughly ensnared. There is little likelihood that a love relationship can survive without a supporting framework of interpersonal skills, work skills, and interests in life. Love provides the bond between people, but their personal attributes provide the structure of the relationship.

The pathology of love relationships is as diverse as human personalities, human interactions, and life situations. It is impossible to encompass the entire field, but it will be worthwhile to make a few generalizations and to describe some common phenomena.

A love relationship that lasts over time comes to a state of equilibrium. A balance is attained between the partners. Depending on the emotional flexibility of the partners, the balance can be static or it can change as the needs of the partners change. Lewis and others (1976) have demonstrated that the flexibility of a family's equilibrium is a good measure of the psychological health of individual family members. Healthy families tend toward flexibility, unhealthy families toward rigidity. Individual members of inflexible families have poorer psychological health than members of flexible families.

The same applies to love relationships. Healthy people who love each other are able to resolve difficulties by compromises that avoid name calling and that enhance the partners' sense of potency. There is open negotiation. Instead of struggling for control, partners interchange roles depending on the present needs of the couple. Each respects the other's autonomy as well as opinions and feelings.

Walster and Walster (1978) use "equity theory" to explain why people seem to get what they feel they deserve from life and from a marital partner. The authors suggest that people select partners with whom they feel equal. One gets according to what one has to offer.

Mental health professionals have also noted that people mate with others of corresponding emotional health. This observation gives us pause when we feel pity for the woman abused by her physically violent spouse, or for the man whose life is made miserable by a shrew. As we examine these relationships, we often find that they involve complementary roles. Sager (1976) postulates that married couples make implicit and explicit contracts with each other. He suggests that each spouse has an unconscious contract that is frequently internally inconsistent because of a person's own contradictory wishes or needs. Implicit in the formation of one-sided contracts is the covert assumption that one's needs will be met in exchange for what one contracts to do for the other. The problem is that the terms of the contract are not known to the partner. When the contract is not fulfilled, psychological symptoms develop, just as they might if a real agreement were broken and a real injury sustained.

The most common pathological love relationship in our culture is the wedding of the hysteric with the obsessive. An hysteric can be broadly caricatured as one who manipulates others to meet his or her needs through histrionics, exaggerated physical attractiveness, coyness, and feigned helplessness. Commonly seen as extroverted and cheerful, these individuals form parasitic, clinging relationships without regard for the partner's needs. They are like little girls seeking omnipotent daddies or little boys seeking a powerful nurturing figure. They are orally fixated, have failed to resolve their oedipal conflicts, and continue to seek the oedipal mother or father.

The obsessive, by contrast, is superficially conforming and has great concern for sameness, stability, and doing right. He or she tends to be humorless, straight-laced, overly concerned with rules, and in control of his or her surroundings. The obsessive is a good boy or girl who has grown up with great respect for the rules of the adult world but with little awareness of their emotional significance. His or her greatest pleasure is often self-righteousness, and righteous indignation the chief outlet for anger. He or she is a good organizer and gives the appearance of a good caretaker. He or she deals with failure to master oedipal conflicts by identification with the feared, threatening parent or by stubborn opposition.

The obsessive (or anal character) looks like a good parent to the hysteric. The hysteric is a welcome relief to the obsessive's permanently gray world. One's soberness and the other's cheerfulness should complement each other nicely. As it becomes apparent that the obsessive is more of a prison warden than a stabilizer for the hysteric, and that the hysteric's cheerfulness lasts only as long as he or she is indulged, one of the partners becomes symptomatic. The hysteric becomes depressed or develops emotionally based physical symptoms. The compulsive becomes angry, feels persecuted, become more rigidly self-righteous, or becomes suspicious of his or her mate's fidelity, as the mate flirts with others to feign independence and to maintain the endless stream of attention necessary to feed his or her self-esteem.

The martyr and the manipulator are another common pathological pair. The hallmark of this relationship is the repeated betrayal of the martyr by the manipulator, who offers a variety of excuses for his or her behavior. At each betrayal, the martyr feels wounded, as if the betrayal were totally unexpected, while the manipulator gives the appearance of remorse and promises never again to repeat the offending behavior, whether it is a drunken binge, writing bad checks, or exhibitionism.

A closer inspection of the martyr reveals an identification with a martyred parent and a sense that life is to be suffered and not enjoyed. One can only expect pain in return for what one gives of one's self. In the absence of the manipulator, these individuals frequently become depressed. Without an external source of pain, they experience the pain of their own self-criticism.

The manipulator, by contrast, sees his or her behavior as the product of urges which he or she can readily rationalize. He or she is not panicked by these impulses. They are welcomed, not defended against. The first drink comes too easily. The bad check is explained by need; besides, it wasn't for very much. The most pathological manipulator is an orally fixated individual with little frustration tolerance and without the apparent burden of conscience. He marries a conscience, perhaps as an attempt to externalize his own primitive self-punishing qualities, and usually succeeds admirably. The manipulator was frequently overindulged or emotionally abandoned as a child and had few limits set for a variety of reasons, including absent or inadequate parents.

The martyr-manipulator relationship can involve any level of psychopathology. It can be the relationship of a prostitute to her pimp-lover, or that of a long-suffering but truly charitable woman to her errant philanthropic husband.

A third type of disharmonious relationship is a swap between two dependent individuals who are unwilling to risk looking for other sources of gratification: the ugly woman and the socially inept man. As a result, they make do with a highly unsatisfactory, but constant and predictable relationship. Each knows the other is too fearful to leave. This knowledge facilitates aggression against each other for its own sake rather than for the sake of improving matters.

A fourth type of pathological love relationships is the uniting of the partners agains the rest of the world—the partners who find a common enemy, be it communism, blacks, or environmental pollution. Each projects his or her aggression on the outside world with the support of the other, and both unite to struggle against the aspect of the external world that they have mutually designated as evil. Should the dominant partner in this type of relationship become psychotic, the more dependent partner may begin to share his or her delusions and hallucinations—the syndrome of *folie à deux* noted earlier. The defense against the common enemy helps avoid dealing with problems in the relationship that would be evident were the couple not so preoccupied. The difficulties that do manifest are blamed not on one's self or one's marital partner but on the stress produced by the enemy's actions or the stress of maintaining an adequate defense. This paranoid stance may be a reflection of severe psychopathology, but the process of externalization by projection is a common defense. In its everyday form, it is called blaming. In its most malignant form, it is pursuit by delusional persecutors.

All four types of pathological love relationship have common elements that differentiate them from healthy love relationships. They are static and repetitive. They are closed systems that do not allow new information to enter and hence perpetuate from generation to generation. The personal inflexibility of the partners creates an inflexible love relationship incapable of changing as the needs of the partners change. Instead, they attempt to maintain the old equilibrium, which, if disturbed, produces symptomatic individuals or symptomatic family relationships.

"Therapeutic" Love

Anxiety and guilt feelings may be indirectly decreased by gaining love, especially if it enhances self-esteem. Fenichel (1945), for example, reported that an imposter was cured when a motherly woman fell in love with him, thereby fulfilling his oedipal wishes. A famous example of the therapeutic value of romantic

love was the cure of Elizabeth Barrett Browning's hysterical inva-
lidism by falling in love and eloping with Robert Browning. One
may speculate that the robust Robert Browning was enough like
Elizabeth's tyrannical father to satisfy her oedipal wishes, but
enough different from him (he was six years younger than Elizabeth) to encourage her functioning as an adult.

Psychotherapists have applied the love principle to their
treatment of patients, reasoning that their patients' problems
stemmed from inadequate parental love (Weiner, 1978). Most efforts of this sort have failed miserably, and mental health professionals generally find they are better off dealing with the damage
caused by lack of love than attempting to make up for what was
reported to be missing (Freud [1921] 1967). Trying to supply the
love missed by a patient as a small child is comparable to supply-
ing an adult pituitary dwarf with growth hormone. Once the personality has crystallized or the bone structure has fixed, one cannot turn back the organism's psychological or physiological processes to insert what was missing. One can only help to compensate
for it or to learn more effective ways to deal with the damage
caused by the lack, whether it is affection or growth hormone.

The author does not deny that a degree of emotional growth
is possible for almost everyone able to function in society, and
that many individuals grow well when accorded the acceptance
often equated with love. This growth does not occur through sup-
plying what was lost. Rather, it occurs through reopening in the
present to that which could not be accepted or dealt with in the
past, and learning new skills to supplement those that were under-
developed.

Conclusions

What can be done to foster healthy love and marital relationships and to prevent the formation of pathological relationships?
We now know enough about mature love and healthy family relationships to educate the public. The most important lesson to
teach is that love is not enough to sustain a love relationship—the
partners must communicate thoughts and feelings and have adequate work and interpersonal coping skills. Knowing how to work
in harmony with another person is the sine qua non of every re-

lationship, whether a job or a marriage. Having the capacity to gratify another person and the ability to deal with frustration are the two interpersonal skills that enable harmonious working together.

We must teach the public that the quality of relationships is more important than their appearance. We must convince our society that one does not capture affection by superficial manipulation of one's appearance or smell, after which one is forever happy exchanging bright, white smiles or inhaling entrancing odors.

We must make it clear that a loving relationship encourages both autonomy and cooperation. It encourages the appropriate interchange and withholding of feelings. It encourages open negotiation, emphasizes the right of every person to his or her point of view, and respects the views of others.

People must become aware that healthy individuals change over time. Change in individuals requires change in relationships, a process requiring willingness to be continually open to one another and to work toward an ongoing compromise. Love is not bliss. It is hard work, facilitated by mutual caring and impelled by mutual need.

We can begin by educating children in schools, young adults in colleges, and parents in parent-education classes. Today's children can learn from their parents and can help work toward a healthier society in which love is based not merely on one's own gain but on enhancement of the other. Altruism is, in the long run, the most effective form of selfishness.

8

Love as a Process of Reducing Uncertainty— Cognitive Theory

Kenneth R. Livingston

Anyone who has ever had more than one romantic relationship is no doubt familiar with their variability over time and across partners. Novels by the thousands and large numbers of films, plays, poems, short stories, soap operas and deep depressions have been produced by artists attempting to detail the endless variations on the romantic theme. The very personal nature of these views of the romantic experience no doubt contributes to the variable ex-

Note: My special thanks to Gwen Broude and Richard Lowry for the extended conversations that helped clarify the arguments presented in this chapter. Thanks also to Martin Ringle for his valuable insights and comments on an early draft of this chapter, and to Diana Abizaid, Roy Hopkins, James Hassett, and John Morris for their reading of an earlier draft. Finally, my appreciation to the friends and more-than-friends who helped encourage, however inadvertently, this view of romantic love.

133

pectations people have of romance, because some of us watch
Woody Allen movies, others read Dostoyevsky, and a few hardy
souls attempt a diet consisting of both.

This sort of variability, even within the same culture, makes
serious treatment by psychologists difficult, which may explain
why we have filled so many fewer reels and pages than artists.
Then again, we just recently took up the challenge. The rest of
humanity has been at it since the first of us wailed a song of loss
or confusion or joy, depending on the particular phase in which
things happened to be. The fact that cries of anguish appear to increase in direct proportion to the population suggests that either
no one has figured it out yet, or that having done so, there was
a failure to communicate the secret to the rest of us. In any event,
the intricacies of the love relationship remain among the most
thoroughly considered, least understood phenomena in the human
experience.

Typically, in a work of this sort, one is supposed to define
the phenomenon under consideration before attempting a discussion of it, but that is far easier to say than to do in this case. Walster and Walster (1978) surveyed a wide range of descriptions of
romantic love and attempted to produce a composite picture of
what they found there. Rubin's (1970) love scale certainly contains, at least implicitly, a definition of the experience. His version
of a definition has the additional advantage of having been vali-
dated by more than one group of researchers (for example, Dion
and Dion, 1975; Goldstein, Kilroy, and Van de Voort, 1976;
Munro and Adams, 1978; Rubin, 1973) and in several different
paradigms. Other scales, less popularly in use, also contain at least
implicit definitions. Without accepting any of these sources as
definitive, it seems clear that some common features or characteristics have begun to emerge, at least in terms of what gets measured by researchers. "Intense absorption in another" (Walster and
Walster, 1978), the desire to confide in one's lover and to be con-
fided in by one's lover, high physiological arousal, greater amounts
of mutual gazing and conversation than are found in nonromantic
relationships, and so on, are commonly identified as descriptors or
indicators of romantic involvement. The cultural stereotype, at
least as I have understood it, includes other characteristics as well:
hypersensitivity to the other's communications, both verbal and

nonverbal; a high level of sensitivity to the needs and desires of the other, and often special effort to gratify those needs and desires; and frequent visual and physical contact, often with associated feelings of excitement and arousal.

However comprehensive a list of this sort, and this one could be more so, it fails to capture the dynamic quality of romantic love. And romantic love is nothing if not dynamic. Consider, then, the following additional factor.

It is possible that one source of variability in conceptions of the romantic experience is the large number of possible combinations of the components listed, plus many more specific ones (such as loss of appetite) not even presented here. Every loving relationship can be characterized by the pattern of components it manifests, and not all such relationships are described by their participants as "romantic." Lee (1977) has attempted to discover meaningful types of such relationships using factor analytic procedures, and the data do suggest the importance of viewing romantic love in the context of other possible arrangements. Nor can one assume that a relationship consists of the same set of components in stable relationship over time. There is some suggestion that the behavior and experience of romantic love have a life cycle during which the components or their relative importance to the experience may shift (Hill, Rubin, and Peplau, 1976). The "life cycle" can be conceived as having three phases. There is an initial phase during which the components that will characterize the relationship are established and organized. The bases for initial attraction have been reasonably well researched (see Berscheid and Walster, 1978; Rubin, 1973), at least with respect to variables like physical attractiveness, proximity, similarity of values, and the like, although considerable theoretical work needs to be done before synthesis is evident in this area. Passing over the second phase for a moment, the final phase, as characterized by Walster and Walster (1978), almost inevitably involves a transformation into some different mode of functioning. People either find other, less passionate ways of defining their relationship, or they are unable to continue it at all. In between the initial attraction and the final resolution of passionate feeling is the phase of romantic love in full flower.

Many approaches have been taken to an understanding of the phenomena described so briefly here, ranging from the phenomenological (Ziller and Rosen, 1975) to the construction of models using sophisticated multivariate statistical techniques (Bentler and Huba, 1979; Tesser and Paulhus, 1976). The goal of this chapter is to grapple with some of the more dynamic aspects of romance, and to do so from what I suppose must be called a cognitive-theoretical perspective. It should soon become apparent, however, that no dissection of the romantic experience is intended by this labeling, and full recognition of the salient emotional character and great complexity of romance is granted implicitly. In particular, I hope to provide an explanation for the cyclical nature of romantic love described earlier, and especially for the nearly inevitable end of the passionate phase of the experience.

In the course of the discussion to follow, several concepts that have come to have multiple sets of connotations play an important role. These include, in particular, uncertainty and information, two concepts that play a central role in the areas of decision theory and information processing theory. Their usage here is not intended to be congruent with their precise mathematical definition in these other areas. A more cognitive psychological definition is implied in which information has the effect of reducing subjective uncertainty, and uncertainty results from a condition of insufficient information for the full evaluation of a given circumstance. The discussion to follow employs these concepts only in this psychological manner.

Toward a Theory of Romance

A good deal of theory and research in the field of psychology points to the importance of uncertainty reduction as a motive across several species (Berlyne, 1960, 1974; Kagan, 1972). The general assumption of this work has been that the experience of uncertainty produces an associated drive state which the organism attempts to reduce. Since the source of the drive is the experience of uncertainty, and since uncertainty exists because more than one event or outcome is possible, the reduction of the "uncomfortable state of uncertainty" (Berlyne, 1974) can be accomplished by selectively gathering information that reduces the number of (subjectively) possible outcomes. The implication of this drive reduction model is that having certainty is rewarding, and that although total certainty is difficult to maintain, it is one goal toward which behavior is directed.

At first glance, a system of this sort makes good evolutionary sense. Situations of uncertainty have considerable potential for danger, and for an organism to be "wired" so as to find uncertainty aversive would presumably lead to the avoidance of dangerous situations and consequent maximization of surviving offspring (see Schneirla, 1959). On closer examination, however, this argument has both logical and empirical flaws.

First of all, it must be pointed out that uncertainty and danger are not in fact equivalent, or even covarying, events. I may be uncertain whether it will be cloudy or sunny tomorrow, but unless I am planning some, for me, unusual activity, there is little danger associated with this uncertainty. By the same token, I may be in danger of a serious accident, while driving, for example, on a holiday weekend, but experience little associated uncertainty. Uncertainty is a psychological state, whereas danger has at least some objective component having to do with well-being. The actual effect of any given situation on behavior must therefore be seen as a (nonlinear?) function of both experienced uncertainty about outcomes and the perceived potential danger associated with those outcomes. Thus the argument that it is adaptive to avoid situations of uncertainty cannot be made on the grounds that situations involving uncertainty are potentially dangerous. There is no evidence that the two covary sufficiently for this to be the case.

On the more empirical side, people can be observed to expose themselves quite deliberately to situations of uncertainty. The examples range from the relatively benign, like betting on football games, to the more serious, like skydiving or asking for a commitment to a relationship from one's partner. At the same time, people engaging in these actions can be seen to behave so as to minimize uncertainties, usually to a degree that reflects the potential danger of the situation. The skydiver, except when in a suicidal frame of mind, can be observed to check and recheck carefully parachute and airplane, the jump site, and so forth, and the gambler gathers at least some information about teams and the point-spread before betting. Yet in both cases, the surest way to minimize uncertainty absolutely is to avoid betting or leaping from a perfectly good airplane in the first place. At the very least, it is clear that the motive to reduce uncertainty does not operate alone in such situations, and it has not been established that the fact that there is some uncertainty does not contribute to the motivation to approach the situation. Given that people do intentionally expose themselves to situations involving uncertainty, the question reduces to whether any logical account of the possible adaptive significance of this tendency can be given.

An argument could be made that a tendency of this sort makes sense across the wide range of behaviors of which an organism is capable. The voluntary victim of uncertainty adjusts his or her estimates of the likelihood of undesirable outcomes over repeated exposures to the situation, often in conjunction with a decrease in associated arousal (for example, see Epstein and Fenz, 1965, for a fine example from the realm of skydiving). These changes occur as a result of repeated exposures to the situation without undesirable consequences, and learning the skills involved in the activity. Skill learning and confidence of this sort can only take place by engaging the situation and coping with its uncertainties. A system that is genetically designed to approach such situations will, in the long run, be better adapted to survive future situations of uncertainty, which in the real world cannot always be avoided. Play in the young of a species often involves uncertainty about outcomes (Bruner, Jolly, and Sylva, 1976), and the value of such activities could also be interpreted in this light. One of the primary roles of parents may, in fact, have to do with making distinctions for the child between truly dangerous situations of uncertainty and those from which valuable lessons might be learned. Furthermore, uncertainties need not concern only physical outcomes. Entertainers, children who recite before the class, and people entering into emotional relationships with others are also exposing themselves to situations of uncertainty where the outcomes are more psychological.

Two features of the argument being developed here bear emphasis since they are crucial to its application to the understanding of romance. Note that uncertainty is seen as a dynamic, shifting factor. It does not continue to operate at the same levels that existed on the first occasion of one's experience of a situation. The second feature of such situations has been implicit thus far, and it concerns the way in which conditions of uncertainty lead to an orientation toward and special attention to situations so character-ized, usually to the accompaniment of heightened physiological arousal (Berlyne and Borsa, 1968). These two factors, and the argu-ment as it has been developed to this point, suggest the following propositions.

- Proposition 1: Individuals orient toward and attend to situations in which some degree of felt uncertainty exists, to the accompa-niment of arousal and in relation to the degree of uncertainty and nature of outcome.
- Proposition 2: Individuals continue to engage such situations so long as they can and do experience the process of the reduction of that uncertainty in a nonthreatening direction.

Although the foregoing propositions are stated in general terms, the concern here is with their application to the romantic experience, and in fact some of the most fascinating illustrations of these principles are found in this area of human experience. From the beginning phases of a romantic involvement, uncertainty has a part to play. If the uncertainty concept is translated into the language of subjective probabilities (Pitz, 1974) it even becomes possible to measure its effects with some degree of precision. A sub-jective probability refers here to "a degree of belief that character izes the observer of an event rather than a characteristic of the event itself" (Pitz, 1974, p. 30), where *degree* of belief reflects the *degree* of uncertainty present in the person's experience of the situ-ation. Subjective probabilities, like their objective counterparts, may range from 0 to 1, and both extremes represent the experience of certainty about outcomes, although the direction of the out-come (an event will or will not occur) is of course different.

Such subjective probabilities play a role even in the initial attraction phase of a relationship. Shanteau and Nagy (1979) mea-sured women's preferences for males as potential dates using as predictors both the rated attractiveness of the man, as is tradition-ally done, and the woman's subjective probability estimate that the male would accept a date with her. These subjective probabil-ities were shown to interact in multiplicative fashion with physical attractiveness to predict preference. Here is a clear example con-sistent with the principle stated Proposition 1. It is not known from Shanteau and Nagy's research whether differences in attention and arousal existed, and this laboratory-based paradigm leaves the dynamic factors of Proposition 2 unexplored. However, the importance of subjective probabilities, even in a relatively impersonal attraction situation, is amply demonstrated.

The central issues being addressed here do include more dynamic factors than these, however. For example, obtaining the answers to the sorts of questions that arise during the initial phase of a relationship (Does she find me attractive? Would he have dinner with me? and so on) obviously reduces the associated uncertainties and thus, according to the propositions, should change one's experience of the situation, in particular the focus of one's attention upon those initial uncertainties. It is a salient characteristic of such relationships that there are a great many such uncertainties, many of which operate simultaneously. Furthermore, whole subsets of such issues are more or less salient depending upon the success or failure of attempts to resolve prior uncertainties. To give a mundane example, uncertainty about whether the partner will spend a romantic spring vacation with one in the Bahamas will increase in salience from the day before the first "date" or outing to the end of the first long weekend spent alone together. To put it another way, information is generally defined as any event that reduces uncertainty, but information about one issue can lead to new uncertainties in regard to other, formerly less salient issues. Subjective probabilities about such outcomes are, however, seldom reduced to 0 or raised to 1 precipitously, and it is the second, *process*-oriented proposition that accounts for the ebb and flow of the romantic experience.

When certainty does not exist, and the individuals involved engage the situation as described in Proposition 1, Proposition 2 states that they will do so only so long as they experience the *process* of reducing that uncertainty. Failure to experience that process can occur in two ways. The couple's communications may be mutual and successful, in which case, for example, uncertainty about a week in the Bahamas gradually drops to zero. This process will be enjoyable, but once certainty is achieved, the process of reducing it ceases and attention is focused elsewhere, in accordance with the first set of principles. Alternatively, there may be no experience of the process because the level of uncertainty increases (ultimately heading toward certainty that the shared trip will not take place) or stabilizes and remains constant. Under any of these circumstances, the orientation and attention to the issue is no longer observed. It is important to emphasize the dynamic nature of this process over time. Until some definite agreement is reached that both parties will, for example, agree to the trip (or whatever), each of them will be constantly shifting his or her subjective estimate of the likely outcome. So long as the trend is *on the whole* toward certainty of the desired outcome (that is, there is a cumulative shift in probabilities, apart from momentary fluctuations), the situation remains engaging.

It is interesting to note here that this process and its effect on attention or vigilance could be rephrased in the language of signal detection and decision theory, an exercise beyond the scope of this chapter. Vickers, Leary, and Barnes (1977) have shown, for example, that certain features of signal detection in a noisy environment show adaptation that is functionally related to changes over time in the probability that an event (signal) will in fact occur. Their analysis leads to the conclusion that the individual in this situation behaves so as to minimize the discrepancy between locally occurring and cumulative probabilities, and furthermore that accuracy is related to measurable dimensions of personality. One of the advantages of the conceptualization offered in this chapter is the possibility of showing concordance with such basic perceptual and cognitive processes, as well as the potential for translation into relatively precise and modelable language.

To summarize to this point, it is argued that the uncertainties that characterize a relationship of attraction and romantic feeling contribute in major ways to the romantic experience. The general effects of uncertainty are not inconsistent with the components of romantic love discussed earlier, including physiological arousal and relatively greater attention to and conversation with the partner than in other relationships. The latter in particular can be viewed in terms of the exchange of information, especially as it relates to altering subjective probabilities about future outcomes in the relationship. Ziller and Rosen (1975), for example, noted a sharp rise in romantic experience by men in two different relationships followed over time after their female partners raised the prospect of an end of the relationship. More will be said about communication and uncertainty later in this chapter.

The shift in focus of uncertainties in the relationship is one way of describing its growth or life cycle, and furthermore it is argued that it is the process of uncertainty reduction, not the having of certainty, that is experienced as engaging and thus maintains the romantic experience. Note that this principle explains why it is that not all romances proceed to the third phase discussed earlier, for once the process of their reduction ceases, remaining uncertainties are not sufficient to maintain orientation to the relationship.

Suddenly, however, an important qualification has appeared on the horizon. This discussion does, after all, concern the dyad, and neither logic nor informal observation nor data from research (for example, Altman, 1973; Ziller and Rosen, 1975) argues for perfect symmetry in the romantic experience. Two people may report being in love to the same degree, but they by no means do so reliably. Furthermore, the quality of the experience may be different for the participants, even if they have the same score on some measure of love. The problem is how to account for such individual differences.

Working from the foundation of the two propositions presented earlier, differences in degree of the romantic experience would be a function of both the levels of uncertainties currently operating in a relationship and the general trends in those levels over time. In addition to these process variables, however, there are also content issues, not unrelated to the risk or reward factors present in the situation. The major concerns and central issues of the relationship may be perceived differently by the participants at any given point in time. For example, suppose "She"* is concerned about the upcoming vacation period and whether their relationship will have developed to the point of making a joint vacation trip. "He" may be aware of this issue, but for him the more salient concern revolves around the degree of long-term commitment to the relationship on her part. They may have identical subjective probability estimates for positive resolution of these is-

*I have used "he" and "she" in this and subsequent examples, but the arguments apply equally to homosexual romantic relationships.

sues and, more importantly, equivalent experiences of the process of the reduction of these uncertainties, and nevertheless may differ in the extent to which they experience being in the throes of a romantic experience. Given that such content issues are crucial to romantic love, how is one to explain these individual differences in focus?

Several possible accounts of such differences are possible, including, for example, the suggestion that such differences are a function of variation in the range of subjective probabilities experienced as rewarding or aversive, or differences in rates of change of such probabilities which are salient or not from the perspective of the second proposition. Such arguments, however, amount to a sort of threshold model, with nearly infinite possibilities for hedging given almost any set of data. However internally consistent such an argument may be, it does not make for a very responsive theory from an empirical viewpoint, and it bears avoiding for that reason. In addition, it equates the concept of uncertainty with the construct of "danger" or aversion in a manner that has already been shown to introduce serious logical and empirical difficulties.

The same problems are *not* encountered if one treats the value of an outcome as logically independent of the uncertainties associated with it. The romantic experience can then be seen as a joint function of the process of reducing uncertainties and the nature of the issue about which uncertainty exists. Furthermore, there is evidence to suggest that such issues in romantic interpersonal situations can be construed quite usefully in terms of their relationship to what Sullivan (1953b) called the "self system" (for example, see Dion and Dion, 1975; Ziller and Rosen, 1975). This interaction is summarized in the third proposition.

- Proposition 3: Individual differences in the romantic experience are a joint function of operation of uncertainty, as described in Propositions 1 and 2, and individual differences in the organization of the self esteem, with particular reference to its sensitivities to esteem and anxiety.

There really is not sufficient space here to explore in detail the full implications of this corollary. The concept of the self system is borrowed relatively unmodified, for purposes of this discussion, from Sullivan (1953b). Sullivan defined the self system as a dynamic set of coordinated processes, developed so as to give coherence to the organism's attempts to meet needs and avoid anxieties. Such a system must be viewed from a developmental perspective, almost by definition, and imperfections of various sorts can and do work into this system over time. However, some weaknesses in the system may be corrected with time and the right set of circumstances. These shifts in the operation and structure of the self system are related to shifts in the kinds of events that tend to focus uncertainties. More will be said about this process in a moment.

By way of illustration, consider the example discussed earlier. "She" is experiencing salient uncertainties about an upcoming vacation, and "He" is experiencing salient uncertainty about the degree of commitment evolving in the relationship. For the sake of argument, let us assume that his concern revolves around the question of whether he is sufficiently valuable to be accepted as an exclusive partner for an indefinite period of time. She, however, is concerned with the perceptions of others, of her self, as these will be affected by whether she goes to the Bahamas alone or with him. It is perfectly possible that the importance for her of the outcome of the vacation trip exceeds the importance for him of the outcome of the commitment issue, and one would then predict a greater degree of romantic feeling on her part than on his, given equivalent experiences for the two of them of the overall process of reducing the uncertainties relevant to their respective concerns.

There are a number of details of this model that remain unspecified here, including the question of just what characteristics of the other in such situations make him or her valuable or not as a partner in reducing uncertainties. However, these are probably related to many of the factors that determine initial attraction (physical presence, personal qualities in social situations, any of a number of traits, and so forth), and as such are not the central concern of this discussion. Suffice it to say that the need for a synthesis of the literature on initial attraction mentioned earlier might well be satisfied by a model based on the propositions presented in this chapter. Perhaps one is attracted initially to persons who show promise of helping one cope with the uncertainties about oneself. These issues, however, must remain unexplored for the present. The central point here is that both the process of reducing uncertainty and the issues about which that uncertainty exists contribute to the intensity and nature of the romantic experience, in accordance with the stated propositions. In the pages that follow, an attempt will be made to explain some of the dynamic phenomena of the romantic experience using these propositions.

The Battle Against Time. The propositions have interesting implications for the course of the romantic experience in a relationship. Earlier discussion emphasized the importance for the romantic experience of the shift in the salience of various components of that experience. It was further argued that the reduction of one set of uncertainties led to the establishment of a new set, at least up to a point. The "point" turns out to be the phase of resolution of the romantic affair. Eventually, the couple has either reduced all the major uncertainties of relevance, and on balance enjoyed the process, or has failed to do so. Resolution of uncertainties may occur in a way that leads either to a favorable or to an unfavorable evaluation of self. Increasing certainty that one is not viewed favorably is likely to be associated with the termination, eventually, of the relationship. Increasing certainty in the opposite direction should in general be associated with its continuation. Note that both processes may occur in the same relationship, with some issues being resolved one way, others in the opposite direction. Whether the relationship continues would then depend upon the balance of such resolutions, as a function of the variables outlined in Proposition 3. Whatever the pattern of uncertainty resolution, the *process* of reducing uncertainty ceases and therefore, according to Proposition 2, so does the person's special engagement in the relationship. The partners in a dyad may reach this point at different times, with consequences to be discussed shortly.

The failure to reduce uncertainties will also be associated with the eventual end of romantic feeling for the same reason. Failure to reduce uncertainty is equivalent to the failure to experience the process of uncertainty reduction. In both the successful and the unsuccessful situations, it is the change in cumulative subjective probabilities that mediates the romantic experience. Since uncertainties must either be reduced or not, it is inevitable that these cumulative probabilities will eventually stabilize, making nearly inevitable the end of the romantic phase of the relationship.

It is the logical necessity of this last statement that under-scores Geraldy's (1939) contention that the romantic affair does continual battle with the passage of time. Unlike the person at a casino gambling table, the individual in a romantic relationship is not faced with objectively established, fixed probabilities, which reset on each throw of the dice or spin of the wheel. The mere pas-sage of time in a relationship with the same person leads to a shift in certain subjective probabilities. If the partner continues to be reliably available, uncertainty reduces even if no other communi-cation is taking place. Only near random behavior or extreme in-consistency on the relevant dimensions of uncertainty can con-tinue to induce in one's lover the feelings of passion that charac-terize romantic involvement, and even this is a highly delicate pro-cess. Unpredictability becomes predictable in its own way and is then no longer a focus for the experience of reducing uncertainty. Just how long all of this takes, and how enjoyable it is, will be in large part a function of the complementarity of the dyad's experi-ence of uncertainty. The crucial hypothesis, in any case, is that it is the eventual loss of the experience of uncertainty reduction that produces the decline of passionate feeling with its associated plea-surable arousal, focused attention, and the like, and the necessity for a change in the definition of the relationship. In this connec-tion, it is interesting to note research with married couples show-ing a decrease in love scores (which have been shown to tap pri-marily the romantic dimension) in the course of a marriage (Cim-balo, Faling, and Mousan, 1976). Passion gives way to companion-ate love in Walster and Walster's (1978) language, or to the search for a new passion.

Vicissitudes of the Romantic Experience. The same set of propositions can also account for the periodic resurgence of in-tensity of romantic experience both within the romantic phase of the relationship and across the longer span of the adult life cycle. As discussed earlier, resolution of one set of uncertainties paves the way for the increased salience of others as yet unresolved. The waxing and waning in salience of foci for uncertainty may overlap in time so that the experience remains at a high level of intensity, or may take on a more cyclical nature.

This apparent cyclicity may be the result of a reemergence of uncertainties after variable periods of time in a relationship. This occurs as a function of shifts in the revelant areas of vulnerability of the self during subsequent stages in the adult life cycle (Levinson, 1978; Vaillant, 1977), an argument that also coincides with Kagan's (1972) contention that foci of uncertainty are subject to change with development. The increase in romantic orientation during middle age (see Munro and Adams, 1978) can be interpreted in terms of a rise in uncertainties about oneself in relation to members of the opposite sex as one enters the second half of life. Whether the target of such feelings remains the same (that is, one's current partner) or shifts will depend upon changes both in the organization of the self and in the character of the partner and his or her ability to satisfy the requirements of the self at that time. In either case, the same principles will govern the course of this new episode. A resurgence of this sort is often associated with other events in the course of a relationship, including, for example, the anticipation of parenthood. The idea of having a (or another) child to "save a marriage" may thus be grounded in a real set of psychological processes. By the same token, it has already been argued that these processes have an inevitable time course, and from this perspective it is not surprising that if the attempt is to save a marriage by making it romantic again, success will usually be temporary.

It is important to point out that the process of uncertainty reduction, which is so central to the arguments presented here, is closely related to patterns of communication between members of a pair. Uncertainty reflects a relative lack of necessary information about outcomes and can thus be reduced not only by observation of another's behaviors but also by listening to what the other says. The verbal communication process is an enormously complex one, however, and little can be done here beyond suggesting the variables likely to be important in understanding its relevance to romantic love.

First, communication, especially verbal communication, is seldom precise and conducted according to the rules of formal logic. The speaker depends heavily on the listener's ability to make inferences about unspoken but intended arguments (for example, see Schank and Abelson, 1978). Inaccuracies and distortions in communication may result either from genuine failures of this inferential process or from systematic distortions introduced by the listener in an attempt to avoid hearing unpleasant messages (Sullivan's "parataxic distortion"). Whether communication is accurate or distorted, by some objective criteria, is not, however, directly relevant to whether the romantic experience occurs. What is important is the effect of a communication on a listener's subjective probability estimates about outcomes in the area under discussion. People often construct idealizations of their partners, especially in the early phases of the relationship, and it has even been suggested that romanticism depends on such idealizations (for example, see Kremen and Kremen, 1971). However, attempts to measure the impact of this variable on the extent to which one is or is not in love have not shown any clearly predictive relationship (Tesser and Paulhus, 1976). The model under discussion here does not depend upon such connections but rather argues that idealizations of one's partner are crucial only to the extent that they affect the experience of uncertainty reduction. A priori, there is no reason why they should do so more often in one direction than another.

Note that the uncertainty variables of Propositions 1 and 2 can affect the frequency and nature of communication as well as being affected by communications. Once "She" no longer experiences personally significant uncertainties in the context of the relationship, her communications designed to elicit information and reduce uncertainty will decline. "He" may thus be hindered in his own attempt to continue the reduction of his uncertainties where those are unresolved. Should this occur, one might expect a decline in his romantic feelings, in accordance with Proposition 2. To the extent that this affects his own verbal and nonverbal behavior, her uncertainties may be increased: he becomes less attentive, passionate, and so forth, making her feel less loved. If, for example, he also behaves so as to reduce his uncertainties about his attractiveness or sexuality by flirting at parties, her own uncertainties may refuel the romantic experience. Such vicissitudes are among the factors that are nicely handled by the propositions presented here.

There is a growing literature on the process of communication exchange which is, at the very least, not inconsistent with this view (see Morton, 1978). This research suggests a change over the course of relationships in the nature of communications, with degree and type of intimacy (descriptive vs. evaluative) and reciprocity of exchange as variables. Further work is needed to tie this work to the dynamic variables outlined here.

The Functional Significance of Romance. I cannot resist making one last argument designed to reinforce those already presented. It stems from the following question: *Why* should the human system be organized in this fashion? In the opening pages of this chapter, the traditional model of uncertainty as a motive force was discussed in terms of its adaptive function, and a few brief remarks were made about the possible adaptiveness of a system like the one outlined here. In the specific case of romantic love, however, the argument can be made more convincingly that it is adaptive for the system to work this way. If one takes it as a given that two parents were more likely than one, in the environment of evolutionary adaptiveness, to raise offspring successfully to childbearing age (Wickler, 1972), then any system, genetically coded, that increases the likelihood of successful pair bonding of potential parents should have considerable adaptive success. The romantic phase of a relationship as outlined here contains many of the features necessary for such success, not the least of which are heightened attentiveness, solicitousness, and communication. These factors could serve to facilitate cooperation in childrearing and, as was already argued above, increased satisfaction of personal needs, which enhances the value of the partner and thus increases behaviors designed to maintain the partnernship. Note further that the dependence of such a system on an uncertainty reduction system like the one outlined here would be extremely elegant—a maximally simple way to mediate a range of complex behaviors and tendencies. The system increases the likelihood of pair bonding but operates so as to reduce the partners' intense absorption in each other after a time, freeing the attentional system for focus on factors likely to affect offspring survival. By the same token, the system serves to monitor potential disruptions of the bond, since increased uncertainties (sometimes experienced and labeled as jealousy) lead to renewal of the romance and associated pair-bonding behaviors.

This is a very sketchy version of what could itself be a complex argument occupying many pages. In particular, it ignores the

considerable range in the nature, and even the significance, of romantic love across the many cultures of the world (Broude, in
press). I am convinced that even this variability offers no serious
challenge to the arguments presented here, but a thorough demonstration must remain for another time.

    Future Directions. There is a great deal of work to be done
on and with the model presented here, in addition to the exploration of the issues just discussed. This mini-theory should have considerable heuristic value for the study of romantic love. I hope
that I do not misrepresent him by suggesting that it is the sort of
generative theory that Gergen (1978) has championed so well.
Among the directions for future exploration is the translation of
these concepts into a more precise language, as suggested earlier in
connection with the work on signal detection. It might then be
possible to revive interest in the testing of such models in the computer simulation paradigm.

    In another direction, the propositions presented here, espe-
cially as they relate to romantic love, are potentially testable in
the real world. However, because they refer to dynamic processes,
and not to structural components, of what must be seen as an
open, interactive system, such testing cannot be expected to occur
in the traditional laboratory paradigms that have provided much
of the data so far available on the subject. The "friend-observer"
approach of Ziller and Rosen (1975) has unexploited potential in
this regard. Although this approach lacks the "objectivity" of
laboratory research, it permits close observation of relationships
on an ongoing basis necessary for the exploration of dynamic processes. Lee's (1977) "story-telling" technique has similar potential
for the retrospective study of the course of romantic love, although
retrospective distortion is also possible in a paradigm of this sort.
Accurately reported daydreaming and fantasy material could provide an important window on the self-system variables outlined in
Proposition 3 and should be examined carefully in this connection.

    Recent advances in complex model building and testing pro-
cedures (Tesser and Paulhus, 1976; Bentler and Huba, 1979) can
also be applied to the model presented in this chapter, provided
measurements are taken at frequent enough intervals and guided
adequately by theory (Smith, 1978). This last qualification is
a crucial one for this approach and highlights what is perhaps the

most important problem to be solved by researchers of the romantic experience. "Being in love" is too often treated as a structural variable rather than a process variable in such research, an approach that seems logically doomed to failure for the simple reason that it misrepresents the phenomena. Early explorations of the model presented here might, for example, focus on the relationship between measured uncertainty about the continuation of the couple's relationship and degree of romantic involvement. Given repeated measurement of such subjective probabilities, cumulative probabilities operating at any point in time could be evaluated (1) in relation to local probabilities (in the manner of Vickers, Leary, and Barnes, 1977), and (2) in relation to measures of both romantic love and the rated importance of the relationship. A simple test of the model might thus be made without wading immediately into the murky waters of the self-system formulations of Proposition 3. At the very least, the development of such procedures should lead to research more suited to the dynamic nature of the experience of romantic love.

9

Toward a Predictive Model of Romantic Behavior

L. Rowell Huesmann

If one wished to generate a great many incredulous, indulgent smiles at a cocktail party, one could hardly do better than to announce the creation of a computer program that simulates love. Man's fascination with the dynamics of love may have begun thousands of years ago, but man's willingness to accept love as a quantifiable phenomenon of predictable occurrence is little greater now than it was then.

Romantic love has been viewed through the ages as a mostly unpredictable but powerful state in which distorted perceptions and illogical behaviors are the norm. Writers from Virgil (*Eclogues* I, 6)—"Love conquers all"—through Shakespeare (*The Merchant of Venice*, II, 6, 36)—"Love is blind"—to Mencken (*Prejudices*, 1919)

—"To be in love is merely a state of perceptual anesthesia"—have reflected the prevailing view of love's irrationality. That such a view of love has been espoused by clever and observant men for centuries should be somewhat discouraging to anyone trying to model love. Yet love is a behavior and should obey the same laws as other behaviors.

Psychologists studying love have offered a variety of definitions of love and explained specific behaviors in a variety of ways, but few attempts have been made to construct formal models of love. The apparent irrationality of love has probably led many to abandon such attempts before they have been begun. In this respect, the study of love has not been very different from the study of many other social psychological phenomena. Too many social psychologists seem to hold the tenet that the cold formalisms of mathematics and computer science can never capture the warmth and diversity of social behavior.

A second factor that has hampered the emergence of formal models of love probably has been the practical difficulties of studying "true love." Longitudinal studies of couples in love are very difficult and costly and, with a few exceptions (for example, Hill, Rubin, and Peplau, 1976), have taken a backseat to studies of transient aspects of romantic attraction. Much of the basic longitudinal data needed to construct an accurate model has not been collected. Studies based on retrospective recall by the subjects have limited validity for such an emotionally charged topic as love. Although the lack of data serves as an excuse for the lack of an accurate model, it cannot serve as an excuse for the lack of any model. In fact, precisely because longitudinal research on love is so difficult, one needs unambiguous theoretical models to guide the empirical research.

None of the foregoing should be taken as a substantive criticism of the theories that have been offered to explain romantic involvement. Instead, the criticism is methodological—that it is time to present general models of love and romantic behavior that are precise, unambiguous, and falsifiable. In the past, only a few attempts have been made in this direction, most notably by Homans (1961) and Levinger and Snoek (1972). More recently, Huesmann and Levinger (1976; Levinger and Huesmann, 1980) have developed an algorithmic model of interpersonal interaction. The remainder of this chapter will use the Huesmann and Levinger model as a framework for an algorithmic process model of love. The value of such a model, I will argue, derives as much from the modes of thinking it forces upon the user as from the predictions it yields.

An Algorithmic Model of Love

Process Models. A process model of behavior is one that explains a subject's behavior in terms of the elementary information processing that the subject is doing. Usually the model is stated as an algorithm; often it can be simulated on a computer. As Huesmann (in press) has argued elsewhere, such models have numerous advantages over descriptive models (for example, structural models or stochastic models). In cognitive psychology, many of the dominant theories of thinking, memory, and problem solving are now stated as process models. However, the intrusion of process models into social psychology has been much less substantial. Huesmann and Levinger's (1976) model for dyadic interaction and Abelson's (1973) models for belief development and attitude change are perhaps the two best-known recent examples.

The advantages of a formal process model derive both from the level of explanation used and the structure forced upon the theorist. Process models explain behaviors in terms of underlying operations that can be performed by information-processing systems. One cannot be ambiguous about such specifications. If one wishes to simulate behavior on a computer with the model, one must be precise and unambiguous or the simulation will never run. As a result of such precision and this finer level of explanation, algorithmic-process models are generally more readily falsifiable than other theories. This is a highly desirable property (Gregg and Simon, 1967) that has too often been missing from theories of love. One of the advantages of an algorithmic model over a mathematical model is that behaviors need not be quantified to be predicted. A process model stated as an algorithm generates behaviors that can be compared directly with observed behaviors. Equally important, because elementary information processes are specified precisely, general laws for behavior according to the model can often be deduced without simulations actually being run.

The State of Love. In studying romantic love, the first two questions probably asked are, "Why do people fall in love?" and "Why do people fall out of love?" Such questions are not precise enough for our purposes though. What does "falling in love" mean? One approach to answering this question is to define a particular state of dyadic interaction, develop a process model for how a pair enters and exits the state, as well as how they behave in the state, and then argue that the state would be perceived by the participants as romantic love. The premise underlying this approach is that "being in love" is an attribution that one makes about oneself and others to explain the behaviors and situations one observes.

What can one say about the state of "being in love"? Certainly it is an interactive state of deep, mutual involvement. However, one is on shaky ground in enumerating more specific indicants of love precisely because different people have different perceptions of love and therefore may make different attributions about the same state. For an attribution of romantic love, an intense sexual desire (at least initially) and an intense longing for the other's presence are probably necessary conditions. Most often, romantic love is a state within which each lover behaves as if the other's well-being and happiness are central, and as if the approval of the other is vital to their own happiness. Rubin (1973) asserts that this complementary needing and giving is the key dimension of romantic love. Other forms of love are less balanced, being weighted more toward giving (as parent for child) or needing (as child for parent). Still, there is a paradoxical nature to the giving-needing balance in romantic love. What appears to be giving from one perspective may be self-satisfying from another. Who is to say that the pleasure a man obtains from giving something to his lover is not as great as the pleasure she obtains from receiving it from him? Of the questionnaire items that Rubin (1973) has found to be best for measuring love, about an equal number have face validity as indicants of giving something to the lover and getting something from the lover. Perhaps the best summary is that romantic love is a state of deep mutual involvement in which exchanges of rewards take place that are highly satisfying to both lovers.

An Exchange Theoretic Model of Love. The algorithmic model of romantic love to be offered here is an exchange theoretic model. Its fundamental assumption is that a mutually satisfying sequence of interactions leads a couple from a state of surface contact with small rewards (Levinger and Snoek, 1972) into the highly rewarding state of deep mutual involvement called love.

The basis of this model of romantic love is Huesmann and Levinger's (1976 ; Levinger and Huesmann, 1980) incremental exchange theory. This theory postulates that a dyadic relationship can best be characterized as a progression through a number of levels of mutual involvement and through states of interaction within each level of involvement. The relationship may reach a steady state, a cycling among a subset of states and levels of involvement, or may eventually terminate. The dynamics of the movement are related to the exchange of rewards that occurs as a result of the behaviors undertaken in each state. Two central premises of the theory are that the actors are primarily self-seeking and that, other things being equal, their interpersonal rewards increase as their mutual involvement deepens. Mutual involvement becomes a psychological concept related to physical and social involvement but fundamentally different. A married couple living together harmoniously may have less mutual involvement than some courting couples and less involvement than at earlier stages of their relationship (or they may have more involvement). Mutual involvement therefore is best measured through the couple's perception of the level of interpersonal rewards available from interacting. As a couple becomes more deeply involved, the rewards exchanged are incremented. The greater the depth of involvement, the greater the exchange of rewards.

States of interaction and levels of involvement are displayed pictorially in Figure 1. Each step on the staircase represents a deeper level of involvement. On a given step, a block of interactions are possible. Each vertical plane in the block denotes a single potential state of interaction in which a variety of potential behaviors are available to the actors. Imagine a couple on the lowest step of the staircase at what Levinger and Snoek (1972) would call the point of surface contact. A variety of factors will influence exactly which state of interaction the couple is in at first. However, the outcome of their first interaction will certainly be a prime determinant of what happens next. A positive experience is likely to lead to other interactions which, if also positive, will eventually lead the couple to interactions on the higher steps of the involve-

Figure 1. A pictorial representation of levels of involvement and
states of interaction in a romantic relationship

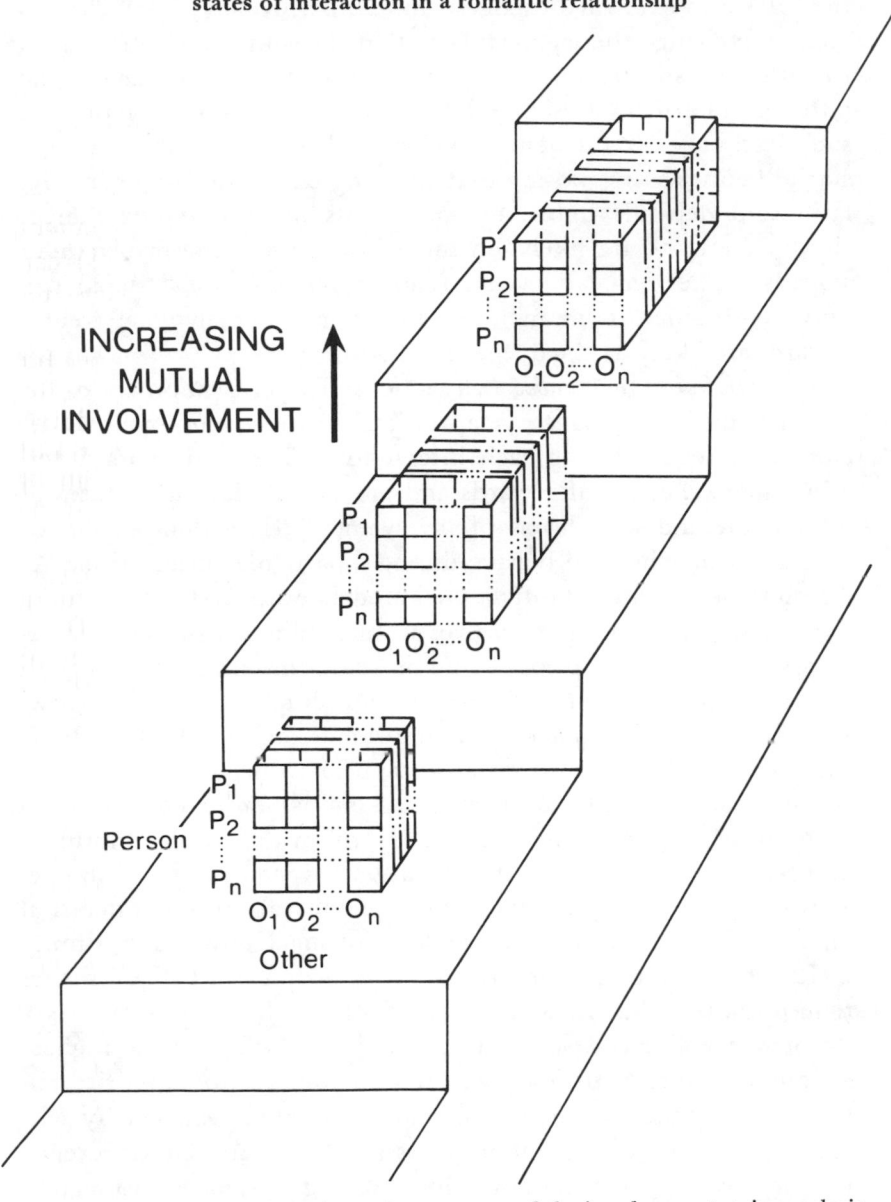

Note: Each vertical matrix on a step of the involvement staircase designates a different state of interaction at that level of mutual involvement. The rows of the matrix denote one person's behavior, the columns denote the other's, and the cells denote the outcomes.

ment staircase. What constitutes a positive experience? As a deriva-
tive of static exchange theory (Thibaut and Kelley, 1959), incremental exchange theory postulates that the value of an interaction
to either person depends upon the rewards they exchange. The
outcome matrices of Figure 1 are a convenient way to represent
such exchanges. Incremental exchange theory goes beyond such
static theories in proposing that the progress of the couple in a relationship depends upon the increments in potential exchanges
they perceive to be likely on the other steps of the involvement
staircase. The deepest levels of involvement (highest steps) can
only be obtained if the man and the woman perceive that greater
rewards are likely at the deeper levels.

   Satisficing in Dyadic Interactions. The critical processes for
each person in a romantic relationship are those employed to decide what to do during each interaction. These behaviors determine the exchanges of rewards and movements into new states of
interaction and new levels of involvement. How does a man or
woman decide how to behave during a particular interaction? As
we must begin with a motivational model, let us first entertain the
hypothesis that each person tries to maximize his or her own rewards. Such an assumption would make our model congruent with
most game theoretic models of behavior (Rapoport, 1966). However, it has the drawbacks that it offends our sensibilities about
the selflessness of love, it does not appear to be the motivational
strategy used for other decisions, and one is hard pressed to conceive of an information-processing algorithm that could determine
in a reasonable amount of time what behavior would maximize rewards. An alternative is suggested by empirical studies of decision
making (Simon, 1955) and problem solving (Newell and Simon,
1972) that seem to demonstrate that people "satisfice" rather
than optimize—that is, when a sufficiently high reward seems likely, people will settle for that reward even if it is not the highest
reward possible. Satisficing and optimizing are not opposite extremes. They both assume people are motivated primarily by self-
seeking. Both require a search of possible behaviors. The difference
is that the optimizer cannot stop searching, no matter how good
the outcome he has found, until he can prove it is the best possible.
For an optimizer, therefore, search may be unbounded. Unless certain special conditions (unlikely ones) are met, one can never be

certain that a local maximum is a global maximum. Although this distinction between optimizing and satisficing may be of negligible importance in most interactions, only a satisficing strategy is computationally plausible for a general model of dyadic interaction. The remaining objection to satisficing, as an underlying motivational strategy for lovers, is that it offends our notions about the selflessness of love. But it will be shown later that satisficing can lead lovers to behave in the most altruistic ways imaginable. If one considers only immediate gratifications, satisficing lovers may seem to do everything without regard for their own well-being according to the incremental exchange model.

Deciding How to Behave in Romantic Relationships. Given that men and women satisfice, how do they decide what to do during a specific interaction? Diverging from classical exchange theories, the model presumes that each lover estimates the utility of each possible outcome not only in the current state but also in likely future states. What makes a future state likely? The subjects apply various heuristics to decide what are likely successors to the current state of interaction. These states are then each examined to determine their utility and their likely successor states. The process repeats itself, and a rapidly expanding tree of potential states of interaction and rewards is constructed in this manner within each person's mind.

The construction of such a search tree need not be a conscious act. The proffered model, like all models, is an analogy. As Schneider and Shiffrin (1977) have argued, many information processes are automatic and relatively impervious to self-perception. Neither the lovers nor observers need be aware of how much the immediate behaviors of the lovers are determined by remote future consequences. The metaphorical descriptions of love as an out-of-control process ("falling in love," "head over heels in love," "crazy about her") are indicative of the limited relation between a lover's behavior and the immediate consequences.

The details of a reasonable heuristic search process for such a tree are too technical for presentation here (see Huesmann, in press). However, some understanding of the search process is necessary for an appreciation of how individual differences affect the decisions a man and woman make when the same potential outcomes are available. Imagine a tree on which each branch represents a potential state of interaction and level of involvement for a man and woman. According to the model, both the man and woman would grow such a tree in their minds, though there is no guarantee that the trees would look very similar. The pair may have quite different conceptions of where their relationship could go. Each can see only his or her own tree, and each always constructs the tree so that the base is the current state. After any interaction, the tree is regrown to reflect any changes with the current state as the new base.

Now consider the woman's problem of deciding what to do next. Her decision-making process can perhaps best be understood as analogous to finding a way to climb a fruit-laden tree. The woman looks up the trunk to the first place it forks. Each branch represents something she could do immediately; but these branches divide as well to denote the man's potential responses. Right after these divisions, she can see fruit that she could have if she got there, but the tree's branches also continue beyond the fruit to diverge again and again. She will have to make other choices, and she can see the branches for the man's responses to these choices and still more fruit of varying size and shape. In fact, the branches continue dividing this way ad infinitum until they disappear into the haze of the distance. The problem for the woman is which way to climb to obtain the most fruit in the long run. Descending from one branch and starting up another may be difficult or impossible in this tree. The woman must not only judge which branches have the most fruit but also guess what her partner will probably do for he controls her climb at every other fork. No matter which way the woman climbs, she may end up empty handed if her man chooses certain branches.

In this way, every potential romantic relationship can be viewed as a fruit-laden tree, but some will be perceived to have so little fruit that climbing them will not even be considered. Thus one question of importance is, What determines a person's initial perception of the fruit available on a tree? Secondly, as one climbs the tree and begins to see better, one may discover that one's perceptions were quite wrong, and the tree is much more or less bountiful than one had thought. Thirdly, while one is climbing one tree, one may suddenly perceive a more fruitful neighboring tree and wish to jump out of the current tree to start up the neighboring tree. All these questions of perception of reward in romantic involvements need to be addressed, but first let us see why different men and women might climb different branches of the same tree.

Individual Differences in Decision Making. There are three individual characteristics that can have vital influences on a man's or woman's decision making independently of who the romantic partner is. One is the depth of search of which a person is capable, and another is the extent to which the individual discounts future rewards in favor of immediate gratifications. Both of these factors determine the person's willingness to delay gratification in a romantic involvement and hence his or her likelihood of reaching a state of "being in love" regardless of the partner. Metaphorically, depth of search amounts to how far one can see out the branches of the tree, but from an information-processing viewpoint it is determined both by the cognitive limitations of the individual information processor and motivational factors. Deeper search requires more effort; yet one who searches deeply is more likely to detect the correct path to reach the desired level of involvement. Discounting of rewards, however, is strictly a motivational problem. Some individuals value a bird in the hand far more than two in the bush. Such discounting of future rewards will make the valuable branches representing deep mutual involvement seem relatively valueless when viewed from afar. As a result, they may never be approached closely enough so that their true value can be seen. The third factor affecting men and women's search of the tree of behaviors is their ability to predict their partners' reactions to their behaviors. The man or woman who can accurately gauge what branch his or her partner will choose is in a much better position to search the tree deeply because the breadth of search can be limited. Unlikely branches can be ignored. What determines one's ability to predict his or her partner's reactions? Although general cognitive abilities undoubtedly play a role, experience is probably the more important factor. People believe the behaviors are most likely that they have seen most often in similar situations (Bandura, 1977). Therefore, in the current model, the subjective probability estimates of the actors are assumed to follow a linear incremental learning curve. Some men and women with learning parameters close to unity change their estimates rapidly on the basis of experience, whereas others with parameters close to zero do not. These individual differences obviously can have a major influence on whether a couple reaches the state of love. For too fast a learner, one bad experience may effectively terminate the relationship by lowering his or her estimates of the partner's behaving nicely. For too slow a learner, changes in the partner's behaviors may not become apparent until too late.

Falling in Love. Romantic love, I have argued, is a state of deep mutual involvement characterized by significant equity in exchanges of rewards. "Falling in love" is the process of moving through rewarding states of interaction and deeper and deeper levels of involvement toward the end state. The theory is that both man and woman are self-seeking satisficers, but that they look far enough ahead in the tree of potential outcomes to see what behaviors will bring them happiness. In the short run, therefore, their behaviors may seem altruistic or purely giving when, in the long run, each is receiving as much as each is giving. That different people fall in love more or less easily can be explained primarily by differences in cognitive skills, differences in discounting delayed gratifications, and differences in perceptions of likely behaviors based on experience. But what determines a person's initial perception of the potential rewards at each level of a relationship? Commonly, exchange theoretic models have associated a reward or cost with each intersection of the two actors' behaviors. The framework within which incremental exchange theory has been cast illustrates the limitations of such a conception. If levels of involvement and states of interaction by themselves are to be desirable, they must possess rewarding properties.

Perceived Rewards in Romantic Interactions. In the context of our algorithmic model of romantic love, reward is a quantity that the actors need in order to be satisfied. A reward may be satisfying because it fulfills basic physiological needs or more abstract needs for actualization, achievement, or affiliation (for example, see Maslow, 1954; McClelland, 1961; Schachter, 1959.) Regardless of why a reward is satisfying, its importance to the progress of a romantic relationship may depend on its type. In a taxonomy proposed by Levinger and Huesmann (1980), three dimensions are suggested for classifying rewards: (1) behavioral versus relational,

(2) coactor dependent versus coactor independent, and (3) direct versus attributional.

Behavioral rewards are those that derive immediately from the behaviors of the lovers. Relational rewards, on the contrary, do not result from specific behaviors but stem from the state of interaction and level of involvement in which the actors find themselves. For example, the very fact of having a "lover" may be intensely rewarding independently of any specific behaviors. In contrast, the immediate gratifications obtained from "making love" would be behavioral rewards. Whereas relational rewards are received continuously as long as the level of the romantic relationship remains unchanged, behavioral rewards are received in distinct quanta. This behavioral-relational distinction is required by the process model of love being proposed. The entries in the exchange matrices of Figure 1 obviously depend on the behaviors represented by the rows and columns, whereas the rewards associated with each step on the staircase depend upon the level of involvement, not on specific behaviors. A relational reward may be activated by a specific event (for example, being seen in public) but it derives from the state of the relationship rather than from the event.

The distinction between rewards that are coactor dependent and coactor independent also originated with computational issues raised by the process model. To what extent can rewards be assigned to a person's payoff matrices and levels of involvement without knowing anything about the person's partner? Thibaut and Kelley (1959) touched on this issue with their discussion of "exogenous" and "endogenous" determinants. Coactor dependency is a more specific distinction illuminated by the process model. Although the value of most outcomes depends very much upon who is the coactor, the value of some does not. For example, the behavioral rewards a man experiences in seeing a particular movie may be independent of which woman accompanies him. More significantly, some components of the relational reward men and women receive from being in love may also be coactor independent (for example, being loved or the status reward of having a lover). In many situations, the dependency of a reward on the coactor may be difficult to measure. Some rewards that are coactor dependent actually depend only on the partner's having a particular characteristic, for example, beauty, power, or empathy. Coactor dependency is perhaps best viewed not as a dichotomy but as a continuum with few rewards falling at either extreme.

Another important distinction necessitated by the process model concerns whether a reward is direct or attributional. Attributional rewards arise from one's own or another's interpretation of an outcome or state. The behavioral rewards for specific outcomes may have both direct and attributional components. For example, sexual caresses produce direct rewards of physical pleasure and allow attributions about one's own desirability and worth to be made. Whereas direct rewards most often result from a single outcome, attributional rewards frequently are based on a sequence of outcomes or state of interaction. Many relational rewards clearly have a large attributional component. Dating a handsome man or beautiful woman is rewarding at least partially because of the attributions others (and perhaps yourself) make about you. By separating out the attributional and direct components of the rewards lovers receive, we can give the process model a more accurate initial reward structure in which some rewards are conditional upon certain attributions being made.

Habituation and Evaluation of Rewards. The foregoing is by no means intended to be a general taxonomy for reward. It does, however, describe the major dimensions of reward with which one must deal in explaining why people fall in love. Another very important point about reward in romantic interactions needs to be made. As exchange theorists have recognized for some time, rewards are not evaluated on an absolute scale and are not constant in value (Brickman and Campbell, 1971; Helson, 1964; Thibaut and Kelley, 1959). The value of any reward, behavioral or relational, direct or attributional, depends upon a person's current comparison level—that is, what they are expecting, are used to, and see available elsewhere. Since habituation is an inevitable fact of life, everyone's comparison levels fluctuate as a function of recent experience. What may have been highly rewarding at one time, may no longer be rewarding because it has been obtained so often. Acts of love that were intensely rewarding to a couple early in a relationship may no longer satisfy them later on. Similarly, the value of status rewards associated with being married or in a relationship may fade with time. The lovers' failure to recognize the inevitability of habituation and to correct their comparison levels for it may, in fact, lead to dissolution of the relationship because higher rewards appear to be available outside the relationship.

The inevitable fluctuation in the value of rewards as a function of previous experience introduces some further complexities into our process model of love. Several models for measuring the value of rewards are available, the most compelling being provided by Kahneman and Tversky (1979) in prospect theory. A major implication of this theory is that a person is most sensitive to gains or losses close to the person's current reference point (comparison level). Another is that people generally underevaluate gains as the gains are farther above the reference point and generally overevaluate the magnitude of losses as the losses are farther below the reference point. A third implication is that people generally act as if probabilities close to zero are higher than they are and as if other probabilities are lower than they are. Each potential reward from a relationship must be reevaluated in line with these principles as it is encountered in the search process the lovers use in deciding how to behave. These constant reevaluations are one reason why the attractiveness for a person of a potential romantic interaction is very sensitive to the person's recent romantic history. To a relatively unhappy person with few recent rewarding experiences, the potential gains from a particular romantic involvement may be evaluated quite highly, whereas the same involvement may be perceived as unrewarding to a person who has recently had a highly rewarding romantic experience.

There is one more aspect of the evaluation of gains and losses that is important in explaining why some people fall in love as they do. I have argued that the likelihood of a man and woman reaching a state of deep mutual love depends critically on their abilities to "look ahead," to estimate what their partner will do, and to delay gratification. For a couple that is falling in love, the pattern of rewards will usually slope sharply upward. Such upward sloping reward functions are customarily indicative of still higher rewards to come. This is true outside the arena of interpersonal relations as well as inside. Consequently, steeply sloping reward functions have obtained secondary reinforcing properties of their own. Western civilizations emphasize growth and achievement as the marks of success even perhaps more than the maintenance of a high reward level. The activity of achieving may sometimes be valued more by the achiever than the outcome itself, and achievement-oriented people may be more satisfied by low behavioral rewards with an apparent steep slope than by higher behavioral rewards with a gradual slope. In terms of our model, some people satisfice on the slope of the reward function instead of looking ahead more deeply and evaluating the total rewards obtainable. The problem this presents for potential lovers is that a steep slope may be local, and, regardless, all such slopes must eventually level off. Too heavy a reliance on the slope of the reward function could produce the classic example of the man who believes he is madly in love with a woman only to discover as soon as a certain level of intimacy is achieved (often sexual) that the relationship is no longer rewarding. Similarly, a woman may leave a reasonably rewarding but unchanging romantic involvement for a new involvement with a steeper slope only to discover that the slope levels off before a comparable reward level is reached. To one who attends more to the slope of the reward function than to the comparative values, "falling in love" will seem more satisfying than "being in love." Those especially prone to this difficulty would be those who greatly value achievement but who have difficulty looking deeply into the future.

A pessimistic view of this model of habituation and reevaluation of rewards in romantic relations would be that no two people can ever be happy for long in a stable relationship. Such a view is misleading. The theory does argue that the value of specific behavioral and relational rewards does not stay constant. But that does not mean that these rewards cannot be replaced with other equally valuable rewards. The real implications of the model are that continuing love requires an ever-changing array of exchanges of behavioral and relational rewards that are mutually satisfying. As lovers habituate to each other's physical presence and sexual attentions, they must supplement these behaviors with other mutually rewarding interactions. On the positive side, habituation to reward levels also means that, no matter how low one's current reward level is, one can be made happy by a little more reward.

Power, Status and Love. In the process of evaluating rewards, we have seen that actors must consider several fundamentally different types of rewards: behavioral, relational, direct, attributional, coactor dependent, coactor independent. Perhaps the most central of these for determining whether or not a couple falls in love are the coactor dependent, relational rewards. These are the rewards the lovers receive simply from being in their current state of involvement with each other. What exactly do the lovers give and receive that is so rewarding? Often among the most important items exchanged are power and status. Although power and status can easily be parameterized within the model, they are elusive, difficult-to-measure concepts. Their determinants differ greatly across sexes, cultures, and time. Certainly wealth and physical attractiveness are important determinants in most settings, but even these may be overshadowed by other factors. Nevertheless, the importance of the power and status of the partners in the development of romantic love seems clear.

As romantic relationships proceed to deep levels of involvement, and the pair conclude they are indeed in love, the power and status of the woman and man can be critical determinants of the relational rewards received by each. First, the greater the power or status of an individual, the greater would be that individual's options for partners, so the more flattering it would be for someone to have that person fall in love with them. This is an attributional, coactor dependent, relational reward. Second, each lover's power or status may "rub off" on the partner or be exchanged for other rewards. One partner may gain power from the other and give status to the other. These are direct, coactor dependent, relational rewards. Such principles could account within our model for the traditional pairing of a wealthy, powerful, but physically unattractive man with a weak, but beautiful young woman. The man's status is enhanced by the attributions he and others may make about his sexuality in attracting the woman, whereas the woman's power is undoubtedly enhanced by her involvement with the man. The interactors' power and status may also affect the value of certain behavioral rewards. For example, the pleasure derived from a sexual interaction may be enhanced by both partners' perception of their power and status. Power and status are valuable commodities in interpersonal interactions and increase one's own value as well as a partner's. From an exchange theoretical viewpoint, it is not surprising that many consider power to be "the ultimate aphrodisiac."

Power and status are relatively stable traits that change slowly over time. A man or woman is not likely to be charismatic one minute and weak the next. Nonetheless, changes may occur and from the viewpoint of our model such changes may have major impacts on relationships. A man who suddenly loses his job or suffers other professional setbacks may value the companionship of his wife more because his self-esteem can be bolstered by her loving him. The status rewards she can give him are now worth more to him. At the same time, the woman may find his companionship less rewarding because he is no longer as powerful. Cultural changes such as America's emerging emphasis on careers for women also may influence relationships because of the power-status exchange. Whereas women used to be valued primarily on the basis of physical attractiveness, social class, wealth, and homemaking abilities, today a man may obtain greater relational rewards of status and power from involvement with a successful professional woman.

Although the partner's power and status may play some role in determining the relational rewards exchanged in almost every love affair, other needs of the lovers cannot be ignored. Furthermore, too large a discrepancy between power or status of the lovers may cause each to make attributions that are destructive of the relationship. An unattractive person may presume that a very attractive partner's interest in him can only be due to his wealth or status. Similarly, a very attractive, low-status individual may attribute a powerful, high-status partner's interest as merely physical. The paradox is that the very differences in power and status that provide the opportunity for a mutually satisfying exchange can destroy any chance of a deep involvement if they are perceived to be the causes of the attraction.

Simulating the Process of Love. The essential elements of the algorithmic, process model of love have now been presented. A man and woman move from a state of surface contact to a state of deep mutual involvement called love in a series of steps involving an incrementing exchange of rewards. The lovers cognitively search the tree of potential future interactions to find a satisficing path of behaviors. The potential rewards at the level of deep mutual involvement must appear satisfying enough to both lovers that alternative directions for the relationship and alternative relationships are passed up. While in love, as during the process of falling in love, the potential exchange of rewards from being in love must be perceived to be so valuable that more immediately gratifying behaviors are passed by. Still, the laws of habituation to reward require that the rewards exchanged constantly change if the state of love is to be maintained. Both men and women are self-seeking satisficers, but in so behaving they satisfy their lovers as well.

A number of simulations of this process model have been run on computers to demonstrate how many of the common phenomena of falling in love are predictable. These simulations have shown, for example, that the apparently altruistic behavior characteristics of lovers are an inevitable concomitant of a relationship in which deeper mutual involvement brings higher rewards and in which the altruistic behavior is necessary to achieve deeper involvement. These simulations also revealed the role of individual differences in falling in love. The farther simulated men or women looked into the future, and the less they discounted delayed rewards, the more likely they were to fall in love (that is, reach the state of deepest mutual involvement). Unlike the predictions of other exchange models, the more each expected the other to behave "altruistically," the more each behaved "altruistically." With regard to the role of similarity between the man and woman, the simulations suggested that one specific type of similarity was particularly important. Payoff correspondence is defined as the extent to which the man and woman receive comparable rewards in the same cell of a payoff matrix or at the same level of involvement. The simulations revealed that the more payoff correspondence there was between a man and woman, the more likely they were to fall in love. Other types of similarity—for example, symmetry of payoffs—had no effect.

The occurrence of behavior that appears altruistic in the immediate context but has been committed in expectation of later gratification presents a definitional problem. Is it altruistic behavior? It fulfills the requirement that a person is sacrificing his own pleasure and enhancing his lover's, but the ultimate aim is self-satisfaction. Actually, the model predicts altruistic behavior in a second situation that may fit the definition better. Although the model asserts that all people satisfice their own rewards, a person in a deep state of love with another might obtain vicarious pleasure from the other's rewards to such an extent that his or her behavior would appear altruistic. The behaviors performed would be those that would give high rewards to the lover at the person's own apparent expense. But, of course, the person would actually again be gratifying himself or herself with the vicarious rewards.

The simulations of romantic interactions also have led to the definition of a number of levels of involvement and states of interaction along the continuum between surface contact and deep romantic love. Recognizing that there may be multiple pathways to the state of deep mutual involvement called love, Huesmann and Levinger (1976; Levinger and Huesmann, 1980) defined a set of states and accompanying transition matrices that partially ordered the levels of involvement along the way to love. Several of the states were viewed as tests that the couple needed to pass before moving to a deeper state of involvement. Interestingly, it was at these points that the simulated couples often stopped progressing to deeper involvement. The important characteristic of these states was that progress to a deeper level of involvement required one of the pair to go out on a limb. High rewards were available if they took a chance and their partner behaved as a lover would, but high costs were possible if the partner did not. Yet one person had to initiate if any progress were to be made. Requests for interaction, disclosures of intimacies, sexual behavior, and commitment behavior all fell in this class. The simulated romantic relationship would often progress to one of these states and no further because neither partner would initiate the needed behavior. What distinguished those relationships that progressed from those that did not were the speed with which the actors changed their estimates of what their coactors would do and the perceived value of a deep involvement. Of course, the greater the perceived value, the more likely the lovers were to overcome the obstacle. More interestingly, if either lover changed his or her expectations about the partner's behavior too rapidly, their relationship was not likely to progress. They would quickly become convinced that their partner's reticence was permanent and stop trying to advance the relationship.

The process model has also been used in attempts to predict the course of specific romantic relationships (Huesmann and Levinger, 1976). However, as with most exchange theoretical models, the difficulties in estimating rewards and options make such applications of problematic value. The major value of the simulations stems from the general principles they elucidate. Nevertheless, if one wishes to predict the likely outcome of a romantic relationship, this algorithmic process model, I would assert, provides the best chance for success. While the matching algorithms based on gross similarity used by computer dating services may be easy to operate and should have some weak validity (since they must measure payoff correspondence to some degree), a more intensive analysis of the couple's reward structures is mandatory for valid predictions.

Conclusions

The process model described in this chapter and the conclusions derived from it may be objectionable to many people. One is on dangerous grounds when one attempts to formalize love. Nevertheless, the model is more precise and unambiguous than others and is in accord with the current cognitive view of man as an information processor. It is generally consistent with our empirical knowledge about love, though its utility in predicting behavior in actual relationships is marginal. The insights into reward, search, decision making, and stages of love provided by the model form a framework for further research. Many of the conclusions drawn from the model will remain speculative until such research is undertaken. Still, the ease with which the incremental exchange model accounts for numerous phenomena of love makes the theory worth maintaining until disconfirmed by data. Perhaps the essence of the model can best be summarized by a quote from Shakespeare (*A Midsummer Night's Dream*, I, 1, 234): "Love looks not with the eyes, but with the mind."

10

Romantic Fantasy in Personality Development

Jerome L. Singer

Although there were accounts of love in the writings of the Greeks and Romans, the classic myths and legends lack a sense of mystery or of romance in the way that we view romantic love today. The *Iliad* or the writings of Ovid were full of adventure, sexual pursuit, and magic, but there was little emphasis on the overestimation of the beloved or on the inner quality of the imagination that characterizes the Romantic Movement of the turn of the nineteenth century or the Renaissance. Love and sex were largely the same thing. When Zeus desired Europa he took the convenient form of a bull to snatch her away. He made no poems or sang no serenades to her. The ancient literature has some instances of tender feeling between a couple but these occur in family situations, such as the parting of Hector and Andromache before he set out to battle with Achilles, or the reunion of Odysseus and Penelope. The love poems of Catullus involve some extravagant metaphors, but there is no overestimation of the beloved who is usually represented as a seductive, fickle, or unavailable courtesan.

One must wait until the medieval period to find early signs in poetry of what we call the romantic attitude or of the elaborate introspection of the lover. Dante's idealization of a young girl he saw only occasionally and her elevation to Heaven in his great epic *The Divine Comedy* represents an early manifestation of this exaggerated elaboration of youthful fantasy into a broader structure that mixes religious symbolism with the kinds of thoughts one has in adolescent fantasies into a unified artistic structure. The sonnets of Petrarch to his Laura or the more extravagant paintings of sheer fantasy of Hieronymus Bosch introduce a "make-believe" dimension more and more. Make-believe and extravagance are perhaps two key features of romanticism—the suspension of judgment, perhaps an exaggeration and idealization that many of us can identify from our own night dreams or reverie meanderings.

In a book that has some of the very poetic and mythic quality he seeks himself to understand, Julian Jaynes (1976) has sought to argue that until somewhere between the first and second millenium B.C. the human brain was not sharply differentiated into two distinctly functioning hemispheres. Human beings did not engage in conscious reflection or introspection; instead they hallucinated their own thoughts and wishes in the form of voices of their tribal chieftains or gods. Following the vast destructions of tight-knit communities by earthquakes and invasions that broke down most of society in the period around 1500 B.C., people were increasingly forced to survive by relying on their own individualized memories, fantasies, and capacities for deception. The notion of "I" began to be introduced in literature during this time since only someone who could mentally remember a series of alternative events while simulating compliance with the wishes of the new lord or conqueror might avoid destruction. In effect, Jaynes' proposal is that self-consciousness is an evolutionary development that is quite recent. One might take this a step further and suggest that even within this framework the romantic attention to elaborate

exploration of one's own fancies and night dreams may reflect
a further differentiation of human capacity, whether or not it involves any actual anatomical changes in the brain structure.

Shakespeare is full of references to the "fantastical," to the
wild flights of imagination and to dreams. Plays like *A Midsummer
Night's Dream* or *The Tempest* have greatly enriched our own culture's capacity for generating imagination and becoming sensitive
to its free play. In Shakespeare's tragedy of young love, *Romeo and
Juliet*, we have not only the exaggerated attribution to the loved
one's appearing—"It is the east and Juliet is the sun"—but also the
speech of Mercutio about Queen Mab with its gossamer and sensu-
ous evocation of the fairies. When Juliet awakes from her drugged
sleep in the tomb of the Capulets, she is momentarily overwhelmed
by her own fantasies of ghosts, a very natural experience that
evokes for all of us similar night terrors.

The origins of romanticism lie in heightened self-consciousness, a readiness to play out extravagant images or to recall night
dreams and fancies aroused by the loved one or by scenery or the
mysterious and unknown. Until the turn of this century, total
darkness following sunset was a characteristic of most human habi-
tation. Cities were not well lighted, the countryside was almost
black at night, and people rarely ventured forth in the evening for
fear of urban marauders or the presumed unhealthy quality of
night air. In homes that were poorly illuminated and heavily dependent on the flickering of firelight, one might indeed become
easily frightened by sudden shadows or flashes of light. Under
these circumstances, the child in bed at night or even young adults
were prey to many fears and fancies.

The romantic movement in literature and music evolved
more self-consciously than it had previously in the twenty years
between 1790 and 1810, a period of tremendous revolution, social
change, and power redistribution in Europe. It was in part a revolt
against the formal classicism so linked to the notion of aristocracy,
a structured hierarchy, and a whole society ruled by kings and nobility. Poets like Wordsworth, Blake, and Coleridge, and soon after,
Keats, Byron, and Shelley reflected the efforts of the change in
power by actively attempting to use their own dreams, their night-
evoked imagery, and indeed their childhood memories to enrich
and enlarge experience. Such efforts had a revolutionary quality at

first, a dethroning of the aristocracy and of the extreme rationalism and formality of the "classical" power structure.

The word *romantic* in itself, traceable to the French word
roman or legend, has a connotation implying a far-off setting in
the days of the ancients, and this provides a clue to the significance of romanticism. It involves storytelling, although not in the
simple fashion of a beginning, middle, and end. It takes on more
of the quality of a dream or fantasy in which unusual or odd turns
of events occur. Strange characters from mythology or legendry
are a part of this type of story. Bizarre and magical poems like
Coleridge's *Christabel* and *The Ancient Mariner* involve an evocation of an imagined past, stimulated by newly discovered paintings
or manuscripts of medieval lore.

In music, Hector Berlioz, one of the few musicians of the
period who had heard and appreciated the mind-stretching explorations in Beethoven's late string quartets, produced his *Fantasic
Symphony* in 1830. Here the music evokes the wild fantasies and
drug-induced imagery of a young man who has taken an overdose
of barbiturates. His mind wanders to scenes of the past, to great
balls, and ultimately to a wild witches' revel where the chilling
medieval chant of the world's end, "Dies Irae," is heard. Today
a film can provide some of this same impact. Indeed, one of the
most haunting scenes of Ingmar Bergman's *The Seventh Seal* occurs
with the march into the town of the black monks whipping chained
penitents, a practice developed to end the great plague, all the while
singing that same haunting chant about the day of judgment.

In summary, the notion of romantic fantasy and of romanticized love involves components of exaggerated and dreamlike evocation of one's thoughts and a heightened self-consciousness in
general, and perhaps reevocation of details from the past. At various times in the reactions of older generations against the romanticism of youth, much is made of the exaggerated attributions of
beauty and the overevaluation of the past and legendary figures.
Shakespeare himself jokes at the ardent adolescent who composes
a poem to his loved one's "eyebrow." The romantic lover is drawn
not just to a high cheekbone or a longing narrowed eye in the loved
one but to the way such features evoke images of the bust of the
Egyptian queen Nefertiti, so long a symbol of beauty. The image
of "star-crossed" young lovers, caught up in their fancies and ex-

travagantly adoring each other in the face of adversity, has become almost an eternal symbol of youth. *Romeo and Juliet* continues to hold the stage and to move us after four hundred years. Edmond Rostand's play, *Les Romantiques*, originally a kind of good-natured spoof of adolescent romanticism, was popular around the turn of the century in Paris. Rewritten and put to music in New York in the 1950s, it has run continuously in Greenwich Village to successive new generations of young lovers under the title *The Fantasticks.*

Romanticism and the Stream of Consciousness

Around the turn of the century, romanticism evolved into an even more self-conscious form. Attention began to be paid in both literature and psychology not only to the products of imagery and fantasy but also to the very process of the ongoing stream of consciousness. The emergence of self-conscious attention to "the remembrance of things past" (Proust) or to specific evocations of the ongoing throught stream by such writers as Dorothy Richardson, Virginia Woolf, and James Joyce, initiated a new era in the writings of fiction that has been an important feature of twentieth-century literature. In this same period, William James introduced the notion of the stream of consciousness as a psychological problem in his *Principles of Psychology*, which was first published in 1890. Within the same decade, Sigmund Freud began the use of the free association method as a part of the psychoanalytic treatment of neurotic patients.

Freud himself, in tracing the origins of his introduction of this procedure, was able to link it to his own reading in adolescence of the writings of Ludwig Bourne, a romanticist of the early nineteenth century. In 1823 Bourne had written: "And here follows the practical application that was promised. Take a few sheets of paper and for three days on end write down, without fabrication or hypocrisy, everything that comes into your head. Write down what you think of yourself, of your wife, of the Turkish War, of Goethe, . . . of the *Last Judgment*, of your superiors—and when three days have passed you will be quite out of your senses with astonishment at the new and unheard-of thoughts you have had.

This is the art of becoming an original writer in three days." (Freud, 1957f, p. 265).

Despite these early beginnings, psychology underwent a fifty-year period of largely ignoring the importance of the ongoing stream of consciousness for developing models of human personality and cognition. Only more recently has there been more extensive recognition of the central role of imagery and ongoing thought as a basic part of human capacity and behavior (Pope and Singer, 1978a, 1978b).

In essence, the new scientific model of the stream of consciousness implies that, first of all, it is possible that the brain is constantly playing and replaying in some form established memories and previous fantasies or thoughts rather than storing them in a fixed location. This ongoing activity, in essence part of the very workings of the brain, may be in a sense a form of alternate stimulation which we must inevitably learn to ignore in the interests of processing new material from the external environment in order to steer ourselves through the world. Nevertheless, there are periods in which the demands of environmental stimulation are reduced or are so redundant that we can in effect pay more attention to the seeming random generator from within. Each time, we become aware of fleeting images, recurrent fantasies, and bizarre associations. This is especially true when we awaken from night dreams, but there are many situations of daytime reverie when similar associations become apparent. In addition, once we have established an orientation, as indeed most creative artists do, to paying more sustained attention to our thoughts and fantasies, we become even more aware of fleeting associations and links of current experiences to experiences from our own past life or to material we have read in books or seen in the cinema or on television.

Although to some extent this inner stream of stimulation is competitive and potentially distracting from some of the information processing that must go on if we are to avoid getting hit by buses as we cross the street or walking into telephone poles, we nevertheless can identify adaptive functions for this ongoing stream of thought. It is possible to identify certain rules for what types of thoughts are more likely to occur regularly. Pope and Singer (1978a) have referred to some of these rules, and Klinger (1978) has pointed to the special importance of a hierarchy of "current concerns" as a principal source for the ideation that recurs in the stream of consciousness. Experimental demonstrations of some of these effects have been reviewed extensively in Pope and Singer (1978a).

A recent, as yet unpublished study by Klos and Singer (1980) attempted to tease out systematically the various components of an earlier experience that recurred in the stream of consciousness of a group of adolescents. Simple incompletion of an ongoing task is more likely to lead to greater recurrence of this situation in later thought samples, a demonstration of the *Zeigarnik Effect*. As part of the experiment, some of these youths had experienced a simulated parent-adolescent conflict which was of a nonconstructive nature in its style of confrontation. Such an experience led to a greater likelihood of this material recurring in later thought. The fact of having undergone such parent-child conflicts recently in simulation (in effect, in imagery) led to further evocation of other parent-related concerns in the life situation of the individual to a greater extent than was evident in the stream of consciousness of those who had not experienced conflict. Finally, these effects of recurrences of fairly recent experiences in the stream of consciousness were especially strong for those adolescents who had undergone recent simulated conflict but who had also reported on questionnaires that they were themselves unhappy with the actual parental figures of their home life.

Studies of this kind provide an increasingly systematic picture that the stream of consciousness is a major arena in which issues of personal significance—some conflictual, some merely involving puzzlement and exploration—are played and replayed. Consider also the possibility that our own thoughts can evoke particular emotions by occasionally surprising us or by providing us with complex and unassimilable material (Izard, 1977; Singer, 1974; Tomkins, 1962, 1963). We can see that the stream of consciousness is a major form of human reality. We live therefore not just with the joys, the surprises, or fears of the material in our physical environment or with the anger or sadness evoked by our inability to escape from frustrating external circumstance. Our own thoughts become similar sources for the positive affects of interest and joy or the negative affects of fear, anger, or sadness. The rate and complexity of material that we have to process as well as its specific content undoubtedly play a role in the range and intensity of our affects.

Part of the function of the stream of consciousness is to explore novel environments and to see where we can find matches from longtime memory that will reduce uncertainty and extreme novelty to manageable proportions. A loud telephone call in the middle of the night will certainly startle a sleeping parent. An initial response to this unexpected stimulus will be surprise and even terror until, as one searches one's long-term memory, one quickly remembers that a son, traveling abroad, had been instructed to telephone as soon as he has arrived safely back in the United States. The experience, then, as one picks up the phone, is not further terror but of joy and excitement as one looks forward to hearing the familiar voice.

Much of our daily life and of the various projects we have undertaken for ourselves lacks the certainty of such expectations. Inevitably therefore our stream of consciousness reverts again and again to these unresolved issues or current concerns, playing out a range of possibilities, some perhaps gloomy and foreboding, others perhaps more wishful and fanciful in a positive sense. In the course of such exploration, we may forge new associational links between events and create new concepts, schema, or in effect, practical plans.

The stream of consciousness therefore is now a central part of any theory of the human personality. Recently even committed social learning theorists, emerging from the more narrow operationalism of American behaviorism, are talking increasingly of notions of self-efficacy (Bandura, 1977). Human beings make choices in their direct interactions with others not only on the basis of an immediate evaluation of the structural characteristics of the situation but also based on days, weeks, indeed years of practice of mental achievements and evaluations which are part of the ongoing thought stream.

From this perspective, we no longer need to view romantic fantasy and at least some of the manifestations of romantic love as inherently "unrealistic" or "escapist." Attention to one's ongoing stream of thought, learning how to identify recurrences in that stream and to manipulate in a playful or planful fashion some of the currents, can yield significant adaptive benefits. The ongoing stream of thought is as much a part of the reality of the human condition as the activities of our senses.

The Sources of Romantic Fantasy

It is increasingly clear that the origins of imaginativeness and the stream of consciousness can be traced to the ongoing make-believe play of children (Singer, 1973; Singer and Singer, 1976). Piaget (1962) early called attention to the two major processes of *accommodation* and *assimilation* through which the child processes information in its earliest years until eventually it moves toward organized and logical thought. Accommodation involves attempts at an imitation of adult movements and gestures, and assimilation links such imitative efforts to the small number of already well-established memory schema available to the child. This effort at assimilation of new material into a relatively limited repertory of memories accounts sometimes for what we consider the quaintness or cuteness of children's play behavior. A four-year-old is seen playing on a kitchen floor, lining up toy soldiers in row after row, ready apparently for combat. Upon inquiry from his mother he replies: "I'm getting all my soldiers ready to rescue Daddy. I hear you talking on the telephone and saying that Daddy was all tied up at work." Two young twin girls in England develop an imaginary playmate called Fetiss with whom they both play together or individually for several years between ages three and five. It should be noted that their mother was pregnant with a third child during the period when the fantasy began.

These early efforts at assimilation undoubtedly lead to bizarre associations and odd connections. Many of these may never be corrected because the children never make them known to adults. Clearly this can account for long-standing distortions and confusions that may be at the least embarrasing or in some cases a source of serious pathology in later life. Inadvertent maternal comments to children touching their genitals, such as "Don't rub so or it will fall off," may become a source of long-standing, uncommunicated, and untested doubts about sexual potency or fears of masturbation.

A great deal of children's play in the first five years of life takes the form of games of making believe and pretending. Extensive research (Singer and Singer, 1976; Singer, 1977; Singer, Singer, and Sherrod, 1980) identified particular patterns of ongoing play that characterize some children more than others. It seems clear that although all children are capable of imaginative and symbolic play for brief periods, some are more prone to engage in it than others and are more consistent in their resort to this type of play. Such evidence suggests that imaginative play is inherently enjoyable and is generally associated with expressions of positive affect, intense interest, and smiling (Singer, 1979). The child who has created a brief miniature world, reducing the external environment from its complexity and confusion to a manageable size and then manipulating this small world in exaggerated fashion under one's own control, evokes the continuing affect of interest, surprise, and joy. The child engaged in make-believe play is already an active romanticist. R. Gould (1972) has assembled transcripts of spontaneous play of children from which they develop a game of "digging for princesses." For the children, the princess is some young, grand, and noble creature, perhaps a little magical in quality and apparently also somewhat confused with treasure and with witches. They create a game of searching to find these creatures by digging.

In the course of imaginative play, children experiment with new combinations of images and ideas, new vocabulary words and sentence structures. Therefore, it is not surprising that one finds that children who are more likely to engage in imaginative play also show a richer and more fluent vocabulary, greater evidence of storytelling capacity in other situations, greater empathy through the role playing inherent in the fantasy games, and a variety of other useful adaptive skills as part of socialization (Singer and Singer, 1976, 1980).

What makes for individual differences in the early resort to imaginative play? It is conceivable that there are constitutional factors that may come into play, although these have not been studied. What is increasingly evident is that although make-believe efforts are inherently part of the information processing of the child, as Piaget (1962) has suggested, the tendency to develop content for use in the game, to sustain play, and in a sense to continue such activities into the early school years is largely a function of parental input. In the research on imaginative play, there are indications that those children who seem happiest and who show leadership and greater cooperation with other children are also those who were more likely to have been exposed to story telling and reading by parents (Singer and Singer, 1976; Shmukler, 1978). In one study (Singer and Singer, 1980), it was found that those children who were relatively heavy watchers of television but who did not show very much influence of the TV action shows on their own aggressive behavior were children whose parents spent time with them reading and telling stories. This storytelling by parents may have presented an alternative form of behavior besides acting it out directly with peers for elaborating on the aggressive material the children saw on television.

Despite the fears of many that exposure to stories and fantasy may lead children away from reality, there seems little evidence from research that this is the case. Instead, accounts of the lives of famous scientists and humanists and artists (Cobb, 1977) indicates a frequent experience of imaginative play and storytelling in the individual's early history. As I have suggested, the manipulation of complex and difficult-to-grasp objects as kings and queens, airplanes, rocket ships, or strange goblins provides the child with some capacity for feeling at least temporary control and gradual assimilation of the material into a set of stored memories and new schema. In a sense, the telling to children of stories about kings or about famous heroes or exciting voyages, which characterizes many relationships between parents and children or, in the past, between uncles and aunts or grandparents and children, may have represented a very similar assimilation attempt by the adults themselves. In the long nights in a rural abode, the older folks might recount Bible stories about far-off lands or might talk about a king who seemed as remote and awesome to them as to the children. In the telling of such a story, the adults have some of the same pleasure of control and manipulation of the remote and powerful as the children get in further replaying the material. The difference may lie in the fact that for children the assimilation process, since it involves so much that is new, takes a longer period of time and is set against a more limited range of memory schema, so that associations are more bizarre and fanciful than they may be for the adults.

From a cognitive affective point of view, we can see that when material that is novel is presented at a moderate pace or under conditions of security and warmth such as occurs with a parent or other adults present, the child may experience brief fear but quickly transfer this to interest and curiosity because of the security of the parents' participation. This is not the case when adults for their own sadistic pleasure undertake to frighten children actively by telling them ghost stories or by tormenting them about possible death or kidnap by fairies or goblins. When Samuel Johnson, the great literary figure of the eighteenth century, was discussing with his friend Mrs. Thrale what book she might buy her young children, he said: "Babies do not want to hear about babies; they like to be told about giants and castles, and of somewhat which can stretch and stimulate their little minds" (Bate, 1977, p. 21).

Children are confronted with a great deal in the world that they cannot make sense of or integrate. This comes furthermore in situations at bedtime. In the darkness, the world seems to disappear for shadows on the wall are confusing and frightening. Since the child may already have heard about goblins or dragons, these night movements may be assimilated into frightenting notions. Older children may take advantage of the fears of the younger ones by identifying strange wind or chimney noises as mysterious and frightening when they themselves have already overcome their own earlier misconceptions. Even at older ages, these childhood night terrors, although better understood, may never be completely relinquished. Certainly the affect associated with such experiences can recur through one's lifetime and indeed can be played upon again and again in literature or theatrical representations. The sinister sexuality of Dracula, a figure who haunted theatergoers and earlier moviegoers in the 1920s and 1930s, reemerged in the 1970s with as great a vividness because it depicts, particularly for girls, some of the mixture of sensuality and initial excitement about sex as well as the terror of the night experienced alone in bed. The demon lover is a symbol going back to medieval days and it recurs frequently in the romantic poetry and novels of the early nineteenth century.

The sources of input into a child's imagination thus become tales told or read by parents, children's lore repeated in darkened rooms, sometimes with malicious intent to tease and frighten, and, in the modern era, television, movies, and popular music. We are just beginning to comprehend the extent to which television, now in effect a member of the family (Singer and Singer, 1980), may be having upon the consciousness of the growing child. Indeed, by one year of age, children are already averaging about an hour a day of watching television, and recent statistics even suggest that by the time they enter school, children will have spent more time watching television than they will ever spend in high school or college. What effect does this prepackaged fantasy have upon imaginative development?

One thing is clear. The play of young children is increasingly characterized by reenactments of scenes from television. Most common are identification in play with superheroic figures—Superman, Batman, the Incredible Hulk, the Bionic Man, or the Bionic Woman. The imaginary playmates of preschool children are increasingly likely to be drawn from such figures. It is even possible that the availability of both male and female superheroes has changed the general tendency of girls from relatively minimal aggression to a more active and often violent role in nursery school play. Boys, unlike girls, still continue to identify primarily with male superheroes and eschew playing one of Charlie's Angels or Wonder Woman (Singer and Singer, 1980).

Imaginary playmates make their appearance somewhere between the ages of two and three and flourish in the preschool years. Data from a study of more than 100 preschoolers (Singer and Singer, 1980) have made it clear that children who have imaginary playmates are less likely to be heavy television watchers. They have an imaginary play situation they can handle and construct themselves. There are other suggestions that imaginary play as part of a child's repertory may be adaptively useful to the child as an alternative to heavy television viewing *or* to the influence upon the child of the viewing of the more violent action programs that are most likely to be correlated with overt aggressive behavior by the child.

Imaginary playmates may arise through compensatory efforts on the part of the lonely child or a child in isolated circumstances. It is also true that parental storytelling and encouragement may provide children with the potential for developing such a playmate. Such fantasy activity may be quite useful and adaptive, whatever its original basis for development. Indeed, research studies indicate that persons who are especially creative are significantly more likely to mention that they had imaginary playmates as children (Singer and Singer, 1976).

Imaginative play and the symbolic games of children provide the bases for a network of associational structures and indeed an entire repertory of potential behavior that can be satisfying to the child. Through pretend play, the child learns that he or she can control and manipulate much of the complex information about his or her own body as well as deal with the painful but exhilarating and healthy movement from the bosom of the family. With the advent of the school years, it is very likely that make-believe play, which is often spoken aloud by children through the kindergarten years, must go underground. That is to say, children have to learn increasingly not to talk aloud in class and indeed they may be shamed by older children to whom they are increasingly exposed if they become engrossed in a fantasy game and imitate the sound effects or say the words aloud. This forces upon them greater resort to private symbolic thinking or egocentric thought, as Piaget (1962) called it.

In this same period, the child is most likely to be learning how to read and to use books to some degree as a further source of imaginative stimulation. In addition to exposure to a broader peer group, the child becomes further assimilated into a new level of culture. In our society, where large segments of the commercial communications industry are now directed at encouraging children to buy "lollipop" music or to respond to particular popular idols on radio and television, there is an earlier thrust toward romantic daydreams than probably ever was the case before in society. Research by Gottlieb (1973) has examined fantasy patterns of elementary and junior high school children and has shown how the heavy emphasis on adventure and exploration in younger children shifts toward romance, particularly for girls, around puberty.

The explosion of availability of communication media undoubtedly has played a role in this development. In the late eighteenth and throughout the nineteenth centuries, the major sources of popular stimulation available to young people in societies with increasing literacy rates (as was the case in England and France) were the popular novels and, somewhat later, the popular women's magazines. Although these romantic materials took the form of elaborate and complex novels such as *Thaddeus of Warsaw*, a favorite of adolescent girls and women in the ninetheenth century, there was really very little alternative form of popular entertainment widely available. Occasional traveling troupes of actors might have a brief effect. A novel of Dickens, however, could be published almost simultaneously throughout England and, within a month or so, in the United States. This made Dickens, during the mid 1800s, the closest thing to a popular television performer or rock-and-roll star of today, even though the vast majority of individuals never saw him. His tours involving readings from his novels were tremendously popular in the 1860s.

The immediacy of the cinema and its miniaturized representation on television has made tremendous changes in the audience accessible to encouragement of romantic fantasy. Even if there once was a so-called latency period in children's development, a presumed decline in sexual interest between ages six and thirteen, it is unlikely that such a repression of interest would be possible today in view of the tremendous stimulation concerning sexuality represented both in movies and on television. A great deal of sexual innuendo and even the meaning of sexual behavior such as can be represented on film may be lost on the relatively young children. Even so, they are increasingly exposed to idealized images of much-sought-after males and females who begin to people their fantasies increasingly, well before the age of twelve or thirteen. Accordingly to our own research, the glossily handsome figures of Donny and Marie are watched by a sizable percentage of preschool children and even more children in their early school ages. Programs like "Charlie's Angels" and "Wonder Woman" are full of sexual innuendo and flamboyant sexual teasings. It is likely that these shows begin to arouse a sense of curiosity in young viewers about what characteristics seem especially desirable in the sexual partner.

With the onset of sexuality and its more grossly physiological manifestations at puberty, children often begin to masturbate. Here it is likely that fantasies now include figures from television and reading or from magazines like *Playboy* or *Penthouse*. Often the masturbatory fantasy may become a regular representation of a famous rock-and-roll or television star. One young woman developed an elaborate fantasy of having intercourse with Mick Jagger, a member of the Rolling Stones. When she began having sexual intercourse regularly as a "groupie" following different bands around, she always reverted, during the act itself, to images of her childhood fantasy of Mick. In the course of her travels as a "groupie," she actually finally encountered the real Mick Jagger. In bed with him at last, she still found it necessary to resort to her *fantasy* Mick Jagger because the real one, after all, was not as prodigiously gifted in bed as she had long fantasized him to be.

In summary, the make-believe play of children gradually merges into unspoken private play and thence to the ongoing stream of thought. In many young people there develops a set toward a moderately well-controlled playful exploration of possibilities through imagery. It seems increasingly clear that this dimension of fantasy is not in itself inherently escapist or self-defeating. Rather it is simply an alternative feature of an adult's behavioral repertoire that permits a sense of control of novelty, exploration of potentiality, and rehearsal or review of past events, material from stories or popular media, or anticipations of upcoming events. Of course, a particular child may use fantasy to escape from a world where he fears he cannot cope or in which he has been manifestly unsuccessful. Research evidence suggests, however, that the very act of elaborating fantasy possibilities may carry with it self-practice in behavior and in the development of cognitive and affective skills that have adaptive values. The data in children's studies suggests that it is the child who *lacks* the capacity for fantasy who is more likely to engage in impulsive behavior and to get into interpersonal difficulties (Singer and Singer, 1976, 1980; Singer and Brown, 1977).

Daydreaming and Romantic Possibility

Adolescence is widely believed to be the period of greatest daydreaming possibility. To the extent that it is possible to measure the amount of time spent in fantasy activity or the variety of fantasies, data seem to support this view (Singer, 1975). The adolescent has by this time a broader range of experience and exposure through books, records, and television or the cinema, to a huge range of desirable life-styles and potential sexual partners, companions, or career choices. At the same time, during the adolescent period in our society, very few strict burdens are placed upon a youngster. In effect, it is unclear to the teenager just what serious limitations the realities of a particular society may impose. This is perhaps less true in many parts of the world than in the more affluent Western, European, or North American countries. Nevertheless, there is increasingly an unclarity about one's future that tantalizes but also may, to some extent, frighten the adolescent.

Fantasy as represented increasingly through the popular media opens vast possibilities. The tall young man who has already shown some skill at basketball can still envision moving on to a professional career. The attractive fifteen-year-old girl who may have won a bathing beauty contest at a local swimming pool or who has been chosen for a leading part in a school play can entertain elaborate visions of a glamorous career in the movies. By the age of twenty or so, many such possibilities are shot down completely. The fantasies may persist, in part because they have been practiced extensively and in part because they bring at least some temporary solace in an otherwise less exciting adult life-style. Nevertheless, it is clear that the more elaborate and extensive fantasies with wide-ranging possibilities are beginning to appear hopeless by early adult life. Perhaps this is somewhat less true for college-educated young adults in American society who enter the world of the glamorous "singles." Exposed as they are to a wide range of magazines and television commercials luring them toward glamorous lives, and possessing at least to some degree enough money or the potential of earning more, this group has engaged increasingly in a postponement of commitment to a more "workaday" adult life-style. It remains to be seen whether economic recession and enforced conservation as a regular way of American life will moderate this trend.

The increasing liberation of women from the pressures to marry early and to accept a secondary role in the economic and power hierarchy of our society may, in a curious way, also play a part in fostering traditional persistence of adolescent fantasy. Magazines like *Cosmopolitan* continue to tantalize the young adult with the possibilities that there is a Burt Reynolds for every girl and that he can be found in a ski lodge or on the beach of the Club Méditerranée at Martinique.

Romantic fantasy, as I have suggested, is a remarkable means of exploring a range of possible futures. To the extent that even with adult commitment some flexibility persists in our society, we find that more and more individuals seeking alternatives are already committed to marriage and family life. Fantasies that in the past would have long disappeared or emerged only in dreams recur increasingly to middle-aged adults who think that, after all, it may still indeed be possible to change a career, to travel, to find a more glamorous spouse than one has settled for earlier. In our society, commercials on television, glamorous movie representations of European or island resort settings, further encourage elaborate romantic fantasies. Even books like Gail Sheehy's *Passages*, which detail later career or social changes yearned for and engaged in by adults, are attractive because they sustain in a great variety of readers the thoughts about alternative life-styles.

It is important to stress that it is not the fantasy process itself that can create difficulties for adults. Rather it is the changing way of life, the actual persistence of material desire through the vast commercialization of our society, and the breakdown of complex ties to an extended family that contribute to the greater rate of individuals' unrealistic fantasies about major life changes. At the same time, it is also true that our society does have flexibility and that finding new partners or sexual adventures and indeed even major career changes are possible in a way never attainable before by grown adults unless they were members of the high aristocracy. Paradoxically, the very realities of our society have created ambiguities that, on the one hand, foster continuation of adolescent fantasies and, on the other, offer certain genuine possibilities for making some of these fantasies into reality.

In a world with such changing rules, it becomes increasingly difficult for an individual to know how far one's fantasies can lead and how to fulfill them without serious harm to family and friends. This seems, to some extent, to be a national dilemma. Similarly, Americans have been prone to assume that there is an endless supply of gasoline at the very modest price they have been paying for years in comparison with the world market. And yet this fantasy is not entirely unrealistic because, under conditions of better organization and planning, energy should be available indefinitely and at reasonable prices.

Detection of maladaptive fantasy, of romanticism gone wild, is easier in the individual whose imagery tends to be monotopical and who clearly shows a dramatic gap between fantasy and capability. Unattractive short men like Napoleon, or like the once well-known theatrical producers Billy Rose and Michael Todd, might share with other young men of comparable physical limitations fantasies of attracting glamorous women. The evidence is clear, however, that for many young men who lack strong business skills, intellectual power, or unusual gifts that the society values *and will pay for*, there is scarcely any hope of attracting beautiful women. If they persist repeatedly in such fantasies to the exclusion of other types of socialization with girls who might indeed be interested, it is clear that they are subject to misguided fantasy and potential delusion. Even Napoleon, for all his successes as a military and political leader, seems never to have been quite sure of the faithfulness of Josephine.

Romantic Fantasy and Romantic Love

In the musical comedy *Fiddler on the Roof*, there occurs a quaint duet between the dairyman Tevye and his wife. She wants to know if he "loves" her. He is puzzled by the question but finally agrees that he does in the sense that he appreciates her cooking, her services to him and faithfulness, warmth in bed, and so on. There is love in the sense of mutual concern and respect, but little romance and certainly no fantasy. Tevye responds to the concrete person much as she is, not what she might be or what she can symbolize. There are no associations or analogies, simply the concrete immediacy of a positive experience.

Romantic love represents an experience that goes beyond this direct form of warmth. It is built around *potentiality*, the touchstone of fantasy, not just what is given but what might be. The role of fantasy as a mind-stretching experience can distort and overidealize an undeserving loved one or it can add an aura of rich color and deepening intensity to an otherwise concretely satisfactory relationship. We live, after all, not just through the concrete satisfactions of physical needs, through the release of an orgasm in a tender sexual encounter, but also in the added meanings engendered by fantasies that anticipate events or see relationships to other experiences and events. "My love is like a red red rose/That's newly sprung in June," writes Robert Burns, or "She walks in beauty, like the night/Of cloudless climes and starry skies," says Lord Byron, each creating a link between a loved one and the memories of natural beauty.

Romantic love in its healthiest form involves an enhancement of experience, acceptance of the "reality" and yet a push toward something beyond. In the sonnet by Shakespeare that begins "My mistress' eyes are nothing like the sun," the poet strives to deny the metaphorical side of love, but the very richness of his imagery belies his effort at "realism." (See Chapter One for the entire sonnet.)

In a sense, we cannot escape our metaphorical capacities. Even the superrealists—the hard-headed businessmen, the stern lawyers, or mechanics—awaken from sleep with a sense of awe and mystery, for the analogizing of their dreams carries them far afield each night. Romantic love, if we give it scope, takes the loved one and puts her into the perspective of a vast symbolic world, an array of implied meanings, revivals of past warmths from childhood and youth, and associations to great literature. Fantasy has a forward-looking thrust as well as a retrospective one and leaves one open to envisioning growth and change in the loved one.

In a period when we face a reshaping of the roles of males and females, the romantic stance may be more adaptive in some ways than the more concrete approach to love. Both partners in a relationship will be changing and developing over a lifetime. The young lover or married man cannot expect that his beloved will remain as comfortable as an old shoe any longer. Shared romantic visions of new possibilities may help young couples grow independently without necessarily growing apart. To understand this possibility, we must examine, finally, the ultimate creative and adaptive powers of imagination and fantasy.

Constructive Uses of Imagery and Romantic Fantasy

In effect, then, romantic fantasy can be viewed as a natural outgrowth of the very process of personality development in our society. As childhood in effect has been extended, the leisure of engaging in fantasy has stretched further and further along in the life cycle. This can present considerable advantages as well as problems. Let us consider some of the adaptive uses of fantasy and positive imagery for self-development and constructive living.

In their very simplest form, daydreams represent a form of self-entertainment under circumstances in which one confronts situations of minimal external input or repetition. A long wait in a bus terminal or a long train ride may become the occasion for elaborate and extended fantasies which actually help the time pass rapidly, as experimental studies have shown (Singer, 1975). Playing with a variety of real or unreal possibilities in one's life through imagery can evoke the emotions of continued interest and joy and give one a sense of aliveness even under circumstances of boring work or tedious delay. The unhappily married adult may find at least temporary surcease from discomfort in playful fantasies of earlier lovers or of potential wild affairs with glamorous or far-off figures like the Aga Kahn or Prince Charles of England. Sarnoff and Sarnoff (1979) have confronted the previously unsayable and propose that masturbation with fantasy can bring satisfaction and peace in situations in which direct sexual activity is precluded by realistic circumstance.

There is a considerable body of research that also points to the relaxing effects of pure fantasy. Researchers are exploring a variety of uses of nature imagery as a means of helping one relax either for therapeutic purposes or in a more general fashion. Extensive psychotherapeutic uses of positive imagery and of a variety of quasi-escapist fantasies have also been increasingly recognized in direct intervention with neurotic patients (Singer and Pope, 1978).

Daydreaming can have more direct implications for action when it is used to explore a range of alternatives in a given situation. One need not confine oneself initially to the most realistic of such alternatives. As a matter of fact, investigators of creativity in scientific and engineering fields have long argued that the more wild the fantasy initially the more likely one is ultimately to come on a genuinely practical solution (Stein, 1975). If one has to try to meet a girl to whom one is attracted, it may not harm the situation to play out in somewhat bizarre detail a variety of approaches. Gradually, one may zero in on something that is feasible and original enough to evoke at least curiosity if not a grossly positive response. Where would Italian culture be today if Dante had made direct overtures to Beatrice instead of tucking her away in his mind and developing an incredibly elaborate superstructure of the afterlife, ultimately assigning her to the Heaven of his poem? We can at least hope that God has rewarded him by putting him alongside her in a real Heaven, if it exists.

For most purposes, fantasy need not be quite so elaborate or bizarre and yet generate sufficient originality. It is clear that some of the ways lovers or married couples sustain their interest over long periods of time is through fantasizing novel interactions for each other. These may range from novel sexual positions through simply forms of travel, new forms of joint social activity such as camping or hiking together, or somtimes simply little humorous intimacies. A husband emerges from the bathroom one morning after shaving to find signs all over the bedroom reading, "Joe is the greatest," "Joe is the supreme lover!" and the like. The art of surprising a loved one with gifts, specially chosen on the basis of careful observation of the other's desires, often comes from the same kind of wide-ranging fantasy. A couple confronted with day-to-day practical problems or problems of illness may create a joint imaginary fantasy of escape about which they can tease each other even though it has no practical possibility. Simply breaking up the mood of depression by engaging in fantasy of a positive kind can at least afford temporary relief but also often suggests other alternatives, once one accepts the possibility of such exploration.

Finally, fantasy has a tremendous power for enriching, from moment to moment, one's daily life experience. Zen Buddhists may be correct in arguing that we often overlook the most direct experience of nature, of simple movements, and of simply momentary experiences, obscuring them with elaborate verbal symbolism or trite phrases. We also minimize the enrichment potential of symbolic elaboration. If one visits Italy, the experience is heightened if the landscape evokes memories of painting by Giotto or Giorgione. The experience of looking at a Tintoretto in a book can be tremendously enhanced if one has seen the painting itself in the Accademia in Venice or on the walls of the Doge's Palace. Replaying these images, book and memory, allows each to enhance the other. In music, one can directly experience the power of a performance of Beethoven's Ninth Symphony because of the use of dynamics, the magnificent development of themes, and the general artistry of the performers. If one also knows that the symphony was written when Beethoven was deaf, and that at its first performance he had to be turned around from the orchestra to see that the audience was wildly applauding, it adds a further dimension to one's experience of the music. Such fantasies about a variety of events can also enhance the experience of literature. Reading a novel, one need not appreciate only the direct story line or the author's use of language. One can at least temporarily enter the novel and become a character, or put the book down for a while and elaborate on alternative plots. In a sense, our fantasy capacity and our romanticism allow us to lead a hundred lives when it would appear on the surface as if we pursue only one existence to its inevitable termination.

11

Romantic Couples
and Group Process

James C. Miller

Many observers have noted that therapy groups are chronically
conflicted about lovers in their midst, and some have postulated
that there is an essential opposition between the romantic couple
and the group (Kernberg, 1977; Braunschweig and Fain, 1971).
On the one hand, groups confer special powers on such dyads and
imbue them with their most optimistic intentions. On the other
hand, they envy these powers and ultimately come to see them as
alien and dangerous to the group mentality.

Since these powers are usually extremely salient to the
group, the relationships between the group and the romantic dyad
are correspondingly volatile. Members may be unable to resolve
the conflict between their wish to use the romantically linked
couple to enhance and perpetuate the group's virtues or to ostra-
cize them as carriers of dissension and change.

One hypothesis about this paradoxical attitude is that it derives from a perceived difference in the potential quality of object

relations in the romantic love relationship compared with those in the collective. As many writers have emphasized (Altman, 1977; Benedek, 1977), the potential for the development of complex, mature object ties in the romantic dyad is limited almost solely by the individual capacities of the partners. This is probably not true for groups, even in situations like intensive group therapy where the goal is to explore object ties as complex as those in the romantic pair. I doubt that there would be much disagreement with the notion that even healthy, mature adults routinely struggle in groups with extremely regressive forces, and that progress is frequently counted in terms of successful regulation of narcissistic concerns rather than the development of more advanced forms of object ties.

I have suggested elsewhere (Miller and others, 1978) that phenomena such as these can be looked at from at least two systems dynamic viewpoints. One, which I have called the individual point of view, details the group from the point of view of the entry or "joining" of the individual to the collective: "The extent to which a person will involve himself in personal commitments to the group, what roles he will take with respect to other members and to the task, as well as a range of conscious and subconscious feelings he may have about the situation, all remain at that instant [of joining] problematic and in need of some kind of resolution" (p. 26). The other, the group point of view, looks at the effects the system task and its associated structure have on various subsectors of an organization. Many times, events that appear to be satisfactorily explained in terms of individual motivation are more usefully and comprehensively viewed in terms of values sought at larger system levels, remaining cognizant of the ultimate effects on the individual. The output from a series of organizational events, beginning with larger systems input, channeled through group structure and finally expressed in group process, may indeed be a series of individual acts. But when seen as leadership acts performing some function for the system, what could be seen as idiosyncratic to the individual becomes more comprehensible in its group context.

From both viewpoints (group and individual), the hypothesis explored is that romantic love relations and group relations have important parallels in origin and function, but that they are alternative and competing strategies for solving many problems of social organization. From the group viewpoint, groups and lovers may be interchangeable in terms of their effectiveness in freeing the individual to engage in new economic units. They differ in that, in most societies, lovers can marry and become a separate economic unit, whereas peer groups remain outside most economic task systems. From the individual viewpoint, a central developmental function of love and peer relations emerges in adolescence and early adulthood, and involves aiding the child's gradual psychological separation from the parents. In this respect, there are important differences between the functions of group and love relations which may contribute to the clinical impression of incompatibility. This chapter will explore the hypothesis that groups, with their regressive potential and pressure, channel members' energies into predominantly pre-oedipal adjustments, where love relations offer the prospect of resolving a wider range of conflicts and facilitating greater conflict-free ego development. These advantages of the dyad lead to their being perceived in groups as privileged and special, as carriers of hope and change, and as keys to the development of creativity and mature self-fulfillment.

The procedure I shall follow is to compare various aspects of the relationship of the individual to the collective with comparable aspects of the relationship to the romantic partner. Thus I shall examine instinctual aspects, with emphasis on relative threats, anxieties, and regressive solutions; levels of object relations, with emphasis on the regulation of narcissistic rewards and injuries; the defensive aspect, with a focus on the predominance of splitting projection and introjection used in groups; and the potential for the growth of a mature commitment to the dyad compared to the demand for more inflexible loyalties and the offer of anonymity and license in the collective.

Drives

Several writers have commented on the sources and nature of threats to the individual posed by groups (Mann, 1967; Slater, 1963; Turquet, 1975). There is substantial consensus that the individual of necessity experiences threats to his or her prior sense of identity in the process of joining a group. As Turquet (1975, p. 97) says of the large group: "This sense of the threat of becoming other than himself, of being in some way altered, pressurized, even diminished, is for the (person) an ever-present experience." The need to find a fit of the individual to multiple, ever-changing roles forms the social framework in which this process occurs.

One particularly useful way of conceptualizing the psychological process by which this "fit" is carried out was proposed by Freud in *Group Psychology and the Analysis of the Ego* (1921). His formula for the "libidinal constitution" of a group was that it consists of "a number of individuals who have put one and the same object in the place of their ego ideal and have consequently identified with one another in their ego" (p. 116). That is, the leader replaces or fulfills the member's ego ideal and governs the ego in its place. It thereby feels appropriate for the member to be governed or led, by means of a process of incorporation or introjection of the leader into the inner life (specifically into the superego or ego ideal) of the member.

For the romantic dyad, there are parallels to this process worth noting, particularly in the early stages of falling in love. As many authors have noted (Kernberg, 1977), there are threats to the lover's prior sense of identity posed by the intimacy and potential for merger in the romantic union. As Freud pointed out, there is a process comparable to replacement of the ego ideal in the romantic relationship, which in a sense creates a form of leadership in both groups and romantic dyads. But from the beginning there are also differences. In the group these processes are fragmented, variegated, and constantly changing, whereas for the couple they can be more integrated, focused, and relatively constant. In the group the incorporative-identificatory process extends to many other people and cannot be integrated to be worked through in relation to one object. In short, processes of splitting and projection are inherent in the formation of groups and may indeed form the basis of their work (that is, they will often not be used defensively), whereas this is not true for the romantic couple. The love relationship can be maintained and can grow without depending so centrally on these processes.

As Turquet (1975, p. 270) noted, because several people are present in a group, "there are many . . . opportunities for the I to project parts of himself onto others. But equally thereby he finds himself fractionated into multiple parts." Large groups seem "to give substance to a fantasy of the [person's] internal world as also vast, unencompassable or boundless." The individual recoils because he "requires of external life in groups a bounded experience to take in as an introject on which to build up his own psychic life-notions of internal boundaries or limitations." Thus in the large group the individual's experience is either "isolated apartness or complete fusion with or loss in." Small groups hold out the same dilemma but are better, according to Turquet, in furthering "a sense of fusion and hence belonging while at the same time offering each individual member a variety of opportunities to implement idosyncratically the roles such a group provides."

What one sees clinically is the ready emergence of such pre-oedipal complementarities which become the cultural fabric of the group: issues of dominance and submission; of sadism and masochism; real dilemmas of sex role de-differentiation; as well as fundamental problems of maintaining one's sense of separate existence. It may be less the ready emergence of these drives than the manner in which they become stable, life-giving patterns in groups, that separates them from romantic dyads. Thoughts, feelings, and fantasies that lovers generally experience as ego alien and ephemeral are often the working assumptions of groups for long periods of time. Establishment of leadership, for example, is establishment of dominance, even if it becomes particularly salient only in pathological instances. By contrast, there is nothing intrinsic to the romantic relationship that forces the emergence of dominance as an issue.

The tendency of groups to free the individual to express sadistic or masochistic drives has impressed many observers. Freud (1921) commented that collectivities tend to put the individual's conscience "out of action," thus freeing up, foremost among many impulses, the sadistic and masochistic ones. This occurs by a process that involves regression, characterized by a pre-oedipal tendency to replace or displace the conscience with here-and-now parental objects. Both Freud and Fenichel (1954) have pointed out that this process is common to love and group relations: "In the state of being in love, in hypnosis, in psychoanalysis, and in the choice of a leader a kind of 'projection of the superego' takes place. Whereas in superego formation an object relation is abandoned and replaced by an ego alteration, here an object relation begins by an object taking over regressively the function of part of the ego" (1954, p. 11). Although this same regressive process can free sado-masochistic drives in both dyadic and group situations, there are factors in the group situation that facilate their expression. In the romantic pair, with normal or neurotic persons, there will be some integration of sado-masochistic and loving impulses around the same object. With the presence of several objects in the group situation, for example, a split between leader and members can further facilitate the expression of less integrated sadistic impulses toward one or the other. Also, as many commentators have observed (Freud, 1921; Janis, 1968), the increased anonymity and social support in groups for the expression of sadistic impulses make their appearance more likely, and make their content more organized and less "pathological" or otherwise deviant.

Janis (personal communication, 1963) has been very explicit about the mechanisms through which groups facilitate and channel sado-masochistic strivings. There arc: greater opportunities for denying personal responsibility; more support for denial of guilt feelings ("everyone does it"); and more opportunity for what Janis calls a "surreptitious form of confession that enables one to unburden himself . . . and . . . enables the group to arrive at much more convincing rationalizations."

One implication of instinctual regression already strongly drawn is that of primitive object relations characterized by processes of incorporation, narcissistic projection, identification, and extreme dependence. In a recent and long overdue discussion about how fundamental and exclusive these primitive processes are to groups (Kernberg, 1979; Shapiro, 1979), there is some agreement that they are fundamental but not exclusive, either in the sense of excluding other less primitive developments in groups, or in the sense of being exclusive to groups compared to romantic love and hypnotic relationships. They are fundamental in at least two senses: (1) Groups cannot be formed without the use of incorporation, projection, identification, and allied processes, which implies that primitive object relationships will be involved in all group situations; and (2) groups, particularly large groups, may be uniquely undifferentiated and unstructured social matrices in which the individual's integrity is most threatened and he is left, ironically, with fewest accessible resources. By contrast, all other relationships that doubtless have primitive aspects to them—romantic love, hypnosis, analysis—have familiar and conventional aspects that ultimately aid the individual in coping with the eruption of primitive material. One moves away from this asocial prototype primarily through the use of defenses at various levels: from the extreme idealization of the leader in the large group with its attendant processes of primitive incorporation and aggression; through Bion's (1959) basic assumption life which the individual shares in a relatively undifferentiated way through contagion and cohesion; to more neurotic-like constellations of defenses involving differentiation (division of labor and function), inhibition, and regulation; and finally to work, involving the acquisition and regulation of appropriated knowledge and skills requisite to complete the task and satisfy group members concerning their participation (Shapiro, 1979).

In the context of primitive object relations, it should not be surprising that satisfaction follows the guidelines set down by the initial narcissistic overestimation of the lover or leader. The psychology of establishing such ties owes a considerable amount to expectations of fulfillment and enhancement of self-esteem. Lovers enter the romantic relationship expecting complete union and self-fulfillment, total love and gratification. Members enter the group wishing to enhance their positive self-images by meaningful involvement in a collective led by the narcissistically fulfilled leader. The investment of the superego in the lover-leader ensures this. What the person wants back is enhanced self-esteem, which can be accomplished in two ways: (1) by the giving over of superego constraints to the leader or lover, freeing the grantor from painful internal conflict, guilt, and self-criticism; and (2) by receiving from the "other" both real and fantasied indications of high regard, of love and special concern. The person may take steps to ensure that love by conformity, fastidiousness, hard work, or the like. Different individuals will require different signs of concern in order to continue to be satisfied (narcissistically enhanced). However, because most groups do not require more from the personal equation in order to carry out their task, the members' interactions with the group are often left at this level, depending as they do entirely on narcissistic dynamics for regulation of the members' participation in the group. One can speculate that individuals with strong narcissistic needs will be attracted to multiple group membership to try to satisfy these needs. My clinical experience has strongly convinced me that groups in particular are strongly affected by the self-esteem needs and regulation of their members. It is no small matter to the individual that he or she has turned to a group for fulfillment of such needs, as Janis (personal communication, 1963) says, "fulfilling the functions of criticising him and showing whether or not he is lovable. . . . The new state of affairs can give rise to blissful feelings of security . . . characterized by a sense of complete unity from fusing the schema of the self with that of the object." It can also give rise to the shock of rejection or absence of appropriate narcissistic gratification, with its attendant rage, guilt, depression, and the like. From this perspective, joining a group may be a substantial emotional gamble in which fantasies of total care and fusion with the rewarding object resulting in highly gratifying narcissistic enhancement are routinely entertained, and just as routinely frustrated. One could say that groups are the perfect environment for the raising of narcissistic concerns and, often enough, for their temporary resolution.

Freud's (1921) view of the cultural prototype for this regressive sequence was what he called the primal horde. He stated the central symbol in primarily genital terms: the strongest male came to dominate the horde and to gain control of all of the horde's women. Thus frustrated, the surbordinate males were forced from the tribe to gratify their sexual needs and establish continuing heterosexual relationships. Thus the incest taboo and exogamy. Freud did not examine the vicissitudes of pregenital needs and drives, even though, of course, the structure of his argument would permit it. The exploration of pregenital dynamics reflected in group life does not require a resolution of the issues raised in biology or sociology as a result of Freud's speculation, but there are some more immediate problems related to it that are of clinical importance. Was Freud calling attention to a causal biosocial given in relation to the primitive processes we observe in groups (that is, do we always observe a *regression* from oedipal issues?) or was it simply an oversight in cataloguing the frustrations and gratifications of wishes at all levels? This is a familiar and important issue for individual psychology as well, one currently receiving comment that is beyond the scope of this chapter. The clinical issue for groups would appear to be to sensitize the observer to a sequence in which the higher level issues may frequently be outside the field of observation: from a primal horde mentality, to the extremely regressive group process that is observed, to the clandestine dyadic arrangements that occur outside the group (exogamously?) as a defense against the regressive processes in the group.

In Freud's view of the primal horde, the dominance of the leader is a given, presumably a biological given. This view allows us to speculate that one function of the leader's demand for loyalty and his prohibition of romantic love relations within the horde had to do with the need for cohesiveness which would have been disrupted by internal pairing. If we now add the intervening picture of the threat of regression in group process, the defensive formation of dyads within the group would again create problems of loyalty and threats to group cohesiveness. Such "pairing" would not be a group culture (not a "basic assumption" in Bion's sense) but instead a threat to group culture. Thus we have more suggestive evidence for our clinical observations of the incompatibility of romantic dyad and group, or rather of dyad-in-group.

Defenses and Work

It is impossible to speak of the vicissitudes of drive expression and regulation, as well as the object relations associated with these drives, without describing in part their correlative defensive processes. Since we have been describing the drive and object relations aspects of collective responses to pairing, we have provided more than a brief introduction to the formation of individual and group defenses. But it remains to take a closer look, and to relate defensive processes in both group and romantic dyad to more sublimatory processes, working through of conflicts, and "work" in the group sense as Bion (1959) described it.

For both romantic pairs and groups, ability to accomplish multiple tasks through establishment of appropriate structure and marshaling of necessary resources forms the framework against which proper functioning is assessed. Ability to carry out problem solving necessary to accomplish the task is the collective analogue to ego-strength in the individual. Collectivities, like individuals, will vary in their abilities to carry out the task: in defining it, in managing the resulting structure, in utilizing resources. Reality test-ing against the external world will vary; members have varying in-terests in accepting responsibility and in differentiating in a manner appropriate to task implementation. In the ideal case where all of these and related abilities are present, the collective can be expected to function at the highest level. As Shapiro (1979) has pointed out, willingness and capacity to take responsibility for differentiating members' roles in relation to task accomplishment will mandate the leader through optimally flexible ego identifications.

For reasons of limited time, resources, or capacities this ideal state is rarely achieved, and inevitably anxieties are aroused and defenses employed. This need not involve observable task failure, as is sometimes assumed. One special incapacity involves tolerat-ing periods of effective work, particularly when such success is construed as, for example, an oedipal victory. Another subtle in-capacity involves role failure, where leadership in effective work is construed in sibling rivalry terms resulting in expressions of envy.

Following Bion's (1959) suggestion that basic assumption life in groups relied heavily on projective identification and other allied primitive defenses, and Jaques' (1955) analysis of systems producing defenses against psychotic anxiety, theory and practice in group dynamics has tended to assume that groups are essentially regressive in nature in their effects on the individual. It has further been assumed that the regression was most accurately character-ized, or in some sense demonstrated, by the pervasive use of primi-tive defense mechanisms like incorporation, introjection, projec-tion, identification, and splitting. There is a decided debt in this to the Kleinian origin of these theories with its emphasis on the ef-fects of very early mental life (see Klein, 1961). And there is also no doubt that the Kleinians found in their analysis of collective life a fertile field of application of their theories. For if the fore-going analysis of collectivities is correct, to study primitive defense mechanisms aroused by them is to study their defining character-istics. An assembly of individuals who had not identified with one another and projected persons/ideas into leadership roles would not be called a group. So also for the romantic dyad: Without the projected idealizations, the primitive identifications resulting in fantasies of fusion and unity and fantasies of enhanced narcissistic fulfullment, we would not call it romantic love.

Since our interest has been in comparing romantic love and group relations, our questions about the characteristic use of defenses can be put in the form of an inquiry into the differences concerning their use in dyads and groups. Although to proceed in this way will be most instructive and least repetitious, we should try to keep in mind the basic similarities in the fashion outlined earlier. Clinical experience seems to indicate that differences appear to emerge and idiosyncratic patterns begin to set in later in the developmental sequence. The fundamental process may be the same, as many observers have pointed out (Freud, 1921; Fenichel, 1954), allowing typical and atypical differences to be established more noticeably later on once the process develops a more coherent form.

Splitting. It has been my experience that differences in splitting between romantic pairs and groups have manifestly to do with numbers, but with an end result that has a substantially divergent psychological form. Simply stated, the transference patterns in romantic pairs are necessarily individual, whereas those in groups are structurally split. So the opportunities for splitting are greater in groups, with a corresponding difficulty in identifying and modifying group splits because of their manifest support in reality. One would expect, then, to find more pervasive and lasting splitting processes in groups, and less effective "observing ego" to chart and resolve (work through) the effects of splitting.

Projection. From the point of view of the use of projection, it seems possible and potentially useful to call attention to an equivalence between leaders and lovers that brings about the same kind of elevation, idealization, and incorporation or primitive identification that endows the leader-lover with special status and powers. Feelings of vicarious worthiness mixed with feelings of extreme unworthiness, feelings of loss of individual distinctiveness and corresponding feelings of merger of identity with the lover-leader are common. A boundary forms around the dyad or group which facilitates splitting and projection of bad objects onto the outside world. With this fundamental process accomplished, the romantic dyad or group projective process can become more differentiated, where intrapsychic structures of the individual play a stronger part, as for example in the superego identification described by Freud (1921). This aspect of the projective process can be more related to task, endowing the leader-lover with authority over collective tasks and permitting division of labor and function among group or dyad members.

Identification. The original set of projections that produce primitive identifications between dyad members or with the leader and the group both assist the participants in joining and help them defend against strong intitial anxieties. Later, identifications are available as defenses against any problems the romantic dyad or group develop in task completion. The more that identification can be within the superego, thus freeing the ego to complete reality plans, the more functional the defense will be.

In comparing romantic dyads and groups with respect to projection and identification, we observe the same framework as with splitting. In each case, the regressive potential and salience of regressive defenses are greater in groups: not only are more potential objects involved with whom to identify on a projective basis but also more members can project potentially destructive impulses onto a single recipient. In addition, as the collective grows larger, reality testing of the thoughts and feelings of other members becomes progressively difficult. In this situation, what could be a comparatively sophisticated superego identification becomes a primitive, largely projectively determined id identification shared in an unthinking and undifferentiated manner by all group members.

Avoidance. In an interpersonal (dyadic or group) situation, members can of course take action to disconnect themselves from the collective as a defense against the anxieties it has aroused. This action can take the physical form of actually leaving the situation, which may be relatively rare because of its uncertain effect both on the perpetrator's inner life and on the other members of the collective. More frequently, the flight takes the form of withdrawal of affect, or fantasy, or thought from the group, or of registering a complaint against further participation. This defense appears to be used equally by romantic dyad and group, but again with a slight edge to group use because of the added anonymity it provides.

If a collectivity has the resources and the opportunities to work through what is of necessity a primitive defensive position, one begins to see evidence of less regressed defenses. A crucial step in this process has to do with the idea of "commitment" or of "joining." When it is possible to make a relatively unambivalent commitment to remain in collective life, working through conflicts despite the inevitable pain and difficulty, one's membership takes on an important new dimension. This dimension involves an assessment on the part of the participants that they are able to continue their participation at some level over the discouraging demands of frustration. The stronger this commitment is, the less blind it will be, and the assessment of resources more accurate. This act of the superego puts the person in the position of being able to work. Without it, extreme defenses of avoidance or of splitting and projection will help to take the person out of the psychological situation. Thus the superego has an important role in determining the framework in which the ego can function in a more mature manner in work.

To the extent to which the individual's superego regresses under the stress of participation, it will of course fail in this function. In my experience, such regression tends to take divergent paths in romantic dyads and groups, with primitive idealizations dominating the love relationship and equally primitive punitive fantasies of retaliation and denigration in group relationships.

There is a relevant superego dimension to what stands as one of the more puzzling paradoxes of Bion's (1959) "basic assumption pairing." It has to do with the idealization-denigration complementarity described above. At a manifest level, the group appears to try to gain the advantages of the romantic dyad: hope, unity, utopia. But there is also a strong prophetic morality to the utopian fantasies, invoving an extreme criticism of the prevailing order, and an equally extreme effort to lead the group out of the lost present to the "promised land" of the future. It seems like an effort magically to synthesize these complementary opposites, and at the same time to capture the magic of the romantic pair for the purposes of the group. It is not surprising that so simple an effort to resolve a complex problem that has important sociological as well as psychological aspects will be fragile and ultimately doomed to failure as a defense. But it is also a good example of basic assumption thinking as Bion has described it, with a single attempt to refuse a split in the superego and to unify dyad and group by allowing the romantic pair to lead.

Summary

Starting from a common observation that groups are often conflicted about romantic pairs, the hypothesis was advanced that groups and dyads may constitute alternative and competing strategies for solving many types of social problems. The subsequent analysis indicated that they are also competing for solving many psychological dilemmas that individuals encounter. With respect to drive regression, groups were hypothesized to provide more frequent and varied opportunities for regression, and generally less resources to work through the regressive pulls, toward development and effective task accomplishment. The extreme threat to the individual posed by the emergence of regressive impulses of dominance and submission, sadism and masochism, fusion and alienation, was found to be greater in groups than in romantic relationships and to be a better fit with their structure and function. Narcissistic concerns are indigenous to groups and provide an important source of secondary gain (or promised secondary gain) for individual participation. Narcissistic dynamics virtually determine the course of development of most groups, whereas for romantic dyads they are an important though less ubiquitous factor.

From the point of view of the development of defenses and ultimately a more conflict-free ego functioning, our exploration again found the romantic pair at an advantage. Groups provide greater opportunities for splitting and projection, and usually less resources to work through the resulting group culture. The process of identification called on by groups is more primitive, supported by inadequate information about both members and leaders. The defense of avoidance is used reciprocally (avoiding group issues by pairing, avoiding issues of intimacy by group membership) but is aided in groups by the additional anonymity provided. Speculation was offered to the effect that love relations' tend to emphasize ego-ideal aspects of the superego, whereas group relations activate or enhance conflicts around its conscience aspects. In this light, Bion's "pairing" was seen as a magical attempt to bring together group and romantic pair into a functional unity, and to resolve splits between ego-ideal and conscience aspects of the superego.

12

Romantic Love as a Social Institution

Anne E. Kazak
N. Dickon Reppucci

Romantic love is often understood as an essentially linear process. We strive for and attain love, revel in its pleasures, and eventually lose love. Whereas other types of love (brother love, mother-child love, love of God) are assumed to be predictable and stable, much like the climate in a particular area, romantic love is different, seasonal rather than climatic.

> *Love is like the falling snow*
> *once it comes it has to go*
> *never say so, it's a lie*
> *love's forever, 'tis time must fly*
> (R. D. Laing, 1976)

As we can mark the beginning of winter by colder weather and winter skies, so too can we identify the early signs of romantic love—warmth, intrigue, and sexual desire. Winter must end. That end is signaled by the decreasing likelihood of freezing temperatures and the arrival of longer days. The end of a love relationship can similarly be noted by increased discontent, a longing for change and a decrease in intensity of desire. While enjoying the pleasures of winter—warm fireplaces and winter sports—or the pleasures of romantic love—passion and a sense of oneness—there is little motivation to anticipate the changing of seasons or the cessation of love. When the end or change occurs, there is a tendency to feel the inevitability of flux and to progress to the next season (spring or the mourning of a lost love). As the linear process of a season or of a love nears its termination, there is little tendency to think of the next winter or to see the enduring cyclical process of romantic love. Our view of the world tends to be one in which we end what was known and move onto something different.

The image of linearity is undermined when time is introduced as an important force and background characteristic. Time punctuates our experiences of romantic love in such a way as to make them appear linear, with definite beginnings, changes, and ends. It is the thesis of this chapter that a more accurate view of romantic love is one that is nonlinear. Rubin (1973) has suggested that we must change our view of love to accept a series of relationships, in each falling in love, loving, and losing love. Since it is our view that romantic love should not be viewed independently of larger social forces, we suggest that within this nonlinear model romantic love functions as a stabilizing force in a society in which individuals often feel rapid flux.

One of the goals of community psychology is to understand social phenomena from several levels of analysis (Rappaport, 1977). In this chapter, we shall utilize previous individual and interpersonal level research findings to pave the way for a collective, or societal, level analysis of romantic love. An assumption of our perspective, again reflecting a basic tenet of community psychology, is that romantic love is intertwined with other aspects of life and has significant interfaces with several of our social institutions. Romantic love cannot be studied meaningfully if it is in isolation from other aspects of human life. Community psychologists have attempted to investigate areas of human life that have often been neglected in the systematic science of psychology. It is our belief that romantic love is an area that has been largely neglected and that merits examination. We shall begin building the background of our perspective by investigating some of the reasons behind the oversight of romantic love in psychology.

Why Study Romantic Love?

It may be that there is no subject as central to our human experience and yet as recurrently incomprehensible as human love. Stressing the importance and pervasiveness of love is nearly impossible to do without appearing trite or repeating tediously what poets have told us more fluently for centuries. Even when we limit our consideration of love to romantic love, its expansiveness persists. Love is compelling and yet strangely sacred and mystical, somehow beyond the realm of usual systematic investigations. We have been taught that love is central to our development and happiness and therefore have developed fairly concrete expectations for the experience of love in our adolescent and adult lives. Although we often assume some underlying communalities in our definitions and sensations of romantic love, our specific experiences of love are generally not shared with others. Love is so central to our lives that we tend not to discuss it casually and so important that perceived failures in attaining the expected state of love are often manifested as severe individual suffering and disappointment.

Psychology as a science and as an art has been dedicated traditionally to understanding human behavior and to alleviating human distress through research findings and psychological intervention, such as psychotherapy. However, psychologists have long been caught in a bind over exactly what areas of human behavior merit investigation. Arenas of human life such as humor and love have often been bypassed by psychologists. Indeed, it is easier to approximate scientific rigor and to feel that our results reflect elucidations of truth when we study cognition, psychophysiology, or memory than it is to assert that we can understand romantic love within the framework of our existing paradigms and research methodologies. There has been a tendency for psychologists to avoid the study of romantic love (this volume is a notable exception) in their pursuits, perhaps for fear of risking alienation and ridicule from the general scientific community. There is some degree of irony in this for the history of psychology has been paved with landmark theories resting upon notions of love. Freud, Bowlby, and Harlow, among others, incorporated love into their theories, and many of the major psychotherapies have allotted love a primary position in their frameworks. Although love has been acknowledged implicitly as important, we have failed to take the additional step of systematically understanding love in a broader and more novel context and of making contemporary contributions to the understanding of love.

One common argument against the study of love is that the phenomenon is so pervasive that it is impossible to know where to begin the investigation. The general idea is that everyone knows what romantic love is, so why bother studying something that we all understand? The same might be said for adolescence. We all remember, probably with some mixed pain and joy, what it was like to pass from puberty to adulthood. Yet, despite this common understanding of the process, we still feel that it is a subject worthy of investigation and express a confidence that our research may help others who have yet to pass through this developmental phase. Why do we not take a similar view of romantic love, arguing that a clearer understanding of what it means to fall in love may help others make sense of their experiences of falling in (and out of) love? Perhaps it is because romantic love continues to be an immediate experience throughout life. We can never be sure that we have closure on romantic love because it can suddenly threaten a marriage that seemed firm or because the power of romantic love (and our lack of control over it) can result in behaviors that seem incomprehensible. An increased understanding of love may destroy some of our illusions of it and may point out directions of change. Change has always been a phenomenon that is at once welcomed and feared, perhaps explaining some of our reluctance to understand romantic love more clearly and to move beyond our linear model.

Senator William Proxmire, a critic external to psychology, attacked a National Science Foundation grant to Elaine Walster and Ellen Berscheid on the topic of love. His comments reflect many of the biases against studying love.

> I object to this not only because no one—not even the
> NSF—can argue that falling in love is a science; not only be-
> cause I'm sure that even if they spend $84 million, or $84
> billion they won't get an answer anyone would believe. I'm
> also against it because I don't want the answer. I believe that
> 200 million other Americans want to leave some things in life
> a mystery and right at the top of things that we don't want to
> know is why a man falls in love with a woman and vice verse.
> So NSF, get out of the love racket. Leave that to Elizabeth
> Barrett Browning and Irving Berlin. Here if anywhere Alex-
> ander Pope was right when he said, "If ignorance is bliss, 'tis
> folly to be wise" [Walster and Walster, 1978, p. viii].

Opinions such as these have elements of truth but they undermine the natural curiosity of scientists as well as the knowledge and means that we have available to understand and explain natural phenomena. There seems to be a strong fear that by studying love we will somehow destroy its spontaneity and magical powers. Although some humor researchers may be absolutely humorless and some researchers in the area of love so infatuated with their pursuits that they fail to experience love, this position is pompous and naive. It is pompous to assume that we are so powerful as researchers that we will be able to destroy an integral part of human experience and naive to believe that we might not be more enlightened by gathering more data on these important realms of human life. In studying romantic love, we must begin with an acceptance of the phenomenon for what it is, allowing the mysticism and pervasiveness of romantic love to foster our understanding of it, rather than allowing them to be obstacles.

Clarifying and Conceptualizing Romantic Love

A preliminary step to formulating a nonlinear, broad perspective on romantic love rests on the substantiation of what is meant by romantic love. We asked forty-eight college students to write down some of their thoughts on romantic love, including definitions of romantic love, to compare these with the diverse definitions offered in the literature. The data we obtained suggest strongly that romantic love is not a clear-cut, singularly understood phenomenon, although there are common threads that pervade the definitions. Our findings reflect both the diversities and similarities of definitions found in the literature (see Blood, 1952; Driscoll, Davis, and Lipetz, 1972; Goode, 1959; Horton, 1973; Murstein, 1974; Pope, in this volume; Rosenblatt, 1967; Walster and Walster, 1978). Romantic love seems to be a dual experience: it is linked strongly to idealization and remoteness but is also characterized by intimacy, both physical and emotional. The definitions that we obtained from college students seemed also to reflect an ambivalence in attitudes toward romantic love. Romantic love is seen as a positive force, evoking happiness and contentedness; it is also seen as a temporary feeling, one that will pass. There is a sense that this temporal nature also is seen as positive.

Although Goode (1959) indicated that romantic love should be seen as a continuum of intensity, the responses of our students seem to suggest that their conceptualization of romantic love is dichotomous in nature. Romantic love is seen as either present or absent in a relationship and is seen as in opposition to other types of love, rather than possessing overlap and communality with them.

The idea that romantic love changes over time in a relationship and that the changes are dramatic is central in the literature on romantic love. Common sense seems to validate this notion and reinforces the linear conceptualization of love relationships. Each person changes over time and this necessarily prompts changes over time in dyadic relationships. The most persistent idea in the literature is that love changes from passionate love to companionate love over the course of a relationship (Walster and Walster, 1978). This change from infatuation and passion to devotion and companionship again suggests linearity. Even when love relationships do not end, the nature of the love bond between two persons changes permanently. Romantic love has been equated with adolescent love (Winch, 1958) and has been identified as the type of love most often leading to marriage (Rubin, 1970). There is a paradox inherent here: People marry for love (romantic love presumably) with the expectation that love should be forever, and yet we also believe that love changes and is not expected to be stable in its form. This paradoxical assumption of forever, and yet not forever, needs to be explored more fully in our understanding of marital relationships for it suggests areas of confusion and frustration. It we assume that many people who marry have experienced romantic love before, what is their understanding of what will happen to this romantic love upon marrying? Although many different attributions can be made for the passing of previous loves, the future cycles of love and changes in love yet to come are often not addressed.

Goldstine and others (1977) identify three stages through which marital and nonmarital relationships pass. Stage 1 is the initial falling-in-love phase during which there is much excitement, uncertainty, and vulnerability. It is a period of self-esteem escalation and high mutuality and idealization. Stage 2 is the period of disappointment and alienation. There is a sense that there are irreconcilable differences between the couple. Disillusionment is prevalent and blaming is likely. Stage 2 is the stage at which couples may split up, or separate and divorce if they are married. For those who survive Stage 2, the final stage (Stage 3) is one in which the couple's expectations for each other become realistic. There is a strong sense of individuality present with a concomitant feeling of security in the relationship. In terms of romantic love, the Goldstine and others (1977) formulation suggests a trend from romantic (passionate) to realistic (companionate) love, but with a distinct intermediary period during which positive feelings of love are less prominent.

In similar fashion Coleman (1977) presents a five-stage model of relationship development. The first stage is Recognition, during which two persons meet and acknowledge that they have common interests and that there is a chemical, physical attraction between them. During the second stage, Engagement, the affection and attraction are readily identifiable and lead to the third stage, Harmony, during which there is an increased intimacy and feelings of pleasure. The fourth phase is Discordance, during which idealization falls away, power struggles emerge, and fears of intimacy surface. The last stage is Resolution, in which a new homeostatic balance is achieved and a more realistic, clearly defined commitment begins.

Knox (1970) conducted a cross-sectional study of dating high school seniors, couples married less than five years, and couples married for more than twenty years, and substantiated the trends described previously. Using the Knox and Sporakowski (1968) Attitudes Toward Love Scale, he found that romantic love did not die in relationships but that conceptualizations of love did change at different points in the relationship. The couples married for less than five years evidenced fewer feelings of romantic love than the other two groups. However, all three groups were found to be more realistic than romantic in their orientation toward love. One interpretation of this study is that romantic love does not die away when more pragmatic types of love emerge but that it may in fact reemerge with an intensity like that characterizing adolescents. Thus, whereas Goldstine and others (1977) and Coleman (1977) do not suggest a return to romantic love, the Knox (1970) research suggests that romantic love may be cyclical and return at a predictable point in the course of a long-term relationship.

Munro and Adams (1978) provide some clues as to factors that may influence the reemergence of romantic love in a marital relationship. They found that feelings of romantic love were lower during periods in a marriage when there is high role structure, such as young married couples with children, and that feelings of romantic love were more common during periods of low role structure, such as dating couples or couples whose children have left home. The suggestion here is also that romantic love reemerges later in the relationship, again refuting the linear model that once romantic love subsides, it will not reappear.

There is a need for a more comprehensive model of changes over the course of relationships and more specific documentation of fluctuations in the course and nature of love over time. Ideally, longitudinal research should follow couples from dating through the decision to live together or to marry and beyond. There is a further need for an understanding of changes in love relationships as they relate to external demands placed upon couples at various points in time. The studies reviewed suggest that many realistic demands confronting young families may contribute to the decrease in feelings of romantic love. We need to understand more thoroughly how financial pressures, childrearing demands, and the integration of work with family life affect feelings of romantic love at various points in the development of a relationship. With the increase in divorce and remarriage in our society (Glick, 1978), it seems imperative to examine the effects that these social trends have upon our attitudes toward romantic love. We know little about how stressors (decisions to have children, divorce, remarriage) affect feelings of romantic love. Indeed, we know surprisingly little about love. There are no data on how many times people fall in love and what changes they observe in first and subsequent loves. There are similarly no data on whether or not the dissolution process and the decision to terminate a relationship affect later relationships and whether or not there are substantial differences in attitudes toward love among those who have ended a marriage in divorce.

The evidence that romantic love increases after twenty years of marriage (Knox, 1970) points to an important role that romantic love may play in relationships and suggests that it may function to alleviate or ameliorate the stresses of later married life and the stresses of retirement, illness, and the "empty nest." The need for idealization and excitement may surface strongly at various points in a relationship and in an individual's life, suggesting a role for romantic love as a stabilizing and comforting force in a period of change and stress. There is a need for further documentation of this reappearance of romantic love in order to flesh out the non-linear model of romantic love.

In any comprehensive understanding of romantic love and the changes that it undergoes, it is important to consider the issue of individual differences in approaches toward love. Goldstine and others (1977) present ten different styles of loving, whereas Lee (1973) suggests three main approaches to love which can be blended into several different types. It is not our intention here to describe fully all the individual differences in approaches to love but to note that these individual differences may be important in viewing relationships over time. It appears important to answer the question of what portion of the variance in predicting changes over time can be attributed to basic differences in what love means to individuals and in how they express their love.

One substantial body of research in the area of romantic love which merits consideration in a broader understanding of romantic love is that concerned with sex differences. Our cultural stereotype has been that women are more romantic than men, but this assumption has been disproven consistently in the literature, with men found to be more romantic than women (Dion and Dion, 1973; Fengler, 1974; Kanin, Davidson, and Scheck, 1970; Kephart, 1967). The focus of these sex differences studies has been on romantic orientation rather than on more quantitative issues such as how frequently each falls in love. For example, Kanin, Davidson, and Scheck (1970) found that men were more romantic in that they tended to fall in love more quickly than women, but that women were more idealistic and more romantic in the long run. This is a consistent theme and is generally explained by differences in the societal meaning placed on involvement and marriage for the two sexes (Dion and Dion, 1973; Fengler, 1974). It is stressed that love and marriage are more important and more serious matters for women than for men and that women are therefore more pragmatic and cautious in their willingness to acknowledge and experience romantic love.

In the data that we collected from college students, we found that the students reported having been in love between two and three times, with no significant differences by sex. A significant sex difference was found for age of respondent at time of first love ($t = 2.87$; $d.f. = 46$, $p < .016$). Women reported first falling in love at a later age ($\bar{x} = 14.8$ years) than did men ($\bar{x} = 11.9$ years). Since both groups reported falling in love the same number of times, there is evidence here to suggest that women fell in love more frequently during their later adolescent years than did men. It may be that women were defining their experiences of romantic love differently from men in that it is surprising that women reported an average age of first love that is close to fifteen, apparently not including junior high "crushes" or early infatuations.

There is evidence that women may be better able to differentiate feelings of liking from feelings of loving (Rubin, 1970). Spaulding (1970) suggests that feelings and behaviors characteristic of romantic love tend to lead to more disturbances in the psychological well-being of men than of women. Hill, Rubin, and Peplau (1976) found the women's feelings of love are far more predictive of the course of a relationship than are men's. In their study of couples living together, they found that women were more likely to perceive difficulties in the relationship and to consider alternatives than were men. The women were also found to be more likely to terminate the relationship.

The literature reviewed on sex differences suggests that this is an area in which further research may help to substantiate the phenomenon of romantic love and place it in perspective. For example, in studies of modern family life, the changing roles of men and women are often discussed in conjunction with changes in the structure and function of the family. The effects of the recent women's movement may be influencing attitudes toward romantic love, and the changing role of women may introduce substantial changes in the process of romantic love in relationships. As women's roles change, men's must also change in order to maintain a homeostatic balance. If, in fact, men become more family oriented (for example, sharing parenting responsibilities, placing less emphasis upon the workplace), then some overall changes in sex-related attitudes toward romantic love may also occur. Marriage may become more important for men, with a move toward increased practicality on their part, and a decrease in romanticism may accompany this shift. Women, at the same time, may become more romantic as they increasingly seek work outside the home and begin to realize that they have more than one option (marriage) in their lives. An alternative view may be that both sexes will come to accept relationships as less permanent if the present trend toward living together and the increasing rate of divorce persists. A larger-scale understanding of romantic love should help people adjust to changes in relationships and in societal patterns, resulting in more successful adaptations to love relationships and less intense misunderstanding and suffering.

Romantic Love Within the Context of Change

We have argued that it is important to understand romantic love and have reviewed some of the literature relevant to an understanding of the development of love relationships. The paradigms that have been presented are characterized by a primarily linear orientation: Love changes form over time and undergoes some substantial shifts in its nature during its transformation. Although the general shift documented is one from passionate to companionate love (Walster and Walster, 1978), there are indications that romantic love may resurface later in relationships (Knox, 1970; Munro and Adams, 1978), suggesting a cyclical and enduring process of change rather than a purely linear approach. This change has been explored to date only at the level of interpersonal relationships. The next step is to examine shifts in romantic love from a broader perspective and to ascertain whether or not romantic love truly undergoes major transformations or whether it recurs in similar forms over time. Thus, having concerned ourselves primarily with interpersonal relationships, we shall now turn to an examination of some societal forces that may elucidate the same process and may clarify the role of romantic love in individuals' lives.

On a societal level, Wilkinson (1978) argues for irrevocable changes in American attitudes toward romantic love. His view is based on the idea that romantic love is related to the frustration of sex drives, which he argues no longer occurs in our society. He found that couples living together (and presumably engaging in as much sexual activity as they desired) had a lower romantic love orientation than they did before living together and fewer feelings of romantic love than did couples not cohabitating. Blood (1952) similarly argued that premarital intercourse was incompatible with romantic love. Twenty-five years later, Blood and Blood (1978) discussed love in a substantially different way. In 1978, they conceptualized romantic love within a more flexible framework of relationships, minimizing the role of romantic love and accentuating the pragmatics of relationships and the overriding importance of attachment and affection. This shift, not acknowledged by Blood in his earlier work, paralleled rather dramatic changes in societal values toward sexuality and cohabitation and may offer support for Wilkinson's (1978) theory. It may also be that romantic love is not as intimately linked with sexual intercourse as was thought at first, but that the romanticism attached to love is a compelling, ongoing process. The increased likelihood of consummating sexual attraction today does not necessarily dictate that attraction will decrease with sexual intimacy. It may be that sexual activity early in a relationship accelerates the passionate to compassionate shift and may bring couples to a Stage 2 (Goldstine and others, 1977) or Discordance (Coleman, 1977) impasse more quickly than if intercourse had not occurred. Our suggestion is that the cyclical process of love may occur nonetheless, and that romantic love may still resurface later in the relationship, if the couple chooses to stay together. Similarly, if the couple chooses not to continue the relationship, it seems likely in a cyclical and enduring process of romantic love that each partner will again experience romantic love with other persons.

Kilpatrick (1974) argues that romantic love is incompatible with our present society for several reasons. He notes that an orientation toward the future is critical for the growth of romantic love and that people are no longer willing to live for the future, preferring to live in the present. Furthermore, an assumption of scarcity is seen as being integral to the prosperity of romantic love. Kilpatrick sees this as being untrue at present, noting that in today's society people generally believe that there is no shortage of goods. A third condition necessary for romantic love to thrive is a sharp polarity between the sexes. The assumption is that romantic love is based on idealization and remoteness from the opposite sex. With the rise of more androgynous values in our society and the meshing of characteristics once assumed to be the province of only one sex, this assumption is not met, according to Kilpatrick. The final missing component needed for the sustenance of romantic love is an individualistic, rather than a communal outlook. Kilpatrick argues that jealousy and possessiveness are critical prerequisites of romantic love and that they are not found in our society with its community orientation, sharing of sexual partners, and group living arrangements.

While Kilpatrick's (1974) arguments are interesting and thought provoking, they suggest a primarily linear approach to changes in love in our society. It is purported that romantic love as we once knew it can no longer exist in our society. The conditions that Kilpatrick cites as antithetical to romantic love seem to be descriptive of American life during the 1960s. Although his analysis may have been accurate in assessing changes from the 1950s to the 1960s, his arguments are now open to debate and fail to anticipate more recent trends in our society as the 1980s begin. Although androgyny may have increased in prominence, it is not clear that this is a lasting change, or a change that is not subject to external forces. It is even less clear that today we feel that there is no shortage of resources or that we are community oriented in our approach to problems. Indeed, the alleged rise of narcissism and introspection and the rapid rise to popularity of business and applied degrees suggest that our orientation may be more individualistic and pragmatic rather than communal and idealistic.

A broader and more cyclical view of romantic love would suggest that romantic love may have decreased during times in which Kilpatrick's (1974) assumptions were met but that it might increase again in prevalence during periods in which societal mores were different. A historical analysis (Levine and Levine, 1970;

Reppucci and Saunders, 1977) of periods of high and low romantic love might prove enlightening. Although much of the desired data on the prevalence of romantic love are not available, it may be that romantic love fluctuates with economic conditions or that it is related to periods of war or peace in our society. Similarly, it may be that within a natural pattern of fluctuation in attitudes toward romantic love different highs and lows are obtained over time. Thus our orientation toward romantic love might rise in the next decade but not to the heights reached several decades ago. Analysis of such sensitive shifts would begin to provide a fascinating picture of changes in romantic love over time. In a seasonal analogy, each winter brings with it colder weather, but some winters are colder than others. Similarly, some periods of high romantic love orientation may be more intense than others. The same analogy could be applied to interpersonal analyses of romantic love in relationships.

Indeed, it is often difficult to ascertain whether societal shifts have lasting impact or whether they are merely part of cyclical processes. The conservatism of the 1950s subsided and was replaced with the liberalism of the 1960s, which gave way to another period of conservatism. There is a popular sense that some of the changes introduced in the 1960s were lasting ones. Thus there is a sense of change along with strong threads of no change. Again, this is much like our consideration of love in a relationship. We expect that love will last and yet we know that there will be changes. Although the 1960s advocated some experimental living arrangements that potentially threatened the structure of the American nuclear family, communal living and group marriages failed to maintain a foothold in our society. Rather than representing novel family forms, some of these alternatives had been popular in previous decades. While authors still debate the issue of whether or not the family is in a period of lasting decadence (Bane, 1976; Lasch, 1977), cohabitation is a phenomenon that appears to have gained some lasting popularity. However, writers in the area (Coleman, 1977; Davidoff, 1977; Hill, Rubin, and Peplau, 1976; Ridley, Peterman, and Avery, 1978) seem to be suggesting that living together is a developmental phase and that it has not replaced marriage as a social institution. This examination of cohabitation points to an apparent change that may represent less of a novel change than was thought at first.

Watzslavik, Weakland, and Fisch (1974) present a systems view of change that appears critical in explaining changes in romantic love, whether the change under consideration is between two persons or in society. They, like Sarason (1972, 1974), note that "the more something changes, the more it stays the same." This seems particularly salient in a discussion of romantic love. We have observed changes in living patterns and societal mores that may have introduced changes in the nature of romantic love. However, the lasting impression is that there has not been as much change as was thought at first. Similarly, it often seems that individuals feel that they will not experience the same sort of love again after a relationship ends but that they do fall in love again. Indeed, it may be that the shift from being in love to falling out of love (a substantial change, it would seem) precipitates the next occurrence of romantic love. As with seasonal change, the more something changes, the more it stays the same. Within our conceptualization of seasons, each winter will eventually be followed by another. Within our view of romantic love, love may be followed by disillusionment but falling in love again seems to be highly probable.

An example of change without change can be seen in the 1978 movie *An Unmarried Woman*. The film was heralded as an acknowledgment of the prevalence of divorce and a documentation of the life of a divorced woman. After only a brief period of pain and uncertainty, the heroine found herself victim to the familiar god of romantic love, this time in the form of an artist. Although the movies suggest that romantic love in a marriage may sour and the marriage may dissolve, the alternative that the heroine chose was to find happiness by falling in love again. Even though she decided at the end not to follow her new love and engage in a marriagelike relationship, the process of idealization, excitement, and romantic intrigue seemed to be critical.

Wilkinson (1976) examined the role that popular music plays in the lives of adolescents, analyzing the top forty songs for the period of 1954–1968, and offered some suggestions as to the stereotypes and values conveyed through these songs. Careful examination suggested that romantic themes were pervasive, although a more thorough examination of trends in music and content of themes may have provided more insight into societal changes. The popularity of old movies (who doesn't like to watch Ginger Rogers and Fred Astaire fall in love again once in a while?) seems to offset the raucousness and blatant sexuality of the now popular punk rock music. The examples of this change-without-change phenomenon are many and may suggest that romantic love plays a role as an important stabilizing force in a society that appears to be undergoing rapid change. The data that we obtained from college students seem to substantiate this idea. Most of the students indicated that although there have been changes in our society and that we have become more practical, romantic love is still alive and well. Most expressed concern that if romantic love as we know it were to erode, it would be hard to reconcile this change.

It seems that the practical and reality-bound part of ourselves often disowns the notions of romantic love such as idealization and undying love. Indeed, romantic love is full of fallacies and "terrible oversimplifications," suggesting that it mirrors what Watzslavik, Weakland, and Fisch (1974) term the Utopia Syndrome. Within the Utopia Syndrome, there is a tendency to see a solution where there is none. Here love is the answer—it conquers all. Those who suffer from the Utopia Syndrome idealize heavily and "question everything but the quest itself." Romantic love forms the basis for most long-term relationships (marriages) and can easily be used unrealistically as a standard by which to view the course of the relationship. Within the enduring and cyclical view of love proposed in this chapter, we view love primarily within the Utopia Syndrome. When love decays, the quest for love continues and romantic love persists. Attempts at first-order change, change that occurs leaving a system unaltered (Watzslavik, Weakland, and Fisch, 1974), are frustrated for they fail to remove us from the romantic love cycle. Indeed, only second-order change, change outside of our present conceptualization of the love relationship, can break the cycle. Second-order changes at an individual level are easier to conceptualize than those at a societal level. Perhaps an individual needs to find new solutions for problems and not seek another love relationship, for the same process is likely to occur with the next love.

It may be that we need not seek a second-order change solution for romantic love at a societal level. The Utopia Syndrome and the idealization it represents serve as protection and needed relief from a pragmatic and stressful world. Although love can blind, it is also a reassuring buffer. This is a function that should not be dismissed lightly. Hall and Taylor (1976) suggest that idealization continues through the divorce process and note that the problem in our society may not be that there is anything intrinsically wrong with love or marriage but that we have come to attach too much importance to these concepts. We tend to believe that without the presence of love (and utopia) as we first knew it, there can be no meaningful relationship.

Watzslavik, Weakland, and Fisch (1974, p. 19) state that "one of the most common fallacies about change is the conclusion that if something is bad, its opposite must of necessity be good." This is pertinent for an understanding of romantic love. Many first-order changes occur in relationships; we dissolve a relationship when it has soured, believing that the same process will not happen again. When we step outside of the relationship and view romantic love from a broader perspective, it becomes clearer that the sequence of falling in love, finding "utopia," and then experiencing deflation of our expectations is a cyclical process. True second-order change is difficult to conceptualize and may not even be something worth striving toward, given the positive aspects of the Utopia Syndrome.

A more in-depth understanding of romantic love and its cyclical process seems to rest upon an acceptance of romantic love as a utopian ideal. Sarason (1972) notes that the utopian ideal is a strong motivating force for change. In the case of romantic love, we must accept this utopianism as a stabilizing force, a respite from daily life. If romantic love is seen not as a dichotomous entity but is viewed within a broader perspective, the outlook for the positive role of romantic love in our lives is brightened considerably.

The Challenge of Viewing Romantic Love Within a Community Context

In many ways, we are back to the original question of why the understanding of romantic love is both important and possible. A review of the literature documenting changes in relationships offered some evidence that a solely linear (passionate to companionate love) model failed to capture some of the cyclical shifts that occur in love over time. Consideration of some shifts in romantic love over time in our society suggested that it is not at all clear that these alleged changes have been long-term in nature. It is suggested that romantic love, at both an interpersonal and societal level, needs to be viewed from a broad model of change, such as that suggested by Watzslavik, Weakland, and Fisch (1974).

Romantic love seems to be a utopian force that is the basis of many marriages—and the root of much discontent when it fails to meet our expectations. Romantic love seems to persist despite changes in our society and merits further investigation from psychologists.

We need to gather more information on the prevalence of romantic love notions in our society today. Past research in this area has been quite narrow in scope. We need to expand our knowledge of romantic love to include variables such as age and socioeconomic status. With the increasing prevalence of divorce and the proliferation of postdivorce family forms, it would be valuable to gather more data on the effects of these changes on attitudes toward romantic love.

Romantic love has become an institution in our society, seen as a prerequisite for marriage and family life. At this time, when many critics are asserting that the family is nearly defunct, romantic love should be incorporated into our study of the family, providing some insights into changes and consistencies over time. The cyclical and enduring process of romantic love might be seen more clearly if we were to study families longitudinally, gathering data descriptive of both their general life situation and their romantic orientations at various times. It may eventually be possible to plan interventions and programs for people at various points in their lives (considering marriage, deciding to have children, dealing with adolescent children, adjusting to life after children grow up) which can incorporate our understanding of romantic love. A more specific understanding of cycles of love would be useful and reassuring in planning therapeutic interventions in general. For example, with an increasing number of young adults postponing marriage or considering lives exclusive of marriage, a model of love relationships that can be used to add some predictability into the lives of such persons could prove useful.

Although romantic love itself need not be the focus of community psychology research endeavors, the nature of romantic love and the utopian ideals it suggests can fit into our existing paradigms. Community psychologists often focus on various forms of alienation and have conceptual frameworks for involving persons in ongoing community processes. We should be able to apply our understanding of romantic love and the utopian ideal in our conceptualization of the psychological sense of community (Sarason, 1974) and the notion of social support networks (Caplan, 1976).

Romantic love may always remain somewhat beyond our grasp if there is truth in Robert Louis Stevenson's words: "Falling in love is the one illogical adventure, the one thing which we are tempted to think of as supernatural in our tried and reasonable world." When understood from the perspective of the Utopia Syndrome and continual change, romantic love need not be seen as a total mystery nor damned as a meaningless concept. Rather, romantic love offers hope for future endeavors aimed at understanding human behavior when it is viewed as a cyclical and enduring process. Like the seasons, it is bound to come again and can be welcomed as a familiar phenomenon.

13

Comparing Romantic
and Therapeutic
Relationships

Linnda Durré

A young man who sought therapy because he feared he might be a homosexual related his suspicions in his first session to his therapist, the renowned Gestalt psychotherapist, Miriam Polster. "Can you help me?" he asked fervently, since he wanted to be heterosexual. "Well, in order for your therapy to work," Dr. Polster replied, "you just may have to risk falling in love with me."

The importance of "falling in love" with one's therapist can be interpreted as positive transference, and its successful resolution in a nonsexual manner is crucial to the process of the therapeutic relationship and the progress that the client will make in therapy. What is love? What are transference and countertransference and what is their impact on psychotherapy?

The Funk and Wagnalls *Standard Dictionary* (1958) defines *love* as "a strong, complex emotion or feeling causing one to appreciate, delight in, and crave the presence or possession of another and to please or promote the welfare of the other." *Romantic* is defined as "characterized or influenced by romance or the *extravagantly ideal* [my italics]; hence impractical, visionary." None of the sources consulted, including Webster's "Unabridged," offered a definition of *Romantic Love* per se.

Transference can be defined as "(1) in general, any displacement of an affect from one object to another, (2) specifically, the displacement of an affect toward the past to the analyst" (Chaplin, 1968, p. 549). Transference, then, is the process by which clients project onto the therapist certain unconscious feelings, characteristics, or dynamics that they experienced as children, usually with an important adult and most frequently with a parent. Transference can be positive or negative. The same dynamic is at work as when these feelings are projected onto a newcomer into one's life who is increasingly perceived as attractive, desirable, and "partnerable."

The term *countertransference* refers to "the analyst's experience of emotional attachment for the patient" (Chaplin, 1968, pp. 120-121). In the broader sense, it can be any emotional response, positive or negative, that is evoked in the therapist by the client, but in common usage and for the purpose of this chapter, countertransference is defined as emotional, physical, and sexual attraction and attachment of the therapist toward the client.

Freud ([1915] 1958) not only acknowledged the similarity between the therapist-client/parent-child relationship but was also acutely aware of the process of the client's falling in love with the therapist. In fact, Freud felt that in positive transference, "falling in love" was inevitable: "It is therefore plain, that he [the therapist] is not to derive any personal advantage from [the therapeutic situation]. The patient's willingness makes no difference whatsoever; it merely throws the whole responsibility on him. Indeed, as he must know, the patient had from the beginning entertained hopes of this way of being cured" [p. 160].

This chapter will explore the similarities and differences between romantic and therapeutic relationships. Probably the most important factors in differentiating between these two situations are the intentions and expectations of the participants. Between lovers, the ultimate goal is union, emotional and sexual. In the psychotherapeutic relationship, however, expectations are quite different. The client, who usually consults a therapist initially for a specific problem, really wants his or her life in general to improve. The ideal aim of the therapist, regardless of the orientation, is to make clients capable of coping with the demands of their lives so that eventually they may "stand alone." Partnering, particularly sexual partnering, has no place in the therapeutic situation.

The Process of Falling in Love

What is the process of "falling in love"? Is there a process? We have all heard of "love at first sight," but for the purpose of this chapter, I have identified six stages of "falling in love": courtship, idealization, acceptance, continuity, crisis, and resolution. These are not necessarily well-defined stages, time-limited or time-related, or even necessarily consecutive. For example, one relationship might begin with an idealization and then follow into a courtship period; difficulties and crises may continue throughout the relationship. But to compare and contrast the love relationships between lover/lover and therapist/client, these six stages will structure the discussion.

Courtship. The "courtship period" may precede or follow the "idealization stage." Basically, in this period, both romantic lovers and the therapist and client are getting to know and trust each other. The foundation of the relationship is established here. Lovers share past experiences, likes and dislikes, hopes and dreams for the future, and consider if the relationship can even *have* a future. If there is compatibility, lovers may ponder living together, marriage, or a deep, permanent bond.

Therapist and client also establish trust and compatability: Can we work together? Do I feel comfortable with this person? The client, as the lover, might decide to withdraw from the relationship if these questions are not answered positively, and find another therapist. The therapist should ask similar questions: Do I feel comfortable with this client? Do I think I can help? Can we work well together? All three questions should be answered positively before therapy continues.

If the therapist does not like or feel comfortable with the client, it may prove damaging to the therapeutic alliance. The therapist can consciously relay to the client—in verbal and non-verbal communications—messages of dislike, impatience, boredom, nonacceptance, resentment, disapproval, fear, and discomfort. This may cause the client to withdraw, not open up, or deal only with "safe" topics. Such a therapist/client relationship may border on the unethical and may be ultimately damaging to the client.

A client and therapist, as in a lover-lover bond, should be able to relate to each other with mutual trust, openness, and compatibility. This brings us to the issue of sharing in both types of relationships.

Sharing. By sharing experiences and ideas, lovers form a bond of compatibility, equality, and mutual support. Similar mutual sharing within the therapist/client relationship is inappropriate and out of place. Certainly, self-disclosure by a therapist can be a powerful tool used to establish empathy and trust, but therapists, as a rule, do not share much of their own experiences. To use a client's session for one's own purposes would be unethical. Even relaying one's likes and dislikes could be detrimental to a client who may seek the acceptance and approval of the therapist and would therefore tailor her or his responses to please the therapist.

It is the client who must do the majority of "sharing." For some, in fact, therapy is a *more* intimate relationship than marriage. One may tell the therapists things that may never be revealed to spouse or partner. A client will relate his or her fears, weaknesses, dislikes, hopes, dreams, strengths, and gains, while the therapist, serving as a mirror, supports, confronts when necessary, and functions as a "reality tester." The one-sidedness of sharing in the therapist/client relationship is opposite to the equality and mutuality of the sharing in the lover/lover relationship. This is an inherent difference in the two relationships. Another major difference is time, as an entity, as a goal, and in its relationship to the future.

Time. Lovers want to spend every possible minute with each other. Being away from each other can be painful, lonely, and alienating. But time belongs to the couple. They can be together as often as they choose. In contrast, a therapist and client are usually together only an hour at a time: once, twice, or three times a week. Daily analysis, at the most, is still only five hours a week.

Time as an entity is very different in the two relationships. Time and its relationship to the future is also different. Lovers may ponder a future together: Will this bond result in a marriage? Should we live together? How many years will this last? Till death do us part? Lovers have the option to consider a future together. Therapist and client, however, do not usually plan a lifelong alliance. Months or a year or two are usually the time expectancy. Certainly, many clients do continue with the same therapist for years; others will call for an occasional "booster shot" session or a short, resuming period while under transient, situational stress. But the goal of therapy is freedom from dependency upon the therapist.

Idealization. In the second stage, both "love" for lovers and transference for clients have begun. This is the "idealization" or "idolization" phase, where the lover regards the object of love as embodying all earthly virtues and as the one person who can give meaning to life. Physical desire is high and attraction is mutual. Depending on the mores of the culture, sexual intercourse may occur or it may be deferred until the couple marries or exchanges vows. However, it is implicitly accepted that a couple "in love" will eventually "become one" through sexual intercourse.

In this period, lovers feel real pain in the absence of the other. They try to look their best and be on their best behavior, they exchange gifts, and they seldom experience a period of time when the other is not in their thoughts. This is also termed the "love is blind" stage. They may see qualities in their beloved that are not really there. They may see what they want to see and hear what they want to hear, molding their partner in their image or vision of what they wish the partner to be. These expectations, which may be high, unrealistic, and/or unfair, can provide much disappointment to the lovers. This usually occurs in the acceptance phase that follows.

For the client, idealization manifests itself in beliefs that the therapist had a happy childhood or certainly one that has been totally and completely resolved and that the therapist has a happy personal life—a happy marriage, good relationships with his chil-

dren, contentment in his work, and so on. In short, the client believes that the therapist is free of problems or any debilitating
pathology. If the therapist were to have an "occasional problem,"
as one woman stated, "it would certainly not be anything that he
couldn't handle."

In the grips of the "idealization" stage, many female clients
have reported seeing their male therapists as "all powerful," "all
wise," and the like. The client places her trust in this omniscient
person who supposedly has the training, education, and skills to
"heal" her. As the relationship is established, she comes to rely
heavily on the therapist for guidance, support, objectivity, empathy, caring, concern, and insight.

As in the romantic love relationship, many of these women
go out of their way to impress and please their therapist. They
may dress up and use makeup to look their most attractive for
each session. They may make or purchase gifts for the therapist,
write poems or keep journal entries about him, indulge in erotic
and masturbatory fantasies, and dress and/or behave seductively in
session. In short, with strong transference, the therapist becomes
a "love object" to the client. "I didn't know what I would do
without him," stated one woman who I interviewed. "He was the
center of my universe." "I did everything with him in mind," related another." "I wanted him to like me," went the standard
reply. "I would do anything to gain his approval and get his attention. Eveything he said was so important to me then."

Some clients resist transference. "Transference resistance" is
defined as "the attempt on the part of the individual being analyzed
to maintain repression over affects or impulses during the process
of transference. Thus the patient may have strong sexual feelings
toward the analyst, but these are kept buried, just as similar feelings toward the parent were repressed" (Chaplin, 1968, pp.
549-550).

Freud considered transference itself as a form of resistance
to therapy. He urged his analysts to use it and work through it,
with no physical contact at all: "To the physician it [positive love
transference] represents an invaluable explanation and a useful
warning against any tendency to countertransference which may
be lurking in his own mind. He must recognize that the patient's
falling in love is induced by the analytic situation and is not to be

ascribed to the charms of her person, that he has no reason whatever therefore to be proud of such a 'conquest' as it would be called
outside analysis. And it is always well to be reminded of this"
[Freud (1915) 1953e, p. 160]. Here Freud draws attention to the
countertransference the analyst may be experiencing within the
"idealization stage." As the more powerful of the two in a thera-
pist/client relationship, the therapist may view the client as "needing to be rescued," "not able to take care of himself or herself,"
"not able to live without him or her [the therapist]," or the therapist may see himself as the only one knowing what is best, good,
right, or necessary for the client. The therapist may also experience physical and/or sexual attraction to the client, and may or
may not choose to relate this to the client.

For most therapists, their countertransference is best dealt
with outside of the client session, either with a supervisor, colleague, or their own therapist. Having to deal with the therapist's
attraction can place a great burden on a client, especially if the
client is not mutually attracted or has enough difficulty dealing
with his or her own sexuality, life, and problems. Many women
I interviewed resented this disclosure by the therapist and felt it
was out of place and that the therapist was using "my time for his
needs."

A therapist walks a thin red line in affirming a client's physical attractiveness and sexuality while at the same time not getting
involved personally. Phrasing the compliment in the objective
rather than subjective style seems to help: "You are a very attractive person" rather than "I am attracted to you" or "I find you
very attractive." Such subjective statements can set up almost
a challenge to some clients to conquer or "seduce" the therapist,
even if the therapist has insisted that there will be no sexual contact between them.

Acceptance. Normally, the idealization stage ends and blends
into the acceptance stage where one's perceptions of the person
are congruent with reality. For some, this stage can be shocking,
disappointing, and full of resentment. "I never knew you were like
that" is a familiar lament. Or, "She's really not that way at all.
She's just under stress."

In a *Los Angeles Times* column, Ellen Goodman (1979) discussed the reasons behind such strong idealization of some couples:

"But maybe they also are afraid that if they let go of their illusions, they will not like each other. We often refuse to see what we might not be able to live with. We choose distortion." The choice is to distort rather than accept. And so the acceptance stage may never be worked out. People will choose to "see what they want to see" and "hear what they want to hear." It may be a delusion, consciously or unconsciously.

For some clients as well as some lovers, part or all of the idealization may *never* end, even when the relationship is over—when either the therapy is terminated (successfully or not) or the love relationship ends in separation, divorce, or death. People may hold on tenaciously to the "image" of their beloved or their therapist. "And what's too painful to remember, we simply choose to forget," sings Barbra Streisand in "The Way We Were."

A successful acceptance stage can be achieved with honesty, openness, mutual support, and direct communication. Time and hard work may also be crucial elements. As Goodman (1979) further states: "I thought about how much human effort can go into maintaining the reality. How much daily energy that might have gone into understanding the reality—accepting it or rejecting it." Here lovers can come to a crossroads which may be part of the "crisis" or "difficulty" stage to be discussed later. Do they accept each and every trait and quality in their partner? Do they even have to? Can they compromise? Do they choose to ignore? Can they laugh about what they do not like—in themselves as well as in their partner? Or do they choose to reject—to leave the partner, either by separation, divorce, or moving out? Transference, like being "in love," may also distort the client's view of the therapist and make "acceptance" difficult.

For some clients, "acceptance" may not be achieved until the therapy has ended. "I just thought that he was the handsomest man I ever saw," one woman told me in an interview for this study. "Then about a year after my therapy was completed, I saw him again, and realized that he was bald, grossly overweight, had bad skin, bad breath, and was a sloppy dresser. A caring, sensitive man, but nothing like what I had imagined. How could I have not seen that?" she asked herself. Many other women shared the same perceptions of their therapists at first: that he was good-looking, kind, understanding, supportive, had no problems of his own, or, as one woman stated, "certainly none that he couldn't solve easily and by himself." They later found out that many of their perceptions were not grounded in reality and some were far from the truth. But transference and countertransference may or may not be related to another aspect of the "acceptance" stage in therapy. For example, can the client accept the therapist who chronically "runs late"? Did the therapist inform the client of this tendency or possibility? Does the therapist make up the time or prorate the session? If a client is obsessive about time, she or he can find another, more punctual therapist, or perhaps the therapist can provide the client with some insight into their obsessiveness-perfectionism, fear of reprisals if they were late, self-righteousness, punishing others, etc.?

What does acceptance of the client by the therapist mean? Can the therapist accept the client's angry outbursts? The "broken records" about things that don't seem to change? The crying spells? The avoidance? Lateness to sessions? Does the therapist accept the client as a person or does the therapist dislike the client? Does the client feel accepted by the therapist? Can the client confide in the therapist and feel safe? The impressions or initial work of the courtship stage discussed previously may be put to the test in the acceptance stage. If these feelings are not worked through, friction, discontent, unsuccessful therapy, and/or termination may result. Successful completion leads to the continuity stage.

Continuity. In the nontherapeutic relationship, this is the "body" as opposed to the "face" of courtship or the "extremities" of termination. It is the daily living with each other, which may last for weeks, months, or years. Although the couple may face disappointments and crises during this period, they choose to continue to work together for a mutually satisfying resolution of their problems. For some, acceptance can occur during or even after the continuity stage. For others, acceptance is in the process of being worked through, or, best of all, this process has already been accomplished. For many couples, this stage bridges decades from courtship/acceptance through the death of one partner. Even today, our society salutes the longevity of the continuation phase through the publicity accorded "silver and golden wedding" celebrations. The lifelong perpetuity of the continuation phase is still an idealization of American culture.

In therapy, however, with its different goal of eventual, healthy separation, continuity is truly a continuation or "midphase" of the process of therapeutically stimulated self-examination by the client. In this stage, the majority of the work is accomplished. Trust has been established; there is an ongoing sense of empathy and understanding. The client continues to peel off layers of self-delusion and is met appropriately with caring, confrontation, and support by the therapist. The client increasingly has the courage to take risks and to deal actively with the issues of her or his growth.

Crisis. Crisis in nontherapeutic interpersonal relationships can originate when one partner sees through the self-imposed pattern of idealization. For example: A woman has envisioned her husband as a dedicated "one-woman man." When she learns that he has one or more relationships outside of their marriage, the shock of disillusion may bring the real picture into focus. Crises may also erupt when one partner in an alliance, from internal stimulus, chooses to make a change in his or her way of life. An example of this is the woman who, having spent twenty years as a dedicated homemaker, chooses to go back to college or to work. When a partner resists change in the other's life-style, a crisis situation can result.

In therapy, crisis can originate from circumstances external to the therapeutic involvement, or from a cross-circuiting of the therapist/client relationship. The external cause for a client's crisis is his or her perceiving a real or threatened change, either self-imposed or super-imposed. A child may leave home, a spouse may institute divorce proceedings, there may be a death in the client's family, or he or she may threaten suicide. The causes are myriad. At these times, clients feel their dependence upon the therapist, whom they have grown to trust, to help them through the crisis. There may be a need for extra emergency sessions and/or telephone calls. Clients may make unreasonable demands on the therapist and feel that they are unable to face the problem or resolve it.

But there is a different type of crisis that can originate within the parameters of therapy itself, when client trauma is created by the ineffective resolution of the countertransference phenomenon by the therapist. Freud was early aware of this potential. In a per-

sonal letter written in 1931 (Freud, 1957c), he advised his student
Ferenczi, who had been employing "mothering" techniques:

> You have not made a secret of the fact that you kiss
> your patients and let them kiss you; I had also heard that from
> a patient of my own. Now when you decide to give a full ac-
> count of your technique and its results, you will have to choose
> between two ways: Either you relate this or you conceal it.
> The latter, as you may well think, is dishonorable. What one
> does in one's technique one has to defend openly. Besides, both
> ways soon come together. Even if you don't say so yourself
> it will soon get known, just as I knew it before you told me.
>
> Now I am assuredly not one of those who from prud-
> ishness or from considerations of bourgeois convention would
> condemn little erotic gratifications of this kind. And I am also
> aware that in the time of the Nibelungs a kiss was a harmless
> greeting granted to every guest. . . . But does that alter the fact
> . . . that with us a kiss signifies a certain erotic intimacy? We
> have hitherto in our technique held to the conclusion that
> patients are to be refused erotic gratifications.
>
> Now picture, what will be the result of publishing your
> technique. There is no revolutionary who is not driven out of
> the field by a still more radical one. A number of independent
> thinkers in matters of technique will say to themselves: Why
> stop at a kiss? Certainly one gets further when one adopts
> "pawing" as well, which after all doesn't make a baby. And
> then bolder ones will come along who will go further, to peep-
> ing and showing—and soon we shall have accepted in the tech-
> nique of analysis the whole repertoire of "demiviergerie" and
> petting parties, resulting in an enormous increase of interest in
> psychoanalysis among both analysts and patients.

Therapists are, after all, also human. And they may experience the excitement of a mutual attraction with a client. What
they do with that attraction separates those with true dedication
to the Hippocratic Oath from those who are more self-serving or
those who are unaware of or choose to ignore their countertransference as well as the client's transference. One therapist, with
whom I became acquainted in a workshop, stated that he knew
a therapist who would immediately refer a client to another prac-
titioner whenever he experienced a physical/romantic "chemistry"
with that client.

But what if the transference and countertransference phenomena become a real love and a mutual romantic attachment?

Since the goals of romantic love and therapy are so different, one of these relationships must be ended, or at least discontinued. It is recommended that both participants enter therapy to make the transition from therapist/client to lover/lover or husband/wife. Couple sessions should be a definite requirement in addition to individual psychotherapy, with either the same or different therapists for each person or, ideally, a dual team of therapists. There are a number of instances of such coupling. Some notable people have married their therapists. Reich's first wife, Bernfeld's last wife, Rado's third wife, and one of Fenichel's former wives were all initially patients. There are many additional examples from modern day life as well.

There are those therapists, however, who—either because they do not work through the countertransference or because some neurotic need of their own—become engaged in a sexual liaison with the client. In these cases, a new crisis situation is generated for the client stemming from the therapeutic situation itself.

In my doctoral dissertation (D'Addario-Durré, 1977), I presented four case histories of women who had had sexual relationships with their male therapists. I also presented data from the questionnaires of sixty-five women who stated that they had been sexually involved with their therapists, and studied in depth the previous literature on the subject. Masters and Johnson (1975, p. 10) point out the extreme vulnerability of the sexually dysfunctional person: "Psychotherapists have long been aware that the sexually dysfunctional individual fearing for his or her manhood or womanhood is particularly prone to a pathologic level of emotional identification with the therapist of choice."

Siassi and Thomas (1973) liken the relationship between a physician and patient to that of a parent and child, both involving helplessness and dependency for survival on a powerful authority figure. They claim that the incest taboo will continue as long as "the nuclear family [remains] the basic unit of society," and that "to equate a sexual relationship between a physician and his patient with the other aspects of sexual freedom betrays ignorance of the basic tenet of society" (p. 1257). Even the fact that "the patient is willing, or may even be the aggressive initiator, is no more valid a justification than the claim of parents who engage in incest that the child was willing or was the initiator" (p. 1256).

Siassi and Thomas (1973) agree that it is the physician who is in control and who has the responsibility to avoid sexual contact which can be exploitative. They also state that the taboo against sexual contact in the therapeutic relationship "is based more on pragmatic than on moral grounds," stressing objectivity in diagnosis, treatment, and prevention, as well as movement toward emotional health through "the establishment of rapport, i.e., a harmonious nonthreatening relationship in which the physician is both an empathic participant and a dispassionate observer" (p. 1257). Sexual contact destroys the objectivity, thereby impairing treatment.

What of the reaction of the female clients who had coupled with their therapists? One of the conclusions of my own study was that the sexual relationships the female subjects had with their male therapists was detrimental, if not devastating, to the personal growth of all four women. The sexual relationships were not physically satisfying to them and there was a significant amount of sexual dysfunction of the clients as well as the therapists. For the female clients, there was frigidity, nonorgasmic responses, and vaginismus. For the male therapists, there was premature ejaculation, priapism, and impotency. The female clients also felt confused and angry about having to pay for therapeutic services concurrent with a sexual relationship, some as much as seventy-five dollars an hour. All four sought out a second therapist (two with men therapists, two with women therapists) to help them deal with the effects of their experiences as well as for their original presenting problems, which had not been resolved. All four spoke highly of their second therapists as people, as well as of their competency as professionals. All four women spoke emphatically against any sexual contact between therapist and client, variously labeling their experience as detrimental, growth-inhibiting, devastating, unethical, and unprofessional.

Resolution. In both romantic love and therapy, there is a resolution to the relationship. In romantic love, the resolution may be the continuity phase with a sense of increasing closeness between the couple as each crisis is met and weathered. This, after all, was the original stated goal of the partners, to go down the years together "in sickness and in health until death do us part."

Another resolution to the romantic condition is separation. This may be initiated by one partner or mutually agreed upon by both. Usually one or both of the partners suffer pain and bereavement as a result of this separation. There may also be feelings of guilt because of the failure of the initial goal of "togetherness."

In therapy, a positive or successful conclusion can be considered to have been reached when client and therapist agree that the client has attained a level of self-awareness and competence to "go it alone," that she or he is no longer dependent upon the therapist. This can occur only when the therapist has led the client through the difficult stage of transference and is fully cognizant of the power of transference to distort the client's perception of reality. During this time, the therapist has also been aware of his own countertransference and has worked out with his own therapist, a supervisor, or colleague any physical or sexual attraction he has felt for the client. A truly satisfactory therapy should be growth-producing for both client and therapist.

A negative termination to therapy is the result in nearly all the cases where the therapist and client have experienced physical and/or sexual intimacy. According to most of these case studies (Belote, 1974; Chesler, 1972; D'Addario-Durré, 1977; Taylor and Wagner, 1976), the therapist initiates the termination because of fear of discovery by his colleagues, his wife, or other clients, or fear of revelation by the female client.

How does this therapist effect termination? In most cases, the therapist very clearly signals that he is "not there" for the client anymore. He is distant, indifferent, bored, disgusted, or unavailable. He does not answer or return telephone calls. Some have abruptly stopped therapy sessions and have cut off all communication with their clients. Others have continued to see the client in therapy but discontinued sexual and/or social contact.

And how does this withdrawal of attention affect the female client? Compounding the pain of rejection by a lover is the overwhelming sense of betrayal by a trusted parent figure. In the words of Chesler (1972, pp. 146–147):

> Although many of the women described being humiliated and frustrated by their therapists' emotional and sexual coldness or ineptitude, it was the therapist, more often than the patient, who ended the "affair." And in every case the woman was further hurt by the abandonment. After the therapist's withdrawal, one woman tried to kill herself; two others lapsed into a severe depression; a fourth woman's *husband*,

who was also in treatment with the same therapist, killed himself shortly *after* if not *because*, he found out about the affair. This particular therapist's rather sadistic and grandiose attempt to cure this woman's "frigidity" one night resulted in her developing a "headache" that wouldn't subside for a year. (Footnote: This therapist systematically had "sex" with as many of his female patients as he could. He also employed them as baby sitters, secretaries, cooks, errand runners, chauffeurs, and so on). His behavior was depressingly typical.

In my research, there were many reports of suicide attempts, severe depressions (some lasting months), mental hospitalizations, shock treatment, and separations or divorces from husbands who just could not understand or could not be supportive. Women reported being fired from or having to leave their jobs because of pressure and ineffectual working habits caused by their depression, crying spells, anger, and anxiety. One woman who participated in my study eventually did commit suicide.

If the client has decided to terminate the relationship, it can be because of disillusionment with her "image" of the therapist, or as one woman stated, "My God was found to have clay feet." She may be dissatisfied with the therapy and/or the sexual relationship (there seems to be a high percentage of sexual dysfunction for both the male therapist and the female client). She too may fear disclosure or discovery by her husband, family, friends, children, neighbors, office staff, or whoever.

In common with the romantic situation, therapy is usually not deemed successful when unilaterally terminated. But unlike most instances of romantic love, the therapeutic involvement is successfully resolved when the client and therapist mutually agree that what they sought to achieve has been accomplished.

Conclusions

Romantic love shares many similarities with the phenomena of transference and countertransference in the therapeutic situation. In both of these relationships, there is an initial "courtship" period, followed by a stage of idealization, manifested in therapy by transference on the part of the client and possible countertransference from the therapist. The third stage is one of acceptance followed by continuity. There may be a crisis stage, where difficulties are encountered and successfully or unsuccessfully worked through. The outcome of this previous stage may result in the resolution or dissolution of the relationship.

The fundamental difference between romantic love and therapy is one of intention about that resolution. Whereas lovers seek union, the ultimate goal of therapy is the separation of client and therapist through the client's achieving independence. The differences also include inequality of roles, power, sharing, and time in the therapist/client relationship as opposed to the optimum equality of roles, power, personal sharing, and time in the lover/lover relationship.

Another basic difference in the romantic and therapeutic conditions is the aspect played by physical acting-out and sexual intercourse. In romantic love, this is, more frequently than not, a condition for the resolution of the relationship, whether positive or negative. Research has proven (Belote, 1974; Chesler, 1972; D'Addario-Durré, 1977; Dahlberg, 1971; Taylor and Wagner, 1976) almost invariably that amatory and sexual interaction between client and therapist dooms the potential for successful therapy and is detrimental if not devastating to the client.

14

Love, Love Problems, and Family Therapy

Donald C. Ransom

Reflecting on romantic love and family therapy brings problems to mind. This may be unfortunate but inevitable, perhaps, since family and marital therapists get involved in people's lives at times of difficulty, pain, and confusion. This particular location in the flow of life partly explains why family therapists and helping professionals in general have developed such a skeptical view of romantic, sentimental, or passionate love.

Focusing on problems and speaking as a clinician, I find that there are two themes that occur most frequently: (1) falling out of love—or losing feeling for one's partner—which is presented directly as such when a discrepancy arises in which either partner feels more in love or loving than the other or is more openly dissatisfied by a lack of such feelings; and (2) problems brought to light by the discovery or disclosure of an affair. Indeed, the two are often related. The most dramatic affairs are sexual, but one's feeling and energy can also become diverted from the primary loved one to work, art, children, and other intense involvements, which may at times be viewed as functional equivalents of an affair.

Deciding how to think about and respond to feelings of love or to romantic relationships and the problems they inevitably bring is not easy. As we shall see, the guidelines available in the marital and family therapy literature are meager. The following case illustrates both the themes mentioned and further provides an example of some clinical issues raised by attempting to deal with love as the problem.

Jim and Linda, a couple with three children who had been married for sixteen years, came into my office and told the following story. Within the past week, Jim had revealed that he was in love with his wife's best friend, Eleanor. The two lovers had known each other for a long time, since Eleanor was married to Jim's cousin, Bill. The two families had always been very close. Jim and Eleanor had been seeing each other secretly for about a year and having sexual relations within the past three months. After the inclusion of sex, their feelings for each other had grown even stronger and now they had decided they wanted to be together. This led to their announcing this fact and the surrounding circumstances to their respective spouses in the past week, precipitating a crisis involving two families. Jim had come in with Linda to see me at her request. It appeared that he had already decided a course of action. He put it more or less this way: "I am very unhappy with my marriage and Eleanor feels the same way about hers. Eleanor and I kind of discovered one another in the middle of all this even though we have known each other in a different way for many years. I make her feel good and I am happy when I am with her. We deserve the chance to start a new life together. I know it will cause problems, especially because of the relations between the two families. I am closer to my cousin's mother and father than I am to my own. But I feel that I am living a lie by staying with my wife and I can no longer go on feeling this way without doing something about it. I am getting more depressed about this each day and something has to be done."

Following this account, Linda responded by saying that she could understand how this might happen and how he might come to believe he felt this way. She, however, was suspicious about the ultimate reality of Jim's feelings and believed he was making a big

mistake. Her grounds for disbelief were in part based on her knowledge of the kind of person she knew Eleanor to be and on what
kinds of needs she believed Eleanor currently had. If Jim really
wanted to leave, she would not try to stop him, but she did not
want him to leave, desiring instead that he stay and that they work
things out. Linda said she was more hurt than angry and more
angry at Eleanor than at her husband. She wanted to put all this
behind them and go on from here and that is why she called me.

When I asked some questions about their marriage and their
life together, no clear complaints emerged. They said their biggest
problem was "communication." Jim described Linda as a fine person, a good mother, an excellent companion with whom he shared
skin diving and hot-air ballooning, and said further that he loved
her very much—but in the wrong way. She said about the same
thing except that she loved him in the right way, even though that
love might not have been well expressed in the past couple of
years. She had gone back to nursing school and had been busy and
the resulting pressure led to changes in the family's routine. Perhaps the marriage had suffered. Somehow I got the message that
she blamed herself more than she blamed him, and now she was
desperately willing to make up for it.

These two persons and their relationship are unique, yet
their dilemma contains themes and issues that are familiar to students of love and of psychotherapy. Thinking about this actual
problem and the problems it in turn raises for the therapist to
whom it was presented provides a means of access to questions
about love and about family therapy. Pursuing the case a bit further reveals something about the relationship between the two.
What can be said about family therapy and romantic love using
this couple as a point of departure? First, a few words about family therapy.

Family Therapy

Within the wide-ranging field generally called psychotherapy, the past twenty-five years have seen a general interest in the
family of those called patients expand to a focus on the family itself as a relevant unit of assessment and intervention. This shift to
a specific concern with the primacy of ongoing relationships has

led to far-reaching conceptual and practical changes in the helping professions. Conceptually, the important difference has been the reversal from viewing the family and other primary relationships in terms of the patient to viewing the patient in terms of those relationships. Figure and ground have become reversed and reversible, and the relevant field of analysis has thereby grown larger and more flexible. Practically, this difference has meant developing new sets of therapeutic techniques aimed at changing patterns of interpersonal relationships directly through working face to face with marital and family members. These developments include a move away from an exclusive concern with families of psychiatric patients to involvement with families and persons with all types of health and personal problems.

One of the most successful developments that has emerged from and in turn shaped these changes is "family therapy." I put quotation marks around the term here initially to indicate that it cannot be taken narrowly to hold any one meaning, yet in the larger picture family therapy has assumed the status of a movement in the field of mental health. In common usage, family therapy refers to both a form of *therapeutic intervention* and a *conceptual approach to human problems*. It is not a therapeutic method in the usual sense. There is no agreed-upon set of procedures followed by practitioners who consider themselves family therapists and no set of techniques to which they jointly adhere. Different therapists approach different families and different problems in a variety of ways.

What is consistent is that, at the conceptual level, family therapy embodies the "family approach." In its simplest statement, this means that problems are understood and addressed as expressions of the universal difficulties that arise in maintaining social relationships and membership in essential human groups. What unifies family therapists is their search for the source of both problems and solutions within recurring patterns of ordinary daily human association.

For the purposes of this chapter, the following combination of focus and purpose will serve as a working definition: *"Family therapy is the process of working at the level of human behavior bounded by intimate relationships, with persons having a history and a future together, in order to influence an agreed upon prob-*

lem" (Ransom and Grace, 1980, p. 250). No important distinction is drawn here between family and marital therapy. The difference is a matter of who is involved and what problems are addressed, since the concepts and techniques employed are shared. This definition also purposefully stretches the everyday meaning of the word *family* (read also *marriage*) into a special type of relationship instead of a particular entity. Marriage and the family are formal institutions that are unquestionably different from and usually more important than other forms of human relatedness. But we know that people can also become involved in relationships that rival the family in intensity, in the achievement of satisfaction and security, and in being demanding. Family therapy is relevant to persons with a wide range of ties with one another, and a workable definition should reflect this scope.

The definition suggested here also uses the terms *influence* and *problem*, instead of terms such as *cure* and *illness*. Family therapy has very little connection with the "mental illness" model. The purpose of family therapy is to introduce the possibility of changes that can take place *between* people in order to resolve problems in living, rather than administering treatments for an illness.

Looking more closely at the types of problems with which family therapy deals further reflects its broad scope. For convenience, four types can be identified. The first includes those problems that are ordinarily described and experienced as belonging to individuals. The family approach views the family and subgroupings within the family as vital sets of relationships involved in the maintenance and expression of one another's symptoms, such as pain, anxiety, depression, illnesses, behavioral abnormalities, and misbehavior. The second type includes problems between pairs of persons expressed as such, for example, parent-child and sibling conflicts or marital tensions and dissatisfactions. Here both the larger family and more limited aspects of it are viewed as contexts and included in any intervention plan. The third type involves family problems per se, in which the group is unable to achieve its shared goals or is unable to sustain itself or supply its members' basic needs, or misuses its members. The fourth type includes problems between one part of the family and another, or between the family and representatives of the community, such as the school, medical care, or the legal system.

Romantic Love

From the previous discussion the picture emerges that family therapy is concerned with common human problems, such as marital tensions and the failure of family members to meet mutually shared needs and achieve common goals, and that family therapists address intimate relations directly to bring about desired changes. Given this emphasis, it is natural to assume that family therapists would be the ideal group to turn to for a discussion of love and its problems and to seek out for suggestions about what can be done when those problems arise. Contrary to such expectations, however, the family therapy literature is nearly devoid of any mention of love, romantic or companionate, or of how to respond to problems of love presented to therapists. This fact grew clear as I began to think about what I had read over the years that might help me with the couple just described, and also help me prepare this chapter.

An incomplete review turned up the following: My library contains forty-three books on marital and family therapy. Looking up the terms *adultery, affair, love, passion,* and *romance* in each index, and further thumbing through each volume, I found that thirty-two contained no references to any of these entries. Of the remaining eleven, four references were incidental and the other seven led to discussions of varying degrees of directness and relevance either to the experience or to the interpersonal process of love.

A look at those discussions is revealing. Three are heavily influenced by the depth or id psychology aspects of psychoanalysis: Framo (1965), Dicks (1967), and Meissner (1978). Three others present ideas developed by Carl Whitaker: Warkenton and Whitaker (1967), Keith and Whitaker (1977), and Napier and Whitaker (1978). Whitaker's thought is difficult to characterize. It is a maverick blend of classical psychoanalytic and existential thinking that builds on the centrality of unconscious needs and wishes while, at the same time, stressing the value of immediate experience and growth as the medium and goal of therapy. The remaining discussion is Haley's (1973) account of the ideas and techniques of Milton Erickson. Haley is the chief architect of the "strategic" or "problem-solving" wing of the family therapy field.

Framo (1965), Dicks (1967), and Meissner (1978) all take up the question of falling in love and getting married from psychodynamic angles. In reading the three, however, as in reading related depth-psychoanalytic discussions of romantic love further removed from the family therapy literature, one gets the idea that the people in question do not relate to one another, but to ghosts, and that they are not in love with one another but with projected aspects of themselves. Further, the therapy described or implied does not relate to the immediate relationship either. For example, Framo (1965) argues that the loved one must combine qualities "which will stimulate the recreation of the childhood, idealized family romance with all its promises of unconditional love; at the same time the prospective mate must be enough like the bad inner object to allow for the eventual penetration of old hatreds" (p. 185). Therapy consists of the exploration of the "relevant motivational formulae in each partner," helping both to "come to terms with their introjects and explicate the meaning of their marital bond" (p. 188). Whatever the meaning, we can expect that it will theretofore have been unconscious and when revealed (through interpretation) by the therapist will prove to be something about which the participants are embarrassed or ashamed.

Dicks (1967) suggests that "the change many lovers feel when the weight of social compulsion comes down after their legal wedding" is based on "the strongly anti-libidinally invested 'social role' derived from parental and religious models, being liable to oust the 'fancy-free' libidinal mutuality of the premarital phase" (p. 121). The universal and actual stresses of being lovers and being married are quickly brushed aside and the couple's failures to cope are viewed as the result of unconscious internalized representations of past experience rather than the struggle with present circumstances.

Meissner (1978) roots his discussion of love and marriage in Freud and Kernberg. He reaches for a "distinction between simple libidinal sexual object attraction and what is referred to in more contemporary terms as a mature and mutual object relationship" (p. 40). It appears to me that this distinction approximates in psychoanalytic terms what Pope refers to in Chapter One of this volume as the difference between "romantic" and "companionate" love. The conclusion reached by Meissner is that "the phenomenon of falling in love is a multidetermined result of a number of dynamic factors, but involves in some significant degree the operation of intense narcissistic needs. The intermeshing of and the responsiveness to such needs play an important part in the choice of marital partner. Each of the partners then seeks—with varying degrees of conscious or unconscious intention—for a mate who promises to provide optimal gratification of such usually unconscious and predominantly narcissistic needs" (p. 42).

Carl Whitaker speaks to questions of love, marriage, affairs, and divorce in a number of his writings. Of the major figures in the family therapy field, he is the one who most consistently meets these issues head on. In a volume edited by Papp, he and David Keith present a case in which an affair is elaborated as "a form of amateur psychotherapy" (Keith and Whitaker, 1977, p. 125). This and related ideas are developed more fully in a book written by Augustus Y. Napier with Whitaker, *The Family Crucible* (1978). The two discuss love and its decay in terms that are connected to what actually happens in a relationship, as well as to the effects of past experiences and unconscious ideas. As "needs for affection; λ desires for freedom; intense anger; sexual cravings; an aching sense of aloneness; bitterness at broken promises; multiple disappointments and humiliations" all add up, "a postponed hunger for life becomes more and demanding as time passes, yet anything that might uncover these needs and frustrations becomes a threat in itself. *So frightening are these tensions that the couple often cannot allow themselves to be consciously aware of them.* All the drama of conflict takes place quietly, implicitly, so that even the participants at times question the reality of their experience" (p. 148). A creative "strategy" that couples use to avoid having to face such problems, while at the same time walking sideways toward them, is the affair. "It is a desperate attempt by the couple to break the marital impasse, one that takes them to the edge of disaster, and often beyond" (p. 149). On the surface, the couple Napier and Whitaker (1978) describe resemble the couple presented at the beginning of this chapter. The affair, like many major marital events, may be intuitively "arranged" by the couple, albeit not deliberately and consciously. Its rough aim is to reintroduce life into a dying and unsatisfying relationship. The forces that lead to an affair are not described as originating in any one person but in a crucible in which both spouses, the spouses' parents, the lover, and the lover's family are all symbolically and politically involved.

Once the affair is revealed, dealing with it presses the couple to communicate on a more profound level than they have in the past. The initial explosion is a message that reverberates in the relationship for awhile and then leads to the possibility of opening up. "They begin to talk more honestly *because they have to*. Their relationship is in such desperate straits, teetering at the edge of separation or divorce, that they overcome timidity and face each other. It is now or never!" (Napier and Whitaker, 1978, p. 161). Thus the search for help is seen as elemental in the creation of an affair: help from the lover and help from those who get involved when the affair is exposed. The open acknowledgment of an affair is a common ticket of admission to marital therapy.

The idea of the "marital impasse" is also helpful. Earlier, Warkenton and Whitaker (1967) proposed that "a normal marriage progresses through a series of impasses as the years go by" (p. 242). One impasse occurs when the "positive transferences" between the couple are gradually exhausted, leading to a "detumescence of 'being in love.'" They call this the "ten-year syndrome" since it usually occurs within that time. At that point, there is likely to be a "civil war" which results in the freeing of both "slaves." If, at this moment, the partners find a deeper person-to-person love for each other, they may well live for ten more years before the next impasse develops. "However, if they do not resolve their 'civil war' at the ten-year level, and just continue living under the same roof, such a continued impasse is likely to result in a perversion of their relationship." Warkenton and Whitaker also state their assumption in another, revealing way: "It is only after a couple has 'fallen out of love' that an adult, warm, loving person-to-person marital relationship is possible for them. In our culture, the ten-year syndrome is probably the first opportunity for a couple to have a really whole-hearted marriage" (p. 242). There is much to ponder in Whitaker's work. It has certainly proved to be relevant for my immediate problem.

The only representative of the "brief," "strategic," or "structural" approach to family therapy who has written about questions of love and love's problems is Jay Haley. In *Uncommon Therapy: The Psychiatric Techniques of Milton H. Erickson, M.D.*,

Haley (1973) presents the most clinically useful account of the "family life cycle" in print and then illustrates a number of problems that can arise at each stage through presentation of a long series of Dr. Erickson's cases. Many of these cases involve problems of love and sexual relations. It is significant that Haley never addresses the experience of love directly, and the treatment strategies credited to Erickson similarly do not deal directly with the resolution of love's difficulties. There is an obvious strategic effort to be indirect, to leave love and matters of personal experience alone while influencing specific patterns of observable behavior through active means.

The view of love and relationships presented by Haley is ethological in tone. Left to their own devices and spared an excess of environmental insults that can intrude from any number of sources, relationships and family life demonstrate a built-in structure that will unfold naturally as time moves along. When that structure is violated, matters must be corrected or symptoms may result. Feelings among the members that occur along the way are almost automatic and epiphenomenal. It is not necessary or desirable to explore them in order to achieve a successful outcome in therapy. One deals instead with the pattern of recurring sequences of behavior with others that sustains a symptom or problem or makes it necessary (functional). This is done largely through suggestion and through prescriptions by the therapists of tasks that patients are ordered to perform.

Why is love missing? The almost total absence of commentary on love in the family therapy literature invites an explanation. There is no single or simple reason why. Reflecting on primary sources in the field and recalling many discussions of both theory and clinical cases, I see three major problems that seem to stand in the way of more direct and meaningful discourse by family therapists on romantic or passionate love: undifferentiated thinking, reductionist thinking, and the tyranny of abnormal norms.

Undifferentiated Thinking. One principle that apparently still needs formal proposal is that falling in and falling out of love can mean many different things depending upon the persons involved and the circumstances of their relationship. Sometimes a relationship, as we ordinarily think of it, is not even necessary, as in the example of the adolescent boy who falls in love with and continually yearns for a girl he does not meet for over a year after the day he first saw her (Coleman and Coleman, 1975, p. 146). In contrast are the couple who fall passionately in love after having known each other and been married for several years. The varieties of romantic love are easily overlooked, it seems, probably because the experience of being-in-love as described by lovers shares universal themes and seems similar from person to person. That similarity of described experience and feeling seems to imply a similarity of underlying "causes." This same idea underlies the assumption that if we look closely and systematically with the correct lenses we can discover the cause of love, from which would follow what needs to be done when love starts to fade. A different idea from modern systems theory, however, proposes that the same state of mind or state in a relationship can result from a number of reasons and be arrived at from a number of different pathways. This principle of "equi-finality" provides an antidote to the "one effect, one cause" model and is useful to keep in mind when thinking about love. It provides a safeguard against the reflexive undifferentiated response to romantic love that is so prevalent in the psychotherapy field, a response that is conventionally as negative and rejecting as it is oversimplified and global.

Reductionist Thinking. A second observation concerning the absence of discussions of love is that the major theories of family therapy automatically redefine and thereby reduce falling in love or falling out of love to a sign or symptom of something else. At the psychoanalytic end of the spectrum, falling in or out of love is a suspicious event raising questions about an immature personality that is unable to relinquish the need for the kind of gratification that should be given up if successful adulthood is to be achieved. Kubie (1956), in his classic chapter in the volume *Neurotic Interaction in Marriage*, defines "being in love" as "an obsessional state which, like all obsessions, is in part driven by anger" (p. 31).

Among family systems therapists, in contrast, falling in love is not discussed because individual-centered motivations and feelings are excluded from their central formulations. It appears that the predominant wing of family systems theory is engaged in a serious effort to see how far it can go in explaining interpersonal behavior without having to resort to any individual variables. Falling out of love is viewed as a sign that the social system is disturbed and needs adjustment. When relations between the generations or factions within the family are corrected and when members assume and enact their proper roles, feelings will follow; love will be restored. Love is not something that needs to be worked out directly. Each approach, then, reduces questions of love to something else, that something having to do with its own preferred formulations.

Ironically, as in classical psychoanalytic treatments of the subject, in a reading of modern family systems therapy it is easy to forget that the marriages and families in question contain real persons actively involved in constructing and maintaining relationships with one another. Both approaches have the built-in propensity to leave the actual persons aside, albeit for widely differing reasons. By now we have some idea of how psychoanalytically oriented family therapists do this. It is worth a moment's digression to balance the discussion with a look at the systems approach.

The predominant metaphor of modern family therapy is that of the "system." Derived from cybernetics and General Systems Theory, the idea of the family as a system has given family therapy an elegant formal language and a set of concepts, including *wholeness, feedback, homeostasis,* and *morphostasis,* that describe how relationships are sustained and changed over time. The theory is abstract and formal. Its application to families is only one exemplification of a scope that strives for universality wherever organized complexity can be found. Until recently, only bits and pieces of the general theory were applied to family processes and family therapy (Ransom and Massad, 1978; Steinglass, 1978). The result of the piecemeal and incomplete application of the idea of system resulted in an overemphasis on the importance of negative feedback, which led to viewing families as far too conservative and resistant to change, and led also to a reification of the family as *the* system that determined what was observed in therapy. Unwittingly, family therapy carried the burden of individual depth psychology and the Freudian equilibrium model in disguise. "Family determinism" arose and stood orthodox psychoanalytic theory on its head. Now, instead of the family's being determined by the unconscious makeup of those who compose it, the individual members' internal states were seen as determined by nonconscious family system needs. The persons in the family became transformed into the "elements of the system," in a sense, servomechanisms to the complex and hierarchically predominant necessities of social organization. The person as a "self" and a constructing actor is denied or ignored. The figure ground reversibility that is the hallmark of General Systems Theory became frozen in one position in its application to family behavior. The ice is thawing slowly.

With this combination of a preference for formal language and abstract description on the one side and the fascination with patterns or organization and techniques for changing them on the other, it is not surprising that much of family therapy has forgotten about the person and forgotten about love. Love is a quality, a subtle shape. It does not yield easily to being reduced to other terms.

Tyranny of Abnormal Norms. One final observation is that, when the subject is brought up, family therapy theorists offer explanations for romantic love without benefit of having first observed and described it as it occurs naturally in normal populations —at least among the population of those who do not come in for therapy. A related ancient problem haunts the understanding of love we are seeking here: therapists are extrapolating from their experience with troubled persons and troubled relationships to universal definitions. (This accounts, in part, for why psychotherapists of nearly all persuasions hold such a negative and rejecting attitude toward romantic love.) Thus, theoretically bent therapists describe what infatuation is, what an affair means, and so on, as if those formulations apply in general. There are simply no means (data) at the present time to tell. Even Whitaker succumbs to the narrowed-down, pathological bias, proposing that "when people 'fall in love,' they experience a bilateral transference relationship with hysterical dynamics in the forefront" (Warkenton and Whitaker, 1967, p. 242). There may well be some truth to this, but, at this point, it seems safe only to say something Murray Bowen (1966) once pointed out: "Whatever love *is*, it is factual that many family members react strongly to statements about it" (p. 351).

Expanding the Boundaries of Family Therapy

Venturing out from the established family therapy literature, where can a family therapist turn for ideas in working with problems that involve romantic love? What other leads can be followed with the couple presented here?

Not too far afield there is much to be gained by studying the work of Bernard Apfelbaum and the Berkeley Sex Therapy Group (for example, Apfelbaum, 1979). Apfelbaum and his colleagues have developed new methods for approaching individuals and couples with sexual problems. Their techniques apply to persons with "sexual dysfunctions," that is, disorders of *sexual performance*, such as impotence and anorgasmia, as well as persons with problems involving *sexual desire*, such as being turned off or being unable to be turned on. Focusing on one major theme raised in the introduction to this chapter—falling out of love, or losing feeling for one's partner—I shall puruse one simple lead: *The same approach that successfully assists partners who are turned off to experience the reemergence of sexual desire might also succeed in assisting partners who have fallen out of love to regain some of the love they have lost.*

The Apfelbaum group's contribution begins with the observation that, regardless of their specific sex problems, sex therapy patients almost universally are consistent in their wish to avoid communicating their frightened, disappointed, helpless, critical, demoralized side; in short, their negative or turned-off side. They fear, for a variety of good reasons, "that thinking or talking about these feelings in a relationship will lead to a more lasting turnoff rather than resolution" (Williams, 1978, p. 481). Therefore, they develop ways of avoiding negative thoughts or, at least, avoid expressing them to their partners, while continuing to pursue the desired state (arousal, erection, orgasm). This special type of avoidance of troubling personal and relationship issues in the service of reaching a desired goal is called *bypassing*. When viewed as a form of sexual response (in contrast to Kaplan's 1974 use of the term to describe the *therapist's* overlooking tensions and conflict in a relationship in the service of restoring sexual functioning), "bypassing can refer to both the ability to overlook tensions in order to become aroused [for an example of this, see Apfelbaum, 1977a] and to the ability to overlook lack of arousal in order to function, as by focusing on sensation" (Apfelbaum, 1977b, p. 97).

An obvious observation about bypassing is that it seems to work for some persons (couples) but not for others, and/or it seems to work sometimes but not at other times. For those for whom bypassing rarely or never works, it seems to have a reverse effect. The attempted solution (albeit unawares) creates an even greater problem. Even when bypassing appears to work, however, a closer look reveals costs and side effects that leave the person and the relationship vulnerable to the kinds of problems bypassing is supposed to avoid. Spontaneous bypassers who can forget difficulties when they arise by shifting into a positive fantasy at the touch of a hand or the sound of a loving word are highly dependent upon proper staging and are vulnerable to slights, plunging moods, and feelings of insecurity when the spell is broken. Those who work hard at bypassing, in contrast, must constantly be on their guard, narrow their focus to tune out any discordant notes in the relationship, and receive constant reassurance that everything is really okay. When this compulsiveness or the necessary feedback breaks down, the situation can rapidly deteriorate.

In response to the near universal reflex to bypass negative and anxiety-provoking aspects of sexual encounters, the Apfelbaum group is developing counterbypassing strategies. "I would say that the main thing we are doing is showing the patient how he can turn on by *including himself* in sexual relationships" (Williams, 1978, p. 479). People learn how to confront their partners with their complaints, insecurities, and doubts—with the kinds of feelings that are very real to them but which they have always suppressed because they have considered both the feelings and their sharing to be countersexual. This is achieved in the therapy through a series of behavioral assignments (homework) and through a lot of exploratory discussion. A task of the therapist is to design situations that intensify each person's mutual conflicts and insecurities in order to reach a level of vivid reality that can be noticed and described. Following this stage, methods of achieving security are discovered and practiced: "We teach the patient to achieve a state we call a *contact turn-on*. If the usual way of turning on is a matter of friction plus fantasy, the contact turn-on is based on friction plus intimacy. *The patient turns on by virtue of being able to express his turned-off emotions to his partner*" (Williams, 1978, p. 481). This communication can have dramatic effects. "It is not uncommon for the patient to finally admit during the genital stroking assignment, 'I am turned off. I find you mechanical, this whole therapy feels mechanical, and I'm getting nothing out of what you're doing now.' Nor is it uncommon for such an admission to be immediately followed by a strong surge of sensation, and a full erection" (p. 482).

This reminds us of the classic confrontation that occurred between the husband and wife described by Napier and Whitaker (1978) in their discussion of the affair in *The Family Crucible*. When they finally had it out with each other after the affair was disclosed, "the two partners fought and cried, talked and searched for an entire night. The next evening, more exhausting encounters. Feelings that had been hidden for years emerged; doubts and accusations that they had never expected to admit articulated . . . they felt alive together for the first time in years. Somewhat mysteriously, they found themselves going to bed together in the midst of a great tangle of emotions—continuing anger, and hurt, and guilt, and this new quality: abandon. The lovemaking was, they were to admit to each other, 'the best it had ever been'" (p. 153).

The first effort to expand the Apfelbaum group's approach to more general issues of marital therapy has been the work of Daniel B. Wile (1978, 1979). Wile starts with the observation that once the spark of love develops into an ongoing relationship, it is inevitable that everyday life will insult lovers with moments when they feel excluded, unappreciated, or disappointed. Couples who do not have a way of recognizing when they are affected by these sorts of exchanges, talking about them, and dealing with them, are subject to an increasing buildup of resentment and alienation leading to a loss of feeling for one another, a loss of faith, and either emotional or actual divorce. Since the general effect of marital discord is to leave both partners feeling stuck, hopeless, and blame-oriented, attributing the problem to their own personal deficiencies or to the deficiencies and unreasonableness of their partners, the task of therapy is to loosen partners from their locked-in perspective by providing them with a noncondemnatory way of making sense out of their own and their partners' behavior. Wile's methods help us to see that, in the case example presented early in this chapter, Linda's annoying question in the first hour, "Do you still love me?" may be the closest this couple has come to recognizing and talking about the important truth that their life together has not achieved the intimacy that both in their own way want.

Circling Back to the Office. Returning to our couple, I now see my task as creating the opportunity to help both partners lay out their intertwined dilemmas for us all to see. The goal would be to find a way to break through the alienation that has been building for several years. After getting a little more background information on the two families involved in the affair, I found myself facing a dilemma. I was ambivalent about how to respond to Jim's being-in-love. Part of me wanted to confirm his experience for what he said it was, and offer simply to deal with the fallout. Another part of me was persuaded that this was a symptom of something else, straight out of Whitaker. I walked the fence offering about five different interpretations of what this development might mean, including just what it looked like on the surface. They probably knew better than I what to make of it, and they could talk it over.

At the end of the hour, I suggested some homework. Since it appeared that Jim was moving out and joining with Eleanor, they were both quite right in assuming that turmoil and pain would result in both families and perhaps beyond. Some of this might be avoided or at least minimized if the two couples would set aside an evening together to sit down and really talk all this out and decide among them how all this could best be handled. I closed by saying I did not want to presume they were coming back, but I would hold an hour open ten days hence.

In the second session, we reviewed the family meeting, which was held as suggested. The discussion that took place there struck Jim as so bizarre that it seemed to have some effect on how he was thinking about the whole situation. At one point his cousin said, "Well, if she's going to fall in love and go off with somebody else, she couldn't have picked a nicer guy." The context of the family meeting also seemed to have the effect of making the lovers look and sound different to each other. I sensed Jim was a little shaken, but he had not changed in his basic position. A third session was planned in order to "deal with the fallout" and help with the transition.

One week later, we all looked for ways that Jim could be a little more sympathetic with himself for leaving his wife and family. As we talked, something slipped out to the effect that he wouldn't mind staying if it weren't for sex. Pursuing that, I learned that sex had been his biggest source of stress for months. His comment about "living a lie" had mainly to do with his feeling about approaching Linda sexually, even though he didn't have his heart in it and didn't really want to. He explained that for some time he had felt no desire for her whatsoever. He believed she had made it obvious that she still wanted sex so he dutifully initiated what would lead to intercourse at about weekly intervals. This always left him feeling guilty and depressed afterward and he could not stand it any more. At one point, he said he could be happy to remain married and be with the family if he could just forget about having to be involved sexually with his wife again, eliminating the whole painful business entirely. He said he knew this was impossible, and Linda was quick to point out that such an arrangement was unthinkable. She still had strong sexual needs and she did not desire to go outside their marriage to have those needs fulfilled. Further discussion led to the discovery, however, that she often acted as if she wanted him sexually when she was really feeling something else, but that she did so because she thought it would help him to know that she still desired and loved him. He, in turn, said that at times he just wanted to give up sex altogether, with everybody, in exchange for peace of mind.

At the end of this third hour, I made a suggestion. Since their remaining days together were apparently numbered, why didn't they play out his fantasy to see what would happen? They could enjoy each other, go skin diving or hot-air ballooning, go out and have fun, sleep together, but eliminate intercourse. Since sex had become such a source of anxiety, it would be interesting to see what Jim would be like relieved of the pressure to engage in it. Jim seemed to like the idea, and Linda thought I was crazy. I asked them to think it over and said I would wait to hear from them before setting up another appointment.

Nine days later, Linda called me and said Jim had decided to stay and that he wanted them to rework their relationship. And, she added, they had decided not to come in for any more sessions for now. I have not heard from them since. A phone call eight months later led to my learning that they were still together, but we did not discuss how they assess their current situation.

Summing Up. Although brief, the therapy approach taken here addresses three levels at the same time, looking for movement within any one or a combination of them. Foremost in mind is the idea that this couple have fallen out of love—have lost feeling, become alienated from each other. There were no doubt good reasons for this and they are multi-leveled and complex.

Of concern with Jim and Linda were: their extended family system, which was very much wrapped up in what was going on; their marital system, which had not constructed a way to make sense out of and deal with worries that were dividing them from the intimacy they once felt for each other; and their personal system, especially their fantasies, which revealed a great deal about how they felt about love and the direction that a solution to love's problems might take.

At the extended family level, little was done except to get the relevant members directly involved with one another over what was happening, but in a way organized by the therapist. This disrupted the extended system's customary responses and led to a different view of what might be happening for at least two of the participants. It is easy to underestimate the degree of disruption that extended families can produce in the love relations of their members. It is often helpful to get them deliberately involved in the therapy process when things get out of hand (see Friedman, 1972; Bowen, 1978).

At the level of marital interaction, the goal was to create a safe environment in order to develop ways of noticing, talking about, and dealing with mutually suppressed worries and complaints. Like many couples, Jim and Linda had not constructed ways of handling discordant issues in their relationship that were free from serious side effects. More than that, both were deliberately bypassing such issues out of a belief that to do otherwise would be counterproductive. For Jim, criticism was confusing and not conducive to a romantic atmosphere. For Linda, it was counter to the spirit of being loyal. For both, it was painful. The important idea for therapy, however, is *not* to sell Jim and Linda on the value of being open and critical; it is rather to step into their immediate and recurring patterns of interaction by reframing what is going on in a way that allows both partners to construct a less accusing and more accepting view of themselves and each other. By denying their important negative feelings they had been excluding an essential side of themselves from their relationship. Such an incomplete self robs the relationship of vital information and of the persons who make it up, precluding the possibility of intimacy. The extent to which Jim and Linda get the chance to express important worries and to be heard within a framework establishing that each has positive intentions and wants the same thing, is the extent to which they may regain some of the love they have lost.

A counterargument proposes that talking about such negative and serious matters may well be incompatible with romantic love, though not with other types of love. Perhaps that is what Warkenton and Whitaker (1967) meant when they said: "It is only after a couple has 'fallen out of love' that an adult, warm, loving person-to-person marital relationship is possible for them. In our culture, the ten-year syndrome is probably the first opportunity for a couple to have a really wholehearted marriage" (p. 242). From several angles, Jim and Linda certainly look like they are facing a marital impasse of the "ten-year" variety, delayed by adjustments and strong defenses until their sixteenth year together. This raises the question whether it is possible to be romantically in love yet be able to deal with all the darkness I am suggesting Jim and Linda need to face.

This brings us to a third level of analysis, the individual psychodynamic level. Here Jim and Linda can be viewed as facing a crisis brought on by a developmental stage transition that is moving them from being in love with love to being in love with each other. Another way of saying this is that they are moving from being hooked on a fantasy or a symbol to being hooked on a real person. Jim knows what he wants and what is missing from his relationship with Linda. He is disappointed but he is unable to express that disappointment, thinking it will only make matters worse. He does not look to his partner or the relationship for explanations of his dissatisfaction. He bears no blame toward Linda. He thinks it is just him, or the inevitable consequence of being married for sixteen years. In fact, this was his most earnest question to me—whether, in my experience, people just get this way after being married for a long time and there's nothing to be done about it. He wants to renew the experience he has lost and he has found someone else with whom he can feel the way he felt toward Linda when they were first married. For him and his idea of love, that is a reasonable solution.

Linda's idea of love is different from Jim's; it is rooted in the wish to be committed. Whether this is because of a long-standing value or because of the role she has moved into in the relationship, or both, we cannot say. She says she loves Jim in spite of his saying he loves her best friend and wants to live with her. She bears no grudge toward him, but only toward Eleanor. This must make Jim wonder what Linda really feels about him. Even though he looks like the "bad guy" here, perhaps what is going on is his attempt to say that he feels ignored or left out. He may feel that he, as Linda's husband, is being used to trigger a fantasy of hers about togetherness. When she goes into this fantasy, she stops communicating with him. She does not tell him what she really thinks about what is going on but only that she loves him and wants him to stay. He then feels alone and cut off, wondering what must be the matter with her when walls of their marriage are tumbling down and she wants to have sex and acts as if she never heard him say he was in love with another woman.

Jim has become a symbol instead of a person to Linda. She is committed to a fantasy about who they are and how they should be and is not connecting with him and with what has been happening for a long time. Ironically, the practical result is the same for both partners. They are pursuing an idea, different for each, which sets the limits on how they can see and be with each other. The result is that they cannot make contact with the excluded side of their partner that does not fit the desired state. Having now lost the fantasy, or being on the brink of having to give it up, the partners now have only each other. The therapy done here initiated the acquaintanceship process at this new level of potentially greater communion.

What About Research? Looking at the family therapy literature on the one side and this unique couple on the other, how could systematic research on romantic love be helpful? The answer is not difficult. Any kind of reliable data on when and how and, perhaps, even why people fall in love would be helpful. So would data on falling out of love, on making a transition to other types of love, and on repairing or regaining love that has faded. As a clinician, however, I can foresee a pitfall along the way to such research that would limit its usefulness in the kind of work described here. The problem is investigating love from too narrow or sectarian a point of view and too strictly from the vantage point provided by a researcher's particular model. Much of the work reviewed in Walster and Walster's *A New Look at Love* (1978) falls into this category. Thus there is a sizable literature on matching of partners and another, separate set of studies on social attraction, designed for the most part to test an abstract and formal hypothesis held by the researcher rather than to discover what is going on from the participants' point of view.

I am not suggesting that romantic love cannot be usefully opened up to scientific investigation. Quite the contrary, I am suggesting the opposite, that we need to be more scientific in our endeavors by observing and describing in detail the varieties of contexts of love for those who experience it rather than falling into generalities or testing hypotheses where they are premature and inappropriate. What the field needs most at this stage is a Studs Terkel of Love, someone to seek out and describe love and lovers in all the richness and variety they contain. I would be eager to read such careful and comprehensive reporting and would expect it to lead to more specific studies later on.

15

Love and the Search for Identity

Hanna Levenson
Charles N. Harris

If one believes in the law of contiguity, then the connection between romantic love and identity is well learned. Whether it be in
the lyrics of ballads, on the pages of "how-to-do-it" manuals, or
on the tongues of our psychotherapy clients, the words *love* and
self constantly appear together. Why? What is there about the nature of human experience that makes love and fears about losing
one's self go together better than love and marriage? The focus of
this chapter is on answering this basic question. The first section
considers the proposition that when people fall romantically in
love they experience a loss of self. The second section examines
the corollary of this notion, namely, that having a solid sense of
identity inhibits one from romantic involvement. And the third
section presents a reconceptualization for understanding the process of individuation-merger.

Romantic Love Experienced as the Loss of Identity

The Experience of Losing Identity. There are many facets to romantic love. Zerof (1978) lists several qualities of romantic love, indicating that it is an unrealistic, unchanging, care-taking attitude, which involves high expectations, ownership, and unconditional acceptance. Ellis (1972, p. 7) outlines the characteristics of the romantic lover as unrealistic, tending to overevaluate the beloved, verbal, esthetic, monogamous, perfectionistic, passionately intense, and often antisexual. In Chapter One, Pope has suggested a working definition of love for this book that includes preoccupation with another person, thinking of the loved one often, and experiencing feelings of despair when separated and a feeling of incompleteness without the loved one. Kilpatrick (1975) goes further in outlining the entire romantic love ideal: "The idea that for every girl there is a boy; that one day they will meet and fall in love and live happily thereafter. . . . The formula hardly varies: A forbidden person, impossible love, forced separation, temporary reunions, and eventual tragic death" (p. 196).

The authors of this chapter believe that one of the primary experential components of romantic love is a sense of losing one's identity. In fact, when people speak of "falling" in love, it is the "self" that is experienced as plummeting toward the ground, and "fall" we must if we are to be truly romantically involved. We do not walk calmly down a flight of stairs or take an elevator—we jump off cliffs, fight dragons, and swallow poisons. But more of this later.

How is the loss of self experienced? There are both positive and negative aspects. The pleasurable feeling involves a loosening of ego boundaries. Perhaps Freud ([1930] 1961) stated it most succinctly in *Civilization and Its Discontents*: "But toward the outside at any rate, the ego seems to maintain clear and sharp lines of demarcation. There is only one state—admittedly an unusual state, but not one that can be stigmatized as pathological—in which it does not do this. At the height of being in love, the boundary between ego and the object threatens to melt away" (p. 13). This loosening of ego boundaries is *enjoyed* as feelings of selflessness and oneness with the beloved, virtually losing one's self into the bond and fulfillment of romantic intimacy. This flow of feeling, surrender to a powerful force and excitement of risk make the lover feel alive in ways he or she has not previously experienced.

However, there are also aspects of losing one's self that are experienced as negative and frightening. As Paul Simon's (1977) lyrics from the song "Slip-Slidin' Away" succinctly convey, "Dolores, I live in fear. My love for you is so overpowering, I'm afraid that I will disappear."* If the pleasurable aspects are in the joy of the falling, the painful ones are in the apprehension of what lies ahead, or more consistent with the analogy, what lies below. Fancher (1973), commenting on Freud's view of happiness, wrote that love seemed like a good compromise between instinctual impulses and relating to people, but "its main drawback was that love puts people at the mercy of the loved one" (p. 226). As a result, one experiences the anxiety, humiliation, and pain of being overtaken, dependent, and vulnerable. Ironically, these are the same states that account for the positive experiences of losing one's self. It appears that the very feelings that impel us to fall deeper and deeper in love are also those that begin to exert a counterforce toward withdrawal. In this chapter's third section, which deals with a reconceptualization of the individuation-merger process, the reason for such similarities in feelings should become more apparent.

The singer of Paul Simon's song fears he will "disappear" because his love is so overpowering. Is there any evidence that there is reason to fear? Does anyone really lose his or her sense of identity? The answer is yes. Not only do people feel *they* are different but they also perceive their environment differently. When we talk of love being blind, we are really saying that the lover attends to selected aspects of the environment previously not recognized and also may not perceive formerly familiar objects. Peele and Brodsky (1975) underline the importance of perception and interpretation of experience in relating love to addiction. Their main thesis is that love is an addiction if the person's attachment to another "is such as to lessen his appreciation of and ability to deal with things in his environment or in himself so that he has become increasingly dependent on that experience as his only source of gratification" (p. 56). In Freud's terminology, this parallels

*© 1977 Paul Simon. Used by permission.

diminished ego functioning. Harding's (1970) definition of love further emphasizes the addiction theme: "To be 'in love' with a man is more than to 'love' him. The state of being in love carries with it a certain element of compulsion and one who is in love, however enraptured he may be, is certainly not free" (p. 36).

The Need to Merge. Given the risks involved, why would someone fall romantically in love? We have categorized the reasons into three major groups: supplies, information, and, most importantly, The Experience itself. There are numerous apparent supplies to be gained from merging with another in romantic love. First, such merger may provide a shortcut to the completion of one's own personality. There is an economical beauty in not having to develop an aspect of one's personality, but finding another who also may be seeking a shortcut to self-actualization. Plato has provided the most vivid imagery for this completion motive. In the *Symposium*, Plato has Socrates explain that there used to be a total being of which half was male and half was female. Zeus, however, to weaken them, cut them in half. "Now when the work of bisection was complete it left each half with a desperate yearning for the other and they ran together and flung their arms around each other's necks, and asked for nothing better than to be rolled into one. So much so, that they began to die of hunger and general inertia, and neither would do anything without the other. And whenever half was left alone . . . it wandered about questioning and clasping in the hope of finding a spare half-woman—or whole woman as we should call her nowadays—or half a man" (Plato, 1961, pp. 543-544).

Jung (1954) wrote eloquently about the archetypal aspects of masculinity (animus) and femininity (anima) and suggested that men and women are attracted to certain aspects in each other in order to make up deficits in their own identities. Jung emphasized that complementary attraction is one of the major motivating forces behind the development of relationships. The theory of complementary attraction has been revered by many (for example Gray and Wheelwright, 1944; Reik, 1945; Winch, 1958). However, as noted by Puckett (1977), many of the findings on complementary attraction have been unsubstantiated by other researchers (Bowerman and Day, 1956; Heiss and Gordon, 1964; Trost, 1967). Levinson (1978), writing on the developmental stages in men's lives, found that one of the tasks of mid-life was to overcome the masculine-feminine polarity and learn to accept the feminine aspects. Levinson acknowledged that this polarity is often reflected in the distinction between thinking and feeling.

A second supply one obtains from merger involves attempts to complete one's self developmentally, not just characterologically. Assuming a psychoanalytic stance, Mahler, Pine, and Bergman (1975) considered the evolution of one's intimate relationships to be related to a repetition of one's earliest connections. They considered that the child goes through various stages of separation-individuation in relationship to significant others which affects all subsequent relationships and spoke of the autistic stage between mother and child when everything is experienced as part of the self. Freud ([1914] 1957g) also described the child's "oceanic feelings of wholeness" as related to the mother. After the autistic stage, Mahler, Pine and Bergman (1975) depicted the symbiotic stage of development wherein the child begins to be more perceptive of its environment but is not yet fully able to delineate inner from outer experience. The three later stages involve a separation phase where there is a progressive discrimination between self and other, a rapprochement period where the child experiences the self as separate but has ambivalence, and the individuated stage. In a dissertation on the intimacy-individuation conflict, Puckett (1977) related Mahler, Pine, and Bergman's developmental stages to the stages of relationships in adulthood. She postulated that elements of all stages exist in adulthood to some degree.

Another supply that may result from merging with another is safety. In certain cultures and societies, such safety may be physical, but in modern Western society, the safety is more psychological in that it provides the expectancy that someone will be there with whom to face the vicissitudes of life. A special case of this psychological safety concerns attempts at resolving conflicts of independence/dependence. Graphic examples can be found in cases of early marriage as a means to escape the parental home without having to gain economic or emotional independence. Similarly, it is quite common for someone who has just left a relationship to fall heels over head in love with someone also on the "rebound." Here the supply obtained is two-fold: avoidance (at least temporarily) of the pain in experiencing the loss, and avoidance (at least temporarily) in dealing with the world alone. In fact, many of the supplies obtained by losing one's self through love involve defending against the threat of loss. To the extent that a person is one with the beloved, there can be no separation. Bowlby (1969) has much to say about the value of this attachment in children and how it provides children with a reassurance that enables them to explore their environment.

As if the economical shortcuts to completion, safety, and identity insurance promised in romantic love were not enough, one also gains immeasurable information about who he or she is or potentially might become. One's uniqueness and specialness become illuminated in the enthralling feedback from the beloved. Erikson (1963) explained that adolescent love appears to be an attempt to achieve identity by "projecting one's diffused ego image on another and by seeing it thus reflected and gradually clarified. This is why so much of young love is conversation" (p. 262). In addition, the sharing of experiences and the attendant understanding heighten the feeling of merger. The shared secrets of life, the pet phrases, and the knowing glances shape one's reality and change subjective idealism into consensual validation. Research substantiates this feeling. People who share experiences or even residential locations come to overevaluate one another (Festinger, Schachter, and Back, 1950). Fromm (1958), in sharing his thoughts on love and psychotherapy, wrote: "When the patient feels love is exactly when he experiences the analyst as being him, as talking from the experience which is shared with him" (p. 133). Thus the information-processing aspects of love are quite important. This area has been predominantly researched by social psychologists, whereas the category of supplies has been more the domain of clinical psychologists.

The third category of motivating forces for the need to merge has been almost the sole province of poets, philosophers, and the lovers themselves. Here we can see the importance of The Experience of losing one's self as a prime motive for falling in love. In fact, we consider The Experience so crucial that it appears to us to be more a drive state than a specific need. The major factor in The Experience of romantic love is the changed state of consciousness—the sensating splendor and expansive feelings of completeness and union. Ellis (1972) captures the essence of this point of view when he states that the romantic lover is frequently (and we would maintain almost always) in love with love, rather than with his beloved.

There have been numerous ways other than The Experience of romantic love through which people have tried to achieve this alteration in consciousness. The pervasiveness and longevity of these methods attest to the power of the drive to merge and lose self-consciousness. In reviewing the literature on meditation, drugs, hypnosis, and orgasm, we have been impressed with the frequency with which these ways of "expanding consciousness" have been compared to and contrasted with the romantic love experience. Professionals who have worked with heroin addicts recognize the "love affair" between the addict and the drug. With many of the more powerfully addictive drugs, there is a periodic fulfillment and obsessiveness that is characteristic of the romantic love experience—the rush, the descent, the loss of self, and the feeling of oneness. Furthermore, there are parallels between the negative aspects of drug addiction and those of romantic love. As Peele and Brodsky (1975) noted, the early pleasures of drug abuse frequently begin to take on a painful neediness, similar to the lover's experience of driven-ness for completion and possession. Fromm (1956) outlined how the escape from separateness through alcohol or drugs leads to more feelings of separateness after the experience is over.

Another way to attempt to lose oneself is through the experience of meditation. As Kilpatrick (1975) noted, there has been a burgeoning of interest in Eastern philosophy and its ideas about the self: " 'Undoing the ego', Meher Baba called it" (p. 139). However, the ready adoption of meditation in our society as a way to achieve instant loss of self-consciousness seems ultimately unfulfilling. As de Ropp (1976) commented in his paper on drugs, yoga, and psychotransformism: "If you sit around like Rodin's thinker, all hunched up, you get nowhere" (p. 167). Another parallel to The Experience of losing oneself in romantic love can be drawn with orgasm. Perhaps it is not clear that any parallels need to be drawn because sex is sometimes confused with romantic love. However, we agree with Ellis's (1972) viewpoint that romantic love is often asexual or even antisexual. Reik (1945) commented on the different aims of sex and love. He reasoned that for sex the aim is a disappearance of physical tension, a discharge and a release, whereas for love the goal is the disappearance of psychical tension, relief. He concluded that sex desires satisfaction whereas love desires happiness. Reich (1975), in his *Function of the Orgasm,* outlined how orgastic potency involves the whole organism, not just the interstitial tissue of the gonads: "Orgastic potency is the capacity to surrender to the *flow* of biological energy, free of any inhibitions; the capacity to discharge completely the dammed up sexual excitation through involuntary pleasurable convulsions of the body" (p. 90, emphasis added). Goethals, in Chapter Sixteen, discusses Arthur Deikman's notions that the experiences of sexual fusion may constitute an altered state of consciousness. Goethals explores the role of "restitutive regression" which can be experienced in the entrance and exit of sexual climax. In fact, intercourse has sometimes been seen as the concrete manifestation of the individuation–merger dilemma. However, some observers of present social interactions conclude that an altered experience of one's self is becoming less a part of sexual enjoyment. May's (1969) view is that at present in our society the orgasm has almost been robbed of any pleasurable sense of a changing consciousness. "This all means that people not only must learn to perform sexually, but must make sure that they can do so without losing themselves in passion or unseemly commitment that may be interpreted as an unhealthy demand upon the partner" (p. 26).

Fromm (1956) felt that all methods such as drugs, meditation, or orgasm were attempts at overcoming separateness, and what they had in common was their intensity, involvement of mind and body, and transitory nature. It seems, however, that romantic love provides one of the most powerful and pervasive means for attaining The Experience in our culture. According to Kilpatrick (1975), the biggest push for The Experience of losing one's self comes from the Human Potential Movement. He criticized such a movement toward what he labels an Eastern philosophy on the grounds that it will lead to "an identity so fluid that it really can't be called an identity (p. 139)."

What is the role of identity in attenuating or potentiating The Experience? First we will consider the notion that the search for identity is in conflict with the romantic love experience.

Search for Identity As the Antithesis of Romantic Love

There are many different types of identity that have been described (for example, collective, social ideal, emotional) and even many definitions of the same type of identity. What most of these have in common, however, is that identity involves a sense of knowing who you are (personal identity) and usually a subjective evaluation of having a life that "hangs together" (what Erikson calls ego identity). Erikson (1963) is perhaps the best-known theoretician on the subject of identity in the human life cycle. He has described a list of ego qualities that emerge during critical periods of development: "A lasting ego identity . . . cannot begin to exist without the trust of the first oral stage; it cannot be completed without a promise of fulfillment" (p. 246). Kilpatrick (1975) aligned himself with Erikson's view of identity when he maintained that identity should involve qualities of sameness, uniqueness, fidelity, and commitment. This approach is consistent with those of Victor Frankl, Rollo May, and most of the Existential writers. This positive view of a lasting identity can be contrasted with that which holds that the idea of a fixed identity is not adaptive in a constantly changing and transient society. Kilpatrick claimed that the Human Potential Movement, represented by such people as Carl Rogers, upholds the concept of a "fluid identity" as more appropriate for our modern times—an identity that abhors permanent and total commitment. When we speak of "losing ourselves" while falling in love, it is the Eriksonian sense of self we feel has been shaken. Horner (1978) defines identity as being the capacity to experience oneself "as separate, real and a whole human being" (p. 14). It is the act of merger with another that violates the sense of separateness and boundedness and causes people to feel that they are losing themselves when they fall in love. What are the positive and negative aspects of having such a sense of identity?

Individuation has been lauded by most of the mental-health behavioral scientists. Such theorists as Jung (1954) and Mahler, Pine, and Bergman (1975) considered individuation the highest form of human development. Similar is Maslow's (1968) view of self-actualization. We find the behaviorists emphasizing the value of assertiveness and proponents of Transactional Analysis praising the evolution of individual identity. There is much research that substantiates that individuation is correlated with better coping skills. For example, Fisher and Cleveland (1968) delineated the effects of being more clearly bounded on one's behavior and effectiveness and functioning. Apparently, lay people recognize the value of having a secure sense of self—witness the popularity of such books as *Looking Out for Number One, How to Say No Without Feeling Guilty,* and *Pulling Your Own Strings.*

Few would argue against the value of most of the aspects of individuation just presented. Why then do people seemingly want to lose themselves? What are the various components of identity definition that may contain negative experiences and consequences? The experience of loneliness can be an offshoot. In discussing the conflict between intimacy versus isolation, Erikson (1963) stated that the avoidance of intimacy because of a fear of ego loss may lead to isolation and self-absorption (p. 264). The Existentialists emphasize the experience of "nothingness and meaninglessness" that can accompany experiential separateness. Some of the negative aspects of a highly developed individual self are emphasized on a sociocultural level by Philip Slater (1976) in his book, *The Pursuit of Loneliness*: "When a value is strongly held, as individualism is in America, the illnesses it produces tend to be treated in the same way an alcoholic treats a hangover or a drug addict his withdrawal symptoms. Technological change, mobility, and individualistic ways of thinking all rupture the bonds that tie a man to a family, a community, a kinship network, a geographical location" (p. 11). Fromm (1956) has stated the negative aspects of individuation quite dramatically by viewing the *awareness* of human separation as the problem of human existence. "The deepest need of man is the need to overcome his separateness, to relieve the person of his aloneness" (p. 8). Furthermore, Fromm theorized that this separate state is a source of shame, guilt, and anxiety. As a clinician, Kaiser (Enelow and Adler, 1965) observed that his patients were isolated. He believed that what drove them "into the office of the psychiatrist is not so much the realistic hope of getting cured as much as to step out of their isolation" (p. xix). As succinctly stated by one of Lair's students (1969),

"I am an identity floating through a void called life, seeing all the beauty, glory, and majesty; yet it signifies nothing for I've never been loved" (p. 237).

Upon inspection, the reasons for developing a clear-cut identity appear quite similar to the motives for immersing oneself in romantic love. Here again, one is seeking the continuity of supplies but from a more stable source—the self. Therefore, there is an emphasis on protecting oneself from loss, which is seen in the reluctance to surrender to another and the tendency to strive for further self-sufficiency. The experience of having a sense of self can also be a powerful motivating force based on survival itself. The knowledge of who one is, and of what one's capabilities and weaknesses are, gives one a sense of control to navigate accurately through life.

We have been describing the nature of The Experience of romantic love and identity, and exploring some of the reasons for striving for each. We have set up a dichotomy between romantic love and identity. In the next section, we shall question the appropriateness of this dichotomy, explore whether romantic love and identity are pathological processes, and suggest a new model.

The Individuation-Merger Process

Pathological or Natural Process. Before a reconceptualization of the individuation-merger process can be presented, it is important to investigate the degree to which romantic love is pathological. Ellis' (1972) description of romantic love is exemplary of most psychological theorists and clinicians who feel that the "ubiquity of ultra-romantic philosophies . . . when combined with the unromantic and often harsh realities of modern life, lead to serious (conscious and unconscious) conflicts and disturbances on the part of virtually all the members of our society" (p. 13). Of his patients, Ellis says: "Romanticism is definitely one of the chief reasons for their being considerably more unhappy and maladjusted than they would be had they more realistic goals of love and marriage" (p. 19). There is ample evidence that people do commit suicide over ill-fated romantic involvements. May (1969) wrote about a paradox of love—"the intensified openness to love that awareness of death gives us and the increased sense of death that love brings" (p. 35).

One has only to skim the myths and stories of romantic love to see how much death is a part of the love experience: Romeo and Juliet, Tristan and Isolde, Zhivago and Lara. In speaking of Tristan and Isolde, who both die—one by a poisoned spear, the other by grief—Kilpatrick (1975) reflected that beyond his love of love Tristan was also in love with death as a return to some kind of narcissistic state "where the distinction between selves is blurred and the world becomes . . . an extension of the self" (p. 210). Common in great stories of romantic love, as well as with the boy and girl next door, is the unfulfilled nature of the relationship, which also sounds quite pathological: the yearning, the obstacles, the unrequited feelings all are part of romantic love. Freud ([1930] 1961) stated that an obstacle is required in order to heighten libido. In fact, by definition, a characteristic of romantic love is unreleased tension. The intensity of such frustration may in fact increase the attraction. In their book, *A New Look at Love*, Walster and Walster (1978) cited numerous studies that strongly suggest that anxiety, frustration, anger, and ambivalence generate fuel for passionate feelings.

In addition to unhappiness, unfulfillment, and death, other "pathological" aspects of romantic love concern the possible outcomes of the interaction between two people who are romantically involved. Sheehy (1976), in her popular book *Passages*, observed that males in our society usually characterize the individuation portion of the conflict. They guard against the flow of merger. Females, however, are viewed as attempting to merge with a strong male as a way to achieve identity. Clinically there are some consistencies that tend to emerge and have implications for the experiencing of romantic love and identity evolution. Men are raised with a rather obvious blind spot which can be best characterized as a softness and ease in dealing with their feelings. Women are more typically sensitized to the importance of empathically dealing with the needs for nurturance and have generally been discouraged from developing a sense of assertion. The stage is set for an individualized type of neediness for men and women which results in numerous problems in the evolution of love relationships. For young adults, these "blind spots" serve as motivating forces for falling in love. They meet that man or woman who characterizes all the undeveloped aspects of their own identity in the beloved. The woman may find her fulfillment in the assertive and performance-oriented male who offers the protection and security of potential or actual success. The male discovers the promise of fulfillment in the woman who provides the soft empathy for his unmet needs for emotional nurturance. Thus the complement is set and romantic love evolves fired from the incompleteness of the individuals and tantalized by the accompanying intermittent affective intensity behind the promise. The true problem emerges when intimacy demands a movement from autistic and symbiotic elements to a recognition of separateness and individuation. The partners discover that in fact their beloved has not conceded the primal love contract, but may seemingly even serve as an impediment to a furtherance of their growth as individuals. The result is one of conflict between continuing the complement and actualizing individualization. The woman is again faced with individual incompleteness as separation-individuation elements intrude. She is likely to begin feeling depressed, "needing space," and wanting to pursue activities that promise the possibilities of experiencing her own energies more fully. Of course, this process works in direct conflict with the male's need for emotional nurturance and closeness as he is faced with the terrifying prospect of feeding himself emotionally. The result is often a regressive return to early experiences of unfulfillment and an internal struggle for homeostasis in dealing with the painful imbalance of individual identity development. The relationship manifests this turmoil in the evolution of a push-pull battle, marked by feelings of ambivalence, fearfulness, and anger, out of the individualized and unfulfilled needs. Perhaps the most blatant instance where these conflicts of identity and intimacy meet head on in an intensifying manner is in the obsessional male and hysterical female relationship. Barnett's (1971) article, "Narcissism and Dependency in the Obsessional-Hysteric Marriage," outlines the tragic story of the male-female relationship in which such conflicts reach increasingly pathological dimensions.

Misery, unfulfilled longing, suffocation of the self, and death all sound rather pathological; however, not all hold that romantic love is a sign of sickness. May (1969) acknowledged that the association between love and death *may be* seen as neurotic by many, but it does appear to be a fundamental and pervasive association. According to May: "This involvement is neurotic only if frozen, or fixated; only if the partners demand that they always live in this level" (p. 36). We agree with May's viewpoint and want to extend it to a consideration of romantic love in general. Falling in love is not pathological per se. Quite the contrary, it appears to us that romantic love provides The Experience of unity and flow that seems to be an essential part of being human. However, romantic love can have unhealthy aspects, especially when it causes a resistance to growth. It has the greatest chance of doing this when the lover continually confuses the experience of "loving being in love" with actual fulfillment and a mature love.

Similarly, the search for identity can have pathological aspects if the individual insulates the self against any loosening of ego boundaries. "Independence carried to its furthest extreme is a defense against commitment" (Shane, 1978, p. 213).

Individuation-Merger Process: A Reconceptualization. We have looked at some of the individual and intrapersonal pathological aspects of romantic love in the context of identity. However, it is our contention that the individuation-merger process is a natural, nonpathological (in most cases), and ongoing human dilemma. We are impressed by the similarities between this basic human dilemma and other dilemmas such as dependence-independence, spontaneity-will, passivity-activity, society-self, wish-reality, and death-life. To some degree, these polarities also mirror anima-animus and Eastern and Western philosophies. One imagines that if a factor analysis were computed on these various dimensions, two orientations would emerge that might be described as "being at one with nature" versus "intentionality." Our society at times emphasizes one pole over the other. For example, the "love generation" of the 1960s was replaced with the "me generation" of the 1970s. Witness the growing number of workshops, papers, and books on, and increased diagnostic use of, the Narcissistic Personality, in contrast to the once more popular Hysterical Character.

What we are lacking are useful models of the individuation-merger process. The word *useful* has two connotations here. The first is heuristic. What model will most readily lead to meaningful research on the subject? Probably the heuristic model will be based on a conflict model that views individuation-merger on opposite sides of some continuum. This model focuses on the role of tension in maintaining a dynamic balance. Walster and Walster's

(1978) equity theory of love (based on a modified, biologically set pleasure principle) is an example of a dynamic interpersonal conflict model. Simply stated, it holds that in a love relationship two people try to establish an actual and psychological balance of costs and benefits. Such a model leads to seeming understanding because it views the world from a Newtonian, mechanistic, linear perspective. The world is seen as being composed of discrete parts that influence one another.

The second connotation of the word *useful* considers what would be the most accurate model of the individuation-merger process. It appears to us that the "two poles" of individuation-merger may be just artifacts of a linear conceptualization of the phenomenon. This conflicting view is inadequate for two reasons. First, romantic love and identity are not two poles, we feel, but rather two overlapping dimensions of the same outlook—they both contain the embellishments of hope and trust. Romantic love is an embellishment on reality. Similarly, the concept of identity is embellished with the meaning and significance of uniqueness, constancy, eternity, choice, and freedom. Not only do love and identity share this romantic quality, they are also dynamically and systemically interdependent. Rather than applying a Newtonian model of discrete qualities influencing one another, we are proposing a model which parallels that of quantum physics. As Capra (1975) states, "Quantum theory thus reveals an essential interconnectedness of the universe. It shows us that we cannot decompose the world into independently existing smallest units. As we penetrate into matter, we find that it is made of particles, but these are not the 'basic building blocks' in the sense of Democritus and Newton. They are merely idealizations which are useful, from a practical point of view, but have no fundamental significance. . . . The universal interconnectedness of things and events . . . seems to be a fundamental feature of the atomic reality" (pp. 137–138).

For example, we accept concepts of time and space as being separate entities in nature. Although we believe in these discrete qualities in order to navigate and understand our environment (heuristic value), such a conceptualization fosters the belief that time and space *really* exist as separate properties in nature. However, Einstein's theory has caused modern physicists to add time to the three space coordinates as a fourth dimension. "Both are intimately and inseparably connected and form a four-dimensional continuum which is called 'space-time'" (Capra, 1975, p. 168).

Applied to the individuation-merger process, this approach views identity and romantic love as part of an interlocking network in which one's sense of identity gains in relationship to The Experience of romantic love and romantic love can only be experienced in terms of an individual's identity. Writers on the subject of this new interlocking network model have concluded that the "two orientations" of individuation-merger might actually be functionally inseparable. Fromm (1956) acknowledged this when he wrote, "Paradoxically the ability to be alone is the condition for the ability to love" (p. 94). And May (1969) said, "The paradox of love is that it is the highest degree of awareness of the individual self and the highest degree of absorption in the other" (p. 62). It is only because Fromm and May are using a linear conflictual model that they saw these relationships as "paradoxical." Although Levinson (1978) wrote of the attachment-separateness *polarity*, he expressed the pseudoparadox when he stated that one cares more deeply for others by caring more deeply for oneself. In listing the "clinically observed characteristics" of self-actualized persons, Maslow (1968) included those attributes of spontaneity, richer emotional reactions, and changed interpersonal relations. As Tillich (1952) said, "The courage to be oneself is never completely separated from the other pole, the courage to be as a part" (p. 123).

The unified dynamic model of merger-individuation perhaps has its greatest applicability in psychotherapy. Clients' fears of losing their identities in the intensity of love, or of being lonely should they want to be independent, need to be reconceptualized and reexperienced. The passion of romantic love is not just the immediate experience of "flow" but rather a new level of consciousness that unites the feeling of merger with that of separation. The experience of romantic love is founded on the reality of an *experiencing self*. Trusting that total experience is the road to transforming romantic love into a more fulfilling and satisfying contact.

16

Love, Marriage, and Mutual Growth

George W. Goethals

I shall discuss in this chapter love, marriage, and a theoretical conception that I am at present calling "mutative relationships." Marriage is defined, for the purpose of this chapter, as an intense psychic and emotional bond between a heterosexual couple. It is what Cuber and Harroff (1965) have defined as a *vital* or *total* marriage and what Fairbairn (1954) and Dicks (1967) would describe as an attitude of mature dependency between differentiated individuals who have the capacity to relate simultaneously upon a social, psychic, and interpsychic level of relationships. This chapter thus proposes that marriage is not only a constantly shifting relationship as it exists in reality but also a relationship in which many different psychological levels and involvements are played out.

Note: Anne Glickman provided editorial help and scholarly collaboration throughout the final writing of this chapter. The members of my graduate seminar at Harvard University, in the course of our discussion of psychoanalytic theory, helped me to untangle and understand, at least in part, the

Perspectives on Love and Marriage

One of the most interesting questions in the literature under consideration is that there have been a number of attempts to define what should exist in a functioning sexual relationship. The works of Masters and Johnson (1966, 1975) and Kaplan (1974) have dealt well with what is involved in the sexual response and also have suggested therapeutic interventions to help loving couples overcome sexual dysfunction. The literature on the physiology of sex is encyclopedic, and no attempt will be made to summarize any of it.

A number of psychoanalytic thinkers have talked in one way or another about what should be involved in an adult genital relationship. Freud, in a number of essays, attempted discussions about adult sexuality and at least hinted at the various elements involved in a love relationship, but his work is clouded by his extremely questionable exposition of female sexuality. Erikson (1950) has offered an operational definition of what should be involved in adult intimacy, and Sullivan (1953b) has made an extremely important distinction, which I have elucidated in an earlier paper (Goethals, 1976), between the developmental tasks involved in being intimate (that is, collaborative) with another human being and the development of what he calls the lust dynamism, the felt need for release of genital tension. Fairbairn (1954, p. 32), in a masterpiece of compression, in one paragraph notes that the adult should not only have a genital attitude that is libidinal but further should have a number of paths to reach the object other than the genitals. Balint, in at least three papers ([1937] 1965a, [1937] 1965b, 1968), has written movingly about what

multiple themes and subtleties of Kernberg's work: Philip Aranow, Catalina Arboleda, Robert J. Blair, Margaret M. Bullitt, Tom Davey, Nancy Davis, Beverly Douhan, Vicki Garvin, Janet Graham, Emily Hancock, Patricia S. Herzog, Sara McLeod, Raquel Ojeda, Suki Parker, Rosemary Sharp, Catherina Ann Steiner, and Dorothy A. Swartz. Josephine Lowndes Sevely made some extremely constructive suggestions. Many of these ideas had their origin in discussions with three of my professional colleagues: Joel H. Feigon, Barbara Massar, and Stuart Pizer.

I also thank Laurie Tiede, who typed the manuscript. My acknowledgment to Donald and Janet, who have permitted me to share aspects of their lives, can be made but never fully.

is involved for an adult in a sexual relationship to permit, in an atmosphere of trust, regression to a state of helplessness. He is referring, of course, to the helplessness that occurs during and shortly after orgasm.

The anomaly is that, on the one hand, we have excellent materials dealing with sexuality, its functioning, malfunctioning, and treatment, and, on the other hand, we have some of the best minds in psychoanalytic thinking addressing *aspects* of intimacy. However, until Kernberg (1974a, 1974b, 1977), no one had attempted to address the psychology of love as part of adult living.

It will be, I think, instructive to understand how I came to have my interest in love relationships and marriage. Some years ago, early in my training, I treated a twenty-year-old male who was in the midst of an extreme depression brought about by the termination of an intial love relationship. I was struck in the course of our relationship with a number of themes. The first was the validity of Freud's dictum, in "Mourning and Melancholia" ([1917] 1957d), that one does not abandon an object position easily, nor give it up without great expenditure of psychic energy. Second, I was interested that this young man, who was extremely intelligent and attractive, did not wish to find a new object and, in many of our sessions, discussed not only the pain of loss but also the intolerable sense of fear he had of ever having to experience such a relationship again. Thus there was not only a kind of object persistency but also a profound sense of object fear. Since this person's psychic integrity can be attested to by the fact that a year later he won a Rhodes Scholarship, this is a case of an otherwise intact person experiencing a combination of fear and depression.

All of us in our work run into cases that have a profound effect upon us because we sense that something very important is going on of a more general nature. After thinking for some years about the issues that I saw involved in this case, I wrote an article (Goethals, 1973) in which I attempted to discuss the fact that being in love was in a sense a two-edged sword. On the one hand, there was a delight in all that loving can mean and in the ecstasies of sexual sharing. On the other, the existential experience of such a state could not prevent any human being from fantasizing about what would happen if this particular object were lost. Despite the limitations of the work of Holmes and Rahe (1967), all of their various samples rated as the most stressful event the loss of a beloved spouse. Therefore, loving and being in love places one in harm's way —that is, at the intersection between ecstasy and despair.

In 1973, I collaborated with two of my colleagues on an article for a book edited by Grunebaum and Christ (Goethals, Steele, and Broude, 1976). In that chapter, we set ourselves the task of reviewing the state of research and theory building that existed at the time, and of trying to bring together certain relatively new theoretical perspectives, including my own, to suggest new directions. Although some of the research reviewed did deal with factors relating to marital satisfaction, most of it dealt with what might be called the psychopathology of marriage. If it did not deal with this concern, it discussed how individual psychopathology caused marital discord. I advanced at that time a theoretical perspective based upon the article I had published earlier (Goethals, 1973), which I called (in full knowledge that I violated the strict biological definition of the term) "A Theory of Symbiosis." This theory derives from a synthesis of the work of Freud, Fairbairn, and Sullivan, and is influenced by the thinking of Dicks. What I said then bears repeating:

> Symbiosis may be described as follows: It consists of a powerful emotional attachment of a positive kind between one object and another. It is characterized as and called *symbiosis* rather than *attachment* because in symbiosis each party provides for the other something that the other does not have. Symbiosis might then be seen as a kind of attachment that, as a prime prerequisite, involves complementation of what exists in one object by what exists in another. Thus, symbiosis can never be seen as an isolated phenomenon. By definition it is not only interpersonal but interpsychic. The world and psyche of one person demand complementation by another for the establishment of a symbiotic field. It follows, of course, that any interference will be vigorously resisted, and, if interrupted, extremely serious revisions of affect or personality, or both, are inescapable [Goethals, Steele, and Broude, 1976, pp. 232-233].

The question involved in making this statement in the context of that particular chapter was whether such a theory could be tested, given the methodological limitations of academic psychology. Given the constraints that method imposes upon data, we concluded, without stating so explicitly, that within the purview of *academic* psychology, this topic could not be researched. One reason is that of all the human relationships, as Dicks (1967) has pointed out, marriage is sui generis. Another is identified by Binstock (1973) in a very moving statement: "There are two relationships that can occupy the center of a life. The quest of them is endlessly compelling. The confusions which occur between them are infinite. One of these relationships is that between mother and infant; the other is that between members of an adult heterosexual couple" (p. 93).

Binstock's observation notes that marriage is not only, as Dicks (1967) has suggested, a sui generis relationship but also that it is constantly changing and can be affected by early experience in one's life with attachment and separation. Despite the work of Bannister (1971) and Ryle (1975), who have attempted to modify Kelly's (1955) grid technique to study marriage, it remains, as a relationship, something that is ever changing. In a very moving little book, de Castillejo (1973) talks about how there can be a *meeting* between people. All of us have had the experience of *meeting* people emotionally and psychically, but it is quite different to meet someone, be intimate with him or her, and then—on the basis of that meeting—form a *continuing* relationship. It has been said by some cynics that the only true relationship that can exist between a heterosexual couple is a meeting followed by a brief affair and a separation. What is common in the thinking of Dicks, Kernberg, and myself is the notion that being in a relationship and continuing a relationship are two entirely different things.

This does not mean, however, that there is not a valid source of data from which to draw observations and bring about a clinical synthesis. The data to which I am referring are clinical data, gathered over time, a task Kernberg accomplishes with great precision in his first two papers (1974a, 1974b). From a methodological point of view, my method is the same, that is, to apply his rich ideas to a couple who are intact and not in psychological distress. It is clinical observation, and time may prove that this may be the only way in which this particular topic, the experiencing of love within the context of a continuing relationship, can be studied. I do not feel that this is a liability. It is high time, in psychology and psychiatry, that we face in a forthright fashion what we can and cannot do within our own fields. Clinical research in clinical psychology is quite frankly in its infancy, but I predict that in the next twenty years, the infant will grow into a vigorous and creative adult.

Mutative Relationships and Marriage

In this discussion, I wish to propose an idea that may be useful in thinking further about love relationships and marriage. I intend first to review some of my own past theoretical thinking, and second to propose and define what I feel is a mutative relationship. These ideas were formulated before I read Kernberg's three papers (1974a, 1974b, 1977). After reading his work, particularly his final paper, I feel able to discuss my own ideas in a fuller fashion, through the use of clinical examples, and also possibly to take Kernberg's work a step further. I say this with full acknowledgment that, from a certain perspective, Kernberg's 1977 paper may have said all there is to say about the subject.

There have been two major influences on my theoretical thinking at its most basic level. One of these is British object relations theory. The other is the work of Sullivan.

Sullivan's work was profoundly infuenced by a number of thinkers; who those thinkers were is found in a book written after his death as a *Festschrift* from his colleagues in the behavioral sciences (Sullivan, 1964). One influence that has not been given nearly enough attention in discussions of Sullivan is the thinking of Lewin (1935) and his conception of the interpersonal field. I am speaking specifically of Sullivan's notions that human beings—by virtue of their evolutionary status—not only are axiomatically interpersonal but they also create in a dyad an interpersonal field: "A" interacting with "B" is not simply "A" plus "B"; it is "A" interacting with "B" to create a third field, "C." A man and a woman represent differentiated individuals as "A" and "B," as well as being in the dyadic field of "C."

Object relations theory has caused me to see Sullivan's adaptation of Lewin's theory as involving not only social interaction but also the effect social interaction can have on both the interpsychic reality between the couple and the intrapsychic balance within each individual. In a continuing relationship, one is relating to the partner and also (catalyzed by the partner) redefining one-self, sometimes in relation to the self and sometimes in relation to the partner.

Having said this, I should like to step further into my ideas about the phenomenon of love as a phenomenon. Although I am ready to accept Slater's (1976) notion that falling in love at first sight is a romantic delusion, I am not prepared to accept the im-plicit premise that follows: that the establishment of intimacy—getting to know one another, getting to trust one another—neces-sarily takes a great deal of time. I do think intimacy involves a syntactic form of what Sullivan has called empathy, and that "understandings" (or "meetings") can be achieved relatively quick-ly between men and women. Conversely, some courtships, and I am speaking here of psychic courtships, may extend over a long period of time. What is common in both situations is that sexual passion becomes a way of expressing what already exists. Good sexual intimacy is essentially related to consummatory psychic fusion or, as Kernberg calls it, *transcendence*, and not related in the least to tension reduction.

This brings me to propose a category of relationship that I am calling, for the purpose of preliminary discussion, the muta-tive relationship, and which I shall now try to define operationally:

1. Its very designation—mutative—implies that this is not only a relationship of intense order but also one that generates changes continually in the three fields that I propose Sullivan implies: the entity made up of the couple and the two separate and distinct individuals.
2. By fact, as well as by design and calculation, the people in such a relationship grow and change. There is a kinetic quality to these relationships.
3. Not only is what happens between the two people colored by what Sullivan calls "friendly wonder" and syntactic empathy but also these qualities are essentially existential. Nothing has to be "worked on."
4. These relationships have tremendous power and scope sexually; they are also sexually exclusive, not by fiat or agreement, but by fact.
5. Both the people and the relationship, taking previous points into account, are constantly open to change and redefinition.

6. There is a high degree of androgyny and empathy in both part-
    ners. They must share a sense of collaboration about their so-
    cial and sexual roles as affected and defined by a highly com-
    plex and changing society.

Such relationships are relatively rare and may represent an end
point on a continuum. However, I think they are possible (Goethals, 1978). Implicit in them are many of the notions from Kernberg's paper (1977) to which I have alluded but have not yet
discussed.

A Mutative Relationship—Donald and Janet

I should now like to turn to a specific clinical case of a mutative relationship, and deal with it purely from the point of view of
what transpired between a couple over a period of five years. Although this particular mutative relationship had as its central feature the experience of change generated by an intense and very
passionate sexual relationship, one should not conclude that this
is the only way mutative relationships can occur. Mutative relationships can occur in any kind of complementarity, and I intend in
the future to discuss several varieties of mutative relationships.
Some background history is in order.

The couple consisted of a male, forty-three years old, and
a female of twenty-seven. Both had been divorced. The reason for
marriage in both cases was religious background which made sexual experimentation outside of marriage forbidden. Having formed
relationships which they hoped would eventuate and fulfill their
emotional and sexual expectations, each got married, and both for
a time experienced some fundamental satisfactions. In both cases,
their spouses refused to accommodate the change in world-view
that developed; they wanted to continue defining the situation in
the terms that existed at the time they got married, and they ignored and denied the inevitable changes brought about by parenting and two-career families. Both divorces were relatively amicable.

The couple came to my attention in an unusual way. They
had heard of my interest in research on marriage and my interest
in talking to couples who perceived themselves to be intensely in
love. They also felt there were some issues between them that
might require some therapeutic attention, but these they consid-

ered to be minor. Since they had volunteered to discuss their marriage and relationship with me, I let them come to see me as they wished, usually once or twice a month, for five years—sometimes as a couple, sometimes singly. As will be noted, their experiencing of each other exemplifies behaviorally and physically some of the constructs of Balint, Kernberg, Winnicott, and myself.

To some extent, the therapeutic aspects of the case were reminiscent of the prayer attributed to the apostle Thomas: "Lord, I believe; help thou my disbelief." In essence, there was so little correspondence between what they experienced together and their previous sexual involvements that there was an air about their relationship of mystery and transcendence, to use Kernberg's terms, which they wanted to test with someone they felt they could trust.

What I propose to do here is to deal with their own account of their experience and to relate it to the appropriate theoretical materials at hand. What follows is a description of several incidents, not necessarily presented in chronological order, most of which occurred over a period of time prior to the couple's deciding to get married. Some features of the case are quite unusual, and still to be explained.

Courtship. Donald and Janet each held doctorates that fitted them to do basic research in either academic or hospital settings. They met as members of a research team involved in highly sophisticated neurological research. They reported that their initial contacts, although warm and friendly, were by no means charged emotionally, sexually, or erotically. They found they could work well and easily together, and that each one's training in his or her specialty complemented rather than duplicated the other person's abilities.

Some comments are required at this point concerning their sexual histories at the time they met. As their marriages deteriorated, both found solace in extramarital relationships. Both reported findings in some instances overt and complete sexual gratification with individuals with whom they could not be intimate or form an intimate relationship. Conversely, both had had relationships that were intimate in the Sullivanian sense but that were found to be unsatisfactory when genital sexuality was added. At the time they met, both were somewhat depressed and, at the time, celibate.

Owing to the nature of their work and its hours, Donald and Janet began to share lunch and dinner together but never at each other's home. They reported feeling tremendously at ease and unpressured by their interaction. They found themselves completely open in talking to each other about the lives they had lived. They both remarked that this candor was very unusual in their experience, since each tended to be, even with close friends, quite reticent. They found this "opening up" to each other extremely refreshing but profoundly puzzling, since, as indicated, this had not been their mode of relating previously.

About six months after they met, an episode occurred which they experienced separately and shared much later as their intimacy evolved. They had been asked by a colleague to sort out some microfilms to construct the bibliography for an article. They were in a small room with very little space. The man became profoundly aware that although his colleague was going about her work calmly, in a completely organized fashion, she was intensely excited sexually. She reports what happened as follows:

> I'd gone to the microfilm files, glad to have Don's company on this extremely dull job and to be with someone I liked. I knew we would be able to chat, and the tedium of the job would be alleviated. I suddenly found myself overwhelmed by an intense genital response. I could feel my genitals becoming drenched and dilated, and I knew that in the cramped quarters in which we were working, my woman's smell could not go unnoticed. What I found myself astonished by was that I felt not a sense of embarrassment or shame but somehow a sense of great pride in revealing to Don later something about my feelings which I at that very moment was suddenly experiencing.

Donald's report of the same incident is as follows: "I felt as though I was being given a gift beyond price. I felt suspended in the here and now. While I had some mild response myself, my most intense feelings were wonderment at her womanhood, the power of her genitals, and her ability to seem proud yet at the same time unexhibitionistic about what was going on." They both reported finishing the job and going back to their research. Instead of experiencing sexual tension, they felt a sense of profound peace and relaxation.

During this period of mutual noninvolvement, both masturbated regularly. Since this masturbation was largely related to tension reduction, it was almost entirely without fantasy. After the incident just reported, both spoke of masturbating for and because of each other. Their fantasies were interesting in that they did not involve sexual scenarios, but rather, in the same mode expressed in leaving the laboratory, a sense of closeness, a sense of sharing, and a surety that the other was experiencing the same thing.

At this point, they discussed an extremely interesting and possibly significant hiatus in their relationship. They both reported knowing it was inevitable that they would be involved sexually; the question was not if but when. They both reported that this was not accompanied by lust or passion, but again by very tender and very gentle feelings toward the other. This, combined with their intellectual colleagueship, gave them what each described as a sense of deep serenity. A kind of Eriksonian basic trust seemed to pervade their interaction. Both reported retrospectively that during this period of time, which lasted approximately a month, if either had asked the other for sexual intercourse, it would have been given joyfully. They spoke of feeling restrained rather than inhibited, of waiting to flower rather than feeling pressured.

Sexual Contact. Their first sexual contact, as will be seen, had profound implications both for the beginning of their relationship and, as it turned out later, for addressing unresolved issues in their adolescence.

Donald invited Janet to come over to his apartment to share an evening listening to music. As they sat down to discuss what they would hear, he suddenly said to her that he desperately wanted physical contact. He says that at that moment he felt completely intoxicated, drawn to her, and found himself with his head buried in her genitals and she lying back and having multiple orgasms. He told her she was beautiful—referring to her genitals—and this intense act by him to her was followed by her giving him fellatio. They reported after the act sitting side by side on the couch, holding each other's hands and laughing. They joked about the fact that they had kissed and loved each other's genitals before they had kissed each other on the mouth.

Aspects of their adolescent experience that were addressed in this particular incident, as well as some of the intricacies of the woman's relationship with her mother, were the following. As a child, Janet was discovered masturbating by her mother, who, from her fundamentalist religious point of view, told the child that what she was doing was sinful, that the part of her body was her "shame." When she was courting her fiancé, and they began to indulge in heavy petting, in feelings of love and adoration she wanted very much to kiss and suck his penis. When she did this spontaneously as they were making love, he pushed her aside and proceeded to masturbate himself in a handkerchief. In Donald's life, a parallel episode occurred. In his late teens, he had his first passionate relationship with a woman, and one evening when they were necking, he exposed his penis and placed her hand on it. She cried out and said, "Put that great big dirty thing away; I can't stand it!" The rest of the evening was, to put it mildly, extremely uncomfortable.

Thus, as Donald and Janet reviewed their rather unusual initial sexual contact, she said to him that her genitals were no longer "it," or no longer "down there," hidden away and shameful, but something she was proud to display and have him enjoy. He in turn suddenly felt the same way about his genitals for the first time in his adult life.

Genitality. Their accounts of first intercourse are equally unusual and thought-provoking. About a week after this initial contact, he invited her again to his apartment. What transpired is best told in his own words:

> I had gotten off work late in the afternoon, and Janet had to work until around 8:30. We agreed to meet at my apartment. I was extremely aware of wanting to see Janet. I know that sounds strange under the circumstances, and probably even stranger when I say that I was not thinking about having sexual intercourse with her. All I knew was that she was going to be with me and spend some time with me, and that was sufficient. I heard her parking her car, and I went to let her in the door. She came walking up the steps in a white dress, laughing. I felt at some level in a state of benign terror. I was not anxious; I was not afraid. But there was something about her skin color, the color of her hair, and the white dress that made her seem to glow. I asked her if she wanted to have a drink. She took me by the hand and said No, she wanted to make love to me. I followed her into the bedroom and we lay fully clothed on the bed. The light in the room was dim. I kissed her and I slowly unbuttoned the front of her dress. She had no underthings on except for her panties. When I had her dress open from the waist to the shoulders, my breath was taken away.

> Her body was incredibly beautiful, and seemed to glow. I felt
> as though I was not only with her but with every fantasy Ru-
> bens ever had when he painted full-breasted, lush women. We
> took off our clothes and with no foreplay whatsoever I im-
> mediately entered her. She began to talk in very sexual terms
> about what was happening and told me to come. I came in an
> immense orgasm. I did not feel that my penis had been in pen-
> etration of her, but rather as though I had been suddenly en-
> gulfed by her. We lay back on the bed and laughed.

In both of their past histories, Donald and Janet revealed that they had been criticized by previous partners for the size of their genitals—she for being too big and uninvolved, he for being painful. Suddenly their genitals were involved in a way that had been completely absent for either of them before, and they felt free to be expressive in the ultimate degree. Janet does not know why she could suddenly talk to a partner in the act of intercourse, but she felt a complete freedom to say and ask anything she wanted.

The Incident of Panic. One of the most interesting issues Donald and Janet discussed with me was their both experiencing, but at different times in the relationship, profound panic. Janet's experience, which happened relatively early in the relationship—before they had gotten married and while they were still living separately—is best described with reference to her own account:

> Donald had gone away for a couple of days to a meet-
> ing in another city. We had arranged to meet at about seven
> o'clock in the evening at his apartment. I woke up that morn-
> ing full of joy and anticipation at his return. It was Sunday
> and therefore I was in my own home and not at work. The
> day passed pleasantly, and the happy mood continued. Sud-
> denly, somewhere between four and five in the afternoon, I was
> seized with a profound case of panic and anxiety. I knew pre-
> cisely when Donald would be back, but somehow I could not
> believe that he, or what we had shared, had existed. I remember
> sitting, shaking, then starting to pace the room. Finally the
> strain became intolerable and I picked up the telephone to call
> his apartment even though I knew he was not there. Much to
> my surprise, he answered the phone, saying he had just walked
> through the door, having caught an earlier flight than he had
> anticipated.

Both members of this couple report a tremendous difference in their feelings as regards being *separated* and being *apart*. When they are absent from each other by mutual consent or professional commitment, there is no anxiety. If they are separated by circumstance, however, both have fantasies about what their lives would be without the other.

Fantasies and Secrets. Shortly after Janet's experience of panic, another act of intercourse occurred which is of significance. Janet had told Donald about a medical convention she had attended some months before, where a group of women had held a party and decided, because of the high quality of the music, to dance together. She danced with a young woman toward whom she suddenly and unexpectedly had strong sexual feelings. Although these were never consummated, nor were any overt advances made, she came away feeling moved by the encounter. Donald recounted to Janet the following dream: "I dreamed you were in an Empire-style bedroom with a very beautiful black woman. She was obviously very taken with you, and proceeded very gently and in a methodical way, although you were resisting, to seduce you. You came to full orgasm in the dream." Donald told this to Janet as they were having intercourse, and she immediately went into a series of intense multiple orgasmic spasms.

Some time after this, what for Don was an astounding experience took place. Their lovemaking was extremely passionate and varied. They would often have intercourse two or three times a night, combining this with other forms of sexual communication. There was a great deal of what might be called Winnicottian play and of laughing and joking; there were also discussions of future plans, as well as talk of past life experiences. One area that had not been discussed, more or less by tacit agreement, was their sexual experiences involving extramarital partners. They had shared, and deeply, the pains and disappointments they had experienced in their marriages.

Donald exhibited a trait, common in males, which may have a deep psychological basis: the feeling that despite clear evidence of one's being a highly satisfactory and providing partner, some other man may have been better endowed and better able to make love. He described to me how listening to a woman talk about previous lovers had always been extremely anxiety producing, and would cause him, as he put it, to "shrivel up." Although these episodes were transitory, and could be worked through, there was a primitive feeling that could only be described as an attenuated form of castration anxiety or a sense of genital inferiority. The paradox was that each of his partners had assured him that on this count he had nothing to worry about.

One evening, after they had made love and were drinking wine and joking, Janet began to laugh. Donald asked her why she was laughing, and she blushed and said that she had to share with him one of the most embarrassing experiences she had ever had in her life, which involved another man. She made it clear that this concerned something sexual, and Donald told me as he heard this how incredibly threatened he felt by the impending disclosure. He said: "I had known that she had had some years before a very painful affair. I'd never known why it was painful, and I had been afraid to ask. I knew it involved someone of high public visibility, and that before the affair she had had some indirect connection with him. I also knew that she wanted to talk to me about him, even though she had not made that explicit, and I could feel myself cringing in anticipation of the resulting anxiety."

Janet had served on a selection committee for a senior post at a university, and the winning candidate had begun to visit her at home. She found herself sexually aroused by him, and during the second or third visit, in a state of intense excitement, they undressed and went to her bed. As she described this, Donald felt intense anxiety. She then went on to describe how, due to her genital size, dilation, and wetness, he kept slipping out of her in the act of intercourse, not only on the first occasion but also on the second and last occasion that they attempted intercourse. She was terribly ill at ease about the whole business and felt a combination of sexual excitement and embarrassment about herself and for her partner, which in retrospect she could view as high comedy.

As Janet recounted this episode, Donald became intensely excited by what she had told him. Identifying with her genital feelings, he turned to her and made love passionately. He subsequently reported that any past sexual experiences they shared with each other always served as a vehicle for intense sexual excitement, which they quite properly labeled a form of verbal foreplay.

Shifts in Orientation. Before elaborating on other critical incidents in this mutative relationship, I shall digress briefly to talk about an aspect of the general emotional tone between these two people, which was characterized by two major shifts in orientation.

When they began their relationship, as many contemporary couples do, they gave each other permission to seek sexual satisfaction elsewhere. They did, however, agree in the light of the intensity of their own feelings and sharings that any outside involvements would be shared. Both reported a complete sense of freedom, while paradoxically being in a state of profound involvement and commitment. Some time later in the relationship, Janet remarked to me that while she could not speak for Donald, the idea of becoming sexually intimate with anyone else was utterly impossible for her. She said it was not that she felt constrained or that she was consciously limiting her behavior; rather, she felt herself in a situation which she succinctly described as involving both freedom and fidelity. In talking through his feelings with me, Donald commented that he had "stopped looking." It was not that he did not enjoy seeing beautiful women, but there was a complete absence of any fantasies about beautiful women whom he might meet socially or professionally.

Another profound shift that came about without any discussion of its occurrence may be of even more interest. Both Donald and Janet could be described as people of high sexual voltage. Consistently during their marriages, and concurrent with affairs they had had, they had masturbated. They had shared this information. Even though they were orgasmic in intercourse with others and received gratification, ultimately they received the most intense gratification from masturbating. In Janet's case, her description of the phenomenon was very similar to that found in *The Hite Report* (1976).

A year or so after their involvement began, in the course of a casual conversation, Janet turned to Donald and asked him when he had last masturbated. In mutual wonderment, they realized they had not masturbated for months and had absolutely no desire to do so. I found this particular aspect of their history extremely intriguing. It exemplifies what Fairbairn (1954) is saying in his cryptic comment about autoeroticism: "Autoeroticism is essentially a technique whereby the individual seeks not only to provide for himself what he cannot obtain from the object, but to provide for himself an object which he cannot obtain" (p. 34). In dealing with each other as differentiated total as well as part objects, neither Donald nor Janet required the supplementation of private fantasy, since what fantasies existed were always shared.

Third-Stage Communication. Another complex level of interaction also began to enter the relationship, and continues to this day. It is what this couple has chosen to call a third-stage level of communication, which takes two characteristics—one very common between couples who are deeply in love, another somewhat unusual though probably not unique to this particular couple. The first is an amazing capacity to read at an almost telepathic level the thoughts and moods of the other. It is what I described earlier in this chapter as "syntactic empathy." However, a particular incident that happened in Janet's life and was then relived in relation to Donald suggests that syntactic empathy can involve not only the existential present but also the past of either individual in a way that defies the barriers of time.

During her high school years, Janet had an idealized deep attachment to a young man two or three years older than she. He was handsome, intelligent, and considered by her and her classmates to be the ideal man. Although he cared about her and was kind to her, in his eyes the relationship was profound friendship rather than the beginning of a possible sexual involvement. He turned to one of her friends for that aspect of his living. Although hurt by his choice, she was able to deal with it.

He went on to a career in the regular armed services as a jet pilot and was well on his way to a stable career. One day when she was alone at home and doing some housework, she was listening to the radio. The regular musical program was interrupted with a news brief, an announcement that on a routine mission the man had been killed when his plane crashed. She reported that she was in the midst of grief and sadness but felt a tremendous need somehow to be close to this idealized and fantasied lover. She went into the bedroom and masturbated, thinking of the times she had spent with him.

When her husband returned, she did not tell him. Some time later in the course of their relationship, she told Donald about the incident and they discussed how, if he had been her husband at that time, she would have told him and how they would have made love together. What is important here is that both of them, in the most careful and minute detail, could describe what would have happened to them in this past had they been able to share it.

Hostility, Anger, Ambivalence. Two or three years after they were married, Janet and Donald went through a very difficult two- or three-month period. Janet was being considered as a candidate for a senior post in another hospital. Donald was somewhat upset about the fact that this meant an end to their collaboration, whereas Janet saw this as a chance, as she put it, to have "a world of my own." Although she reassured Donald that part of their work would continue to be collaborative, she felt the need as a person to have something that was completely her own. During this period, since the selection process was lengthy, she felt unsexual, irritable, and withdrawn. She asked Donald to deal with her and bear with her, saying that once things were over, she would be again available. He felt profoundly ambivalent about this whole situation. On the one hand, he wanted to be supportive, to be "the rock" that she asked; on the other hand, he felt somehow that his own emotional needs were unmet. He could understand the legitimacy of the situation, but irrationally he felt let down and neglected.

When Janet won the post, they went out to celebrate with friends. Before they had gone out, she had acknowledged to him that without his help and support during the time of transition, she might well have collapsed. During the course of the evening, however, as they joyously celebrated with friends, she made no allusion in the presence of others to the support Donald had given her, or to the acknowledged cost it had placed on his own emotional structure. As they were driving home, he told her he felt bereft and neglected, that he was extremely angry with her for not recognizing his help. She in turn replied that it was her day, her job, and damn it, she was going to enjoy it. They proceeded to express their anger openly with each other, and then decided to sleep separately. The next morning, the storm had passed, and they could reconcile and reconstitute.

Throughout the course of their relationship, as they continued to externalize and act upon erotic feelings, as the stresses and strains of their independent professional careers took time and energy and occasionally gave each a feeling of frustration and loss, they were able to articulate their anger and condolence about not being where they once were. They could talk about their professional admiration for each other's advancements, and enjoy them, but at the same time be angry that such advancements might give them less time together. Their capacity to externalize their anger and ambivalence, as well as their capacity to have intense sexual contact, is a characteristic of this couple. Dick once made the comment that the opposite of love is not hate but indifference. This is a couple who can externalize anger, fight it out, but are never indifferent to each other.

Theoretical Issues of the Case

I should like now to turn to the incidents in the history of this couple which, in my framework, would be a mutative relationship (Goethals, 1978) and which Kernberg (1977) describes in his third paper dealing with the psychology of love. In the course of this section, I want both to discuss the interaction of the couple as it might be interpreted theoretically and to add some of their own interpretations and observations as to what went on between them.

Earlier in this chapter, in discussing the work of Slater (1976), I suggested that love relationships could be formed in quite different ways—that meetings as described by de Castillejo (1973) could occur, yet there might be other relationships that took longer to unfold, even though when consummated they might be as intense and passionate as those that had more apparent immediacy.

The initial weeks and months of this couple's relationship bear close scrutiny. They met in a working situation and found that there was indeed an *intimacy* in the sense that Sullivan (1953b) describes it and I have attempted elsewhere to elaborate (Goethals, 1976). Their work was not only collaborative but also complementary. Second, there was an openness on which both could remark, knowing it was new and novel and yet feeling completely safe and comfortable within its field. Third, there could be acknowledgment of genitality and sexual arousal in an atmosphere of pride and self-esteem. Finally, when sexual contact was made, it was made in a somewhat unusual way. In discussing this period of time, the couple raised with me the question of whether they were involved in some kind of very subtle, nonverbal form of courtship. The intense first sexual contact, I think, can be explained as analogous— but now between a more normal couple—to the case of the obsessional patient described by Kernberg (1974a). In both instances, there was a relationship with a differentiated whole object and then a capacity for intense mutual genital identification and closure with the other. A comment made by Erikson (1963, p. 265) explains this beautifully: "When Freud said 'love,' he meant *genital* love and genital *love*; when he said love *and* work, he meant a general work-productiveness which would not preoccupy the individual to the extent that he loses his right or capacity to be a genital and loving being. Thus we may ponder, but we cannot improve on 'the professor's' formula." This initial stage also conforms remarkably to Fairbairn's (1954, p. 32) description of mature love:

> In the mature individual on the other hand . . . the genital organs provide a path of least resistance to the object—but, in this case, only in parallel with a number of other paths. The real point about the mature individual is not that the libidinal attitude is essentially genital, but that the genital attitude is essentially libidinal. There is thus an inherent difference between the infantile and the mature libidinal attitude arising out of the fact that, whereas in the case of the infant the libidinal attitude must be of necessity predominantly oral, in the case of the emotionally mature adult libido seeks the object through a number of channels, among which the genital channel plays an essential, but by no means exclusive, part. Whilst, therefore, it is correct to describe the libidinal attitude of the infant as characteristically oral, it is not correct to describe the libidinal attitude of the adult as characteristically genital. It should properly be described as "mature." . . . It is not in virtue of the fact that the genital level has been reached that object-relationships are satisfactory. On the contrary, it is in virtue of the fact that satisfactory object-relationships have been established that true genital sexuality is attained.

Finally, what happened between the couple is a vivid illustration of the incorporation of lust dynamism into an already established intimate relationship, as viewed by Sullivan (1953b).

It is rather clear in this relationship that this couple portrays the multiple transactions that Kernberg describes in his discussion of passion. This is related to the fact of sexual intercourse and orgasm, but, in addition, their account shows an ability to deal, sometimes in unexpected ways, with their fantasies. As Kernberg (1977, pp. 103-104) has so clearly defined it: "Under optimal circumstances, the intensity of sexual enjoyment has an ongoing renovative quality which does not depend on the 'mechanical features' of sexual gymnastics, but on the couple's intuitive capacity to weave changing personal needs and experiences into the complex net of heterosexual and homosexual, loving and aggressive, aspects of the total relationship expressed in unconscious and conscious fantasies and their enactment in their sexual relations."

In our discussion about this aspect of their relationship—the capacity for intense eroticism, multidimensional in its scope—what puzzled Janet and Donald was not its existence but rather how and why this happened between them and never at any other time in their sexual histories. Although we talked about this numerous times, the closest they could come to articulating what they felt was to say that, for reasons unknown to either of them, they felt a complete sense of safety and security with the other. Janet remarked that she always knew exactly where Donald was and, in knowing this, felt she could express anything and everything that was her being.

Earlier in this chapter and in the body of the case, I have alluded to the fact that being in love is, in a sense, being "in harm's way." The panic that both of them felt was this amalgam, which I feel is so true in an intense love relationship, of profound ecstasy with the anticipation of possible loss. They feel that by externalizing this fear and dealing with it, they have been able not only to see themselves as a devoted couple but also to understand the irrational anxieties each can have at times about the other. This is certainly reminiscent of much of Dicks' (1967) thinking about the need for each spouse to tolerate the infantile residuals in the other.

There is another aspect of this fantasy world which, in this case, I think is quite remarkable. This involved Donald's radical change in response to Janet's previous sexual history. In my estimation, this is related to the strength of the couple's relationship when addressing unresolved oedipal and castration anxieties in the midst of the world of sexual passion. This is consistent both with my thinking and with Kernberg's (1977) discussion of how in sexual passion the oedipal aspects can be worked through and the couple can feel part of a unity, not only with themselves but with the mysteries of their parents' sexual relationship: "The shared experience of orgasm includes, in addition to the temporary identification with the sexual partner, the transcendence from the experience of the self into that of the fantasied union of the oedipal parents, as well as the transcendence of the repetition of the oedipal relation to abandonment of it in a new object relation that reconfirms one's separate identity and autonomy. In sexual passion, time-determined boundaries of the self are crossed and the past world of object relations is transcended into a new, personally re-created one" (p. 98).

The segment of the case that deals with the fighting and the mutual feelings of hostility and ambivalence related to Janet's job change is instructive in two ways. First, it suggests—as Kernberg (1977) has pointed out—that among the most profound strains upon a love relationship are the pressures of the modern world and the role changes demanded of both men and women. Although Kernberg is not explicit about the remedy to this, he *is* about the situation: "The social, cultural, and professional development and success of women in our society, then, may threaten traditional, culturally sanctioned and reinforced protection of men against their oedipal insecurity and fears and against their envy of women in the broadest sense; and the changing reality of their life faces both participants with the potential reactivation of conscious and unconscious envy, jealousy, and resentment, which dangerously increase the aggressive components of the love relation" (p. 109). What seems to me critical in this relationship as it continues is that the couple's constant capacity to deal with issues of hostility, competition, and the very ambivalence of being in a relationship as demanding as theirs openly places them in a position where they exemplify what I call the *mutative*. It must be emphasized that this relationship is not an endurance contest; rather it demonstrates that contemporary couples, when they can externalize the negative aspects of their relationship, given a firm foundation of passion and tenderness, can face the inevitable transitions of life and career.

I have saved for the final part of my discussion, for reasons that will become obvious, an aspect of the intervention that I have left so far without comment. This has to do with Donald's report of the very unusual visual impressions he had of Janet as she came into his apartment, and of his feelings when he undressed her. As he talked about this with me, he made an allusion, as reported in the case, to feeling he was with a woman who was out of a fantasy of Rubens. This relates to two issues of importance. First, it relates to Deikman's (1977) suggestion that in sexual relationships altered states of consciousness can exist. Although Deikman largely focuses upon the phenomena associated with orgasm, it seems logical that altered states of consciousness can also exist in intense experiences of sexual excitement. Second, Donald's comment about seeing his beloved's body is tremendously reminiscent of a clinical fragment in Kernberg's (1977, pp. 96–97) work:

> The patient, a college professor in his late thirties, shortly before setting out on a professional trip to Europe had become engaged to a woman he felt very much in love with. On his return, he described an experience he had when visiting the Louvre and seeing there for the first time Mesopotamian miniature sculptures from the third millennium before our era. At one point, he had the uncanny experience that one of these tiny sculptures, the body of a woman whose nipples and navel were marked by tiny precious stones, resembled the body of the woman he loved. He had been thinking about her, longing for her as he walked through the practically deserted halls, and while he was looking at the sculpture, a wave of erotic stimulation seized him, together with an intense feeling of closeness with her. . . . The sense of sexual excitement had become fused with the sense of oneness, of longing and yet closeness with the woman he loved, and through the oneness and love he had been permitted entrance into the transcendent world of beauty.

Thus Donald and Janet saw themselves as Kernberg's analys- and did, not only in relation to each other as lovers but also in relation to lovers at all ages over time. I should like to make one final comment about this aspect of their relationship as I conclude this chapter, which is in the same area as the observation I have reported and Kernberg has remarked upon. One of the couple's friends gave them a book of erotic pictures ranging from antiquity to the present. The book contained hundreds of such pictures. They both read and enjoyed looking at these, separately and together. One evening Donald said, "I want you to write down on a slip of paper the picture that you feel is most moving and most related to us." Janet did this without hesitation. She said, "Please do the same for me"; he did. They exchanged the slips of paper. Out of a thick volume, they had picked the identical picture.

Martin Buber had expressed the same idea at the level of poetry: "But when the perfect encounter is to occur, the gates are unified into one gate of actual life and you no longer know through which you have entered."

17

Love and the Dynamics of Personal Growth

Mihaly Csikszentmihalyi

"Any theory of love must begin with a theory of man," says Fromm (1956, p. 7). He is right, of course, because any description of human activity will make sense only within a particular set of assumptions about what human beings are. So before talking about love, one ought to say what one thinks people are; and before *that*, one should say a few words about the theoretical framework one is about to use.

Setting the Stage: An Epistemological Excursion

The progress of knowledge, or the system of explanation people create to account for facts, has never followed a line of

straight, incremental growth. We have had instead a series of dialectic swings in which explanations for experienced events are first
based on one set of assumptions about the nature of reality, and
these are soon replaced by an entirely different set. It seems that
human comprehension is unable to cope with the various dimensions of reality simultaneously, and is forced instead to adopt partial perspectives which emphasize one dimension to the exclusion
of others in different segments of historical time.

Sorokin (1937), for instance, has shown that in the past
twenty centuries Western thought has alternated between periods
in which all interpretations of fact were based on the evidence of
the senses, or empiricism, and periods in which mystical vision,
or faith in supernatural revelation, or the logical operations of reason were held to constitute the framework within which facts
were to be explained. It is not true, on Sorokin's evidence, that
empiricism—or the scientific perspective that every educated person now takes for granted—has grown steadily from early humble
beginnings to its present state of preeminence. What seems to have
happened instead is that periods of intense empirical activity, as in
the third century A.D., have yielded to centuries in which empirical thought was practically never used to explain complex events,
and mysticism, fideism, or rationalism were predominant instead.
It is as if each of these frameworks for explanation—or epistemologies—offers a seductive promise to make sense of the world and
of our experience in it, and so people choose one of them for this
purpose until they realize its limitations, at which point the former epistemology is entirely rejected, and a new one becomes en-
throned in its place. Rarely has anyone succeeded in viewing the
world from all possible angles at the same time.

This bias would not matter so much if those who use any
one epistemology were aware of their inevitable self-imposed limitation. Problems arise only when the mystic insists that reality is
"nothing but" that slice of it which he has allowed himself to see,
or when the scientist begins to take his or her empirical view of
reality too seriously and consequently confuses symbol and substance. When epistemologies rigidify into "nothing but" world
views, the thinker becomes encapsulated by his own thought
(Royce, 1964). As a result, experience loses its rich texture,

thought becomes unable to relate adaptively to its real environment, and much unnecessary argument ensues among the blind cohorts attempting to describe the transcendental elephant.

These rather obvious reflections are in order, I think, as a preamble to discussing romantic love. For among the important "facts" of human experience, few are as dependent as love is on the particular epistemological position of the viewer. Love has been "seen" as nothing but a result of body chemistry by some (and by most people in certain periods of time); by others it has been seen as a fulfillment ordained by God; it has been seen as a mystical union of unfolding potentialities and as a rational contract for mutual benefit. It might seem flippant to suggest that all of these perspectives are equally valid. Yet it seems undeniable that each explanation *can* be right. To understand the phenomenon of love in all its complexity one must be willing to accept the fact that human behavior is motivated by reason, faith, and intuition as well as by hormones, and that these processes are basically irreducible to each other; they are more independent of each other than, say, photosynthesis as a form of energy transformation is of digestion, or any of these is of the steam engine.

In the historical period in which we happen to live, love has been generally viewed exclusively through the lens of empiricism—or, to be more exact, through the lens of a particular stage in the development of the empirical sciences. Thus the kinds of events surrounding the manifestations of love, which in former centuries minstrels, poets, or saints have described in terms of a variety of explanations, have all been reduced to a limited set of biological functions. Everyone is familiar, for example, with the great Freudian simplification that accounts for every facet of the relationship between two people—as well as for much else—in terms of the vicissitudes of repressed libido.

The "debunking" perspective of psychoanalysis has been, of course, often salutary. Petrified myths of previous orthodoxies were cluttering the landscape. We should not, however, carve another idol with which to replace them—a myth should help the mind grow, not be its despot.

What is limiting about reductionistic approaches such as the psychoanalytic one is that any meaningful change in the human condition is ruled out in advance. If one assumes that the only real pleasure a person can experience is the libidinal one, and that all the complexities of behavior are "nothing but" displacements or sublimations of the original instinctual drive, then psychologists must limit themselves to viewing all new manifestations of behavior as a transformation of the one original source of all behavior. While such a stance *might* be the correct one, it goes against the grain even of the empirical epistemology, whose most basic rule is never to foreclose judgment.

The other main reductionistic doctrine of our times is behaviorism. Modern behaviorism has dispensed with the concepts of need and instinct. Its reductionism derives from the basic assumption that any stimulus acquires its reinforcing value exclusively from the previous history of the experiencing organism. This perspective also denies, in principle, that the organism can learn to relate to a novel stimulus in a new way, as a function of current experience as well as a past conditioning.

Contemporary accounts of behavior are based on a *closed* view of human nature. They assume that needs, motivations, and rewards are set by genes and prior experience. Whatever the organism encounters later in life will have no chance to modify the already established structure of needs and reward contingencies. Every new experience will derive its meaning only from its relation to a set pattern of motivations.

An alternative to this perspective is an *open* view of behavior, which assumes that persons learn new "needs," motivations, and rewards in the course of their development, and that these emerging motivational systems must be understood in their own right, rather than explained away solely in terms of past conditions of the organism (Csikszentmihalyi, 1978b). Emergent motivation as an explanatory concept makes sense if we consider the following argument. During the course of development, a person is continuously faced with stimuli that demand some sort of response yet have very tenuous associations with the person's instinctual needs or history of reinforcement. Nevertheless, it makes sense to assume that the person's first responses to novel stimuli will be made in terms of an already established motivational system—he or she will behave according to a "closed" model of behavior. But if the stimulus is rich enough and allows for a great variety of responses, the person might begin to respond to it in terms of motivations *that he or she could never have imagined to exist*, and these emerging motives will be more essential to sustaining the response than any of the previously established response configurations.

In practice, we all know how this works. For example, every year tens of thousands of young people put on a diving mask for the first time to duck below the surface of the sea and gingerly explore the underwater environment. Some of them will return year after year and become confirmed skin or scuba divers. Why? Because floating in water harks back to the blissful amniotic stage? Because it serves to sublimate a repressed libidinal design? Because it is linked with a chain of previously reinforcing stimuli? Well, perhaps all of these reasons explain a small proportion of the phenomenon. But what is more salient is that the confirmed diver is one who has discovered under water a whole new set of experiences for which his previous life could never have prepared him: a way of breathing, moving, seeing, and communicating that is utterly unprecedented. Discovering a unique set of opportunities for action, and thus of previously unimaginable experience, is the main motivation of the diver. The same motivation seems to propel the mountain climber, the chess player, the composer of music and all the rest of us at least some of the time (Csikszentmihalyi, 1975). This is roughly what is meant by emergent motivation: a process in which previously neutral stimuli become reinforcing because they produce new experiences.

This long detour was necessary because nowadays it would be almost impossible to start a discussion of love without having an implicit understanding that, after all, love is basically *nothing but* a superstructure built on libidinal foundations. I want to make clear at the outset that, in my opinion, such an assumption misses the point. Just as in architecture, that which is built on the foundation of love is usually more significant, interesting, and enlightening than what lies underneath. If we were to find out that the Parthenon is build on the same foundation as a Kentucky Fried Chicken stand, this would not force us to conclude that the two structures were equivalent.

At the risk of seeming to evade the topic, let me give one last example to illustrate the concept of emergent motivation with a case that is, in many ways, similar to the phenomenon of love, yet is simpler to grasp. It concerns the way people relate to food. In all taxonomies of basic instincts or drives, hunger and sex are usually at the top of the list. Thus food has been rightly considered to be one of the most effective primary reinforcers. Now if one adopts a closed, reductionistic perspective on behavior, then all our dealings with food will be explained in terms of its ability to reduce hunger by raising the blood sugar level, and so forth. Eating at an elegant restaurant, cooking a gourmet meal, breaking the host during Mass, or sharing a snack with a friend would all be instances of "feeding your face," reducible to a viscerogenic or libidinal oral need. It is likely that all human dealings with food originated with the homeostatic pleasure derived from reducing hunger. This is, in an evolutionary perspective, the "foundation" upon which all food-related behaviors are based. But it is just as important to realize that with the passage of time such behaviors cease to be motivated exclusively by the "closed" instinctive or libidinal source. When people discover how to combine new flavors in gourmet cooking, they create a reward system based on criteria of which they had not been aware before. A family holiday dinner produces experiences of sociability that go far beyond caloric rewards. When food is used as a symbol of status, of friendship, of community, or personal skill, of world-view (as vegetarians or macrobiotic believers do), then the rewards of food cannot be reduced any longer to a simple set of preexisting needs but should be considered in light of emerging motives that people discover as they interact with the possibilities in their environment.

Needless to say, one advantage of the open perspective on behavior advanced here is that it takes account of change, both ontogenetically and phylogenetically. Its use allows us to recognize that persons are profoundly modified by their interactions with one another, with the features of the natural environment, and with the systems of thought, belief, and action present in their culture. All these interactions generate motives and rewards that cannot be reduced to previously existing constellations of motives or rewards. To understand complex human behavior, such as love, we need to approach its rich manifestations with respect, so as not to miss the tenuously emerging reality that can so easily be overshadowed if we look only for the older, more established needs and motives.

The perspective to be developed here need not conflict with those presented elsewhere in this volume. We would agree, for instance, with the position taken by Friedlander and Morrison that "a frustrated need state . . . is an integral part of the romantic love experience." There is no question that frustrated needs, a searching for self-esteem, and a host of other antecedent conditions predispose one to fall in love. The only argument to be made here is that none of these reductionistic explanations deals with the phenonenon in its entirety. For once a person, for whatever reasons, does get around to falling in love, a new set of experiences is triggered off. When this happens, love *may* become an entirely new ball game. It can provide a set of rewards, rules, and motives of its own that entirely supersede the original needs that made one fall in love in the first place. At that point, a love relationship becomes a genuine growth experience because it provides the person with feelings, thoughts, goals, and desires that he or she would never have otherwise.

A Definition of Love

Recent psychological writing on love presents a strange paradox. The issue of the causes and consequences of love are eagerly debated, and scholars ask themselves whether love is a "good" or a "bad" thing (for example, Casler, 1973). Yet very rarely is love defined, and, when it is, the definition remains vague or fails to capture the phenomenon. Lacking a clear concept of what the object of discussion is, the writers' conclusions often produce sensations akin to what Alice must have felt in Wonderland.

Those who do define love typically use some variation built on the Greek conceptions of *eros* or *agape*, the first referring to self-fulfillment through another human being, the second to self-surrender for the sake of the other (Tillich, 1957). The *agape* concept, for instance, informs the definitions of most clinically oriented psychologists. Fenichel (1945, p. 84): "One can speak of love only when consideration of the object goes so far that one's satisfaction is impossible without satisfying the object, too." Sullivan (1953a, pp. 42–43): "When the satisfaction or the security of another person becomes as significant to one as is one's own satisfaction or security, then the state of love exists." And Fromm (1956, p. 26): "Love is the active concern for the life and the growth of that which we love."

The problem with these definitions is that they rely on internal processes of evaluation and decision which are exceedingly difficult to study. How does one know to what extent someone else considers the "satisfaction" of the "object," or is concerned for the "life and growth" of the beloved? As a reaction to such problems, experimental psychologists have tended to formulate their definitions within the theoretical frameworks of physiology, attribution theory, behaviorism, or a combination thereof. A contemporary definition of "passionate love" (which, alas, seems to have very little kinship with *eros*) runs something like this: "(1) He is physiologically aroused, and (2) he concludes that love is the appropriate label for his aroused feelings" (Walster, 1971, p. 85). Or, "Love might be analyzed as the mutual tendency of two individuals to reinforce each other" (Skinner, 1953, p. 310). Such definitions certainly assume less about the inner states of the psyche, but their greater concreteness conceals a strange conceptual fuzziness. A "mutual tendency to reinforce each other" can be found among people who consciously pursue their self-interest without in the least caring for each other. Besides, mutuality is hardly a prerequisite for love. Are we to gloss over such inconsistencies in order to have a "neat" definition?

We shall try to approach love in as concrete a way as possible without violating the integrity of the concept—which is based on experience refined by thought over the centuries. Two definitions will be advanced, one for "love" in general, in the sense of *agape*, and the second for "romantic love." As one might expect, the two are quite different. Although empirically the two processes might overlap entirely, analytically they are quite distinct.

We speak of love in the broader sense *when a person invests attention in another person with the intention of realizing that person's goals*. The crucial variable in this definition is *attention*. It is crucial because every person has a limited supply of attention to invest in percepts, thoughts, or actions. Attention is practically indivisible: at any given moment, one cannot pay attention to more than a few stimuli at the same time (Binet, 1890; Kahneman, 1973). What a person can experience and accomplish in his or her lifetime is limited by the sum of discrete moments in which attention can be invested. Hence the allocation of attention over time determines the content of a person's live (James [1890] 1950; Csikszentmihalyi, 1978a). Attention is usually directed by intentions that tend to maximize one's own goals, but this is not the case in love.

Hence love is one of the most intriguing processes in psychology, because it involves the investment of a scarce resource necessary for survival (that is, attention) in goals that do not necessarily benefit the individual directly. At least this is what the *concept* of love is all about. Whether such a thing exists empirically or not is a question that can only be answered by empirical means.

We speak of romantic love *when a person cannot control his or her attention being invested in another person, yet enjoys the experience*. The essential fact about romantic love is its spontaneous, almost "helpless" character. Intentionality, which is often present in love, is antithetical to romantic love. If one must self-consciously intend to pay attention to a person, it is a sure sign that romantic love is not involved. Lovers are supposed to walk with their heads in the clouds, their minds filled with thoughts of the beloved. They are clumsy, distracted, unrelated to their surroundings, because their attention is not invested in the environment; it is focused on the object of love. And even if the lover tries to switch the focus of his or her psychic energy, the effort will typically be in vain.

Yet this state of "possession," this inability to control one's attention, which otherwise would be intolerable, is experienced as enjoyable in romantic love. True, the lover might suffer and pine if his or her attention is not returned by the beloved, but were there a choice, a true lover would not choose to end the experience, however painful, because even pain is enjoyable in the total context of the experience.

The difference between love and romantic love are now obvious: the first might be spontaneous or voluntary, the second is always spontaneous; the first must be directed primarily by the love object's interests, the second might or might not; the first need not be enjoyable, the second always is. In other words, the criterion of love is striving to realize the other's goals, the criterion of romantic love is spontaneity and enjoyment. When all three conditions are satisfied at the same time, love and romantic love are both present, merged in the same act of attention.

This definition clearly distinguishes between romantic love and those behavioral manifestations that one commonly identifies with it, but which do not meet the criteria. Sex, for instance, may occur in a context of love and/or romantic love, or it may not; sex and love are independent analytically, even if empirically they may co-occur at better than statistical chance levels. Every time sex is not spontaneous (that is, one must invest attention in "wanting" to do it), or is not enjoyable, romantic love is lacking. (It should be noted that enjoyment and pleasure are not the same thing. Enjoyment, as Aristotle pointed out, is a holistic—therefore also cognitive and emotional—experience one derives from an action, whereas pleasure is a passive physiological experience. Thus one can enjoy sex even without the full dimension of pleasure so prominently emphasized by current opinion on the subject.) And every time one partner is unconcerned about the other's goals, love is lacking in the sexual act.

By the same token, romantic love is independent of the "dating complex," that vast behavioral simulation which takes up so much of the psychic energies of adolescents. As several researchers have noted, teenage "love" relationships tend to be calculated rather than spontaneous, and the partner tends to be self-consciously seen as a trophy of personal prowess rather than a person whose goals one intends to enhance. Enjoyment is usually not derived from the relationship itself, but from the reflected peer group prestige it provides (Offer and Offer, 1968; Josselson, Greenberger, and McConochie, 1977). Of course, this conceptual sleight of hand, which disguises entirely different phenomena under the label of "love," is not limited to adolescence; it pervades adult relationships as well.

Love and Evolution

Our definition of love is not a behavioral one, and thus it contradicts the praxis of modern psychology. We are asserting that one cannot meaningfully decide whether or not a person is in the state of "love" by using observable evidence alone. Since what we call love is a state of the total information-processing system, or *self*, it is only within that system that the evidence lies. Behavior might offer valuable clues as to the state of the system, but it cannot provide conclusive proof. Behavior alone cannot tell us what a person's intentions are, whether the investment of attention is willed or spontaneous, and whether the experience is enjoyable or not. Only the person involved, reflecting on the state of his or her own self, has access to all the relevant data. Unfortunately, there is no foolproof way for the psychologist to extract this information, hence the obvious methodological difficulties of the phenomenological approach adopted here.

The only way to justify this approach is by assuming that people are able to describe the states of their own selves with tolerable accuracy, and that they are willing, by and large, to share such a description. These assumptions give rise to a method that is admittedly shaky, but any other alternative ends up reducing complex events, such as love, to a simplified form that distorts the original phenomenon beyond recognition.

Love in humans is obviously continuous with "instinctive" behaviors. It is likely that love has evolved out of what ethologists have been calling "attachment behavior" (for a review of this field, see Rajecki, Lamb, and Obmascher, 1978). Our willingness to invest attention in someone else's goals even at the cost of our own is based on the same altruistic behavior that evolutionary pressures have supported in ants, birds, and nonhuman mammals (Hamilton, 1964; Trivers, 1971; Wilson, 1975). Romantic love, or the seizure of our psychic energy by a conspecific in an enjoyable context, is based on the instinctive sexual attraction that ensures reproduction in all dimorphous species. Yet with humans a new level of complexity is present and must be accounted for. For one thing, people can dissemble, that is, they can send out consciously misleading information about their inner states. They can feign love or hate, and thus behavior ceases to be a reliable measure of the state of their selves. Whether man developed the ability to deceive only in the last few millennia, as Jaynes (1976) maintains, or whether it is a much older phylogenetic skill (Premack and Woodruff, 1979), it is one that seems to have been perfected by man relatively recently.

Deceit is an important factor because it implies intentionality, that is, the capacity to process in consciousness different information sequences relating to future action and then choose to invest attention in one of them. This in turn implies "voluntary" action that cannot any longer be reduced to spontaneous behavior.

Another dimension of human love that seems to have emerged relatively late in evolutionary history is its motivational flexibility. Sexual attraction in other animal species is triggered by fairly specific signals, such as certain scents, color displays, or behavior patterns. The same spontaneous releasers are still active in stimulating attraction between humans, as witness the huge success of the cosmetic and apparel industry and the popularity of nightclubs and discos. But what is astounding is the enormous variety of reasons why people "fall in love." The shape of a nose, a lock of hair, a particular inflection of the voice, a common interest in poetry can serve to capture a person's attention. Or to move to the more complex motivational plane on which Shakespeare's Othello explained the mutual attraction that bound him to Desdemona: "She lov'd me for the dangers I had pass'd, and I lov'd her that she did pity them." To reduce the variety of reasons to some set of preexisting genetic instructions is to misunderstand the emergent nature of human motivation. People fall in love for reasons that could not be predicted even by knowing all the facts of their lived experience, simply because these reasons can be utterly novel and unique. Love, like any other experience, is as complex as the consciousness that processes it.

Finally, the kind of enjoyment that results from romantic love is also an emergent phenomenon. We have no knowledge of what enjoyment nonhuman animals derive from their interactions, and there is no way of finding out. Some writers rule out the possibility that even the highest primates have any experience analogous to love; they are said to lack choice, preference, or conscious attachment (Pierre-Grassé, 1964). Others interpret the evidence to indicate that animals can develop social bonds based on "affection" independently of sexuality (see Griffin, 1976). But even the most strict reductionist must agree that in humans the situation is quite different. The variety of stimuli that can provide positive feedback in human interaction is practically endless; for this reason, discussion of this variety will be saved for the next section.

But what does it mean, from an evolutionary perspective, to say that love is an emergent phenomenon not reducible to instinctual processes? It means that, as a result of selective pressures, humans have developed a novel system for controlling their expenditure of energy. Their actions are no longer determined entirely by past solutions coded in the genes, to be reenacted when the environment produces the appropriate cues. "Phyletic memory" (Marais, 1969) is no longer the main guideline to action. For better or for worse, humans have perfected the capacity to respond to their environment in "nonhuman" ways. Consciousness has allowed us to do what Piaget calls de-centering, that is, to consider objects or events from viewpoints not given in our previous experience. This capacity is what allows us to transcend our origins; it is the cutting edge of evolution.

It is probably that, as most psychologists would claim, the reasons given by lovers for their feelings might be easily explained in terms of sublimation, attribution effects, or cognitive dissonance theory. The more sexually repressive a society is, the more people will have to explain even their sexual attraction in idealized terms. The fewer reasons there might be for loving a man, the more ardently the lover will justify her choice. The less conscious a man is of the reasons he is attracted to a woman, the more far-fetched excuses he will invent to rationalize his actions. All of these "debunking" explanations are accurate as far as they go. But as "nothing but" accounts, they do not reveal all that is going on. For despite these humble beginnings, love can emerge as an experience in which people truly discover how to appreciate, learn from, and enjoy those very fictions that they have created.

An evolutionary approach leads one further to ask: What is the survival advantage of love? If reproduction and mutual protection can be ensured by sexual and social bonding, for what reason did the more complex phenomenon of romantic love emerge? Answers to these questions must, of course, remain speculative. But it seems evident that as the human species developed more complex cognitive skills, instinctive bonding was no longer a satisfactory way of bringing people together. As humans began to reflect, and to invent concepts like "soul," "the sacred," and "freedom of will" to describe possibilities suggested by their experiences, it became natural to extend these concepts to the relationship between sexes. Thus romantic love was slowly "invented" in the process of applying new conceptual categories to old instinctive behaviors. That this invention was positively selected for in the course of sociocultural evolution might be explained in terms of the general selection for conceptual order. When a man accepts the fact that "empathy" or "spiritual values" are viable concepts, it becomes easier for him to believe that his relationship with a woman involves such processes. To believe that his interactions with others do not conform with these more complex emotions would cause an internal inconsistency that requires attention (that is, psychic energy) to be resolved, and thus produce entropy, or decreased efficiency, in the information-processing system that is consciousness. It is perfectly possible to argue that love, as we have come to know it, "emerged" out of selective pressures without endorsing a reductionist conclusion. For as soon as the cognitive and emotional expectations of love are superimposed on the instinctive bonds of sexuality, the relationship between people is qualitatively changed. It makes no sense to expose the instinctive roots of love and say: "See! That's all there is. Just sex." There is that, of course, but there is also more: roots and flowers are an inseparable whole. So when some psychologists pounce with glee on the ecstatic love poems of a St. Theresa or a St. John of the Cross and conclude that "this does not seem much different [from] the avid descriptions of Fanny Hill" (Casler, 1973, p. 15), they are missing the point. What is different between the mystic's vision of love and that of a whore is not its original motivation, which has been built into our makeup through eons of selective pressures. The important difference is what has been added onto the instinctual foundation. To miss the emergent goals and motives represented by such pioneers of love is to miss the course of evolution.

This is not to say that love is a powerful, stable motivating force in human affairs. Because of its recent emergence in phylogenetic history, its hold is unpredictable and fragile. Witness the enormous increase in divorce rates as soon as economic and political pressures to maintain marital systems are removed. It is clear that the institutions of marriage and family were shaped and are maintained by stark survival pressures, not by the emergent emotion of love (Csikszentmihalyi, 1970). Yet this somber fact does not imply that love will never be able to support human institutions. It just says that consciousness will have to complexify much further before what is now a rare exception can become the general norm.

The Dynamics of Enjoyment

There is a beautiful old French song that says: "Pleasures of love last but one instant long, the pains of love last the whole life through." This is a recurrent theme in human experience, expressed in art and folk wisdom, thus the chances are that it reflects a real situation. How can we reconcile it with the definition of romantic love that stresses enjoyment? There are several reasons why love can easily degenerate into a painful experience. First of all, the loss of control over one's attention characteristic of romantic love usually coexists in consciousness with a variety of expectations about the person who is the focus of attention. We tend to project onto the beloved all our hopes, all of our desires. Idealization and frustration are central to the romantic love experience. Unrealistic expectations will be inevitably shattered in the course of prolonged interaction. Love by itself cannot be a solution to a person's desires; the relationship must be actively nurtured if it is to keep providing enjoyment. Those who cling passively to it as their only hope for salvation are bound to be disappointed, and thus will join the dirge about "the pains of love." Moreover, the experience of love does not occur in a vacuum. It takes place in a vortex of pressures which interfere with love's demands on attention. The social institutions we have created to cope with survival problems—work, family, social and political organizations—all make demands on attention through their obligations, thereby reducing the amount of psychic energy we can use to experience love relationships. Institutions bind our attention in routine patterns, leaving little spontaneous attention. Therefore, those who expect love to solve all their problems end up disappointed by the fragility of their dream.

Given these difficulties, what can one do to keep romantic love alive, and to enjoy it in its most complex forms? This question presents an immediate problem. If romantic love is a spontaneous experience, as our definition requires, it would seem that there is nothing we can consciously do without destroying it. This is a limitation one must face. There is no sensible way to make oneself "fall in love" more easily, more often, or for a longer time. Any strategy to achieve such an effect would be self-defeating. Yet it is possible to make love more rich, more enjoyable, more fulfilling once the experience is established. We cannot make love happen, but we can nurture it after it is born.

To get the most out of the experience of romantic love is not difficult, at least in principle. It requires the same steps that are needed to make any experience more enjoyable. We have found that whenever a person has fun—whether it is dancing or playing chess, climbing a mountain or studying in a classroom—a similar set of inner experiences and environmental conditions is present (Csikszentmihalyi, 1975, 1976, 1978c; Csikszentmihalyi and Larson, 1978; Mayers, Csikszentmihalyi, and Larson, 1978). The experience of enjoyment—or *flow*, as we came to call it—is characterized above all by a deep, spontaneous involvement with the task at hand. In flow, one is carried away by interaction, to the extent that one feels immersed in the activity—the distinction between "I" and "it" becomes irrelevant. Attention is focused on whatever needs to be done, and there is not enough left over to worry or to get bored or distracted. In a state of flow, a person knows what needs to be done and knows whether the goals are being achieved or not—the feedback is clear. Yet the question of whether one is doing well or not seems to matter little; in flow, a person does not worry about his or her performance. The sense of time becomes distorted: hours seem to pass by in minutes, but afterward one might feel than an eternity has elapsed. The ego that surveys and evaluates our actions disappears in the flow of experience; one is freed of the confines of the social self and may feel an exhilarating sense of transcendence, of belonging to a larger whole.

These qualities describe how people feel when they enjoy what they are doing. Surgeons in the operating room or laborers on the assembly line use the same words to describe their work when it is enjoyable and rewarding. Needless to say, the experience of flow sounds very similar to what people say about how it feels to be in love. Common to the two states is the spontaneous investment of attention, the loss of self with concomitant intimations of transcendence, and, of course, the enjoyment. Is flow a variety of love, or love a form of flow? The question is one of definition, and thus perhaps not very important. What does matter is whether we can understand romantic love better by using the knowledge we have about the flow experience.

What we know about flow is that whether it is present or not depends a great deal on two conditions: how the activity is structured objectively, and how the person perceives the structure of the activity. For instance, every game is structured so as to make the focusing of attention on the play activity easy, and it provides clear goals, rules, and feedback. These structural features engage the player's attention, producing the flow experience. However, a person might restructure stimuli in his or her consciousness so as to produce flow without assistance from prestructured patterns in the environment and thus experience flow outside of ready-made cultural platforms. This is what children, yogis, mathematicians, artists—and countless unsung "average" people—can do at times.

A decisive structural factor for enjoyment is the balance of challenges and skills. At any given moment, we process in consciousness two crucial pieces of information: What can be done here? And, What could I do? The first question deals with the opportunities for action in the environment, or challenges. The second concerns one's own capacity to act, or skills. When challenges overwhelm skills we feel anxious, when skills outweigh challenges we feel bored. Flow occurs when we come close to matching the two. Here again we meet the external/internal dialectic of flow: Challenges and skills are partly objective features of the situation, partly they are the results of one's subjective attitude. The two are related, and both are important in producing the experience. For instance, a chess player can enter flow more easily in a chess tournament than in a dentist's waiting room, because the tournament presents him with a manageable task appropriate to his skills. But even at the dentist's, he could experience flow if he restructured the situation to optimize its potential challenges: by playing out a game in his head, by focusing his attention on a challenging article in a magazine, by flirting with the nurse, or by making critical observations to himself about the decorating scheme in the waiting room.

An essential feature of this structure of challenges and skills is that their balance is not static. If the complexity of challenges one faces does not increase with time, flow gives way to boredom. As we practice an activity, our skills in it increase until they outweigh the challenges. Hence, to maintain flow, there must be provisions made to find new things to engage our attention and skill, lest what used to be fun drift into tedium. For a climber, this means new peaks to ascend, more difficult faces to scale, or perhaps developing an interest in teaching others to climb, or in the esthetic, historical, or scientific dimensions of the mountain. Pleasure can be repeated again and again, as instinctual tensions build up and demand to be released; enjoyment, however, must grow in order to survive. Unless the experience becomes more complex, it stops providing enjoyment.

This model of the flow experience suggests, first of all, that in order to keep love enjoyable—that is, to keep it going at all, since enjoyment is necessary for romantic love to exist—one needs to be confronted by challenges appropriate to one's skills. Of course, any fool can fall in love. But to keep being in love one must be either very clever, or extremely simple. The innocent who does not feel he has any skills need never become bored by the object of his love. He can keep experiencing flow because, at least subjectively, his skills never grow and hence love never loses its freshness. Most of us, however, have lost this simple innocence and would easily tire of a relationship that failed to provide new opportunities for action.

But what challenges and what skills are relevant to being in love? As previously noted, romantic love is essentially attention focused on another person. Thus the "activity" of love consists in thinking about, looking at, and interacting with the object of one's attention. It follows that the challenges relevant to the activity of love must refer to aspects of the other person, or of the interaction. At the most basic level, the opportunities for action are given by the body of the beloved. In this age of specialization, some people are said to be "legmen" because their focus of attention in women is on the lower extremities. Others prefer buttocks, bosoms, or other anatomical configurations. This is fine as far as it goes, but it becomes difficult to envision a sustained love relationship built on the appreciation of a single physical detail. Even the whole body, with all its wonderfully different stimuli, eventually runs out of challenges to engage the skills of the lover. Thus a relationship in which attention is focused only on physical experiences tends to become boring sooner or later. To keep love fresh each partner must grow, that is, provide new challenges to the lover; and the lover must learn new skills to appreciate and respond appropriately to the changing ways of the beloved. The dimensions of growth are as many as the potentialities of human beings: emotional, artistic, intellectual, moral, as well as physical. Lovers can draw on all of these possibilities to enrich each other's mutual enjoyment.

Different historical periods have perfected techniques for increasing the potential challenges in one or the other of these dimensions. The *Kama Sutra* and *The Joy of Sex* teach how to make the physical side of a relationship more complex. Japanese women (or at least some of them) learn how to make even the most mundane daily acts occasions for graceful performance. The great invention of courtly love in medieval provence established new "games" of interpersonal relationship with difficult and exciting rules. The salons of the eighteenth century evolved somewhat less stringent but even more complex rules based on sparkling conversation and esoteric interests. In our own time, romantic love is becoming more complex thanks to the ever greater liberation of women. As women take on a wider range of responsibilities, they present greater and more varied challenges to men, thus enriching relationships—at least with liberated men who have the skills to match these emerging opportunities for interaction. Goethals' moving description of Donald and Janet's relationship in Chapter Sixteen is a good illustration of how two people can grow in skills by making a physical relationship more complex. What Goethals means by a "mutative relationship," I think, is the prerequisite for the survival of romantic love: an interaction that remains enjoyable because the challenges and skills are in a dynamic balance.

In other words, to keep romantic love alive the partners must grow, and each must be sensitive to the growth of the beloved. If this happens, almost infinite opportunities for enjoyable interaction will unfold. Sharing a conversation, a meal, a vacation, or even household chores can become the setting for flow. But recognition of the potential for growth in love must be qualified by recognition of the difficulties involved. To preserve love one has to provide new challenges and learn new skills. One must be constantly sensitive to the dynamics of the relationship. All of this requires attention, and attention is a form of energy that is in limited supply. We need to do our work, to monitor our inner states, to raise our children, to keep our home in order, and even to relax from all the other demands on our attention. How much of it can we spare to keep love alive? It is not suprising that so often, at the first signs of strain or boredom, most people withdraw their psychic energy from the relationship and let love wither away.

It is now time to raise the issue that several psychologists have debated in recent years: Is love good? (See Curtin, 1973.)

Or, as the question is often phrased, Does love contribute to mental health? Neither of these questions actually makes much sense. Nobody really knows what is "good" or what is "mental health." But we can say that when love is spontaneous and enjoyable—that is, when it is love at all—then it is as good a thing as any person can experience. But perhaps the questions should be stated in relative terms: Given all the demands on a person's attention, is it better to allocate some of it to nurture love, or is it better to invest it elsewhere? Even this formulation, which an economist might appreciate, is just barely sensible. It assumes a knowledge we simply do not have. Love might be better for some people some of the time, but it is foolhardy to generalize even in a relative way.

Of course, falling in love is a dangerous proposition. Those who take the concept of "mental health" seriously, and believe that a safe, well-balanced, adjusted self is the ultimate goal, will no doubt have many cogent qualms about the experience. But, let's face it: everything worth achieving in life is dangerous. Everything enjoyable (as opposed to merely pleasurable) requires one to extend oneself. To grow is always risky, because one must abandon the well-learned habits of a former self and venture into new realms of feeling and action. Of course, one can lose oneself, one can get hurt. Those are the chances a person takes for wishing to be more than he or she already is.

It might be foolhardy, but if I had to take a stand, I would come out on the side of romantic love. There are many ways of experiencing flow, many ways to grow while enjoying life. But perhaps there is no way that is as enjoyable as through interaction with other people. We can expand our intellectual skills by playing at mathematics or chess, we can perfect our esthetic sensitivities with music or poetry, we can stretch our physical limits in sports. But there is no better way of becoming a whole human being than by paying attention to another.

Only from an intimate relationship with another person can one learn to use all the hidden potentialities of one's self—to integrate the *animus* with the *anima* (as Levenson and Harris describe in Chapter Fifteen), to act out one's compassion and one's craziness, to exercise all the options of being that in everyday life lie buried under the pall of social expectations.

The analysis so far has been restricted to romantic love. We have tried to see how it can survive by becoming more complex and thus stimulating mutual growth. But romantic love, with all its power and its potential for promoting growth, can also be a cruel experience. Like all creative processes, it can destroy as well as nurture. If the two partners fail to grow apace, there is no way to keep the relation alive. In our hedonistic age, where one's fulfillment takes precedence over everything else, romantic love can easily become a narcissistic interlude. The option that was not considered, but might be in many ways the best, is to transform romantic love into just love. This requires, however, changing the rules of the game. A genuine love relationship need no longer be spontaneous or enjoyable. It can be sustained by the will to help the beloved reach his or her goals. It could be that this form of love is the best game yet devised through the process of evolution. But it is a very complicated one, and it definitely deserves a story all its own.

18

New Frameworks for Inquiry

Kenneth S. Pope

What do we know (or question, or wonder about) here at the end of the book that we didn't at the beginning? Each chapter has covered its own territory. These chapters, written by people selected for their diverse specializations and perspectives, work together to bring forth issues crucial to a better understanding of romantic love.

The first issue, of course, is one of definition. The "working definition" offered in the first chapter is characteristic of an overwhelming number of those presented in works on romantic love: it is almost solely a description of how a person feels. It represents a certain kind of phenomenological approach. Though elaborated, clarified, and qualified throughout the rest of the chapter, the heart of this working definition is clearly:

> A preoccupation with another person. A deeply felt desire to be with the loved one. A feeling of incompleteness

without him or her. Thinking of the loved one often, whether
together or apart. Separation frequently provokes feelings of
genuine despair or else tantalizing anticipation of reuniting.
Reunion is seen as bringing feelings of euphoric ecstasy or
peace and fulfillment.

The chapters in this volume have made obvious the degree
to which studies of romantic love might more productively be
based upon definitions that attempt the difficult work of specifying more than just the "feeling" side of love. Essentially, the working definition says: one person thinks a lot ("preoccupation";
"often") about someone else and experiences many feelings (desire, incompleteness, despair, anticipation, ecstasy, peace, and fulfillment). More precise and useful definitions (particularly for research) will characterize the attachment itself (Rizley's definition
asserts it to be "rapidly formed, temporarily robust"), the cognitive processes (Csikszentmihalyi sets forth a one-sentence definition: "We speak of romantic love when a person cannot control
his or her attention being invested in another person, yet enjoys
the experience"), and the interaction between the lover and loved
one (Huesmann defines romantic love in terms of the incremental
"exchanges of rewards").

Assumptions, Models, and Methods of Research

Ironically, although most definitions of romantic love seem
too exclusively phenomenological, most research has downplayed
this aspect. The chapters in this volume present numerous ways in
which romantic love is affected by historical, biological, economic,
sociological, and psychological factors. And yet, as Farber stresses
in his analysis, the research tends to rely on questionnaires, rating
scales, and personality inventories (many of which were prompted
by Rubin's 1970 landmark undertaking of the "Measurement of
Romantic Love"). The focus is on the psychosocial and demographic correlates of falling in and out of love, and leaves relatively unexamined how lovers experience this phenomenon. Artistic
and literary sources (see the introductory chapter; also sections of
the chapters by Geller and Howenstine and by Singer) provide numerous themes for research on the phenomenology of love.

Goethals and Ransom, in their chapters, have presented detailed case histories that show forth the delicate movements, sudden lurches, and complex textures of the relationship between lovers. Such case histories not only make our understandings of love more vividly personal but also suggest specific hypotheses that can be evaluated in light of further research. From such accounts have come, for instance, notions of how personality styles (see Weiner's chapter) influence romantic loving and how romantic relationships seem to pass through predictable stages (to be discussed later in this chapter).

Elaborate models of romantic loving, with specific implications that can be tested, are still rare. Those that are presented (for example, in the chapters by Huesmann and Livingston) or reviewed (for example, Homans, 1961; Tesser and Paulhus, 1976; Bentler and Huba, 1979) in this volume often seem to have a cold artificiality upon first reading, an effect due in large part, no doubt, to the apparent discrepancy between our own deeply personal experience of loving and the remorselessly objective statements on the page, and also to our suspicion that some deeply private mystery is being violated or devalued. Their benefit, however, is in their aim of blending both general (not applying to one person alone but to human experience more broadly) and specific (offering us fully descriptive, predictive, or explanatory propositions that can be tested "in the real world"). By bringing these models into frequent contact with materials from the case histories mentioned earlier, we can refine, elaborate, and, in a very limited sense, test them.

Progress toward a more complete evaluation of our notions about romantic love depends upon the development of a wider variety of investigative strategies. As the contributions to this volume have made clear, the going is slow. Huesmann notes that "longitudinal studies of couples in love are very difficult and costly and, with a few exceptions (for example, Rubin, Hill, and Peplau, 1976) have taken a backseat to studies of transient aspects of romantic attraction." Reviews in this volume of such methods as "friend-observer" (Ziller and Rosen, 1975) and "storytelling" (Lee, 1977) show movement in an encouraging direction.

The need, however, is not only for the development and use of a more diverse set of research techniques but also for an enlarged scope. As Farber concludes, "relevant research in the last decade has focused almost exclusively on the nature of romantic love in high school or college students." Research studies should reflect the fact that people do fall in love in their twenties, thirties, forties, and beyond. And, as the chapters by Friedlander and Morrison and by Singer maintain, the phenomenon of romantic love may flower suddenly in the life of the young adult, but it has its roots deep in the life of the child.

Scientific investigations of romantic love are not only excessively limited to a particular age range but also in a narrow way focused on heterosexual pairings. Few careful studies of homosexual romantic relationships emerge from the reviews of research literature in this volume. But these in particular (for example, Masters and Johnson's conclusions that homosexual lovers tend to be more attentive to the needs of their partners; or Peplau and her colleagues' finding that women involved in long-term relationships with other women report high levels of emotional and sexual satisfaction as well as equality of power) suggest a neglected area of research useful to our understanding of romantic love generally and, more specifically, of those factors that make it satisfying to the participants.

Investigations are further improved when the focus on romantic love in the life of the individual is broadened to include reference to other species, to our biological heritage, and to an evolutionary perspective. It can of course be argued, as in Weiner's chapter: "Romantic love involves the bonding or attachment of persons, but it is more than an epiphenomenon of the biological drive for perpetuation of the species. Romantic love encompasses a range of behavior that transcends pairing for reproduction, safety, or security. It is a uniquely human experience." And yet who can look at the sciomyzid fly (who brings forth from his mouth a white foam, fashions it into a decorative pie, and, when his prospective partner becomes preoccupied eating this gift, begins to mount her) or the black widow spider (who devours her mate after sex, a result, Woody Allen concludes, of terrible postcoital depression) and fail to learn something about certain kinds of romantic relationships? Two fundamental questions in this regard are: To what extent are our romantic inclinations genetically patterned? And, to what extent is romantic love adaptive for the individual or species? Livingston sets forth one of the central themes within this framework: "If one takes it as a given that two parents were more likely than one, in the environment of evolutionary adaptiveness, to raise offspring successfully to childbearing age (Wickler, 1972), then any system, genetically coded, that increases the likelihood of successful pair bonding of potential parents should have considerable adaptive success." Such themes, and the emerging evidence concerning their validity, are most fully represented in the chapters by Rizley, Livingston, and Csikszentmihalyi.

Unresolved Issues

Taken as a whole, the chapters have displayed major unresolved issues with a sharpened focus but with a bewildering array of seemingly contradictory evidence. Satisfying resolution of these issues waits on the careful application of improved research perspectives and strategies, as discussed in the previous section.

Mature or Immature? First, to what degree is romantic love immature? Friedlander and Morrison are among those who develop the idea that romantic love expresses the more primitive, selfish, and immature aspects of human personality. Its value, they assert, is in its potential as an aid in the transition to higher developmental levels. Geller and Howenstine, likewise, delineate romantic love's potential to help move the person toward maturation: "In our time, the creative and constructive role that romantic love can play in fostering personal integration needs to be reaffirmed." Whereas Friedlander and Morrison argue that such "mature" qualities as "intimacy, reciprocity, and a full knowledge and appreciation of the beloved" preclude romantic love, Weiner is among those who develop the view that adult romantic love is characterized by "the satisfaction of one's beloved's needs being of equal importance to the satisfaction of one's own (a form of altruism)." Rather than being the expression of an immature personality or a transition from lower to higher levels of development, romantic love, in this view, occurs within the context of maturity. As Weiner puts it: "A prerequisite to adult love is the development of a certain level of intrapsychic and interpersonal maturation." Another approach to this issue stresses neither the "maturity" nor the "immaturity" of romantic love, but rather treats these concepts as inapplicable, only apparently in conflict, or as not significant. Huesmann, for example, finds that "both man and woman are self-seeking satisficers" who look ahead to see what behaviors will make them happy. Such behavior may seem altruistic; in the long-run each receives as much as each gives. He summarizes: "These simulations have shown, for example, that the apparently altruistic behavior characteristic of lovers is an inevitable concomitant of a relationship in which deeper mutual involvement brings higher rewards and in which the altruistic behavior is necessary to achieve deeper involvement."

Idealistic or Realistic? A second unresolved issue is whether romantic love is essentially realistic or idealistic (or otherwise un-realistic). The introductory chapter developed, on the basis of lit-erature from an early historical period, the theme of lovers know-ing each other realistically and intimately. The contrary view is carefully argued by Friedlander and Morrison: "Idealization and fantasy are the sine qua non of the romantic love experience. . . . In order to permit the attribution of such idealized characteristics to the romantic love object, the individual selected to serve this func-tion is often one who is not readily available or knowable. In this way, a relative lack of familiarity and partial knowledge of the ro-mantic object serve to facilitate the process of idealization." Liv-ingston is among those who find no necessary link between love and idealization: "People often construct idealizations of their partners, especially in the early phases of the relationship, and it has been suggested that romanticism depends on such idealiza-tions. . . . However, attempts to measure the impact of this vari-able on the extent to which one is or is not in love have not shown any clearly positive relationship."

A Strengthened or Weakened Sense of Identity? A third un-resolved issue is the degree to which romantic love strengthens or weakens the lover's sense of self. Livingston stresses the "vulner-ability of self" within romantic relationships. Uchalik and Living-ston discuss such common situations as "the woman who has sac-rificed her independence and made much of her sense of worth dependent on her spouse"; and Levenson and Harris, who devote their chapter solely to this issue, assert that "one of the primary experiential components of romantic love is a sense of losing one's identity." Yet romantic love also appears to be the source of the strengthening of identity and the fulfillment of self: "In short, the full expression of intimacy within a romantic love relationship appears to satisfy and fulfill the self" (Farber); "Only from an intimate relationship with another person can one learn to use all the hidden potentialities of one's self" (Csikszentmihalyi). Again, it is possible to maintain that romantic love is not limited to *either* the loss *or* the fulfillment of the sense of self, but may involve both. This "you're both right" stance seems to make most sense if romantic love is viewed not as a static state but as a process.

The Process of Romantic Loving

So often romantic love is presented as a yes-or-no concept, a static experience, a steady state having a set of attributes (as in the working definition of the introductory chapter). It is like a huge barrel: you fall into it, then, after some time, you fall out of it. As mentioned earlier, the research to date has largely occupied itself with attempting to catalogue what sorts of people under what sorts of conditions are apt to fall into this barrel, and to determine how long the barrel is likely to hold them before dumping them out, and where they are likely to fall (for example, into mature or companionate love, into depression, into a stifling marriage).

The authors of this volume have drawn forth a less prevalent view of love which furnishes a promising context for future research. Simplified, this idea holds love to be less a "thing," a goal, a steady state, and more a process. People are construed less as passively or helplessly falling in or out, and are seen as more actively engaging in love.

Again and again, each chapter's vocabulary expresses this view. Geller and Howenstine, drawing on Schafer, discard the notion of love as an anthropomorphized or reified entity and speak not of "romantic love" but rather of "men loving." Their attempt to use only verbs and adverbs when referring to love stresses the active, evolving nature of loving. Goethals stresses the "kinetic quality" of romance; Uchalik and Livingston note the potentially damaging effects of viewing romantic love "as a goal, rather than a process"; Huesmann discusses this "process model"; and Livingston emphasizes the "dynamic aspects" of love ("It is the process of uncertainty reduction, not the having of certainty, that is experienced as engaging and thus maintains the romantic experience.").

Such an increased emphasis upon questions of how people engage in the loving processes suggests, in turn, an increased research emphasis upon stages in the life-cycle. Chapters Two through Five and also those by Weiner and Kazak and Reppucci (drawing variously on the pioneering work of Freud, Piaget, Erikson, Levinson, Gould, and Vaillant) explore the manner in which our movement through stages or phases affects our ways of loving and our experience of that process.

The process of loving, like that of living, may fall into some sort of identifiable, or even predictable, patterns or stages. This volume has presented or reviewed some initial attempts to discern within the development of romantic relationships reliable phases (for example, Weiner; Coleman; Livingston; Goldstine and others). Such phases tend to be ordered in a progressive, beginning-to-end array. The final stage contains such options as "dissolution of the relationship" or "progression to mature or companionate love." Kazak and Reppucci, however, suggest that the process of loving may be more accurately viewed as cyclical. Thus "stages" may not be limited to single positions in the order of development but may appear, disappear, and reappear later, like seasons.

The idea that romantic love is a process in which people engage rather than a state into and out of which people passively fall is reminiscent of the relatively recent evolution of cognitive psychology. Held as self-evident for so long, the idea has faded that perception is the passive reception of "outer" events. Rather, the organism is construed as internally generating "schema" and actively attempting to match these successfully against stimuli. What we see is not so much a picture painted by external reality as it is an internally produced hypothesis (based upon a number of factors, including our past experience) which we put to constant test through our actions.

Our understanding of romantic love may be ready to undergo a similar evolution. If so, some unresolved issues will appear quite differently within the new framework. For instance, it may become less useful to direct our efforts toward determining whether romantic love belongs to the idealistic or realistic category. Romantic loving may include images of the beloved that are not best understood as passively received and helplessly held "truths" or "fictions" (idealizations) but rather as hypotheses, as active attempts at intimate understanding that occur between a lover who is constantly changing over time and a beloved, who is likewise changing. Such images may furthermore influence both lover and beloved. As Singer puts it: "Romantic love represents an experience that goes beyond this direct form of warmth. It is built around *potentiality*, the touchstone of fantasy, not just what is given but what might be."

Conclusion

The research and theory discussed within the volume provide us with the elements for a better understanding of romantic love, suggest creative approaches to the bewildering tangle of controversies in this area, and provoke us toward exciting and badly needed research possibilities. Up until the last decade or so, romantic love suffered sad and seemingly inexplicable malignant neglect by psychology in particular and the scientific disciplines more generally. That period of scientific misanthropy is over, and high time. What Kierkegaard would have us believe about our efforts to close the door to love in our individual lives may also describe the result of excluding it from our common research endeavors and scientific understandings:

> *To cheat oneself out of love is the most*
> *terrible deception; it is an eternal loss*

References

Abelson, R. P. "The Structure of Belief Systems." In R. C. Schank and K. M. Colby (Eds.), *Computer Models of Thought and Language*. San Francisco: Freeman, 1973.

Adams, V. "Erikson Sees Psychological Danger in Trend of Having Fewer Children." *New York Times*, August, 4, 1979, p. 17.

Albee, E. *The American Dream and The Zoo Story*. New York: New American Library, 1961.

Alexander, R. D. "National Selection and Social Exchange." In R. L. Burgess and T. L. Huston (Eds.), *Social Exchange and Developing Relationships*. New York: Academic Press, in press.

Alexander, R. D., and Noonan, K. M. "Reconstructing Human Sexual and Social History." In N. Chagnon and W. Irons (Eds.), *Evolutionary Biology and Human Social Behavior*. North Scituate, Mass.: Duxbury Press, 1979.

Altman, L. C. "Some Vicissitudes of Love." *Journal of the Psychoanalytic Association*, 1977, *25*, 33–52.

Altman, R. "Reciprocity of Interpersonal Exchange." *Journal of the Theory of Social Behavior*, 1973, *3*, 249–261.

Apfelbaum, B. "On the Etiology of Sexual Dysfunction." *Journal of Sex and Marital Therapy*, 1977a, *3* (1), 50–62.

Apfelbaum, B. "Sexual Functioning Reconsidered." In R. Gemme and C. Wheeler (Eds.), *Progress in Sexology*. New York: Plenum, 1977b.

Apfelbaum, B. "Why We Should *Not* Accept Sexual Fantasies." In B. Apfelbaum, M. H. Williams, and S. E. Greene (Eds.), *Expanding the Boundaries of Sex Therapy*. Berkeley, Calif.: Berkeley Sex Therapy Group, 1979.

Apfelbaum, B., Williams, M. H., and Greene, S. E. (Eds.). *Expanding the Boundaries of Sex Therapy*. Berkeley, Calif.: Berkeley Sex Therapy Group, 1979.

Askew, M. W. "Courtly Love: Neurosis as Institution." *Psychoanalytic Review*, 1965, *52*, 19–29.

Ausubel, D. P. *Theory and Problems of Adolescent Development*. New York: Grune & Stratton, 1954.

Averill, J. R. "Grief: Its Nature and Significance." *Psychological Bulletin*, 1968, *70*, 721–748.

Bacon, F. *Selected Writings of Francis Bacon*. New York: Modern Library, 1955. (Originally published 1597.)

Balint, M. *Thrills and Regressions*. New York: International Universities Press, 1959.

Balint, M. "Early Developmental States of the Ego: Primary Object-Love." In M. Balint (Ed.), *Primary Love and Psychoanalytic Technique*. New York: Horace Liveright, 1965a. (Originally published 1937.)

Balint, M. "On Genital Love." In M. Balint (Ed.), *Primary Love and Psychoanalytic Technique*. New York: Horace Liveright, 1965b. (Originally published 1937.)

Balint, M. *The Basic Fault: Therapeutic Aspects of Regression*. London: Tavistock, 1968.

Balswick, J. "How to Get Your Husband to Say I Love You." *Family Circle*, 1979, *2*, 110–111.

Bandura, A. *Social Learning Theory*. Englewood Cliffs, N.J.: Prentice-Hall, 1977.

Bane, M. *Here to Stay*. New York: Basic Books, 1976.

Bannister, D., and Fransella, F. *Inquiring Man: The Theory of Personal Constructs*. Baltimore: Penguin Books, 1971.

Barnett, J. "Narcissism and Dependency in the Obsessional-Hysteric Marriage." *Family Process*, 1971, *10* (1), 75–84.

Barzun, J. *Classic, Romantic and Modern*. Chicago: University of Chicago Press, 1961.

Bate, W. J. *Samuel Johnson*. New York: Harcourt Brace Jovanovich, 1977.

Becker, E. *The Denial of Death*. New York: Free Press, 1973.

Bell, R. R. "Female Sexual Satisfaction As Related to Levels of Education." *Sexual Behavior*, November, 1971, pp. 6–14.

Bell, R. R., and Chaskes, J. B. "Premarital Sexual Experience Among Coeds, 1958 and 1968." *Journal of Marriage and the Family*, 1970, *32*, 81–84.

Belote, B. "Sexual Intimacy Between Female Clients and Male Psychotherapists: Masochistic Sabotage." Unpublished doctoral dissertation, California School of Professional Psychology, San Francisco, 1974.

Benedek, T. "Parenthood As a Developmental Phase." *Journal of the American Psychoanalytic Association*, 1959, 7, 417–423.

Benedek, T. "Ambivalence, Passion and Love." *Journal of the Psychoanalytic Association*, 1977, *25*, 53–80.

Bentler, P. M., and Huba, G. J. "Simple Minitheories of Love." *Journal of Personality and Social Psychology*, 1979, *37*, 124–130.

Bergis, I. *Combat in the Erogenous Zone*. New York: Knopf, 1972.

Berlyne, D. E. *Conflict, Arousal, and Curiosity*. New York: McGraw-Hill, 1960.

Berlyne, D. E. "Information and Motivation." In A. Silverstein (Ed.), *Human Communication: Theoretical Explorations*. Hillsdale, N.J.: Erlbaum, 1974.

Berlyne, D. E., and Borsa, D. M. "Uncertainty and the Orientation Reaction." *Perception and Psychophysics*, 1968, *3*, 77–79.

Berscheid, E., Stephan, W., and Walster, E. H. "Sexual Arousal and Heterosexual Perception." *Journal of Personality and Social Psychology*, 1971, *20*, 93–101.

Berscheid, E., and Walster, E. H. "A Little Bit About Love." In T. L. Huston (Ed.), *Foundations of Interpersonal Attraction*. New York: Academic Press, 1974.

Berscheid, E., and Walster, E. H. *Interpersonal Attraction*. (2nd ed.) Reading, Mass.: Addison-Wesley, 1978.

Bettelheim, B. *The Empty Fortress*. New York: Free Press, 1967.

Binet, A. "La concurrence des états psychologiques." *Revue Philosophique de la France et de l'Étranger*, 1890, *24*, 138–155.

Binstock, W. A. "On Two Forms of Intimacy." *Journal of the American Psychoanalytic Association*, 1973, *21*, 93–107.

Bion, W. R. *Experiences in Groups*. New York: Basic Books, 1959.

Black, H., and Angelis, V. B. "Interpersonal Attraction: An Empirical Investigation of Platonic and Romantic Love." *Psychological Reports*, 1974, *34*, 1243–1246.

Blood, B., and Blood, M. *Marriage*. (3rd ed.) New York: Macmillan, 1978.

Blood, R. "Romance and Premarital Intercourse: Incompatibles?" *Marriage and Family Living*, 1952, *14*, 105–107.

Blos, P. *On Adolescence: A Psychoanalytic Interpretation*. Glencoe, Ill.: Free Press, 1962.

Bowen, M. "The Use of Family Theory in Clinical Practice." *Comprehensive Psychiatry*, 1966, 7, 345–374.

Bowen, M. *Family Therapy in Clinical Practice*. New York: Jason Aronson, 1978.

Bowerman, C., and Day, B. "A Test of the Theory of Complementary Needs As Applied to Couples During Courtship." *American Sociological Review*, 1956, *21*, 602–605.

Bowlby, J. *Attachment and Loss*. London: Hogarth Press, 1969.

Braunschweig, D., and Fain, M. *Eros et Anteros*. Paris: Petite Bibliothèque Payot, 1971.

Brickman, P., and Campbell, D. T. "Hedonic Relativism and Planning the Good Society." In M. H. Appley (Ed.), *Adaptation-Level Theory: A Symposium*. New York: Academic Press, 1971.

Broderick, C. B. "Socio-Sexual Development in a Suburban Community." *Journal of Sex Research*, 1966, *2*, 1–24.

Broderick, C. B., and Fowler, S. E. "New Patterns of Relationships Between the Sexes Among Preadolescents." *Marriage and Family Living*, 1961, *23*, 27–30.

Broderick, C. B., and Rowe, G. P. "A Scale of Preadolescent Heterosexual Development." *Journal of Marriage and the Family*, 1968, *30*, 97–101.

Bronfenbrenner, U. "Freudian Theories of Identification and Their Derivatives." *Child Development*, 1960, *31*, 15–40.

Broude, G. "Male-Female Relationships in Cross-Cultural Perspective: A Study of Sex and Intimacy." *Behavioral Science Research*,
in press.

Broverman, I. K., and others. "Sex-Role Stereotypes and Clinical
Judgments of Mental Health." *Journal of Consulting and Clinical Psychology*, 1970, *34*, 469–474.

Brozan, N. "A Study of the American Man." *New York Times*,
January 19, 1979, p. A14.

Bruner, J. S., Jolly, A., and Sylva, K. *Play: Its Role in Development and Evolution*. New York: Basic Books, 1976.

Burgess, E. W., and Wallin, P. *Engagement and Marriage*, Philadelphia: Lippincott, 1953.

Burns, R. B. "Attitudes to Self and Attitudes to Others." *British
Journal of Social and Clinical Psychology*, 1976, *15*, 319–321.

Burton, R. "The Anatomy of Melancholy." In A. M. Witherspoon
and F. Warnke (Eds.), *Seventeenth-Century Prose and Poetry*.
New York: Harcourt Brace Jovanovich, 1963.

Byrne, D. *The Attraction Paradigm*. New York: Academic Press,
1971.

Campbell, J. (Ed.). *The Portable Jung*. New York: Viking Press,
1971.

Capellanus, A. *The Art of Courtly Love*. (J. Perry, Trans.) New
York: Norton, 1969. (Written early thirteenth century.)

Caplan, G. *Support Systems and Community Mental Health*. New
York: Behavioral Publications, 1976.

Capra, F. *The Tao of Physics*. Westminster, Md.: Shambhala Publications, 1975.

Carey, J. T. "Changing Courtship Patterns in the Popular Song."
American Journal of Sociology, 1969, *74*, 720–731.

Casler, L. "Toward a Re-evaluation of Love." In M. E. Curtin
(Ed.), *Symposium on Love*. New York: Behavioral Publications,
1973.

Chaplin, J. P. *Dictionary of Psychology*. New York: Dell, 1968.

Chesler, P. *Women and Madness*. New York: Avon Books, 1972.

Cimbalo, R. S., Faling, V., and Mousan, P. "The Course of Love:
A Cross-Sectional Design." *Psychological Report*, 1976, *38*,
1292–1294.

Clarke, A. C. "An Examination of the Operation of Residential

Propinquity as a Factor in Mate Selection." *American Sociological Review*, 1952, *17*, 17-22.

Cobb, E. *The Ecology of Imagination in Childhood*. New York: Columbia University Press, 1977.

Coleman, A., and Coleman, L. *Love and Ecstasy*. New York: Seabury Press, 1975.

Coleman, J. S., and others. *Youth: Transition to Adulthood*. Chicago: University of Chicago Press, 1972.

Coleman, S. "A Developmental Stage Hypothesis for Nonmarital Dyadic Relationships." *Journal of Marriage and Family Counseling*, 1977, *3*, 71-76.

Conger, J. J. *Adolescence and Youth: Psychological Development in a Changing World*. New York: Harper & Row, 1973.

Conger, J. J. "Sexual Attitudes and Behavior of Contemporary Adolescents." In J. J. Conger (Ed.), *Contemporary Issues in Adolescent Development*. New York: Harper & Row, 1975.

Coombs, R. H., and Kenkel, W. F. "Sex Differences in Dating Aspirations and Satisfaction with Computer Selected Patterns." *Journal of Marriage and the Family*, 1966, *28*, 62-66.

Csikszentmihalyi, M. "Sociological Implications in the Thought of Teilhard de Chardin." *Zygon*, 1970, *5* (1), 130-147.

Csikszentmihalyi, M. *Beyond Boredom and Anxiety: The Experience of Play in Work and Games*. San Francisco: Jossey-Bass, 1975.

Csikszentmihalyi, M. "What Play Says About Behavior." *Ontario Psychologist*, 1976, *8* (2), 5-11.

Csikszentmihalyi, M. "Attention and the Wholistic Approach to Behavior." In K. S. Pope and J. L. Singer (Eds.), *The Stream of Consciousness*. New York: Plenum, 1978a.

Csikszentmihalyi, M. "Intrinsic Rewards and Emergent Motivation." In M. R. Lepper and D. Greene (Eds.), *The Hidden Costs of Reward*. New York: Erlbaum, 1978b.

Csikszentmihalyi, M. "Phylogenetic and Ontogenetic Functions of Artistic Cognition." In S. Madeja (Ed.), *The Arts, Cognition and Basic Skills*. St. Louis, Mo.: Cemrel, 1978c.

Csikszentmihalyi, M., and Larson, R. "Intrinsic Rewards in School Crime." *Crime and Delinquency*, 1978, *24* (3), 322-335.

Cuber, J. F., and Harroff, P. B. *Sex and the Significant Americans:*

A Study of Sexual Behavior Among the Affluent. Baltimore: Pelican Books, 1965. (Hardcover edition published as *The Significant Americans.*)

Curtin, M. E. *Symposium on Love.* New York: Behavioral Publications, 1973.

D'Addario-Durré, L. J. "Sexual Relations Between Female Clients and Male Therapists." Unpublished doctoral dissertation, California School of Professional Psychology, 1977.

Dahlberg, C. C. "Sexual Contact Between Patient and Therapist." *Medical Aspects of Human Sexuality,* 1971, *5* (7), 34–56.

Davidoff, I. "Living Together As a Developmental Phase: A Wholistic View." *Journal of Marriage and Family Counseling,* 1977, *3,* 67–76.

de Castillejo, I. C. *Knowing Woman: A Feminine Psychology.* New York: Harper & Row, 1973.

de Ropp, R. S. "Drugs, Yoga and Psychotransformism." In J. Needleman and D. Lewis (Eds.), *On the Way to Self Knowledge.* New York: Knopf, 1976.

de Rougement, D. *Love Declared.* Boston: Beacon Press, 1963.

de Rougement, D. *Love in the Western World.* New York: Fawcett World Library, 1969.

Deikman, A. J. "Bimodal Consciousness." In R. E. Ornstein (Ed.), *The Nature of Human Consciousness.* New York: Viking Press, 1974.

Deikman, A. J. "Bimodal Consciousness and the Mystic Experience." In P. R. Lee and R. E. Ornstein (Eds.), *Symposium on Consciousness.* Baltimore: Penguin Books, 1977.

Dicks, H. V. *Marital Tensions: Clinical Studies Towards a Psychological Theory of Interaction.* New York: Basic Books, 1967.

Dion, K. L., and Dion, K. K. "Correlates of Romantic Love." *Journal of Consulting and Clinical Psychology,* 1973, *41,* 51–56.

Dion, K. L., and Dion, K. K. "Self-Esteem and Romantic Love." *Journal of Personality,* 1975, *43,* 39–57.

Dohrenwend, B. S., and Dohrenwend, B. P. (Eds.). *Stressful Life Events.* New York: Wiley, 1974.

Donaldson, E. T. "The Myth of Courtly Love." *Ventures,* 1965, *5,* 16–23.

Donelson, E. "Social Responsiveness and Sense of Separateness." In E. Donelson and J. E. Gullahorn (Eds.), *Women: A Psy-*

chological Perspective. New York: Wiley, 1977.

Donne, J. "Poems." In A. M. Witherspoon and F. Warnke (Eds.), *Seventeenth-Century Prose and Poetry.* New York: Harcourt Brace Jovanovich, 1963. (Originally published 1633.)

Dosamentes-Alperson, E. "The Intrapsychic and the Interpersonal in Psychotherapy." *American Journal of Dance Therapy*, 1979, *3*, 20-31.

Douvan, E., and Adelson, J. *The Adolescent Experience.* New York: Wiley, 1966.

Dreyer, P. H. "Changes in the Meaning of Marriage Among Youth: The Impact of the Revolution in Sex and Sex Role Behavior." In R. E. Grinder (Ed.), *Studies in Adolescence.* (3rd ed.) New York: Macmillan, 1975.

Driscoll, R., Davis, K., and Lipetz, M. "Parental Interference and Romantic Love: The Romeo and Juliet Effect." *Journal of Personality and Social Psychology*, 1972, *24*, 1-10.

Droscher, V. B. *They Love and Kill.* New York: Dutton, 1976.

Dunphy, D. C. "The Social Structure of Urban Adolescent Peer Groups." *Sociometry,* 1963, *26*, 230-246.

Durkheim, E. *Suicide.* New York: Free Press, 1951.

Ehrmann, W. *Premarital Dating Behavior.* New York: Holt, Rinehart and Winston, 1959.

Elkind, D. "Egocentrism in Adolescence." *Child Development*, 1967, *38*, 1025-1034.

Elkind, D. "Adolescent Cognitive Development." In J. F. Adams (Ed.), *Understanding Adolescence.* Boston: Allyn & Bacon, 1968.

Elkind, D. *Children and Adolescents: Interpretive Essays on Jean Piaget.* New York: Oxford University Press, 1970.

Elkind, D. "Understanding the Young Adolescent." *Adolescence,* 1978, *13*, 127-134.

Ellis, A. *The American Sexual Tragedy.* New York: Lyle Stuart, 1962.

Ellis, A. "Romantic Love." In J. A. Gould and J. J. Iorio (Eds.), *Love, Sex and Identity.* San Francisco: Boyd & Fraser, 1972.

Enelow, A. J., and Adler, L. M. "Forward." In L. B. Fierman (Ed.), *Effective Psychotherapy: The Contribution of Hellmuth Kaiser.* New York: Free Press, 1965.

Epstein, S., and Fenz, W. D. "Steepness of Approach and Avoidance Gradients in Humans as a Function of Experience." *Journal of Experimental Psychology*, 1965, *70*, 1-12.

Erikson, E. H. *Childhood and Society*. New York: Norton, 1950.

Erikson, E. H. "The Problem of Ego Identity." *Journal of the American Psychoanalytic Association*, 1956, *4*, 56-121.

Erikson, E. H. *Identity and the Life Cycle* (selected papers). Psychological Issues Monograph 1. New York: International Universities Press, 1959.

Erikson, E. H. *Childhood and Society*. (2nd ed.) New York: Norton, 1963.

Erikson, E. H. "Youth and the Life Cycle." In D. E. Hamachek (Ed.), *The Self in Growth, Teaching and Learning*. Englewood Cliffs, N.J.: Prentice-Hall, 1965.

Erikson, E. H. *Identity: Youth and Crisis*. New York: Norton, 1968a.

Erikson, E. H. "The Life Cycle." In *International Encyclopedia of the Social Sciences*, Vol. 9, pp. 286-292. New York: Macmillan and Free Press, 1968b.

Fairbairn, W. R. D. *An Object Relations Theory of Personality*. New York: Basic Books, 1954.

Fancher, R. E. *Psychoanalytic Psychology*. New York: Norton, 1973.

Farber, B. A., and Geller, J. D. "Student Attitudes Toward Psychotherapy." *Journal of the American College Health Association*, 1977, *25*, 301-307.

Farber, L. H. *Lying, Despair, Jealousy, Envy, Sex, Suicide, Drugs, and the Good Life*. New York: Harper & Row, 1976.

Fengler, A. P. "Romantic Love in Courtship: Divergent Paths of Male and Female Students." *Journal of Comparative Family Studies*, 1974, *5*, 134-139.

Fenichel, O. *The Psychoanalytic Theory of Neurosis*. New York: Norton, 1945.

Fenichel, O. *The Collected Papers of Otto Fenichel*. New York: Norton, 1954.

Festinger, L., Schachter, S., and Back, K. *Social Pressures in Informal Groups: A Study of Human Factors in Housing*. New York: Harper & Row, 1950.

Fisher, S., and Cleveland, S. *Body Image and Personality*. New York: Dover, 1968.

Ford, C. S., and Beach, F. A. *Patterns of Sexual Behavior*. New York: Harper & Row, 1951.

Fowles, J. *The Aristos: A Self Portrait in Ideas*. Boston: Little, Brown, 1964.

Framo, J. L. "Rationale and Techniques of Intensive Family Therapy." In I. Boszormenyi-Nagy and J. L. Framo (Eds.), *Intensive Family Therapy: Theoretical and Practical Aspects*. New York: Harper & Row, 1965.

Freud, E. L. (Ed.). *Letters of Sigmund Freud*. New York: Basic Books, 1961.

Freud, S. *Group Psychology and the Analysis of the Ego*. London: Hogarth Press, 1921.

Freud, S. "Contributions to the Psychology of Love: A Special Type of Choice of Objects Made by Men." In E. Jones (Ed.), *Collected Papers*. Vol. 4. London: Hogarth Press, 1953a. (Originally published 1910.)

Freud, S. "Contributions to the Psychology of Love: The Most Prevalent Form of Degradation in Erotic Life." In E. Jones (Ed.), *Collected Papers*. Vol. 4. London: Hogarth Press, 1953b. (Originally published 1912.)

Freud, S. "Contributions to the Psychology of Love: The Taboo of Virginity." In E. Jones (Eds.), *Collected Papers*. Vol. 4. London: Hogarth Press, 1953c. (Originally published 1918.)

Freud, S. "The Dynamics of Transference." In E. Jones (Ed.), *Collected Papers*. Vol. 8. London: Hogarth Press, 1953d. (Originally published 1912.)

Freud, S. "Observations on Transference Love." In E. Jones (Ed.), *Collected Papers*. Vol. 2. London: Hogarth Press, 1953e. (Originally published 1915).

Freud, S. "The Unconscious." In E. Jones (Ed.), *Collected Papers*. Vol. 4. London: Hogarth Press, 1953f.

Freud, S. "Group Psychology and the Analysis of the Ego." In J. Strachey (Ed.), *The Complete Psychological Works of Sigmund Freud*. Vol. 18. London: Hogarth Press, 1957a. (Originally published 1921.)

Freud, S. "Introductory Lectures on Psychoanalysis: Lecture XX. The Sexual Life of Human Beings." In J. Strachey (Ed.), *The Complete Psychological Works of Sigmund Freud*. Vol. 16. London: Hogarth Press, 1957b. (Originally published 1916.)

Freud, S. Letter to S. Ferenczi. In E. Jones, *Life and Work of Sigmund Freud*. Vol. 3. New York: Basic Books, 1957c.

Freud, S. "Mourning and Melancholia." In J. Strachey (Ed.), *The Complete Psychological Works of Sigmund Freud*. Vol. 14. London: Hogarth Press, 1957d. (Originally published 1917.)

Freud, S. "New Introductory Lectures on Psycho-analysis: Lecture XXXI. The Dissection of the Psychical Personality." In. J. Strachey (Ed.), *The Complete Psychological Works of Sigmund Freud*. Vol. 22. London: Hogarth Press, 1957e. (Originally published 1933.)

Freud, S. "A Note on the Prehistory of the Technique of Analysis." In J. Strachey (Ed.), *The Complete Psychological Works of Sigmund Freud*. Vol. 18. London: Hogarth Press, 1957f. (Originally published 1920.)

Freud, S. "On Narcissism: An Introduction." In J. Strachey (Ed.), *The Complete Psychological Works of Sigmund Freud*. Vol. 14. London: Hogarth Press, 1957g. (Originally published 1914.)

Freud, S. "On the Universal Tendency to Debasement in the Sphere of Love." In J. Strachey (Ed.), *The Complete Psychological Works of Sigmund Freud*. Vol. 11. London: Hogarth Press, 1957h. (Originally published 1912.)

Freud, S. "Splitting of the Ego in the Process of Defence." In J. Strachey (Ed.), *The Complete Psychological Works of Sigmund Freud*. Vol. 23. London: Hogarth Press, 1957i. (Originally published 1940.)

Freud, S. "Three Essays on the Theory of Sexuality: III. The Transformations of Puberty." In J. Strachey (Ed.), *The Complete Psychological Works of Sigmund Freud*. Vol. 7. London: Hogarth Press, 1957j. (Originally published 1905.)

Freud, S. "The Future Prospects of Psychoanalytic Therapy." In J. Strachey (Ed.), *The Complete Psychological Works of Sigmund Freud*. Vol. 11. London: Hogarth Press, 1957k.

Freud, S. "Some Character Types Met with in Psychoanalytic Work." In J. Strachey (Ed.), *The Complete Psychological Works of Sigmund Freud*. Vol. 14. London: Hogarth Press, 1957l.

Freud, S. "Libidinal Types." In J. Strachey (Ed.), *The Complete Psychological Works of Sigmund Freud*. Vol. 19. London: Hogarth Press, 1957m.

Freud, S. "Female Sexuality." In J. Strachey (Ed.), *The Complete Psychological Works of Sigmund Freud.* Vol. 21. London: Hogarth Press, 1957n.

Freud, S. "Recommendations to Physicians Practicing Psychoanalysis." In J. Strachey (Ed.), *The Complete Psychological Works of Sigmund Freud,* Vol. 12. London: Hogarth Press, 1957o.

Freud, S. "The Unconscious." In J. Strachey (Ed.), *The Complete Psychological Works of Sigmund Freud.* Vol. 14. London: Hogarth Press, 1957p. (Originally published 1915.)

Freud, S. "The Dynamics of Transference." In J. Strachey (Ed.), *The Complete Psychological Works of Sigmund Freud.* Vol. 12. London: Hogarth Press, 1958. (Originally published 1915.)

Freud, S. *Civilization and Its Discontents.* New York: Norton, 1961. (Originally published 1930.)

Freud, S. *Group Psychology and the Analysis of the Ego.* New York: Bantam, 1965. (Originally published 1921.)

Freud, S. *Group Psychology and the Analysis of the Ego.* New York: Liveright, 1967. (Originally published 1921.)

Friedan, B. "Does Equality for Women Have to Threaten Men?" *Family Circle,* 1979, *2,* 1–6.

Friedenberg, E. Z. *The Vanishing Adolescent.* Boston: Beacon Press, 1959.

Friedman, E. H. Engagement and Disengagement—Family Therapy with Couples During Courtship." In F. D. Andres and J. P. Lorio (Eds.), *Georgetown Family Symposia.* Washington, D.C.: Georgetown Family Symposia, 1972.

Fromm, E. *The Art of Loving.* New York: Harper & Row, 1956.

Fromm, E. "Love in Psychotherapy." *Merrill-Palmer Quarterly,* 1958, *4* (3), 125–136.

Frye, N. *Anatomy of Criticism.* Princeton: Princeton University Press, 1957.

Gediman, H. K. "Reflection on Romanticism, Narcissism, and Creativity." *Journal of the American Psychoanalytic Association,* 1975, *23* (2), 407–423.

Geraldy, P. "L'Amour." In W. Geofferey (Ed.), *The Compleat Lover.* New York: Harrison-Hilton Books, 1939.

Gergen, K. J. "Toward Generative Theory." *Journal of Personality and Social Psychology,* 1978, *36,* 1344–1360.

Glick, P. *The Future of the American Family*. Report presented to Select Committee on Population, House of Representatives, May 23, 1978. Washington, D. C.: Bureau of the Census, 1978.

Goethals, G. W. "Factors Affecting Permissive and Nonpermissive Rules Regarding Premarital Sex." In J. M. Henslin (Ed.), *Sociology of Sex: A Book of Readings*. New York: Appleton-Century-Crofts, 1971.

Goethals, G. W. "Symbiosis and the Life Cycle." *British Journal of Medical Psychology*, 1973, *46*, 91-96.

Goethals, G. W. "The Evolution of Sexual and Genital Intimacy: A Comparison of the Views of Erik H. Erikson and Harry Stack Sullivan." *Journal of the American Academy of Psychoanalysis*, 1976, *4* (4), 529-544.

Goethals, G. W. "A Review of Some Issues Relating to Intimacy: A Memorandum to Professor Carol Gilligan." Department of Psychology and Social Relations, Harvard University, May 1978.

Goethals, G. W. "Male Object Loss: A Special Case of Bereavement, Anxiety and Fear." Unpublished paper, Harvard University, 1979a.

Goethals, G. W. "Syntactic Empathy and Personal History: A Dimension of Intimacy." Unpublished paper, Harvard University, 1979b.

Goethals, G. W., Steele, R. S., and Broude, G. J. "Theories and Research on Marriage: A Review and Some New Directions." In H. Grunebaum and J. Christ (Eds.), *Contemporary Marriage: Structure, Dynamics, and Therapy*. Boston: Little, Brown, 1976.

Goldenberg, H. *Contemporary Clinical Psychology*. Monterey, Calif.: Brooks/Cole, 1973.

Goldstein, M., Kilroy, M. C., and Van de Voort, D. "Gaze as a Function of Conversation and Degree of Love." *Journal of Psychology*, 1976, *92*, 227-234.

Goldstine, D., Larner, K., Zuckerman, S., and Goldstine, H. *The Dance-Away Lover*. New York: Ballantine Books, 1977.

Good, L. R. "Belief in Romantic Love." *Psychology*, 1976, *13* (1), 6-7.

Goode, W. "The Theoretical Importance of Love." *American Sociological Review*, 1959, *24*, 38-47.

Goodman, E. "The Real Versus the Really." *Los Angeles Times*, Sept. 30, 1979.

Gorney, R. "Affective and Psychosocial Implications of Television,

Culture, and the New Biology: A Condensed Synopsis of a Summary of a Précis of an Outline." Paper presented at 2nd annual meeting of the Langley Porter Institute Alumni Faculty Association, San Francisco, April 1979.

Gottlieb, S. "Modeling Effects upon Fantasy." In J. L. Singer, *The Child's World of Make-Believe*. New York: Academic Press, 1973.

Gould, R. *Child Studies Through Fantasy*. New York: Quadrangle Books, 1972.

Gould, R. L. "The Phases of Adult Life: A Study in Developmental Psychology." *American Journal of Psychiatry*, 1972, *129*, 521–531.

Graham, J. "My Dear and Only Love." In A. M. Witherspoon and F. Warnke (Eds.), *Seventeenth-Century Prose and Poetry*. New York: Harcourt Brace Jovanovich, 1963.

Graves, R. *Poems 1970–1972*. New York: Doubleday, 1973.

Gray, H., and Wheelwright, J. "Jung's Psychological Types and Marriage." *Stanford Medical Bulletin*, 1944, *2*, 37–39.

Greenburg, D. *How to Be a Jewish Mother*. Los Angeles: Price/Stern/Sloan, 1964.

Gregg, L. W., and Simon, H. A. "Process Models and Stochastic Theories of Simple Concept Formation." *Journal of Mathematical Psychology*, 1967, *4*, 246–276.

Griffin, D. R. *The Question of Animal Awareness: Evolutionary Continuity of Mental Experience*. New York: Rockefeller University Press, 1976.

Group for the Advancement of Psychiatry. *Normal Adolescence: Its Dynamics and Impact*. New York: Scribner's, 1968.

Guntrip, H. *Schizoid Phenomena, Object Relations and the Self*. New York: International Universities Press, 1969.

Haley, J. *Uncommon Therapy: The Psychiatric Techniques of Milton H. Erickson, M.D.* New York: Ballantine Books, 1973.

Haley, J. *Problem-Solving Therapy: New Strategies for Effective Family Therapy*. San Francisco: Jossey-Bass, 1976.

Hall, J., and Taylor, S. "When Love is Blind: Maintaining Idealized Images of One's Spouse." *Human Relations*, 1976, *29* (8), 751–761.

Halverson, J. "Amour and Eros in the Middle Ages." *Psychoanalytic Review*, 1970, *57*, 245–258.

Hamilton, G. V. *A Research in Marriage*. New York: A. and C.

Boni, 1929.

Hamilton, W. D. "The Genetic Evolution of Social Behavior." *Journal of Theoretical Biology*, 1964, *7*, 1-51.

Harding, M. E. *The Way of All Women*. New York: Putnam's, 1970.

Harlow, H. F. "The Nature of Love." *American Psychologist*, 1958, *13*, 673-685.

Harlow, H. F. "Love in Infant Monkeys." *Scientific American*, 1959, *200*, 68-74.

Heiss, J., and Gordon, M. "Need Patterns and the Mutual Satisfaction of Dating and Engaged Couples." *Journal of Marriage and the Family*, 1964, *26*, 337-339.

Helson, H. *Adaptation-Level Theory*. New York: Harper & Row, 1964.

Hendin, H. *The Age of Sensation*. New York: McGraw-Hill, 1975.

Hill, C. T., Rubin, Z., and Peplau, L. A. "Breakups Before Marriage: The End of 103 Affairs." *Journal of Social Issues*, 1976, *32* (1), 147-168.

Hite, S. *The Hite Report: A Nationwide Study of Female Sexuality*. New York: Macmillan, 1976.

Hobart, C. W. "The Incidence of Romanticism During Courtship." *Social Forces*, 1958, *36*, 362-367.

Holmes, T. H., and Rahe, R. H. "The Social Readjustment Rating Scale." *Journal of Psychosomatic Research*, 1967, *11*, 213-218.

Homans, G. C. *Social Behavior: Its Elementary Forms*. New York: Harcourt Brace Jovanovich, 1961.

Homer. *The Odyssey*. (Samuel Butler, Trans.) New York: Pocket Books, 1969.

Horner, A. *Being and Loving*. New York: Schocken Books, 1978.

Horton, M. "Alternatives to Romantic Love." In M. Curtin (Ed.), *Symposium on Love*. New York: Behavioral Publications, 1973.

Huesmann, L. R. "Process Models of Social Behavior." In N. Hirschberg (Ed.), *Multivariate Methods in the Social Sciences: Applications*. Hillsdale, N.J.: Erlbaum, in press.

Huesmann, L. R., and Levinger, G. "Incremental Exchange Theory: A Formal Model for Progression in Dyadic Social Interaction." In L. Berkowitz and E. Walter (Eds.), *Advances in Experimental Social Psychology*. Vol. 9. New York: Academic Press, 1976.

Hurowitz, L., and Gaier, E. L. "Adolescent Erotica and Female Self-Concept Development." *Adolescence*, 1976, *11*, 497-508.

Ishida, Y. "Physician-Patient Sexual Relations." *Medical Aspects of Human Sexuality,* 1974, *8* (10), 103.

Izard, C. *The Face of Emotion.* New York: Appleton-Century-Crofts, 1971.

Izard, C. *Human Emotions.* New York: Plenum, 1977.

Jacobs, A., and Sachs, L. B. (Eds.). *The Psychology of Private Events.* New York: Academic Press, 1971.

James, W. *The Principles of Psychology.* New York: Dover, 1950. (Originally published 1890.)

Janis, I. L. "Group Identification Under Conditions of External Danger." In D. Cartwright and A. Yander (Eds.), *Group Dynamics: Research and Theory.* New York: Harper & Row, 1968.

Jaques, E. "Social System Defenses Against Persecutory and Depressive Anxieties." In E. Jaques *New Directions in Psychoanalysis.* New York: Basic Books, 1955.

Jaques, E. "Death and the Mid-life Crisis." *International Journal of Psychoanalysis,* 1965, *46,* 502–514.

Jaynes, J. *The Origins of Consciousness.* Boston: Houghton Mifflin, 1976.

Jersild, A. T. *The Psychology of Adolescence.* (2nd ed.) New York: Macmillan, 1963.

Johnson, S. "The Metaphysical Poets." In A. M. Witherspoon and F. Warnke (Eds.), *Seventeenth-Century Prose and Poetry.* New York: Harcourt Brace Jovanovich, 1963. (Originally published 1779.)

Jong, E. *Fear of Flying.* New York: Holt, Rinehart and Winston, 1973.

Josselson, R., Greenberger, E., and McConochie, D. "Phenomenological Aspects of Psychosocial Maturity in Adolescence." *Journal of Youth and Adolescence,* 1977, *6* (2), 145–167.

Joyce, J. *Ulysses.* New York: Modern Library, 1961. (Originally published 1914.)

Jung, C. G. "Marriage as a Psychological Relationship." In H. Read, M. Fordham, and G. Adler (Eds.), *The Collected Works of C. G. Jung.* Vol. 17. New York: Pantheon Books, 1954.

Jung, C. G. "The Stages of Life." In J. Campbell (Ed.), *The Portable Jung.* New York: Viking, 1971.

Kafka, F. *The Great Wall of China.* New York: Schocken Books, 1946.

Kagan, J. "The Concept of Identification." *Psychological Review,*

1958, *65* (5), 296–305.

Kagan, J. "Motives and Development." *Journal of Personality and Social Psychology*, 1972, *22*, 51–66.

Kahne, H. "Economic Perspectives on Roles of Women in the American Economy." *Journal of Economic Literature*, 1975, *13*, 1249–1292.

Kahneman, D. *Attention and Effort*. Englewood Cliffs, N.J.: Prentice-Hall, 1973.

Kahneman, D., and Tversky, A. "Prospect Theory: Analysis of Decisions Under Risk." *Econometrica*, 1979, *47*, 263–292.

Kanin, E., Davidson, K., and Scheck, S. "A Research Note on Male-Female Differentials in the Experience of Heterosexual Love." *Journal of Sex Research*, 1970, *6*, 64–72.

Kaplan, H. S. *The New Sex Therapy: Active Treatment of Sexual Dysfunctions*. New York: Brunner/Mazel, 1974.

Keith, D. V., and Whitaker, C. "The Divorce Labyrinth." In P. Papp (Ed.), *Family Therapy: Full-Length Case Studies*. New York: Gardner Press, 1977.

Kelly, G. *The Psychology of Personal Constructs*. New York: Norton, 1955.

Kennedy, E. "The Looming 80s." *New York Times Magazine*, Dec. 12, 1979, pp. 68–69, 110–120.

Kephart, W. "Some Correlates of Romantic Love." *Journal of Marriage and the Family*, 1967, *29*, 470–474.

Kernberg, O. F. "Borderline Personality Organization." *Journal of the American Psychoanalytic Association*, 1967, *15*, 641–685.

Kernberg, O. F. "Factors in the Psychoanalytic Treatment of Narcissistic Personalities." *Journal of the American Psychoanalytic Association*, 1970a, *18*, 51–85.

Kernberg, O. F. "A Psychoanalytic Classification of Character Pathology." *Journal of The American Psychoanalytic Association*, 1970b, *18*, 800–822.

Kernberg, O. F. "New Developments in Psychoanalytic Object Relations Theory." Paper presented at 58th annual meeting of American Psychoanalytic Association, May 1971.

Kernberg, O. F. "Early Ego Integration and Object Relations." *Annals of the New York Academy of Sciences*, 1972, *193*, 233–247.

Kernberg, O. F. "Barriers to Falling and Remaining in Love."

Journal of the American Psychoanalytic Association, 1974a, *22*, 486-511.

Kernberg, O. F. "Mature Love: Prerequisites and Characteristics." *Journal of the American Psychoanalytic Association*, 1974b, *22*, 743-768.

Kernberg, O. F. "New Developments in Psychoanalytic Object Relations Theory. Part II: Instincts, Affects and Object Relations." In O. F. Kernberg, *Object Relations Theory and Clinical Analysis*. New York: Jason Aronson, 1976a.

Kernberg, O. F. *Object Relations Theory and Clinical Psychoanalysis*. New York: Jason Aronson, 1976b.

Kernberg, O. F. "Boundaries and Structure in Love Relations." *Journal of the American Psychoanalytic Association*, 1977, *25*, 81-114.

Kernberg, O. F. "Large Group Processes: Psychoanalytic Understanding and Applications." Paper presented at 66th annual meeting of American Psychoanalytic Association, New York, 1979.

Kiell, N. *The Universal Experience of Adolescence*. New York: International Universities Press, 1964.

Kilpatrick, W. "The Demythologizing of Love." *Adolescence*, 1974, *9* (33), 25-30.

Kilpatrick, W. *Identity and Intimacy*. New York: Dell, 1975.

Klein, M. *The Complete Works of Melanie Klein*. New York: Delacorte Press, 1961.

Klinger, E. "Modes of Normal Conscious Flow." In K. S. Pope and J. L. Singer (Eds.), *The Stream of Consciousness*. New York: Plenum, 1978.

Klos, D. S., and Singer, J. L. "Determinants of Adolescents' Ongoing Thought Following Simulated Parental Confrontations." Unpublished paper, 1980.

Knox, D., Jr. "Conceptions of Love at Three Developmental Levels." *Family Coordinator*, 1970, *19*, 151-156.

Knox, D., Jr., and Sporakowski, M. H. "Attitudes of College Students Toward Love." *Journal of Marriage and the Family*, 1968, *30*, 638-642.

Koenigsberg, R. A. "Culture and Unconscious Fantasy: Observations on Courtly Love." *Psychoanalytic Review*, 1967, *54* (1), 36-50.

Kohlberg, L. "Stage and Sequence: The Cognitive-Developmental Approach to Socialization." In D. A. Gaslin (Ed.), *Handbook of Socialization Theory and Research*. Chicago: Rand McNally, 1969.

Kohut, H. *The Restoration of Self*. New York: International Universities Press, 1977.

Kremen, H., and Kremen, B. "Romantic Love and Idealization." *American Journal of Psychoanalysis*, 1971, *31*, 134–143.

Kris, E. "On Preconscious Mental Processes." In D. Rapaport (Ed.), *Organization and Pathology of Thought*. New York: Columbia University Press, 1951.

Kubie, L. S. "Psychoanalysis and Marriage: Practical and Theoretical Issues." In V. W. Eisenstein (Ed.), *Neurotic Interaction in Marriage*. New York: Basic Books, 1956.

Laing, R. D. *Do You Love Me?* New York: Ballantine Books, 1976.

Lair, J. *I Ain't Much, Baby—But I'm All I've Got*. Greenwich, Conn.: Fawcett Crest, 1969.

Landis, C. "Psychoanalytic Phenomena." *Journal of Abnormal Social Psychology*, 1940, *35*, 17–28.

Larson, D. A., Spreitzer, E. A., and Snyder, E. E. "Social Factors in the Frequency of Romantic Involvement Among Adolescents." *Adolescence*, 1976, *11*, 7–12.

Lasch, C. *Haven in a Heartless World*. New York: Basic Books, 1977.

Lasch, C. *The Culture of Narcissism*. New York: Norton, 1978.

Lasègue, C., and Falret, J. "La folie à deux." *American Journal of Psychiatry*, 1964, *121*, supplement 2–23. (Originally published 1877.)

Lee, J. A. *The Colours of Love: An Exploration of Ways of Loving*. Toronto: New Press, 1973.

Lee, J. A. "A Typology of Styles of Loving." *Personality and Social Psychology Bulletin*, 1977, *3*, 173–182.

Levine, M., and Levine, A. *A Social History of the Helping Services*. New York: Appleton-Century-Crofts, 1970.

Levinger, G., and Huesmann, L. R. "An 'Incremental Exchange' Perspective on the Pair Relationship: Interpersonal Reward and Level of Involvement." In K. J. Gergen, M. S. Greenberg, and R. H. Willis (Eds.), *Social Exchange: Advances in Theory and Research*. New York: Winston, 1980.

Levinger, G., and Snoek, J. D. *Attraction in Relationship: A New Look at Interpersonal Attraction.* Morristown, N.J.: General Learning Press, 1972.

Levinson, D. J. "The Age Thirty Transition—An Unexpected Opportunity and Burden of Adult Development." Paper presented at the annual meeting of the Western Psychological Association, San Francisco, April 1978.

Levinson, D. J., and others. *The Seasons of a Man's Life.* New York: Knopf, 1978.

Lewin, K. *A Dynamic Theory of Personality: Selected Papers.* (D. K. Adams and K. E. Zener, Trans.) New York: McGraw-Hill, 1935.

Lewis, C. S. *The Four Loves.* New York: Harcourt Brace Jovanovich, 1960.

Lewis, C. S. *The Allegory of Love.* New York: Oxford University Press, 1977.

Lewis, J. M., and others. *No Single Thread.* New York: Brunner/Mazel, 1976.

Lewis, R. A., and Burr, W. R. "Premarital Coitus and Commitment Among College Students." *Archives of Sexual Behavior*, 1975, *4*, 73-79.

Lidz, T. *The Person.* (rev. ed.) New York: Basic Books, 1976.

Loewald, H. W. *Psychoanalysis and the History of the Individual.* New Haven, Conn.: Yale University Press, 1978.

Luckey, E. B., and Nass, G. D. "A Comparison of Sexual Attitudes and Behavior in an International Sample." *Journal of Marriage and the Family*, 1969, *31*, 364-379.

McCall, G. J. "A Symbolic Interactionist Approach to Attraction." In T. L. Huston (Ed.), *Foundations of Interpersonal Attraction.* New York: Academic Press, 1974.

McCary, J. L. *Freedom and Growth in Marriage.* Santa Barbara, Calif.: Hamilton, 1975.

McClelland, D. C. *The Achieving Society.* New York: Free Press, 1961.

McDavid, J. W., and Harari, H. *Social Psychology.* New York: Harper & Row, 1968.

Maddock, J. W. "Sex in Adolescence: Its Meanings and Future." *Adolescence*, 1973, *31*, 327-333.

Mahler, M. S., Pine, F., and Bergman, A. *The Psychological Birth of the Human Infant.* New York: Basic Books, 1975.

Malcolm, H. *Generation of Narcissus.* New York: Little, Brown, 1971.

Mann, R. D. *Interpersonal Dynamics and Group Development.* New York: Wiley, 1967.

Marais, E. N. *The Soul of the Ape.* New York: Atheneum, 1969.

Marmor, J. "The Feeling of Superiority: An Occupational Hazard in the Practice of Psychotherapy." *American Journal of Psychiatry,* 1953, *110* (5), 370-373.

Martin, P. A. *A Marital Therapy Manual.* New York: Brunner/Mazel, 1976.

Masih, V. K. "Imaginary Play Companions of Children in Piagetian Theory and the Helping Professions." *Proceedings of the Seventh Interdisciplinary Conference,* Vol. I, University of Southern California, 1978.

Maslow, A. *Motivation and Personality.* New York: Harper & Row, 1954.

Maslow, A. H. *Toward a Psychology of Being.* New York: Van Nostrand, 1968.

Masters, W. H., and Johnson, V. E. *Human Sexual Response.* Boston: Little, Brown, 1966.

Masters, W. H., and Johnson, V. E. "Principles of the New Sex Therapy." Address to the American Psychiatric Association—Sex Therapy Session, Anaheim, Calif., May 1975.

Masters, W. H., and Johnson, V. E. *Homosexuality in Perspective.* Boston: Little, Brown, 1979.

May, R. *Love and Will.* New York: Dell, 1969.

Mayers, P., Csikszentmihalyi, M., and Larson, R. "The Daily Experience of High School Students." Paper presented at the annual meeting of the American Educational Research Association, Toronto, 1978.

Mead, M. *Culture and Commitment: A Study of the Generation Gap.* New York: Doubleday, 1970.

Meichenbaum, D. "Why Does Using Imagery in Psychotherapy Lead to Change?" In J. L. Singer and K. S. Pope (Eds.), *The Power of Human Imagination: New Methods in Psychotherapy.* New York: Plenum, 1978.

Meissner, W. W. "The Conceptualization of Marriage and Family Dynamics from a Psychoanalytic Perspective." In T. J. Paolino and B. S. McCrady (Eds.), *Marriage and Marital Therapy: Psy-*

choanalytic, Behavioral and Systems Theory Prespectives. New York: Brunner/Mazel, 1978.

Mencken, H. L. *Prejudices: First Series.* New York: Knopf, 1919.

Miller, J. C., and others. *Reparation and Change: Psychological Aspects of Social Innovation.* Washington, D.C.: CEGO Publications, 1978.

Minuchin, S. *Families and Family Therapy.* Cambridge, Mass.: Harvard University Press, 1974.

Mitchell, J. "Adolescent Intimacy." *Adolescence,* 1976, *11,* 275-280.

Morton, T. L. "Intimacy and Reciprocity of Exchange: A Comparison of Spouses and Strangers." *Journal of Personality and Social Psychology,* 1978, *36,* 72-81.

Morton, W. *Love in Epigram.* Chicago: McClurg, 1899.

Munro, B., and Adams, G. R. "Love American Style: A Test of Role Structure Theory on Changes in Attitudes Toward Love." *Human Relations,* 1978, *31,* 215-228.

Murstein, B. *Love, Sex and Marriage Through the Ages.* New York: Springer, 1974.

Nadelson, T., and Eisenberg, L. "The Successful Professional Woman: On Being Married to One." *American Journal of Psychiatry,* 1977, *134,* 1071-1076.

Napier, A. Y., and Whitaker, C. A. *The Family Crucible.* New York: Harper & Row, 1978.

Neugarten, B. (Ed.). *Middle Age and Aging.* Chicago: University of Chicago Press, 1968.

Newell, A., and Simon, H. A. *Human Problem Solving.* Englewood Cliffs, N.J.: Prentice-Hall, 1972.

Offer, D., and Offer, J. "Profiles of Normal Adolescent Girls." *Archives of General Psychiatry,* 1968, *19,* 513-522.

Offer, D., and Freedman, D. X. (Eds.). *Modern Psychiatry and Clinical Research.* New York: Basic Books, 1972.

Orel, H. (Ed.). *Thomas Hardy's Personal Writings: Prefaces, Literary Opinions, Reminiscences.* Lawrence, Kansas: Regents Press, 1969.

Ornstein, R. E. *The Psychology of Consciousness.* New York: Viking Press, 1971.

Ortega y Gasset, J. *On Love.* New York: New American Library, 1957.

Parsons, T., and Bales, R. F. *Family, Socialization and Interaction*

Process. New York: Free Press, 1955.

Pearson, C., and Pope, K. *Who Am I This Time?* New York: McGraw-Hill, 1976.

Peele, S., and Brodsky, A. *Love and Addiction*. New York: Taplinger, 1975.

Peplau, L. A., and others. "Loving Women: Attachment and Autonomy in Lesbian Relationships." *Journal of Social Issues*, 1978, *34*, 7–28.

Phillips, D., with Judd, R. *How to Fall out of Love*. Boston: Houghton Mifflin, 1978.

Piaget, J. *The Psychology of Intelligence*. London: Routledge & Kegan Paul, 1950.

Piaget, J. *The Origins of Intelligence in Children*. New York: International Universities Press, 1952.

Piaget, J. *Play, Dreams and Imitation in Early Childhood*. New York: Norton, 1962.

Pierre-Grassé, M. *La vie amoureuse des animaux: Les vertebres*. Paris: Hachette, 1964.

Pitz, G. F. "Subjective Probability Distributions for Imperfectly Known Quantitics." In L. W. Gregg (Ed.), *Knowledge and Cognition*. Hillsdale, N.J.: Erlbaum, 1974.

Plato. *The Collected Dialogues*. New York: Bollingen Foundation, 1961.

Pope, K. S., and Singer, J. L. "Some Dimensions of the Stream of Consciousness: Towards a Model of Ongoing Thought." In G. Schwartz and D. Shapiro (Eds.), *Consciousness and Self-Regulation*. New York: Plenum, 1978a.

Pope, K. S., and Singer, J. L. (Eds.). *The Stream of Consciousness*. New York: Plenum, 1978b.

Premack, D., and Woodruff, G. "Does the Chimpanzee Have a Theory of Mind?" *Behavioral and Brain Sciences*, 1979, in press.

Puckett, J. R. "The Intimacy/Individualization Conflict: A Study of the Relationship Between Level of Self-Actualization and Couple Interaction." Unpublished doctoral dissertation, California School of Professional Psychology, 1977.

Rajecki, D. W., Lamb, M. E., and Obmascher, P. "Toward a General Theory of Infantile Attachment: A Comparative Review of Aspects of the Social Bond." *Behavioral and Brain Sciences*, 1978.

Ransom, D. C., and Grace, N. T. "Family Therapy." In G. M. Rosen, R. H. Layton, and J. P. Geyman (Eds.), *Behavioral Science in Family Practice.* New York: Appleton-Century-Crofts, 1980.

Ransom, D. C., and Massad, R. J. "Family Structure and Function." In R. E. Rakel and H. F. Conn (Eds.), *Family Practice.* (2nd ed.) Philadelphia: W. B. Saunders, 1978.

Rapoport, A. *Two-Person Game Theory.* Ann Arbor: University of Michigan Press, 1966.

Rappaport, J. *Community Psychology: Values, Research and Action.* New York: Holt, Rinehart and Winston, 1977.

Reich, W. *Character Analysis.* New York: Farrar, Straus and Giroux, 1949.

Reich, W. *The Function of the Orgasm.* New York: Pocket Books, 1975.

Reik, T. *Psychology of Sex Relations.* New York: Holt, Rinehart and Winston, 1945.

Reik, T. *Of Love and Lust.* New York: Farrar, Straus and Giroux, 1957. (Originally published 1941.)

Reik, T. *Of Love and Lust.* New York: Pyramid Books, 1976. (Originally published 1941.)

Reiter, E. O., and Kulin, H. E. "Sexual Maturation in the Female: Normal Development and Precocious Puberty." *Pediatrics Clinics of North America,* 1972, *19,* 581-603.

Reppucci, N. D., and Saunders, J. T. "History, Action and Change." *American Journal of Community Psychology,* 1977, *5,* 399-411.

Ridley, C., Peterman, D., and Avery, A. "Cohabitation: Does It Make for a Better Marriage?" *Family Coordinator,* 1978, *27,* 129-136.

Rieff, P. *Freud: The Mind of the Moralist.* New York: Doubleday, 1961.

Rilke, R. M. *Duino Elegies.* New York: Norton, 1978.

Rosenblatt, P. "Marital Residence and the Functions of Romantic Love." *Ethnology,* 1967, *6,* 471-480.

Roth, P. *Portnoy's Complaint.* New York: Random House, 1969.

Royce, J. R. *The Encapsulated Man.* New York: Van Nostrand, 1964.

Rubin, Z. "Measurement of Romantic Love." *Journal of Personality and Social Psychology,* 1970, *16* (2), 265-273.

Rubin, Z. *Liking and Loving: An Introduction to Social Psychology.* New York: Holt, Rinehart and Winston, 1973.

Rubin, Z. "From Liking to Loving: Patterns of Attraction in Dating Relationships." In T. L. Huston (Ed.), *Foundations of Interpersonal Attraction.* New York: Academic Press, 1974.

Russell, B. *The Conquest of Happiness.* New York: Liveright, 1930.

Ryle, A. *Frames and Cages: The Repertory Grid Approach to Human Understanding.* New York: International Universities Press, 1975.

Sager, C. J. *Marriage Contracts and Couple Therapy.* New York: Brunner/Mazel, 1976.

Sarason, S. B. *The Creation of Settings and the Future Societies.* San Francisco: Jossey-Bass, 1972.

Sarason, S. B. *The Psychological Sense of Community: Prospects for a Community Psychology.* San Francisco: Jossey-Bass, 1974.

Sarnoff, S., and Sarnoff, I. *Sexual Excitement, Sexual Peace.* New York: Evans, 1979.

Schachter, S. *The Psychology of Affiliation.* Stanford, Calif.: Stanford University Press, 1959.

Schachter, S. "The Interaction of Cognitive and Physiological Determinants of Emotional States." In L. Berkowitz (Ed.), *Advances in Experimental Social Psychology.* New York: Academic Press, 1964.

Schafer, R. "The Psychoanalytic Vision of Reality." *International Journal of Psychoanalysis*, 1970, *51*, 279-297.

Schafer, R. *A New Language for Psychoanalysis.* New Haven, Conn.: Yale University Press, 1976.

Schank, R. C., and Abelson, R. P. *Scripts, Plans, Goals and Understanding.* Hillsdale, N.J.: Erlbaum, 1978.

Schneider, W., and Shiffrin, R. M. "Controlled and Automatic Information Processing: I. Detection, Search, and Attention." *Psychological Review*, 1977, *84*, 1-66.

Schneirla, T. C. "An Evolutionary and Developmental Theory of Biphasic Processes Underlying Approach and Withdrawal." In M. R. Jones (Ed.), *Nebraska Symposium on Motivation.* Lincoln: University of Nebraska Press, 1959.

Seeman, M. V. "Delusional Loving." *Archives of General Psychiatry*, 1978, *35*, 1265-1267.

Sevely, J. L., and Bennett, J. W. "Concerning Female Ejaculation and the Female Prostate." *Journal of Sex Research*, 1978, *14* (1), 1-20.

Shakespeare, W. *The Merchant of Venice*. In G. B. Harrison (Ed.), *The Complete Works of Shakespeare*. New York: Harcourt Brace Jovanovich, 1948. (Originally published about 1598.)

Shakespeare, W. *A Midsummer Night's Dream*. In G. B. Harrison (Ed.), *The Complete Works of Shakespeare*. New York: Harcourt Brace Jovanovich, 1948. (Originally published about 1600.)

Shakespeare, W. *Hamlet*. New York: Washington Square Press, 1957. (Originally published 1602.)

Shakespeare, W. *The Complete Works of Shakespeare*. Chicago: Scott, Foresman, 1961.

Shakespeare, W. *Antony and Cleopatra*. Baltimore: Penguin Books, 1970. (Originally published 1607.)

Shane, M. *Lovers as Friends*. New York: 1978.

Shanteau, J., and Nagy, G. F. "Probability of Acceptance in Dating Choice." *Journal of Personality and Social Psychology*, 1979, *37*, 522-533.

Shapiro, R. L. "Small Group Regression and Mature Group Functioning." Paper presented at 66th annual meeting of American Psychoanalytic Association, New York, 1979.

Sheehy, G. *Passages*. New York: Bantam Books, 1976.

Shippers, L. "The Permanence of Change and the Adolescent Experience." *Adolescence*, 1978, *13*, 143-148.

Shmukler, D. "The Origins and Concomitants of Imaginative Play in Young Children." Unpublished doctoral disseration, University of Witwatersrand, South Africa, 1978.

Siassi, I., and Thomas, M. "Physicians and the New Sexual Freedom." *American Journal of Psychiatry*, 1973, *130* (11), 1256-1257.

Silverman, I. "Physical Attractiveness and Courtship." *Sexual Behavior*, September 1971, pp. 22-25.

Simon, H. A. "A Behavioral Model of Rational Choice." *Quarterly Journal of Economics*, 1955, *69*, 99-118.

Singer, J. L. *The Child's World of Make-Believe*. New York: Academic Press, 1973.

Singer, J. L. *Imagery and Daydream Methods in Psychotherapy and Behavior Modification.* New York: Academic Press, 1974.

Singer, J. L. *The Inner World of Daydreaming.* New York: Harper & Row, 1975.

Singer, J. L. "Imagination and Make-Believe Play in Early Childhood: Some Educational Implications." *Journal of Mental Imagery*, 1977, *1*, 127–144.

Singer, J. L. "Affect and Imagination in Play and Fantasy." In C. Izard (Ed.), *Emotions in Personality and Psychopathology.* New York: Plenum, 1979.

Singer, J. L., and Brown, S. L. "The Experience-Type: Some Behavioral Correlates and Theoretical Implications." In M. A. Rickers-Orsiankina (Ed.), *Rorschach Psychology.* (2nd ed.) Huntington, N.Y.: Krieger, 1977.

Singer, J. L. and Pope, K. S. "The Use of Imagery and Fantasy Techniques in Psychotherapy." In J. L. Singer and K. S. Pope (Eds.), *The Power of Human Imagination.* New York: Plenum, 1978.

Singer, J. L., and Singer, D. G. "Imaginative Play and Pretending in Early Childhood: Some Experimental Approaches." In A. Davids (Ed.), *Child Personality and Psychopathology: Current Topics.* Vol. 3. New York: Wiley-Interscience, 1976.

Singer, J. L., and Singer, D. G. *Television, Imagination and Aggression: A Study of Preschoolers' Play.* Hillsdale, N.J.: Erlbaum, 1980.

Singer, J. L., Singer, D. G., and Sherrod, L. R. "A Factor Analytic Study of Pre-Schoolers' Play Behaviors." *Academic Psychology Bulletin*, 1980, *2*, 143–156.

Skinner, B. F. *Science and Human Behavior.* New York: Macmillan, 1953.

Slater, P. *Microcosm.* New York: Wiley, 1963.

Slater, P. *The Pursuit of Loneliness: American Culture at the Breaking Point.* (rev. ed.) Boston: Beacon Press, 1976.

Smith, E. R. "Specification and Estimation of Causal Models in Social Psychology: Comment on Tesser and Paulhus." *Journal of Personality and Social Psychology*, 1978, *36*, 34–38.

Sontag, S. *Against Interpretation.* New York: Delta, 1966.

Sontag, S. *Styles of Radical Will.* New York: Farrar, Straus and Giroux, 1969.

Sorenson, R. C. *Adolescent Sexuality in Contemporary America.*

New York: World, 1973.

Sorokin, P. A. *Social and Cultural Dynamics*. Vol. 2. New York: American Book Company, 1937.

Spaulding, C. "The Romantic Love Complex in American Culture." *Sociology and Social Research*, 1970, *55*, 82-100.

Stein, M. I. *Stimulating Creativity Group Procedures*. Vol. 2. New York: Academic Press, 1975.

Steinglass, P. "The Conceptualization of Marriage from a Systems Theory Perspective." In T. J. Paolino and B. S. McCrady (Eds.), *Marriage and Marital Therapy: Psychoanalytic, Behavioral and Systems Theory Perspectives*. New York: Brunner/Mazel, 1978.

Stone, L. J., and Church, J. *Childhood and Adolescence: A Psychology of the Growing Person*. New York: Random House, 1957.

Strupp, H. H. "Specific vs. Nonspecific Factors in Psychology and the Problem of Control." *Archives in General Psychiatry*, 1970, *23*, 393-401.

Suckling, J. "The Letters of Sir John Suckling." In A. M. Witherspoon and F. Warnke (Eds.), *Seventeenth-Century Prose and Poetry*. New York: Harcourt Brace Jovanovich, 1963. (Originally published 1658.)

Sullivan, H. S. *Conceptions of Modern Psychiatry*. (2nd ed.) New York: Norton, 1953a.

Sullivan, H. S. *The Interpersonal Theory of Psychiatry*. New York: Norton, 1953b.

Sullivan, H. S. *Schizophrenia as a Human Process*. New York: Norton, 1962.

Sullivan, H. S. *The Fusion of Psychiatry and Social Science*. New York: Norton, 1964.

Tavris, C. "Men and Women Report Their Views of Masculinity." *Psychology Today*, 1977, *10*, 34.

Taylor, B. J., and Wagner, N. N. "Sex Between Therapists and Clients: A Review and Analysis." *Professional Psychology*, November 1976, pp. 593-601.

Tennov, D. "Sex Differences in Romantic Love and Depression Among College Students." Paper presented at 81st annual meeting of the American Psychological Association, Montreal, Sept. 1973.

Tesser, A., and Paulhus, D. "Toward a Causal Model of Love."

Journal of Personality and Social Psychology, 1976, *34*, 1095–1105.

Thelan, M. H., Dollinger, S., and Roberts, M. C. "On Being Imitated: Its Effects on Attraction and Reciprocal Imitation." *Journal of Personality and Social Psychology*, 1975, *31* (3), 467–472.

Thibaut, J. W., and Kelley, H. H. *The Social Psychology of Groups.* New York: Wiley, 1959.

Tillich, P. *The Courage to Be.* New Haven, Conn.: Yale University Press, 1952.

Tillich, P. *The Dynamics of Faith.* New York: Harper & Row, 1957.

Tillich, P. *Systematic Theology.* Vol. 3. Chicago: University of Chicago Press, 1963.

Toffler, A. *Future Shock.* New York: Random House, 1970.

Toffler, A. "A New Kind of Man in the Making." *New York Times Magazine,* March 9, 1980, pp. 24–30.

Tomkins, S. S. *Affect, Imagery, Consciousness.* Vols. 1 and 2. New York: Springer, 1962, 1963.

Trivers, R. L. "The Evolution of Reciprocal Altruism." *Quarterly Review of Biology*, 1971, *46*, 35–37.

Trost, J. "Some Data in Mate Selection." *Journal of Marriage and the Family,* 1967, *29*, 739–755.

Turquet, P. "Leadership: The Individual and the Group." In G. S. Gibbard, J. J. Hartman, and R. D. Mann (Eds.), *Analysis of Groups: Contributions to Theory, Research, and Practice.* San Francisco: Jossey-Bass, 1973.

Turquet, P. "Threats to the Individual in the Large Group." In L. Kreeger, *The Large Group.* London: Constable, 1975.

U.S. Bureau of the Census. *Statistical Abstract of the United States: 1975.* (96th ed.) Washington, D.C.: U.S. Government Printing Office, 1976.

Vaillant, G. *Adaptation to Life.* Boston: Little, Brown, 1977.

Vergil. *Eclogues.* In H. H Warwick (Ed.), *A Vergil Concordance.* Minneapolis: University of Minnesota Press, 1975. (Written about 40 B.C.)

Vickers, D., Leary, J., and Barnes, P. "Adaptation to Decreasing Signal Probability." In R. Mackie (Ed.), *Vigilance.* New York: Plenum, 1977.

Walster, E. "Passionate Love." In B. I. Murstein (Ed.), *Theories of Attraction and Love*. New York: Springer, 1971.

Walster, E., Aronson, V., Abrahams, D., and Rottman, L. "The Importance of Physical Attractiveness in Dating Behavior." *Journal of Personality and Social Psychology*, 1966, *4*, 508–516.

Walster, E., and Walster, G. W. *A New Look at Love*. Reading, Mass.: Addison-Wesley, 1978.

Wanderer, Z., and Cabot, T. *Letting Go*. New York: Putnam's, 1978.

Warkenton, J., and Whitaker, C. A. "The Secret Agenda of the Therapist Doing Couples Therapy." In G. H. Zuk and I. Boszorymenyi-Nagy (Eds.), *Family Therapy and Disturbed Families*. Palo Alto, Calif.: Science and Behavior Books, 1967.

Watzslavik, P., Weakland, J., and Fisch, R. *Change: Principles of Problem Formation and Problem Resolution*. New York: Norton, 1974.

Weinberg, M. S. *Sex Research: Studies from the Kinsey Institute*. New York: Oxford University Press, 1976.

Weiner, M. F. *Therapist Disclosure*. Woburn, Mass.: Butterworths, 1978.

Weitzman, L. J., Eifler, D., Hokada, E., and Ross, C. "Sex Role Socialization in Picture Books for Preschool Children." *American Journal of Sociology*, 1972, *77*, 1125–1150.

Wexler, J., and Steidl, J. "Marriage and the Capacity to be Alone." *Psychiatry*, 1978, *41*, 72–81.

Whitehead, A. N. *Science and the Modern World*. New York: New American Library, 1925.

Wickler, W. *The Sexual Code*. New York: Doubleday, 1972.

Wile, D. B. "Is a Confrontational Tone Necessary in Conjoint Therapy?" *Journal of Marriage and Family Counseling*, 1978, *4*, 11–18.

Wile, D. B. "An Insight Approach to Marital Therapy." *Journal of Marriage and Family Therapy*, 1979.

Wilkinson, M. "Romantic Love: The Great Equalizer? Sexism in Popular Music." *Family Coordinator*, 1976, *25*, 161–166.

Wilkinson, M. "Romantic Love and Sexual Expression." *Family Coordinator*, 1978, *27*, 14–149.

Williams, J. H. *Psychology of Women*. New York: Norton, 1977.

Williams, M. H. "Individual Sex Therapy." In J. LoPiccolo and L. LoPiccolo (Eds.), *Handbook of Sex Therapy*. New York: Plenum, 1978.

Wilson, E. O. *Sociobiology: The New Synthesis*. Cambridge, Mass.: Harvard University Press, 1975.

Wilson, E. O. *On Human Nature*. Cambridge, Mass.: Harvard University Press, 1978.

Winch, R. F. *Mate-Selection: A Study of Complementary Needs*. New York: Harper & Row, 1958.

Winnicott, D. W. "The Depressive Position in Normal Emotional Development." *British Journal of Medical Psychology*, 1955, *28*, 89-100.

Winnicott, D. W. "The Development of the Capacity for Concern." *Bulletin of the Menninger Clinic,* 1963, *27*, 167-176.

Winnicott, D. W. *Playing and Reality*. New York: Basic Books, 1971.

Winthrop, H. "Love and Companionship." In II. A. Otto (Ed.), *Love Today*. New York: Dell, 1973.

Woodworth, R., and Schlosberg, II. *Experimental Psychology*. New York: IIolt, Rinehart and Winston, 1954.

Zerof, H. G. *Finding Intimacy*. New York: Random House, 1978.

Ziller, R., and Rosen, J. "Monitoring the Meaning of Love." *Journal of Individual Psychology*, 1975, *31*, 51-64.

Index